BARTENDER'S GUIDE

AN A TO Z COMPANION TO ALL YOUR FAVORITE DRINKS

John K. Waters

Avon, Massachusetts

DEDICATION
This book is dedicated to Chuck Bethel,
my former partner in crime, creator of the infamous DC-10,
and the best bartender I ever worked with.

.

Published by Adams Media, an F+W Publications Company
57 Littlefield Street
Avon, MA 02322
www.adamsmedia.com

ISBN 10: 1-59869-764-1
ISBN 13: 978-1-59869-764-3

Printed by KHL Printing Co Pte Ltd, Singapore.

J I H G F E D C B A

Contains portions of material adapted and abridged from *The Everything® Bartender's
Book* by Jane Parker Resnick, Copyright © 1995 by F+W Publications, and *The Every-
thing® Cocktail Parties and Drinks Book* by Cheryl Charming, Copyright © 2005 by F+W
Publications.

Please enjoy alcohol responsibly,
and only if you're of legal age.

*This title is available at quantity discounts for bulk purchases.
For information, please call 1-800-289-0963.*

Contents

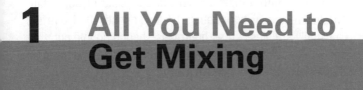

1 All You Need to Get Mixing

BAR **BASICS**

The craft of mixing drinks is straightforward and relatively easy to master. In fact, most of the 2,000 recipes in this book require only a few basic skills that anyone can learn.

TERMINOLOGY

SHOT: Equal to 1½ fluid ounces, or a jigger.

JIGGER: Both a measurement and a piece of bar equipment. In a recipe, a jigger equals 1½ fluid ounces. It also refers to a usually stainless steel, hourglass-shaped double cup that holds an ounce of fluid in one side and an ounce and a half in the other. Jiggers now come in a variety of sizes, from ½ ounce by 1 ounce to 1 ounce by 2 ounces.

PONY: Equal to one fluid ounce. It's used rarely these days, but you might run across this term in an old bar guide.

DASH: Technically, a dash equals $1/32$ of a fluid ounce, but who has time to measure that? Basically, it's just enough liquid to add a little color or flavor.

SPLASH: Couple of dashes.

FILL OR TO FILL: When a drink recipe calls for, say, "club soda to fill," it means that you should add enough soda to reach the top of the glass.

GARNISH: Typically, it's a piece of fruit used to adorn the drink. But garnishes can take the form of vegetable pieces, bits of candy, special cookies—just about anything that will enhance a drink's visual appeal.

TWIST: A slice of citrus peel that is squeezed—literally twisted—over a drink, and then added directly to the drink or run around the rim. Twisting the peel releases flavorful oils and aroma. Although in this book we used the phrase "garnish with a twist," a twist is not really a garnish, which is arguably optional, but an essential ingredient.

ON THE ROCKS: It seems obvious, but just in case, "rocks" are ice cubes. A drink served "on the rocks" is served with ice.

UP OR STRAIGHT UP: Served without ice.

FROZEN: A "frozen" cocktail is one that is prepared in a blender with crushed ice.

HIGHBALL: A drink made with one kind of liquor topped with a mixer. Highballs are usually served on the rocks in a highball glass. Often not stirred, they are always served with a sip stick. Think scotch and soda or screwdriver.

COCKTAIL: A drink made with a variety of liquors, mixers, and other ingredients, combined in a variety of ways in a variety of glassware. Basically, a cocktail is any mixed drink that's not a highball. Cocktails may be stirred, shaken, or frozen (blended with ice). Think martini and margarita.

SHOOTER: A drink designed to be consumed in one gulp. Served without ice in a shot glass or old-fashioned glass.

MIXER: A mixer is the nonalcoholic main medium of many cocktails. Mixers range from plain and fizzy water to sodas, like Coca-Cola and 7-Up, to just about any fruit juice. In a gin and tonic, the mixer is the tonic water; in a screwdriver, it's the orange juice; in an Irish coffee, it's the coffee. All highballs include mixers, but some cocktails do not.

RIMMING: Many drinks are served in glasses with a coating of salt or sugar on the rims. The process of getting those dry ingredients to stick to the glass is called "rimming." Typically, it involves rubbing a wedge of lemon or lime around the rim of the glass, and then dipping the glass upside down into some salt, sugar, and sometimes other ingredients, which sticks to the wet rim.

MUDDLING: The technique of gently crushing fresh ingredients, such as mint leaves, with other ingredients to release their oils or essence. It's done with the back of a spoon or a wooden pestle (called a muddler) in the bottom of an old-fashioned glass, a small bowl, or a mixing glass. Other ingredients are then added on top. Note: Heavy metal muddlers are available, but they tend to scar the glass. Using a wooden muddler or a bar spoon's muddler end can spare your glassware.

FROSTING: A frosted glass is covered in a very thin layer of ice. That layer is produced by dipping the glass in water and placing it in a freezer for about half an hour.

TECHNIQUES

BUILT

Most highballs are simply assembled, or "built," right in the glass in which they will be served. One of the reasons using the proper glass is so important is that it determines the proportions of ingredients in many drinks.

Here's how to do it: Fill the glass with ice. Pour in the liquor. Fill the glass with the mixer. Add the garnish. Some recipes call for the drink to be stirred, but most do not. If the drink must be stirred and the mixer is carbonated, stir gently to preserve the bubbles.

STIRRED

Some drinks simply must be stirred with ice to blend and chill the ingredients properly. Combined and mixed in a separate glass, the stirred drink can be served straight up in a cocktail glass or on fresh ice in an old-fashioned glass.

Here's how to do it: Nearly fill a cocktail shaker with ice. Add the ingredients in the order given in the recipe. Stir with the straight end of a bar spoon. Some recipes call for a gentle stir, but most want you to give the drink a hard spin. Now hold a strainer over the glass and pour the blended ingredients into the serving glass. Add the garnish.

SHAKEN

The ingredients of some cocktails just have to be shaken together with ice to mix them properly—sugar, cream, some fruit juices, and egg whites, for example.

Here's how to do it: (This technique employs a two-piece Boston shaker, not the one-piece European version.) Nearly fill the glass side of a shaker with ice. Add the ingredients in the order given in the recipe. Place the stainless steel side over the top of the glass side and press down to form a seal between the two. Hold the shaker firmly with one hand on the top and one on the bottom, and shake it up and down. You should feel the ice and liquid sloshing hard between the two sides of the shaker. And it'll get pretty cold.

Now hold the glass side upright and tap the metal top with the heel of your hand to break the seal. Chilled by the ice, the metal side has contracted, increasing the strength of the seal, so it might take a couple of thumps to get it loose. (That's why flashy bartenders can spin those two-piece shakers without spilling.) Turn the whole thing over so the contents end up in the metal side. Put the strainer in place, and strain the drink into the glass.

Shake most drinks vigorously to a slow count of ten. Drinks with hard-to-combine ingredients, such eggs and cream, should be shaken longer and harder.

BLENDED

Combining ingredients in a blender with some ice and giving it all a whirl produces the "frozen" cocktail. Although it's true that you could blend just about any drink—even a highball—some drinks were designed for the blender.

Here's how to do it: Simply add all the ingredients to a clean blender. If you're using fresh fruit, it goes in first, followed by the alcohol. Add the ice last. The trick is not to add so much ice that you dilute the drink. You can always add more. Run the blender for about 10 seconds on the lowest setting, then switch to a higher setting for another 10 seconds or until the drink is smooth. Add more ice as needed through the opening in the lid while the blender is running. When the ingredients are combined to the right consistency, pour the drink into the glass, garnish, and serve immediately. Another trick: If the drink recipe calls for a complicated garnish, assemble it first so that the drink can be served as soon as it is blended.

If you're using a blender, always add the ice and frozen fruit slowly. Commercial blenders are designed to buzz right through them, but they tend to bog down consumer-grade machines.

LAYERED

Layering is a technique that involves floating colored liqueurs, and sometimes other ingredients, one on top of another, to form distinct layers visible in the glass. Think pousse café. The trick is to know the specific gravity or weight of each liqueur, to combine them from heaviest to lightest.

Here's how to do it: Layer the liqueurs over one another, pouring them carefully over the back of a spoon, starting with the heaviest and finishing with the lightest.

FLAMING

A few of the drinks listed in this book call for a layer of alcohol floating on top of the drink to be set aflame. Flamed drinks have been around for decades. They're dramatic, which is probably the reason behind the practice in most cases, but in some drinks the fire can have an essential effect on the flavor.

Here's how to do it: One approach is to warm the alcohol you wish to ignite in a spoon, which causes fumes to rise from the liquor, which will easily catch fire. Using a long, barbecue match or lighter, you light the liquor and pour it into the drink.

Another approach is simply to light high-alcohol spirits, such as 151, that you have floated on the glass. The spoon approach allows you to light just about anything, but there's a danger of spilling as you pour the flaming alcohol into the glass.

ALWAYS TAKE GREAT CARE when flaming a drink. Do it away from all open liquor bottles. Be sure that the flame has gone out and the glass is safely cooled a bit before drinking.

PLANNING A COCKTAIL PARTY

Cocktail parties are back in a big way! But for many, planning one can be downright nerve-racking. But if you've stocked your bar with the basics, and you have the right tools, glasses, and mixers, the refreshments, at least, should be a breeze.

KEEP IT SIMPLE

A good cocktail party can have somewhere between fifteen and forty people, and will last no longer than two to three hours (to keep the energy and conversation level up). You can never fully anticipate what your guests will want to drink, but when alcohol is free, they tend to be satisfied with whatever you serve. The bigger the party, the fewer drink choices you should provide.

CALCULATING AMOUNTS

You will, of course, need to know the number of guests you expect to calculate the amount of liquor you'll need to have on hand. Typical cocktail party guests will consume about two drinks each. One bottle of wine holds four glasses, and a 750 ml bottle of liquor will yield about twenty-five shots. If you decide to provide a specialty drink, count on every person trying at least one.

STOCKING AND EQUIPPING A BAR

Whether you've decided to build a stand-alone wet bar in your rec room, or you're just mixing cocktails in the kitchen, it makes sense to invest in a few tools of the mixologist's trade.

TOOLS

Chances are you already have a number of the basic bar tools: a paring knife and cutting board, a blender, a refrigerator, and measuring spoons and cups. But no well-equipped bar would be without a few essential specialty utensils.

SHAKER: This is a must-have; you can't shake a cocktail without a shaker. There are two types: the European (or French) shaker and the Boston (or American) shaker. The European version is a single metal or glass container with a two-piece metal lid designed for straining and pouring.

Both for its versatility and a certain coolness factor, you'll want the Boston shaker. It consists of two separate, open tumblers, one glass, and the other metal. You can use the glass side for stirred drinks; in the recipe, it'll be called a "mixing glass."

STRAINER: To get your shaken cocktail from the shaker to the glass without the used ice, you need a strainer. Strainers are perforated metal paddles designed to fit over the opening of a cocktail strainer. A loose wire spring looped along the edge of one side helps the strainer to fit into the shaker cup.

JIGGER: Used for measuring liquor, a jigger is a stainless steel, hourglass-shaped double cup that holds an ounce of fluid in one side and an ounce and a half in the other. Jiggers come in a variety of sizes, from ½ ounce by 1 ounce to 1 ounce by 2 ounces. Many bartenders simply use a shot glass to measure, but a jigger can help your accuracy.

BAR SPOON: A bar spoon is more than just a spoon. Its long stem makes it perfect for stirring cocktails in a tall mixing glass or Collins glass. The bowl of the spoon can be used as a muddler, as can the other end. Its twisted handle may be used to slow liqueurs poured into layered drinks (though pouring over the back of the spoon is the most common method).

MUDDLER: Muddlers come in two forms: a small wooden pestle shaped like a baseball bat, and a metal version with a flat, bumpy end. The wooden version works very well and is less likely to scar your glassware than the metal version.

RIMMER: Rimmers are designed for creating a salted or sugared rim on a cocktail glass. They typically come with two or three round compartments, one containing a donut-shaped sponge for the juice or water used to wet the rim, and other compartments that hold salt and/or sugar. The glass is placed top-down first on the sponge section for wetting, and then dipped into the salt or sugar.

FRUIT-JUICE EXTRACTOR OR CITRUS REAMER: Highly recommended. A number of drinks call for a fresh squeeze or two of juice, and unless you're a weight lifter, a citrus reamer is *the* utensil for getting every last drop from that lime.

BOTTLE/CAN OPENERS AND CORKSCREWS: Old-fashioned bottle openers that also open cans are still a bar staple. Wine is an ingredient in a number of cocktails, so you'll also need a corkscrew. You probably already have a "wing" corkscrew in a drawer in your kitchen. That's the one with two little arms that rise up as you twist in the screw. The most professional corkscrew is the "waiter's" version, a three-in-one gadget that opens wine and other bottles, and cans. But there have been so many innovations in the past few years that you now have a lot of options, including new lever-style corkscrews, twist-style corkscrews, pump-style wine openers, and a range of uncorking "machines."

DECANTERS (BOTTLE POURERS): They're not absolutely necessary, but they're nice, especially if you're taking a turn behind the bar during a social gathering.

SIP STICKS: A short, thin straw usually made of plastic. They are served with highballs and cocktails and used for sipping and/or stirring.

SWIZZLE STICKS: A small spear-like stick with a flat, paddle-shaped end. They are added to cocktails to hold fruit, or as stirrers in tall glasses. They are usually made of plastic, but other materials, such as glass and wood, are sometimes used. The designs of the paddle ends vary widely.

ICE BUCKET AND TONGS: Ice should be thought of as an ingredient, and you'll want all your ingredients close at hand when you start mixing.

NAPKINS/COASTERS: No bar setup would be complete without something to set the drink on.

MIXERS

The well-stocked bar will include any of the following mixers:

JUICES: Orange, grapefruit, cranberry, pineapple, lemon, lime, and tomato juice or V8. Fresh squeezed fruit juice will elevate a drink beyond the ordinary. The average lemon or lime will yield about an ounce of juice; an orange will yield between 1½ and 3 oz. of juice, depending on its size.

CARBONATED BEVERAGES: Club soda, tonic water, Coca-Cola or other cola, 7-Up or Sprite, and ginger ale.

DAIRY: Milk, half-and-half, cream, whipped cream, and even ice cream.

COFFEE, TEA, HOT CHOCOLATE: Essentials for a number of winter favorites.

PREPARED DRINK MIXES: Prepared drink mixes, such as a daiquiri or Bloody Mary mix, range from okay to terrible. Rose's Lime, a sweetened lime concoction, and sweet-and-sour mix are bar staples, but you can even substitute homemade versions of these ingredients to great effect. Make your own sour mix by combining about eight ounces of lemon juice with two tablespoons of sugar. The sweetened lime mix is a combination of eight ounces of lime juice with two tablespoons of sugar. Make your own version of a Collins mix by combining one ounce of lemon juice with a teaspoon of superfine sugar and three ounces of club soda.

SIMPLE SYRUP: Many professional bar setups include a bottle of sugar water called "simple syrup," which they use to sweeten drinks when sugar is called for. Because the sugar is already dissolved, it mixes better than dry sugar. To make your own, heat two cups of water in a saucepan, and slowly add a pound of granulated sugar until it is completely dissolved. The syrup can be stored in a bottle in a cool place.

FLAVORING INGREDIENTS

BITTERS: Bitters are a witch's brew of roots and barks, berries and herbs. Bitters add a kick of flavor to the mixed drinks they accompany, always in dashes. The most common type of bitters is Angostura, made in Trinidad. Two that are sometimes used are Peychaud's, from New Orleans, and Orange Bitters, an English product. Bitters do contain some alcohol.

GRENADINE: This blood-red syrup made from pomegranates is an essential ingredient in a number of drinks, not just for its sweet flavor, but for visual effects.

VERMOUTH: The dry variety is essential for martinis; the sweet a requirement of the Manhattan.

CONDIMENTS: The following list of cocktail condiments should be part of every bar setup: • Table salt • Coarse salt • Table sugar • Superfine sugar • Cinnamon • Nutmeg • Horseradish • Tabasco

GARNISHES: Whether it's a garnish, which does affect the flavor of a drink, or a decorative bit of "garbage," which doesn't, every bar should have a few key fruits on hand, and even a few vegetables. • Lemons • Limes • Olives with pimentos • Cucumber peel • Pearl onions • Oranges • Celery stalks • Mint leaves • Black olives • Red maraschino cherries

GLASSWARE

Almost as important as what is in the drink is what the drink is in. And this isn't just about aesthetics. Glassware has a big influence on how the drink . . . well . . . *works*.

BRANDY SNIFTER: Brandy snifters range considerably in size, from 5 to 25 ounces, so preference must be a guide. The short stem allows your hand to warm the brandy. The narrower mouth of the glass holds the aroma. Typical size: 17.5 ounces.

CHAMPAGNE FLUTE: Taller and narrower than the Champagne glass, the flute is designed to preserve the wine's bubbles, and to show them off as they rise to the surface. Typical size: 7–10 ounces.

CHAMPAGNE GLASS: A shallow, stemmed, wide-mouthed glass designed to allow the carbonation of the wine to escape. Typical size: 4–6 ounces.

COLLINS GLASS: Shaped the same as a highball glass, but taller and often frosted nearly to the top, the Collins glass gets its name from the Collins family of drinks. Nowadays, a Collins glass is used for a number of cocktails, such as the Mai Tai. Most bars use the Collins glass to serve soft drinks and plain juice. Typical size: 10–14 oz.

CORDIAL GLASS: Sometimes called a "pony" or a sherry glass, this small, stemmed glass is preferred for aperitifs, ports, and sherry—think before- and after-dinner drinks. These types of drinks are, by definition, small, and the size of the sherry glass is right for the typical portion. The tapered shape of the glass also enhances the aroma of the drink. Typical size: 3–4 ounces.

HIGHBALL GLASS: A highball glass is a short, straight-sided glass almost universally used for on-the-rocks drinks like a scotch and soda or a gin and tonic—in other words, highballs. But it's also used for a wide range of cocktails that need to be served on ice. It's the glass of choice for everything from Planter's Punch to a Bloody Mary. Typical size: 8–10 oz.

HURRICANE GLASS: This tall, elegantly cut specialty glass is named for the hurricane lamp, whose shape it resembles. It is designed for tropical drinks, such as its namesake Hurricane. Typical size: 15 oz.

IRISH COFFEE GLASS: The Irish coffee glass or mug is a soul-warming container for all hot drinks. It offers enough volume for the right proportions of spirits and nonalcoholic ingredients and its handle allows you to hold the glass while the drink is still properly hot. Typical size: 8–10 ounces.

LIQUEUR GLASS: A 1-ounce liqueur glass is also known as a cordial glass or a "pony." Pour a pousse-café in the pony for the strangest combination behind the bar.

MARGARITA GLASS: The margarita glass is a kind of cocktail glass. Slightly larger and rounded, it has a broad rim for holding salt. It's also used for daiquiris and other fruit drinks. This might be the best glass to choose when the recipe calls for a "large cocktail glass." Typical size: 12 oz.

MARTINI OR COCKTAIL GLASS: This glass is the symbol of drinking establishments throughout the world. Designed like an upside down Chinese straw hat on a stem, it holds the ingredients—usually served straight up—over a wide surface so they are least likely to separate. The stem allows you to hold the glass without warming the drink. Martinis, Manhattans, Metropolitans, and gimlets are a few of the many drinks served in a cocktail glass. Typical size: 4–12 oz.

OLD-FASHIONED GLASS: Short and squat, the old-fashioned glass is named for the venerable Old-Fashioned, but it's also called a "rocks" glass, because it is the universal vessel for liquor served straight over ice, or with a splash. The old-fashioned glass is also used for a range of cocktails served on the rocks. Typical size: 4–8 ounces.

PARFAIT GLASS: The parfait, while certainly not a bar essential, is appropriate for a number of festive, blended concoctions. It has an inward curve, a steep rim, and a larger, rounded bowl. Often used for drinks containing fruit or ice cream. Typical size: 12 ounces.

PILSNER GLASS: Beer is served in a mug or pilsner-style glass, but so are some cocktails. Typical size: 16 ounces.

POUSSE-CAFÉ GLASS: A narrow, specialty glass used primarily for layered concoctions, such as its namesake. Its tallish, narrow shape increases the ease of layering ingredients. Typical size: 6 ounces.

SHOT GLASS: A very small glass used for serving liquor straight up, and often for measuring cocktail ingredients. Double sized shot glasses also work for some layered drinks. Typical size: 1–2 ounces.

SOUR GLASS: Named for the Whiskey Sour, this short, stemmed glass is also known as a "delmonico." It has a wide opening, similar to a champagne flute. It's just the right size to hold the ingredients of its namesake cocktail, with or without ice, but it is the glass of choice for a range of cocktails. Typical size: 5 ounces.

WINE GLASS: A red wine glass (8-10 ounces) typically is balloon-shaped; white wine glasses (6-8 ounces) are more elongated and tapered. For cocktail recipes calling for a wine glass, but not specifying the type, go with one of the all-purpose wine glasses that are also available.

2 The Recipes

A-1 COCKTAIL

MARTINI

MAKES 1 DRINK

1 oz. gin
½ oz. Grand Marnier
dash lemon juice
dash grenadine

Pour ingredients into a shaker with ice. Shake well and strain into a chilled martini glass.

ABBEY COCKTAIL

MARTINI

MAKES 1 DRINK

1¼ oz. orange juice
1¼ oz. gin
2 dashes orange bitters

Pour ingredients into a shaker with ice. Shake well and strain into a chilled martini glass. Garnish with a maraschino cherry.

ABBOT'S DREAM

HIGHBALL

MAKES 1 DRINK

2 oz. Irish cream liqueur
1 oz. Frangelico
½ oz. banana liqueur
½ oz. cream

Pour all ingredients into a blender with a cup of ice. Blend until smooth and pour into a highball glass.

ABILENE

HIGHBALL

MAKES 1 DRINK

1½ oz. dark rum
2 oz. peach nectar
3 oz. orange juice

Pour all ingredients into an ice-filled highball glass. Stir well.

ACAPULCO

MARTINI

MAKES 1 DRINK

1¾ oz. light rum
½ oz. triple sec
½ oz. fresh lime
    juice
1 tsp. sugar

Pour ingredients into a shaker with ice. Strain into a chilled martini glass or serve on the rocks.

ACAPULCO CLAM DIGGER

OLD-FASHIONED

MAKES 1 DRINK

1½ oz. tequila
3 oz. tomato juice
3 oz. clam juice
¾ tbs. horseradish
splash fresh lemon
    juice
Worcestershire
    sauce to taste
Tabasco sauce to
    taste

Pour all ingredients into an ice-filled old-fashioned glass. Garnish with a slice of lemon. (Substitute: 6 oz./ Clamato juice for tomato and the clam juices.)

ACE OF SPADES

COLLINS

MAKES 1 DRINK

1 oz. Crown Royal
1½ oz. Amaretto
cola

Pour Crown Royal and Amaretto into an ice-filled Collins glass. Add the cola to fill and stir. Garnish with a sprig of mint.

ACE VENTURA

MARTINI

MAKES 1 DRINK

¼ oz. vodka
¼ oz. tequila
¼ oz. rum
dash Sambuca Red
dash Sambuca Blue
dash Sambuca Green
dash Sambuca Black
dash Sambuca White
dash Sambuca Gold
Sprite

Fill ¼ of a large, chilled martini glass with ice. Add the vodka, tequila, and rum. Add the Sprite until the glass is three-quarters full. Add the Sambuca in layers. Garnish with an umbrella and serve with a bendable straw.

ADAM

MARTINI

MAKES 1 DRINK

2 oz. dark rum
1 oz. lemon juice
1 tsp. grenadine

Pour ingredients into a shaker with ice. Shake well and strain into a martini glass.

ADAM AND EVE

MARTINI

MAKES 1 DRINK

1 oz. Forbidden
    Fruit Liqueur
1 oz. gin
1 oz. brandy
dash lemon juice

Pour ingredients into a shaker with ice. Shake well and strain into a martini glass.

ADIOS

COLLINS

MAKES 1 DRINK

2 oz. sweet-and-
    sour mix
½ oz. vodka
½ oz. light rum
½ oz. blue curaçao
½ oz. gin
club soda

Pour the first five ingredients into a Collins glass. Add a splash of club soda and stir gently.

ADIRONDACK MINT

IRISH COFFEE

MAKES 1 DRINK

1 oz. Godiva
    Chocolate Liqueur
1 oz. peppermint
    schnapps
2 oz. hot chocolate

Pour all ingredients into an Irish Coffee glass or mug and stir. Top with whipped cream.

ADMIRAL

MAKES 1 DRINK

1 oz. rye whiskey
2 oz. dry vermouth
juice of ½ lemon

Pour ingredients into a shaker with ice. Shake well and strain into a sour glass. Garnish with a lemon twist.

ADMIRAL NELSON'S BREW

IRISH COFFEE

MAKES 1 DRINK

1 oz. spiced rum
½ oz. applejack
8 oz. hot unfiltered apple cider

Pour first two ingredients into an Irish Coffee glass or large mug. Add the hot cider and stir. Garnish with a cinnamon stick and an orange slice.

ADONIS

MARTINI

MAKES 1 DRINK

1 oz. dry sherry
½ oz. sweet vermouth
½ oz. dry vermouth
2 dashes orange bitters

Pour all ingredients into an ice-filled shaker and stir well. Strain into a chilled martini glass.

AFFAIR

MARTINI

MAKES 1 DRINK

1 oz. strawberry schnapps
1 oz. cranberry juice
1 oz. orange juice

Pour all ingredients into an ice-filled shaker and stir well. Strain into a martini glass.

AFFAIR TO REMEMBER

HIGHBALL

MAKES 1 DRINK

*2 oz. strawberry
  liqueur
2 oz. orange juice
2 oz. cranberry
  juice
club soda*

Pour first three ingredients into a highball glass and stir. Fill with club soda.

AFFINITY

MARTINI

MAKES 1 DRINK

*2 oz. scotch
½ oz. sweet
  vermouth
½ oz. dry vermouth
3 dashes bitters*

Pour ingredients into a shaker with ice. Stir and strain into a martini glass.

AFTER FIVE

MARTINI

MAKES 1 DRINK

*1 oz. Irish cream
  liqueur
1 oz. Kahlua
1 oz. peppermint
  schnapps*

Pour all ingredients into an ice-filled martini glass. Stir gently.

AFTERNOON DELIGHT

MARTINI

MAKES 1 DRINK

*1 oz. banana vodka
  or rum
1 oz. banana
  liqueur
1 oz. white crème
  de cacao
1 scoop of banana
  ice cream
1 scoop of chocolate
  ice cream*

Pour all ingredients into a blender and blend until smooth—thick, but drinkable. For a creamier drink, add milk or half-and-half until the mixture reaches your preferred consistency. Serve in a large martini glass.

AGENT ORANGE

COLLINS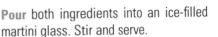

MAKES 1 DRINK

*1½ oz. Southern
    Comfort
1½ oz. Tennessee
    whiskey
8 oz. orange juice*

Pour first two ingredients into an ice-filled Collins glass. Add orange juice to taste. Garnish with an orange twist.

AGGRAVATION

MARTINI

MAKES 1 DRINK

*1¼ oz. scotch
¼ oz. coffee
    liqueur*

Pour both ingredients into an ice-filled martini glass. Stir and serve.

AK-47

COLLINS

MAKES 1 DRINK

*¹/₃ oz. brandy
¹/₃ oz. whiskey
¹/₃ oz. gin
¹/₃ oz. vodka
¹/₃ oz. rum
¹/₃ oz. bourbon
¹/₃ oz. Cointreau
¹/₃ oz. lime
fill with club soda*

Pour first eight ingredients into an ice-filled shaker. Shake well and strain into a Collins glass. Top off with the club soda and serve.

ALABAMA COCKTAIL

MARTINI

MAKES 1 DRINK

*1½ oz. brandy
½ oz. lemon juice
½ tsp. powdered
    sugar
splash curaçao*

Pour ingredients into a shaker with ice. Stir well and strain into a chilled martini glass.

ALABAMA FIZZ

HIGHBALL

MAKES 1 DRINK

juice of ½ lemon
1 tsp. powdered
  sugar
2 oz. gin
club soda

Pour first three ingredients into an ice-filled shaker. Shake well and strain into a highball glass over ice. Fill with club soda and garnish with two sprigs of mint.

ALABAMA RIOT

MARTINI

MAKES 1 DRINK

2 oz. Southern
  Comfort
1 oz. peppermint
  schnapps
1 oz. vodka
8 oz. fruit punch
1 oz. lime juice

Pour the fruit punch into a large martini glass filled with ice. Add the Southern Comfort, peppermint schnapps, and vodka. Stir and top with lime juice.

ALABAMA SLAMMER

HIGHBALL

MAKES 1 DRINK

1 oz. Southern
  Comfort
1 oz. Amaretto
½ oz. sloe gin
splash lemon juice

Pour first three ingredients into an ice-filled highball glass and stir. Add the lemon juice.

ALABAMA SLAM SHOOTER

SHOT

MAKES 1 DRINK

½ oz. Southern
  Comfort
1 oz. Amaretto
½ oz. sloe gin
splash lemon juice

Pour all ingredients into an ice-filled shaker and stir. Strain into a shot glass. Add lemon juice.

ALAMO SPLASH

COLLINS

MAKES 1 DRINK

1½ oz. tequila
1 oz. orange juice
½ oz. pineapple
*   juice*
splash lemon-lime
*   soda*

Pour ingredients into a shaker with ice. Stir and strain into a Collins glass over ice.

ALASKA

MARTINI

MAKES 1 DRINK

2 oz. gin
¾ oz. yellow
*   Chartreuse*
2 dashes orange
*   bitters*

Pour ingredients into a shaker half filled with ice. Shake well and strain into a martini glass.

ALBEMARLE FIZZ

HIGHBALL

MAKES 1 DRINK

juice of ½ lemon
1 tsp. powdered
*   sugar*
2 oz. gin
1 tsp. raspberry
*   syrup*
club soda

Pour first four ingredients into an ice-filled shaker. Shake and strain into a highball glass over ice. Fill with club soda.

ALCUDLA

MARTINI

MAKES 1 DRINK

2 oz. dry gin
1 oz. Galliano
1 oz. crème de
*   banane*
1 oz. grapefruit
*   juice*

Pour ingredients into a shaker with ice. Shake and strain into a martini glass. Garnish with a grapefruit twist.

ALEXANDER COCKTAIL

COLLINS

MAKES 1 DRINK

1 oz. gin
1 oz. crème de cacao
1 oz. sweet cream

Pour ingredients into a shaker with ice. Shake very well. Strain into a martini glass.

ALEXANDER NEVSKY

MARTINI

MAKES 1 DRINK

2 oz. Stolichnaya raspberry vodka
1 oz. gin
4 fresh raspberries

Pour vodka and gin into a shaker with ice. Shake and strain into a chilled martini glass over the fresh raspberries. Optional: Sprinkle a few drops of Framboise or Kirschwasser over the top of the drink.

ALEXANDER THE GREAT

COLLINS

MAKES 1 DRINK

½ oz. crème de cacao
½ oz. coffee liqueur
½ oz. cream
1½ oz. vodka

Pour ingredients into a shaker with ice. Strain into a martini glass.

ALFIE COCKTAIL

COLLINS

MAKES 1 DRINK

1½ oz. lemon vodka
dash triple sec
1 tbs. pineapple juice

Pour ingredients into a shaker with ice. Shake and strain into a martini glass.

ALFONSO

WINE

MAKES 1 DRINK

1 oz. Dubonnet
2 dashes bitters
1 tsp. sugar
Champagne (iced)

Pour the bitters and the sugar into a wine glass. Add the Dubonnet and a tsp. of crushed ice. Fill the glass with Champagne and stir gently. Garnish with a lemon twist.

ALGONQUIN

MARTINI

MAKES 1 DRINK

1½ oz. rye whiskey
1 oz. dry vermouth
1 oz. pineapple
  juice

Pour ingredients into a shaker with ice. Shake well and strain into a martini glass.

ALGONQUIN BLOODY MARY

HIGHBALL

MAKES 1 DRINK

2 oz. vodka
4 oz. tomato juice
juice of ½ lime
1½ tsp. Worcester-
  shire sauce
6 dashes Tabasco
  sauce
salt (to taste)
pepper (to taste)

Pour ingredients into a shaker with ice. Shake very well and strain into a highball glass over ice. Garnish with a lime wedge.

ALHAMBRA ROYALE

IRISH COFFEE

MAKES 1 DRINK

1½ oz. cognac
1 cup hot chocolate
whipped cream
orange peel

Fill an Irish Coffee glass or mug with hot chocolate almost to the brim. Twist an orange peel over the mug and add it to the chocolate. In a ladle, warm the cognac over hot water. Light the warmed cognac and pour into the mug. Blow out the flame and top with the whipped cream.

ALOHA BUBBLY

COLLINS

MAKES 1 DRINK

*2 oz. dry white
wine
2 oz. pineapple
juice
2 oz. club soda
½ tsp. sugar*

Pour the last three ingredients into a Collins glass and stir well. Add crushed ice and the white wine. Add additional club soda to fill and stir again. Garnish with a whole strawberry.

ALICE IN WONDERLAND

IRISH COFFEE

MAKES 1 DRINK

*5 mint leaves
2 spoonfuls simple
syrup (page 13)
2 lime slices
1 oz. light rum
hot green tea
honey*

In an Irish coffee glass or mug, muddle the mint in the simple syrup with the lime slices. Add the rum. Pour in the green tea. Add the honey to taste.

ALIZE MARTINI

MARTINI

MAKES 1 DRINK

*2½ oz. Alize
1 oz. vodka*

Pour all ingredients in a martini glass and stir.

ALL AMERICAN

COLLINS

MAKES 1 DRINK

*1 oz. bourbon
whiskey
1 oz. Southern
Comfort
2 oz. cola*

Pour all ingredients in an old-fashioned glass and stir.

ALLEGHENY

COLLINS

MAKES 1 DRINK

1 oz. dry vermouth
1 oz. bourbon
   whiskey
1½ tsp. blackberry
   brandy
1½ tsp. lemon juice

Pour ingredients into a shaker with ice. Shake and strain into a martini glass. Garnish with a lemon twist.

ALLIGATOR

COLLINS

MAKES 1 DRINK

3 oz. vodka
2 oz. triple sec
2 oz. melon liqueur
1 oz. orange juice
   (no pulp)
1 oz. Sprite
1 oz. sweet-and-
   sour mix

Pour all ingredients into an ice-filled Collins glass and stir. Garnish with an orange slice.

ALMOND DELIGHT

SOUR GLASS

MAKES 1 DRINK

1½ oz. Sambuca
3 oz. Amaretto

Pour ingredients in a sour glass.

ALMOND GROVE

COLLINS

MAKES 1 DRINK

1 oz. Amaretto
1 oz. crème de
   coconut
dash cocoa powder

Pour ingredients into a shaker with ice. Shake well and strain into a martini glass. Garnish with grated nutmeg.

ALMOND JOY

MAKES 1 DRINK

½ oz. Amaretto
½ oz. white crème
    de cacao
2 oz. light cream

Pour ingredients into a shaker with ice. Shake and strain into a martini glass.

ALMOND JOYTINI

MARTINI

MAKES 1 DRINK

1 oz. coconut rum
1oz. Amaretto
1 oz. crème de
    cacao
2 oz. half-and-half

Pour ingredients into a shaker with ice. Shake well and strain into a martini glass.

ALMOND KISS

MAKES 1 DRINK

1 oz. Malibu rum
hot chocolate
whipped cream

Pour first two ingredients into an Irish coffee glass or mug. Top with whipped cream.

ALOHA

MAKES 1 DRINK

½ oz. dark rum
¼ oz. dry vermouth
¼ oz. cognac
¼ oz. gin
½ oz. lime juice
1 oz. club soda

Pour ingredients into a shaker with ice. Shake and strain into a large martini glass. Garnish with a slice of lime.

ALPINE LEMONADE

COLLINS

MAKES 1 DRINK

1 oz. vodka
1 oz. gin
1 oz. rum
2 oz. lemonade
2 oz. cranberry
*   juice*

Pour ingredients into a shaker with ice. Shake very well and strain into a Collins glass over ice.

ALTERNATINI

MARTINI

MAKES 1 DRINK

3 oz. vodka
1 tsp. white crème
*   de cacao*
½ tsp. sweet
*   vermouth*
½ tsp. dry vermouth

Pour ingredients into a shaker with ice. Shake well and strain into a chilled martini glass rimmed with sweetened cocoa powder. Garnish with a Hershey's Kiss.

ALYESKA'S BUTTERED RUM

IRISH COFFEE

MAKES 1 DRINK

2–3 tbs. buttered
*   rum mix*
1½ oz. spiced rum
hot water
whipped cream

Pour first two ingredients into an Irish coffee glass or mug and fill with hot water. Top with whipped cream.

AMARETTO SOUR

SOUR

MAKES 1 DRINK

1½ oz. Amaretto
1 oz. Rose's Lime

Pour ingredients into a shaker with ice. Shake well and strain into a sour glass over ice. Garnish with a lemon wedge and a cherry.

AMARETTO STINGER

MARTINI

MAKES 1 DRINK

2 oz. Amaretto
*2 oz. white crème
 de menthe*

Pour ingredients into a shaker with ice. Stir and strain into a martini glass.

AMBASSADOR

COLLINS

MAKES 1 DRINK

2 oz. tequila
orange juice
1 tsp. simple syrup

Pour ingredients into a Collins glass over ice. Garnish with an orange slice.

AMBER AMOUR

COLLINS

MAKES 1 DRINK

1½ oz. Amaretto
*½ oz. sweet-and-
 sour mix*
club soda

Pour first two ingredients into a Collins glass over ice. Top with club soda and stir. Garnish with a cherry.

AMBROSIA

HIGHBALL

MAKES 1 DRINK

1 oz. applejack
1 oz. brandy
dash triple sec
juice of 1 lemon
*Champagne
 (chilled)*

Pour first four ingredients into an ice-filled shaker. Shake well and strain into a highball glass over ice. Fill with Champagne and stir gently.

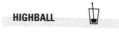

AMER PICON COCKTAIL

MARTINI

MAKES 1 DRINK

2 oz. Amer Picon
1 oz. lime juice or
*   juice of ½ lime*
1 tsp. grenadine

Pour ingredients into a shaker with ice. Shake well and strain into a martini glass.

AMERICAN BEAUTY

MARTINI

MAKES 1 DRINK

1 oz. brandy
½ oz. dry vermouth
¼ tsp. white crème
*   de menthe*
1 oz. orange juice
1 tsp. grenadine
½ oz. tawny port

Pour the first five ingredients into an ice-filled shaker. Shake well and strain into a martini glass. Float the port on top.

AMERICAN COBBLER

WINE

MAKES 1 DRINK

1½ oz. bourbon
1 oz. Southern
*   Comfort*
2 dashes peach
*   brandy*
4 dashes lemon juice
simple sugar (to
*   taste)*
club soda

Pour the first five ingredients into an ice-filled shaker. Shake well and strain into a large wine glass or goblet over ice. Fill with club soda. Garnish with a peach slice and a mint leaf.

AMERICAN FLAG

CORDIAL

MAKES 1 DRINK

1 oz. grenadine
1 oz. Parfait Amour
1 oz. maraschino
*   liqueur*

Layer ingredients in order in a cordial glass or pousse.

AMERICAN FLYER

WINE

MAKES 1 DRINK

1½ oz. light rum
1 tbs. lime juice
½ tsp. simple syrup
Champagne or
    sparkling wine

Pour first three ingredients into an ice-filled shaker. Shake and strain into a chilled wine glass. Fill with the Champagne.

AMERICAN GROG

IRISH COFFEE

MAKES 1 DRINK

1½ oz. rum
1 sugar cube
¼ lemon
boiling water

Put the sugar cube into the bottom of an Irish coffee glass or mug. Add the lemon juice, and then the rum. Fill the mug with the hot water.

AMERICAN LEROY

HIGHBALL

MAKES 1 DRINK

1 oz. Kahlua
1 oz. vodka
1 oz. Irish cream
1 oz. crème de
    cacao

Pour all ingredients in a blender. Blend until smooth and pour into a highball glass.

AMERICAN ROSE

WINE

MAKES 1 DRINK

1½ oz. brandy
½ tsp. Pernod
1 tsp. grenadine
½ peach, fresh,
    peeled and
    mashed
Champagne or
    sparkling wine

Pour first four ingredients into an ice-filled shaker. Shake well and strain into a chilled wine glass. Fill with Champagne and garnish with a peach slice.

AMERICAN SWEETHEART

MAKES 1 DRINK

1 oz. bourbon
1 oz. Southern
  Comfort
dash dry vermouth
sweet-and-sour mix

Pour ingredients into a shaker with ice. Shake well and strain into an old-fashioned glass over ice.

AMERICANA

COLLINS

MAKES 1 DRINK

¼ oz. Tennessee
  whiskey
1 tsp. fine sugar
dash bitters
Champagne, chilled

Pour the first three ingredients into a Collins glass over ice. Stir until the sugar dissolves. Fill with Champagne.

AMERICANO

OLD-FASHIONED

MAKES 1 DRINK

1 oz. Campari
½ oz. sweet
  vermouth
club soda

Pour Campari and sweet vermouth in an old-fashioned glass over ice. Stir. Top with club soda. Garnish with an orange slice.

ANACONDA

SHOT

MAKES 1 DRINK

¹/₃ oz. rum
¹/₃ oz. Goldschlager
¹/₃ oz. green crème
  de menthe

Pour all ingredients into a shot glass.

ANATOLE COFFEE

WINE

MAKES 1 DRINK

½ oz. cognac
½ oz. coffee
    liqueur
½ oz. Frangelico
iced coffee
whipped cream

Pour first three ingredients into a blender with ice. Blend thoroughly. Pour into a large wine glass. Top with the whipped cream.

ANGEL'S DELIGHT

MARTINI

MAKES 1 DRINK

1¼ oz. cream
¾ oz. triple sec
¾ oz. gin
2–3 dashes
    grenadine

Pour ingredients into a shaker with ice. Shake well and strain into a chilled martini glass.

ANGEL'S FALL

MARTINI

MAKES 1 DRINK

1½ oz. Amaretto
¾ oz. gin
¾ oz. vodka
¼ oz. 151 proof rum
¼ oz. dark rum
¼ oz. light rum
1½ oz. grenadine
splashes cranberry,
    pineapple, and
    grapefruit juices

Pour all ingredients into a blender with ice. Blend until smooth and serve in a large martini glass.

ANGEL'S KISS

CORDIAL

MAKES 1 DRINK

¼ oz. crème de
    cacao
¼ oz. Parfait Amour
¼ oz. brandy
¼ oz. cream

Layer ingredients in order in a cordial glass.

ANGEL'S LIPS

OLD-FASHIONED

MAKES 1 DRINK

3 oz. Benedictine
1½ oz. Irish cream
*   liqueur*

Pour ingredients in an old-fashioned glass over ice. Stir gently.

ANGEL'S TIT

PARFAIT

MAKES 1 DRINK

1½ oz. dark crème
*   de cacao*
cream

Pour crème de cacao into a parfait glass. Layer the cream on top and garnish with a cherry.

ANGEL'S WING

CORDIAL

MAKES 1 DRINK

½ oz. white crème
*   de cacao*
½ oz. brandy
1 tbs. light cream

Layer in order in a cordial glass.

ANJORSKA

HIGHBALL

MAKES 1 DRINK

1 1/3 oz. Bacardi
*   Limon*
2/3 oz. Passoa
1 2/3 oz. sweet-
*   and-sour mix*
1 2/3 oz. cranberry
*   juice*
2/3 oz. grape juice

Pour all ingredients into a highball glass over ice. Garnish with a slice of lime.

ANKLE BREAKER

OLD-FASHIONED

MAKES 1 DRINK

2 oz. 151 proof rum
1 oz. cherry brandy
1 oz. lime juice
1 tsp. simple syrup

Pour ingredients into a shaker with ice. Shake and strain into a chilled old-fashioned glass.

ANN SHERIDAN COCKTAIL

MARTINI

MAKES 1 DRINK

juice of ½ lime
1/3 oz. orange
* curaçao*
2/3 oz. white rum

Pour ingredients into a shaker with ice. Shake and strain into a martini glass.

ANTE

MARTINI

MAKES 1 DRINK

1¼ oz. calvados or
* apple brandy*
½ oz. Dubonnet
¼ oz. Cointreau
1 dash bitters

Pour ingredients into a shaker with ice. Stir well and strain into a martini glass.

ANTIBES

OLD-FASHIONED

MAKES 1 DRINK

2 oz. gin
¾ oz. Benedictine
2½ oz. grapefruit
* juice*

Pour ingredients into a shaker with ice. Stir well and pour into a chilled old-fashioned glass. Garnish with an orange slice.

ANTIFREEZE

MAKES 1 DRINK

1 oz. triple sec
1 oz. blue curaçao
6 oz. orange juice

Pour ingredients into a shaker with ice. Stir and strain into a highball glass over ice.

AODA SHOP COLA (NONALCOHOLIC)

MAKES 1 DRINK

¼ tsp. vanilla
extract
½ tsp. cherry
juice
cola
lemon wedge
for garnish

Fill a highball glass with ice. Add cherry juice and vanilla extract. Top with the cola. Garnish with the lemon wedge.

APERITIVO

MAKES 1 DRINK

3 oz. gin
1 oz. white
Sambuca
4 dashes orange
bitters

Pour ingredients into a shaker with ice. Stir and strain into a chilled martini glass. Garnish with an orange twist.

APHRODITE'S LOVE POTION

MAKES 1 DRINK

1½ oz. brandy
dash bitters
5 oz. pineapple
juice

Pour ingredients into a highball glass with ice and stir. Garnish with a cherry and an orange slice.

APOCALYPSE

MARTINI

MAKES 1 DRINK

1 oz. peppermint
   schnapps
¾ oz. Kahlua
½ oz. vodka
½ oz. bourbon
   whiskey

Pour ingredients into a shaker with ice. Stir well and strain into a martini glass.

APOCALYPSE NOW (SHOOTER) **SHOT**

MAKES 1 DRINK

¹/₃ oz. dry vermouth
¹/₃ oz. tequila
¹/₃ oz. Irish cream
   liqueur

Pour the first two ingredients into a shot glass and stir. Slowly add the Irish cream liqueur to fill.

APOLLO 13

CHAMPAGNE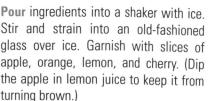

MAKES 1 DRINK

2 oz. white rum
2 oz. cream
½ oz. Grand
   Marnier
½ oz. Galliano
splash grenadine

Pour ingredients into a shaker with ice. Shake well and strain into a Champagne flute. Garnish with a cherry.

APPLE BLOSSOM

OLD-FASHIONED

MAKES 1 DRINK

2 oz. brandy
2 oz. apple juice
1 tsp. lemon juice
   or juice of ½
   lemon

Pour ingredients into a shaker with ice. Stir and strain into an old-fashioned glass over ice. Garnish with slices of apple, orange, lemon, and cherry. (Dip the apple in lemon juice to keep it from turning brown.)

APPLE BLOW

MARTINI

MAKES 1 DRINK

1½ oz. applejack
1 tbs. lemon juice
1 egg white
1 tsp. powdered
    sugar
1 oz. apple juice
6 oz. club soda

Pour ingredients into a shaker with ice. Shake well and strain into a martini glass.

APPLE BRANDY COCKTAIL

MARTINI

MAKES 1 DRINK

1½ oz. apple
    brandy
1 tsp. grenadine
1 tsp. lemon juice

Pour ingredients into a shaker with ice. Shake and strain into a martini glass.

APPLE BRANDY COOLER

COLLINS

MAKES 1 DRINK

2 oz. brandy
1 oz. light rum
1 oz. dark rum
4 oz. apple juice
½ oz. lime juice
1 tsp. simple syrup

Pour all ingredients except the dark rum into an ice-filled shaker. Shake well and strain into a chilled Collins glass. Float the dark rum on top. Garnish with a slice of lime.

APPLE CART

OLD-FASHIONED

MAKES 1 DRINK

1 oz. apple brandy
¾ oz. Cointreau
½ oz. lemon juice

Pour ingredients into a shaker and stir well. Pour into a chilled old-fashioned glass over ice.

APPLE COLADA

MAKES 1 DRINK

*2 oz. apple
    schnapps
1 oz. coconut
    cream
1 oz. half-and-half*

Pour ingredients into a blender with two cups of ice. Blend until smooth and pour into a Collins glass. Garnish with an apple slice and a cherry. (Dip the apple in lemon juice to keep it from turning brown.)

APPLE DAIQUIRI

MAKES 1 DRINK

*2 oz. light rum
¾ oz. calvados
½ oz. lemon juice
1 tsp. simple syrup
    (to taste)*

Pour ingredients into a shaker with ice. Shake well and strain into a chilled martini glass. Garnish with an apple slice. (Dip the apple in lemon juice to keep it from turning brown.)

APPLE DAIQUIRI

MARTINI

MAKES 1 DRINK

*1½ oz. light rum
1 oz. lime juice or
    juice of ½ lime
½ oz. calvados
1 tsp. fine sugar*

Pour ingredients into a shaker half filled with ice. Shake well. Strain into a martini glass. Garnish with an apple slice. (Dip the apple in lemon juice to keep it from turning brown.)

APPLE FIZZ

MAKES 1 DRINK

*2 oz. apple brandy
4 oz. apple juice
½ tsp. lime juice
sparkling water*

Pour all ingredients into a highball glass over ice. Garnish with a slice of lime.

APPLE GRANNY CRISP

MARTINI

MAKES 1 DRINK

1 oz. apple
   schnapps
½ oz. brandy
½ oz. Irish Cream
2 scoops of vanilla
   ice cream
graham cracker
   crumbs
whipped cream

Pour first five ingredients into a blender with crushed ice. Blend until smooth and poor into a large martini glass. Top with whipped cream and a dash of cinnamon.

APPLE KNOCKER

HIGHBALL

MAKES 1 DRINK

1½ oz. vodka
2 tbs. apple cider
1 tsp. lemon juice
1 tsp. strawberry
   liqueur

Pour ingredients into a shaker with ice. Shake well and strain into a highball glass over ice.

APPLE MARTINI

MARTINI

MAKES 1 DRINK

2 oz. gin or vodka
1 oz. green-apple
   schnapps

Pour ingredients into a shaker with ice. Shake well and strain into a chilled martini glass. Garnish with green apple peel.

APPLE PIE

MARTINI

MAKES 1 DRINK

1 oz. rum
½ oz. sweet
   vermouth
1 tsp. apple brandy
1 oz. lemon juice or
   juice of ½ lemon
½ tsp. grenadine

Pour ingredients into a shaker with ice. Shake well and strain into a martini glass.

APPLE PIE À LA MODE

MARTINI

MAKES 1 DRINK

¾ oz. spiced rum
½ oz. apple
   schnapps
2 oz. apple juice
2 tbs. apple pie
   filling
1 oz. coconut cream
1 oz. heavy cream
dash cinnamon

Pour ingredients into a shaker with ice. Blend until smooth and creamy. Pour into a large, chilled martini glass. Garnish with an apple slice and a cinnamon stick. Dip the apple in lemon juice to keep it from turning brown.

APPLE PIE MARTINI

MARTINI

MAKES 1 DRINK

3 oz. vanilla-
   flavored vodka
½ oz. calvados
½ oz. dry vermouth

Pour ingredients into a shaker with ice. Shake and strain into a chilled martini glass. Garnish with a thin slice of apple. (Dip the apple in lemon juice to keep it from turning brown.)

APPLE SAUCE

COLLINS

MAKES 1 DRINK

1 oz. spiced rum
3 oz. apple sauce
4 oz. sweet-and-
   sour mix
¼ oz. triple sec

Pour ingredients into a blender with 12 oz. of ice until slushy. Pour into a Collins glass.

APPLECART

MARTINI

MAKES 1 DRINK

1 oz. applejack
1 oz. triple sec
1 oz. lemon juice

Pour ingredients into a shaker with ice. Shake well and strain into a martini glass.

APPLETINI

MARTINI

MAKES 1 DRINK

2 oz. sour apple
schnapps
1 oz. vodka
dash sweet-and-
sour mix

Pour ingredients into a shaker with ice. Shake well and strain into a martini glass.

APRICOT COCKTAIL

MARTINI

MAKES 1 DRINK

1½ oz. apricot
brandy
1 tsp. gin
juice of ¼ lemon
juice of ¼ orange

Pour ingredients into a shaker with ice. Shake well and strain into a martini glass.

APRICOT COOLER

HIGHBALL

MAKES 1 DRINK

2 oz. apricot brandy
½ oz. grenadine
4 oz. lemon and
lime club soda

Pour brandy and grenadine into a highball glass over ice and stir. Fill with soda.

APRICOT FIZZ

HIGHBALL

MAKES 1 DRINK

2 oz. apricot brandy
1 oz. lemon juice
1 oz. lime juice
1 tsp. fine sugar
4 oz. club soda

Pour the juices, sugar, and liquor into an ice-filled shaker. Shake well and strain into a highball glass over ice. Add club soda and stir. Garnish with lemon slice.

APRICOT LADY

OLD-FASHIONED

MAKES 1 DRINK

1½ oz. white rum
1 oz. apricot brandy
1 tsp. triple sec
½ oz. lemon juice
1 egg white

Pour ingredients into a shaker with ice. Shake well and strain into an old-fashioned glass over ice. Garnish with an orange slice.

APRICOT SPARKLER (NONALCOHOLIC) OLD-FASHIONED

MAKES 1 DRINK

2 oz. apricot
   nectar
1 oz. lemon
   juice or juice
   of ½ lemon
club soda

Pour juices into an ice-filled shaker. Shake well and strain into an old-fashioned glass over ice. Add club soda and stir gently. Garnish with a lemon twist.

AQUARIUS

OLD-FASHIONED

MAKES 1 DRINK

1½ oz. blended
   scotch whiskey
½ oz. cherry brandy
1 oz. cranberry
   juice

Pour ingredients into a shaker with ice. Shake well and strain into an old-fashioned glass.

AQUEDUCT

MARTINI

MAKES 1 DRINK

1½ oz. vodka
1 tsp. white
   curaçao
1 tsp. apricot
   brandy
1 tbs. lime juice

Pour ingredients into a shaker with ice. Shake well and strain into a martini glass. Garnish with a lemon twist.

ARC DE TRIOMPHE

MARTINI

MAKES 1 DRINK

²/₃ oz. calvados
¹/₃ oz. lemon juice
1 tsp. sugar

Pour ingredients into a shaker with ice. Shake and strain into a martini glass.

ARCADIA

MARTINI

MAKES 1 DRINK

1½ oz. gin
½ oz. Galliano
½ oz. crème de
   banane
½ oz. grapefruit
   juice

Pour ingredients into a shaker with ice. Shake well and strain into a martini glass.

ARCHBISHOP

OLD-FASHIONED

MAKES 1 DRINK

2 oz. gin
1 oz. green ginger
   wine
1 tsp. Benedictine

Pour into an ice-filled old-fashioned glass. Stir well.

ARCTIC CIRCLE

HIGHBALL

MAKES 1 DRINK

1 oz. vodka
½ oz. lime juice
ginger ale

Pour vodka and lime juice into an ice-filled highball glass. Add ginger ale to fill. Garnish with crushed mint leaves.

ARKANSAS AVALANCHE

HIGHBALL

MAKES 1 DRINK

3 oz. Goldschlager
7 oz. Sprite
2 oz. grenadine

Pour ingredients into a shaker with ice. Shake and strain into a highball glass.

AROUND THE WORLD

MARTINI

MAKES 1 DRINK

¾ oz. dark rum
¼ oz. cognac
1¼ oz. orange juice
1 oz. sweet-and-sour mix
¼ oz. crème de noyaux

Pour ingredients into a blender with crushed ice until smooth. Pour into a large, chilled martini glass.

ARTILLERY

MARTINI

MAKES 1 DRINK

2 oz. gin
½ oz. sweet vermouth
dash bitters

Pour ingredients into a shaker with ice. Shake well and strain into a martini glass.

ARUBA

MARTINI

MAKES 1 DRINK

2 oz. gin
½ oz. white curaçao
½ egg white
1 oz. lemon juice
1 tsp. orgeat syrup

Pour ingredients into a shaker with ice. Shake well and strain into a chilled martini glass.

ASSASSIN

MARTINI

MAKES 1 DRINK

*¹/₃ oz. Jack
Daniel's whiskey*
¹/₃ oz. tequila
*¹/₃ oz. peppermint
schnapps*
cola

Pour ingredients into a martini glass. Stir well.

ASTERIX

HIGHBALL

MAKES 1 DRINK

*²/₃ oz. Finlandia
vodka*
*²/₃ oz. Pisang
Ambon*
fill with Sprite
dash lemon juice

Pour all ingredients into a highball glass over ice.

AUNT AGATHA

OLD-FASHIONED

MAKES 1 DRINK

1¼ oz. dark rum
2 oz. orange juice
3 drops of bitters

Pour into an old-fashioned glass over ice. Float bitters and garnish with an orange slice.

AUTUMN IN NEW YORK

IRISH COFFEE

MAKES 1 DRINK

1 oz. applejack
½ oz. Tuaca
hot apple cider
whipped cream

Pour the applejack and Tuaca into an Irish coffee glass or mug. Add the hot cider to fill. Top with whipped cream.

AVIATION

MAKES 1 DRINK

2 oz. gin
½ oz. maraschino
*   liqueur*
¼ oz. lemon juice

Pour ingredients into a shaker with ice. Shake well and strain into a martini glass. Garnish with a cherry.

AXIS KISS

MAKES 1 DRINK

dash Amaretto
*   almond liqueur*
dash crème de
*   cassis*
chilled Champagne

Pour Amaretto and crème de cassis in a Champagne flute. Top with the Champagne.

B

B & B

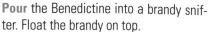

MAKES 1 DRINK

½ oz. brandy
½ oz. Benedictine

Pour the Benedictine into a brandy snifter. Float the brandy on top.

B. V. D. COCKTAIL

MAKES 1 DRINK

¾ oz. dry gin
¾ oz. dark rum
¾ oz. French
*   vermouth*

Pour ingredients into a shaker with ice. Stir well and strain into a martini glass.

B-52 SHOOTER

SHOT

MAKES 1 DRINK

½ oz. coffee
   liqueur
½ oz. Irish cream
   liqueur
½ oz. orange
   liqueur

Pour ingredients into a shaker with ice.
Stir well and strain into a shot glass.

BABY BELLINI (NONALCOHOLIC)

CHAMPAGNE

MAKES 1 DRINK

2 oz. peach
   nectar
1 oz. lemon
   juice or juice
   of ½ lemon
sparkling cider,
   chilled

Pour peach nectar and lemon juice
into a Champagne flute. Add sparkling cider to fill. Stir gently.

B

BABY DOE COLADA (NONALCOHOLIC)

MARTINI

MAKES 1 DRINK

2 oz. strawberries
3 oz. sweet-and-
   sour mix
2 oz. heavy cream
splash 7-Up

Pour ingredients into a blender with
ice. Blend until smooth and creamy.
Sugar the rim of a martini glass and
pour in the mixture. Garnish with
slice of lime.

BABYFACE MARTINI

MARTINI

MAKES 1 DRINK

3 oz. strawberry
   vodka
½ oz. dry vermouth
¼ tsp. maraschino
   liqueur

Pour ingredients into a shaker with
ice. Shake well and strain into a chilled
martini glass. Garnish with a whole
strawberry.

51

BACHELOR BUZZ (NONALCOHOLIC) IRISH COFFEE

MAKES 1 DRINK

1½ oz. espresso
½ oz. raspberry
   syrup
½ oz. hazelnut
   syrup
4 oz. hot
   chocolate

Pour espresso and hot chocolate into an Irish coffee glass or mug. Add the syrups and stir. Top with whipped cream.

BACHELOR'S BAIT MARTINI

MAKES 1 DRINK

2 oz. gin
3 dashes orange
   bitters
dash grenadine
1 egg white

Pour ingredients into a shaker with ice. Shake well and strain into a chilled martini glass.

BAILEY'S COMET SHOT

MAKES 1 DRINK

1½ oz. Bailey's
   Irish cream
   liqueur
¹/₈ oz. 151 rum
pinch of cinnamon

Pour the Bailey's into a shot glass. Float the 151 rum on top. Light the rum. Sprinkle cinnamon over the flame to create tiny firework-like sparkles (the comet effect). Allow the flame to die and then drink. Be careful of glass's hot rim. Wait until the fire has died down to drink the shot.

BALALAIKA MARTINI

MAKES 1 DRINK

½ oz. vodka
½ oz. Cointreau
½ oz. lemon juice

Pour ingredients into a shaker with ice. Shake well and strain into a martini glass.

BALI HAI

COLLINS

MAKES 1 DRINK

2 oz. light rum
1 oz. Aguardiente
2 oz. lime juice
2 oz. lemon juice
1 tsp. orgeat syrup
1 tsp. grenadine
Champagne or
    sparkling wine

Pour all ingredients except the Champagne into an ice-filled shaker. Shake well and strain into a Collins glass. Add Champagne to fill.

BALLET RUSSE MARTINI

MARTINI

MAKES 1 DRINK

2 oz. vodka
½ oz. crème de
    cassis
4 dashes lime juice

Pour ingredients into a shaker with ice. Shake well and strain into a martini glass.

BALMORAL

MARTINI

MAKES 1 DRINK

1½ oz. scotch
½ oz. sweet
    vermouth
½ oz. dry vermouth
2 dashes bitters

Pour ingredients into a shaker with ice. Stir and strain into a martini glass.

BALTIMORE BRACER

MARTINI

MAKES 1 DRINK

1 oz. brandy
1 oz. anisette
1 egg white

Pour ingredients into a shaker with ice. Shake well and strain into a martini glass.

BALTIMORE EGGNOG

MAKES 1 DRINK

1 oz. Jamaican rum
1 oz. brandy
1 oz. Madeira
1 egg
1 tsp. powdered
    sugar
¾ cup milk

Pour ingredients into a shaker with ice. Shake well and strain into a Collins glass. Top with a dash of nutmeg.

BAMBOO MARTINI

MAKES 1 DRINK

1 oz. dry sherry
1 oz. dry vermouth
dash orange bitters

Pour ingredients into a martini glass. Stir. Garnish with a lemon twist.

BANANA BANSHEE

MAKES 1 DRINK

2 oz. banana
    liqueur
2 oz. white crème
    de cacao
2 oz. light cream

Pour ingredients into a shaker with ice. Shake well and strain into a highball glass.

BANANA BERRY MARGARITA

MAKES 1 DRINK

1 whole banana
$^1/_3$ cup mixed
    berries
1¼ oz. silver
    tequila
½ oz. blue curaçao
½ oz. Chambord
1 oz. sweet-and-
    sour mix
splash orange juice

Pour ingredients into a blender with ice. Blend until slushy. Pour into a margarita glass. Garnish with a slice of lime.

BANANA BLISS

MARTINI

MAKES 1 DRINK

*1 oz. brandy
1 oz. banana
 liqueur*

Pour ingredients into a shaker with ice. Stir and strain into a martini glass.

BANANA COLADA

COLLINS

MAKES 1 DRINK

*2 oz. light rum
2 oz. coconut
 cream
1 banana, sliced
4 oz. pineapple
 juice*

Pour ingredients into a blender with ice. Blend thoroughly and pour into a Collins glass. Garnish with a slice of pineapple, a cherry, and a straw.

BANANA COW

MARTINI

MAKES 1 DRINK

*1½ oz. light rum
1 oz. crème de
 banane
1 oz. cream*

Pour ingredients into a shaker with ice. Shake well and strain into a martini glass. Garnish with a slice of a banana.

BANANA DREAM

MARTINI

MAKES 1 DRINK

*2 oz. Irish cream
 liqueur, chilled
½ oz. light rum
1 tbs. banana
 liqueur
½ banana, diced*

Pour ingredients into a blender with ½ cup crushed ice until smooth. Serve in a martini glass.

BANANA ITALIANO

MARTINI

MAKES 1 DRINK

1½ oz. Galliano
1 oz. crème de
banane
1 oz. half-and-half

Pour ingredients into a blender with ice until smooth. Pour into a chilled martini glass.

BANANA SPLIT

IRISH COFFEE

MAKES 1 DRINK

1 oz. banana
liqueur
½ oz. grenadine
6 oz. hot chocolate

Pour ingredients into an Irish coffee glass or mug. Top with whipped cream and cherry.

BANNOCKBURN

MARTINI

MAKES 1 DRINK

1 oz. scotch
dash Worcestershire
sauce
tomato juice

Pour ingredients into a martini glass. Garnish with a slice of lemon.

BANSHEE

MARTINI

MAKES 1 DRINK

2 oz. crème de
banane
1 oz. white crème
de cacao
1 oz. light cream

Pour ingredients into a shaker with ice. Shake well and strain into a martini glass.

BARBARELLA

OLD-FASHIONED

MAKES 1 DRINK

2 oz. Cointreau
1 oz. Sambuca,
 white

Pour ingredients into a shaker with ice. Shake and strain into a chilled old-fashioned glass.

BARBARY COAST

MARTINI

MAKES 1 DRINK

1 oz. gin
½ oz. scotch
½ oz. light rum
½ oz. white crème
 de cacao
1 oz. light cream

Pour ingredients into a shaker with ice. Shake well and strain into a martini glass.

BARBED WIRE

MARTINI

MAKES 1 DRINK

3 oz. vodka
½ tsp. sweet
 vermouth
½ tsp. Pernod
½ tsp. Chambord
 Raspberry
 Liqueur

Pour ingredients into a shaker with ice. Shake well and strain into a chilled martini glass. Garnish with a lemon twist.

BARBERSHOP POLE

SHOT

MAKES 1 DRINK

¼ oz. grenadine
¼ oz. white crème
 de cacao
¼ oz. cherry brandy
¼ oz. chocolate-
 flavored vodka
1 chocolate malted
 ball (like a
 Whopper)

Layer the grenadine, crème de cacao, cherry brandy, and vodka in that order into a tall shot glass. Gently garnish with the candy, which forms the top of the "barbershop pole."

BARBICAN

MARTINI

MAKES 1 DRINK

3½ oz. scotch
½ oz. Drambuie
1 oz. passion fruit
  juice

Pour ingredients into a shaker with ice. Shake well and strain into a martini glass.

BARELY LEGAL

COLLINS

MAKES 1 DRINK

1 oz. Amaretto
1 oz. 151 rum
Dr. Pepper or
  Mr. Pibb

Pour the Amaretto and rum into a Collins glass over ice. Add Dr. Pepper to fill and stir.

BARKING SPIDER

COLLINS

MAKES 1 DRINK

1½ oz. tequila
  (Tarantula Azul,
  preferred)
1½ oz. blue curaçao
¾ oz. 151 proof rum
dash triple sec
dash sweet-and-
  sour mix
splash orange juice

Pour ingredients into a Collins glass over ice.

BARN BURNER

IRISH COFFEE

MAKES 1 DRINK

1 oz. Southern
  Comfort
6 oz. hot apple
  cider

Pour ingredients into an Irish coffee glass or large mug. Stir gently.

BARN DOOR

HIGHBALL

MAKES 1 DRINK

1½ oz. vodka
pineapple juice
splash cranberry
juice

Pour ingredients into a highball glass over ice. Add pineapple juice to fill. Float the cranberry juice on top.

BARNUM

MARTINI

MAKES 1 DRINK

3 oz. gin
½ oz. apricot
brandy
4 dashes bitters
4 dashes lemon
juice

Pour ingredients into a shaker with ice. Shake well and strain into a chilled martini glass. Garnish with a lemon twist.

BARON COCKTAIL

MARTINI

MAKES 1 DRINK

½ oz. dry vermouth
½ tsp. sweet
vermouth
1½ tsp. triple sec
1½ oz. gin

Pour ingredients with ice into a shaker. Stir and strain into a martini glass. Garnish with a wedge of lemon.

BARONIAL

MARTINI

MAKES 1 DRINK

2 oz. Lillet
1 oz. gin
splash Cointreau
dash bitters

Pour ingredients into a shaker with ice. Stir and strain into a martini glass.

BARRACUDA BITE

COLLINS

MAKES 1 DRINK

*1½ oz.151 proof
    rum
1½ oz. vodka
½ oz. lime juice
½ oz. grenadine*

Pour ingredients into a shaker with ice. Stir gently and strain into a Collins glass over ice.

BASIN STREET

MARTINI

MAKES 1 DRINK

*2 oz. bourbon
1 oz. triple sec
1 oz. lemon juice*

Pour ingredients into a shaker with ice. Shake and strain into a martini glass.

BAT BITE

HIGHBALL

MAKES 1 DRINK

*1¼ oz. dark rum
4 oz. cranberry
    juice*

Pour ingredients into a highball glass. Garnish with a wedge of lime.

BAY BREEZE

HIGHBALL

MAKES 1 DRINK

*1½ oz. vodka
pineapple juice
cranberry juice*

Pour vodka into a highball glass over ice. Add pineapple juice to fill. Finish with a splash of cranberry juice.

BAY CITY BOMBER

PARFAIT

MAKES 1 DRINK

½ oz. vodka
½ oz. rum
½ oz. tequila
½ oz. gin
½ oz. triple sec
1 oz. orange juice
1 oz. pineapple juice
1 oz. cranberry juice
1 oz. sweet-and-
    sour mix
¼ oz. 151 proof rum

Pour all ingredients except the 151 rum into a blender with a cup of ice. Blend until smooth and pour into a parfait glass. Float 151 rum and garnish with a cherry and an orange slice.

BAZOOKA BOMBER

OLD-FASHIONED

MAKES 1 DRINK

½ oz. banana
    liqueur
½ oz. triple sec
dash grenadine

Pour all ingredients into an old-fashioned glass over ice.

BB GUN

COLLINS

MAKES 1 DRINK

1 oz. Sambuca
1 oz. vodka
1 oz. tequila
splash lime juice
splash lime Cordial
splash club soda

Pour all ingredients into a Collins glass over ice. Stir well.

BBC

MARTINI

MAKES 1 DRINK

1 oz. Bailey's Irish
    cream liqueur
1 oz. dark rum
1 oz. banana
    liqueur
1 banana
3 oz. piña colada
    mix

Pour the banana and the banana liqueur into a blender and spin into a thick paste. Add the Bailey's, piña colada mix, and rum. Blend until well mixed. Add a cup of crushed ice and blend until smooth. Serve in a large martini glass. Garnish with a sprig of mint.

BEACH BLANKET (NONALCOHOLIC) HIGHBALL

MAKES 1 DRINK

4 oz. white
   grape juice
3 oz. cranberry
   juice
club soda

Pour juices into a highball glass over ice. Add club soda to fill. Stir gently. Garnish with a slice of lemon, a slice of lime, and a cherry.

BEACH BUM
MARTINI

MAKES 1 DRINK

2 oz. light rum
½ oz. triple sec
½ oz. lime juice
dash grenadine

Pour all ingredients into a shaker half filled with ice. Shake well and strain into a martini glass rimmed with sugar.

BEACH COOLER
HIGHBALL

MAKES 1 DRINK

1 oz. 151 proof rum
1 oz. Cointreau
1½ oz. lime juice
2 oz. papaya nectar

Pour ingredients into a blender with about a cup of ice. Blend until slushy and pour into a highball glass.

BEACH CRUISER
COLLINS

MAKES 1 DRINK

1¼ oz. spiced rum
4 oz. pineapple
   juice
3 oz. cranberry
   juice

Pour ingredients into a shaker with ice. Shake and strain into a Collins glass. Garnish with a pineapple wedge.

BEACHCOMBER

MARTINI

MAKES 1 DRINK

1½ oz. light rum
½ oz. maraschino
liqueur
1 tsp. fine sugar
½ oz. lime juice

Pour ingredients into a shaker about half filled with ice. Shake well and strain into a martini glass.

BEAM ME UP SCOTTY

SHOT

MAKES 1 DRINK

½ oz. coffee
liqueur
½ oz. crème de
banane
½ oz. Irish cream

Pour ingredients into a shaker with ice. Shake well and strain into a shot glass.

BEARDED CLAM

MARTINI

MAKES 1 DRINK

1 oz. Crown Royal
1 oz. Amaretto
splash cranberry
juice

Pour ingredients into a martini glass over ice. Stir gently.

BEAUTY ON THE BEACH

HIGHBALL

MAKES 1 DRINK

1 oz. white rum
1 oz. Southern
Comfort
1 tbs. Grand
Marnier
1 tsp. lemon juice
2 dashes orange
bitters

Pour ingredients into a shaker with ice. Shake well and strain into a highball glass.

BEE STINGER

MARTINI

MAKES 1 DRINK

½ oz. white crème
    de menthe
1½ oz. blackberry
    brandy

Pour ingredients into a shaker with ice. Stir and strain into a martini glass.

BEER BELLY MARGARITA

MARGARITA

MAKES 1 DRINK

1½ oz. tequila
2 oz. Mexican beer
juice from half a
    lime
3 oz. sweet-and-
    sour mix

Pour ingredients into a blender with about a cup of ice. Blend until smooth. Pour into a margarita glass rimmed with kosher salt. Garnish with a slice of lime.

BEE'S KNEES

MARTINI

MAKES 1 DRINK

1½ oz. white rum
¼ oz. lemon juice
½ oz. honey

Pour ingredients into a shaker with ice. Shake and strain into a martini glass.

BEETLEJUICE

COLLINS

MAKES 1 DRINK

½ oz. vodka
½ oz. melon liqueur
½ oz. blue curaçao
½ oz. raspberry
    liqueur
½ oz. cranberry
    juice
sweet-and-sour mix

Fill a Collins glass with ice and add the vodka. Fill the glass ¾ full with the sweet-and-sour mix. Add the rest of the ingredients one at a time. Garnish with a pineapple spear and a cherry.

BEIGE RUSSIAN

HIGHBALL

MAKES 1 DRINK

1 oz. vodka
1 oz. Tia Maria
chocolate milk

Pour vodka and Tia Maria into a highball glass over ice. Add milk to fill. Stir.

BELLINI

CHAMPAGNE

MAKES 1 DRINK

2 oz. peach nectar
½ oz. lemon juice
chilled Champagne

Pour the juices into a Champagne flute. Stir. Add Champagne to fill. Stir gently.

BELLINSKI

WINE

MAKES 1 DRINK

1 oz. peach vodka
3 oz. peaches,
*   puréed or*
*   mashed*
1 tsp. maraschino
*   liqueur*
Champagne (brut)

Spoon the peaches into a large, chilled wine glass. Add the maraschino liqueur and the vodka. Stir. Add cold Champagne to fill.

BELMONT

MARTINI

MAKES 1 DRINK

2 oz. gin
½ oz. raspberry
*   syrup*
¾ oz. light cream

Pour ingredients into a shaker half filled with ice. Shake well. Strain into a martini glass.

BELMONT (NONALCOHOLIC)

COLLINS

MAKES 1 DRINK

3 oz. cran-raspberry drink
1 oz. club soda
1 scoop vanilla ice cream

Pour ingredients into a blender without ice. Blend thoroughly. Pour into a Collins glass.

BERLIN MARTINI

MARTINI

MAKES 1 DRINK

1½ oz. vodka
¹/₃ oz. blackberry brandy
splash black Sambuca

Pour ingredients into a shaker with ice. Stir well and strain into a martini glass. Garnish with a fresh blackberry.

BERMUDA ROSE

MARTINI

MAKES 1 DRINK

1¼ oz. dry gin
¼ oz. apricot nectar liqueur
¼ oz. grenadine

Pour ingredients into a shaker with ice. Shake well and strain into a martini glass.

BERMUDA TRIANGLE

OLD-FASHIONED

MAKES 1 DRINK

1 oz. peach schnapps
½ oz. spiced rum
3 oz. orange juice

Pour ingredients into an old-fashioned glass over ice.

BERRY BORDELLO

COLLINS

MAKES 1 DRINK

1 oz. strawberry
    vodka
½ oz. raspberry
    vodka
½ oz. raspberry
    liqueur
cranberry juice

Pour the first three ingredients into a Collins glass over ice. Add cranberry juice to fill and stir. Garnish with blueberries, raspberries, or a strawberry on the rim.

BÉSAME (KISS ME)

HIGHBALL

MAKES 1 DRINK

2 lime wedges
5–6 raspberries
1½ oz. Agavero
passion fruit juice
dash Chambord

Muddle limes and raspberries into a highball glass. Add Agavero. Add passion fruit juice to fill. Top with a splash of Chambord. Pour this mix into a cocktail shaker with ice. Shake well and strain back into the highball glass.

BET THE LIMIT

SHOT

MAKES 1 DRINK

½ shot tequila
½ shot Cointreau

Pour ingredients into a shaker with ice. Stir and strain into a shot glass.

BETSY ROSS

MARTINI

MAKES 1 DRINK

2 oz. brandy
1½ oz. port
dash triple sec

Pour ingredients into a shaker with ice. Stir well and strain into a martini glass.

BETWEEN THE SHEETS

MAKES 1 DRINK

¾ oz. brandy
¾ oz. light rum
¾ oz. triple sec
½ oz. lemon juice

Pour ingredients into a shaker with ice. Shake well and strain into a chilled martini glass. Garnish with the lemon twist.

BIG APPLE

PARFAIT

MAKES 1 DRINK

2 oz. apple brandy
½ oz. Amaretto
3 oz. apple juice
1 tbs. apple sauce

Pour ingredients into a shaker with ice. Blend until smooth. Pour into a parfait glass. Garnish with a dash ground cinnamon.

BIG BIRD

HIGHBALL

MAKES 1 DRINK

1 oz. banana
    schnapps
pineapple juice
orange juice

Pour the schnapps into a highball glass. Add pineapple and orange juice to fill.

BIG CHILL

COLLINS

MAKES 1 DRINK

1½ oz. dark rum
1 oz. coconut
    cream
1 oz. orange juice
1 oz. cranberry
    juice
1 oz. pineapple
    juice

Pour ingredients into a blender with about a cup of ice. Blend until smooth. Serve in a tumbler or Collins glass. Garnish with a pineapple wedge and a cherry.

BIG DIPPER

MAKES 1 DRINK

1 oz. Pusser's rum
1 oz. brandy
1 tbs. lime juice
½ tsp. sugar
dash Cointreau
club soda

Pour first five ingredients into a shaker with ice. Shake and strain into an old-fashioned glass over ice. Add club soda to fill.

BIG DOG

HIGHBALL

MAKES 1 DRINK

1 oz. Kahlua
1½ oz. vodka
milk
cola

Pour the Kahlua and vodka into a highball glass over ice. Add milk to within a half inch of the rim. Add a splash cola and stir.

BIG EASY

HIGHBALL

MAKES 1 DRINK

1 oz. Southern
    Comfort
1 oz. grenadine
cola

Pour Southern Comfort and grenadine into a highball glass over ice. Add cola to fill. Garnish with a cherry.

BIJOU

MARTINI

MAKES 1 DRINK

1 oz. gin
1 oz. Chartreuse
1 oz. sweet
    vermouth
1 dash orange
    bitters

Pour ingredients into a shaker with ice. Stir well and strain into a martini glass. Garnish with a cherry and lemon twist.

BIKINI

MARTINI

MAKES 1 DRINK

1 oz. white rum
2 oz. vodka
½ oz. milk
1 tsp. sugar
juice of ½ lemon

Pour ingredients into a shaker with ice. Shake and strain into a martini glass. Garnish with a lemon twist.

BIKINI (NONALCOHOLIC)

MARTINI

MAKES 1 DRINK

*5 oz. peach
    nectar*
*1 oz. raspberry
    syrup*
*1 oz. fresh
    lime juice*

Pour ingredients into a shaker half filled with ice. Shake well and strain into a martini glass.

BIRD OF PARADISE

MARTINI

MAKES 1 DRINK

¾ oz. tequila
*¾ oz. white crème
    de cacao*
½ oz. Amaretto
1 oz. cream

Pour ingredients into a shaker with ice. Shake well and strain into a martini glass.

BISHOP

HIGHBALL

MAKES 1 DRINK

4 oz. red wine
2 oz. orange juice
*1 oz. lemon juice or
    juice of ½ lemon*
1 tsp. fine sugar

Pour juices and sugar into a shaker nearly filled with ice. Stir and strain into a highball glass over ice. Add red wine to fill. Garnish with slices of orange and lemon.

BISTRO SIDECAR

MARTINI

MAKES 1 DRINK

1½ oz. brandy
½ oz. Tuaca
½ oz. Frangelico
splash lemon juice
splash simple syrup
wedge of tangerine,
*   squeezed*

Pour ingredients into a shaker with ice. Shake and strain into a sugar-rimmed martini glass. Garnish with a roasted hazelnut.

BITTERS HIGHBALL

HIGHBALL

MAKES 1 DRINK

¾ oz. bitters
ginger ale

Pour ingredients into a highball glass over ice. Stir. Garnish with a lemon twist.

BITTERSWEET MARTINI

MARTINI

MAKES 1 DRINK

1 oz. sweet
*   vermouth*
1 oz. dry vermouth
lemon twist

Pour ingredients into a shaker with ice. Stir and strain into a martini glass. Garnish with a lemon twist.

BLACK AND WHITE MARTINI

MARTINI

MAKES 1 DRINK

3 oz. vanilla vodka
1 oz. crème de
*   cacao*

Pour ingredients into a shaker with ice. Shake and strain into a chilled martini glass. Garnish with black and white licorice candies.

BLACK DEATH

COLLINS

MAKES 1 DRINK

½ oz. vodka
½ oz. Southern
  Comfort
½ oz. Amaretto
½ oz. curaçao
½ oz. triple sec
cranberry juice

Pour ingredients into a shaker with ice. Shake and strain into a Collins glass over ice.

BLACK DEVIL

MARTINI

MAKES 1 DRINK

2 oz. dark rum
½ oz. dry vermouth

Pour ingredients into a shaker with ice. Stir and strain into a martini glass. Garnish with a pitted black olive.

BLACK DOG

MARTINI

MAKES 1 DRINK

3 oz. light rum
½ oz. dry vermouth

Pour ingredients into a shaker with ice. Stir well and strain into a chilled martini glass. Garnish with a pitted black olive.

BLACK FEATHER

MARTINI

MAKES 1 DRINK

2 oz. brandy
1 oz. dry vermouth
½ oz. Cointreau
1 dash bitters

Pour ingredients into a shaker with ice. Stir and strain into a martini glass. Garnish with a lemon twist.

BLACK FOREST CAKE

MAKES 1 DRINK

¹/₃ oz. cherry
   whiskey
²/₃ oz. Swiss
   chocolate
   almond liqueur
6 oz. hot chocolate

Pour ingredients into an Irish coffee glass or mug. Top with whipped cream and garnish with a cherry and chocolate sprinkles.

BLACK HAWK

MARTINI

MAKES 1 DRINK

1½ oz. blended
   whiskey
1½ oz. sloe gin

Pour ingredients into a shaker half filled with ice. Stir and strain into a martini glass. Garnish with a cherry.

BLACK JACK

MARTINI

MAKES 1 DRINK

1½ oz. scotch
1 oz. Kahlua
½ oz. triple sec
½ oz. lemon juice

Pour ingredients into a shaker with ice. Shake well and strain into a martini glass.

BLACK LACE

MARTINI

MAKES 1 DRINK

2 oz. black
   Sambuca
1 oz. crème de
   banane
1 oz. peach
   schnapps
juice from ½ lemon

Pour ingredients into a shaker with ice. Shake well and strain into a chilled martini glass.

BLACK MAGIC

COLLINS

MAKES 1 DRINK

*2 oz. Blavod black
vodka*
½ oz. grenadine
7-Up

Pour the Blavod and grenadine into a Collins glass over ice. Fill with 7-Up and stir. Garnish with a maraschino cherry.

BLACK MAGIC SHOOTER

SHOT

MAKES 1 DRINK

2 oz. vodka
1 oz. coffee liqueur

Pour ingredients into a shaker half filled with ice. Shake well and strain into a shot glass.

BLACK MARIA

SNIFTER

MAKES 1 DRINK

2 oz. light rum
*1 oz. coffee-
flavored brandy*
*3 oz. strong black
coffee*
2 tsp. fine sugar

Pour all ingredients into a brandy snifter and stir. Add ice.

BLACK MARTINI

MARTINI

MAKES 1 DRINK

*1 oz. Blavod black
vodka*
*1 oz. raspberry
liqueur*
1 oz. triple sec
*2 oz. sweet-and-
sour mix*

Pour ingredients into a shaker about half filled with ice. Shake and strain into a martini glass. Sometimes served in a sugar-rimmed glass.

BLACK MONDAY

MARTINI

MAKES 1 DRINK

1 oz. dark rum
½ oz. black
   Sambuca
1 tsp. cherry
   brandy
½ oz. lemon juice

Pour ingredients into a shaker with ice. Shake well and strain into a martini glass.

BLACK ROSE

COLLINS ▮

MAKES 1 DRINK

²/₃ oz. Parfait
   Amour
²/₃ oz. gin (or
   vodka)
²/₃ oz. lemon juice
²/₃ oz. simple syrup
1¹/₃ oz. pineapple
   juice
club soda

Pour first five ingredients into a shaker with ice. Shake well and strain into a Collins glass over ice. Top with the club water and garnish with a cherry and mint sprig.

BLACK RUSSIAN

OLD-FASHIONED

MAKES 1 DRINK

1½ oz. vodka
1 oz. coffee liqueur

Pour ingredients into an old-fashioned glass and stir. Serve straight up or on the rocks.

BLACK THORN

OLD-FASHIONED ⎍

MAKES 1 DRINK

1½ oz Irish
   whiskey
1½ oz. dry
   vermouth
3 dashes Pernod
3 dashes bitters

Pour ingredients into a shaker with ice. Stir and strain into an old-fashioned glass over ice.

BLACK TURNCOAT

OLD-FASHIONED

MAKES 1 DRINK

2 oz. tequila
juice of ½ lime
splash water
cola

Pour the tequila and lime juice in an old-fashioned glass over ice. Add a splash water and stir. Top with chilled cola. Garnish with a lime twist.

BLACK VELVET

HIGHBALL

MAKES 1 DRINK

6 oz. stout or dark
  porter (chilled)
6 oz. Champagne or
  sparkling wine
  (chilled)

Pour the stout and the Champagne into a highball glass at the same time. Do not stir.

BLACK WATCH

MARTINI

MAKES 1 DRINK

1½ oz. scotch
1 oz. coffee brandy
splash club soda

Pour ingredients into a shaker with ice. Stir and strain into a martini glass.

BLACK WIDOW

MARTINI

MAKES 1 DRINK

¾ oz. dark rum
½ oz. Southern
  Comfort
1 oz. sweet-and-
  sour mix

Pour ingredients into a shaker with ice. Shake and strain into a martini glass. Garnish with a lemon twist.

BLAME IT ON RIO

COLLINS

MAKES 1 DRINK

¼ oz. vodka
¼ oz. spiced rum
¼ oz. Malibu rum
¼ oz. Amaretto
¼ oz. peach schnapps
¼ oz. banana liqueur
1½ oz. pineapple
    juice
club soda

Pour all ingredients except the club soda into a shaker with ice. Shake well and strain into a Collins glass. Top with a splash club soda and garnish with a lime twist.

BLARNEY STONE

MARTINI

MAKES 1 DRINK

2 oz. Irish whiskey
½ tsp. Anisette
½ tsp. Cointreau
½ tsp. maraschino
    liqueur
dash bitters

Pour ingredients into a shaker half filled with ice. Shake well and strain into a martini glass. Garnish with an olive.

BLEEDING HEART

OLD-FASHIONED

MAKES 1 DRINK

½ oz. Aalborg
    Akvavit
½ oz. cherry brandy

Pour ingredients into an old-fashioned glass. Serve straight up.

BLINDER

HIGHBALL

MAKES 1 DRINK

2 oz. scotch
5 oz. grapefruit
    juice
1 tsp. grenadine

Pour the first two ingredients into a high-ball glass over ice. Add grenadine and stir gently.

BLING BLING

MAKES 1 DRINK

2 oz. vodka
2 oz. white grape
    juice
2 oz. 7-Up

Pour all ingredients over ice into a high-ball glass. Stir gently.

BLISS

COLLINS

MAKES 8 DRINKS

2 liters pink
    lemonade
8 oz. vodka
4 oz. blue curaçao

Chill all ingredients. Pour into a large bowl or pitcher. Serve in tumblers or Collins glasses filled with ice.

BLITZ

SHOT

MAKES 4 DRINKS

1 oz. tequila
1 oz. rum
1 oz. gin
1 oz. vodka
1 oz. cranberry
1 oz. sweet-and-
    sour mix
splash tonic water

Pour all ingredients except the tonic into a shaker with ice. Shake and strain into four shot glasses. Top each shot with a splash tonic water. To drink: Instead of salt, start with a lick of sugar, toss back the shot, then suck a lime.

BLIZZARD

HIGHBALL

MAKES 1 DRINK

½ oz. white crème
    de cacao
½ oz. Chambord
¼ oz. vodka
¼ oz. Kahlua
a cup or so of cream
    or whole milk

Pour ingredients into a shaker with ice. Shake well and strain into a highball glass over ice.

BLOOD AND SAND

MARTINI 🍸

MAKES 1 DRINK

¾ oz. scotch
   whiskey
¾ oz. Cherry
   Heering
¾ oz. sweet
   vermouth
¾ oz. orange juice

Pour ingredients into a shaker with ice.
Shake and strain into a martini glass.

BLOODY BULL

HIGHBALL 🥃

MAKES 1 DRINK

2 oz. vodka
3 oz. tomato juice
2 oz. beef bouillon
dash Worcester-
   shire sauce
dash Tabasco sauce

Pour all ingredients into a highball glass
over ice and stir well. Garnish with a lime
wedge.

BLOODY MARY

HIGHBALL 🥃

MAKES 1 DRINK

2 oz. vodka
4 oz. tomato juice
½ oz. lemon juice
dash Worcestershire
   sauce
dash Tabasco sauce
shake salt and
   pepper
shake celery salt

Pour all ingredients into a highball glass
over ice and stir well. Garnish with a celery stick and a lime wedge.

BLOODY VIPER

WINE 🍷

MAKES 1 DRINK

4 oz. Tabasco
   extra spicy Bloody
   Mary mix
1½ oz. vodka
½ oz. Pernod
cracked pepper

Pour liquids into a shaker with ice. Pour
over ice in a large wine glass or goblet,
sprinkle with pepper. Garnish with a cor-
nichon (gherkin pickle).

BLOWJOB

MAKES 1 DRINK

½ oz. vodka
½ oz. coffee brandy
½ oz. coffee
    liqueur

Pour ingredients into a shaker half filled with ice. Shake well and strain into a shot glass.

BLUE BAZOOKI

MARTINI

MAKES 1 DRINK

1½ oz. Mandarin-
    flavored vodka
1½ oz. blue curaçao
splash orange juice
4 oz. sparkling
    mineral water

Pour the vodka, blue curaçao, and a generous splash of orange juice into a cocktail shaker containing ice made from mineral water. Add the 4 oz. of mineral water and shake well. Strain into a sugar-edged martini glass.

BLUE BLAZER

IRISH COFFEE

MAKES 1 DRINK

2½ oz. rye or
    bourbon
2½ oz. boiling
    water
1 tsp. powdered
    sugar
lemon peel

Start with two large mugs with handles. Put the whiskey in one mug, and the boiling water in the other. Light the whiskey and mix both ingredients by pouring them from one mug to the other. If done properly, it will look like a continued stream of liquid fire. Add sugar and garnish with lemon twist.

BLUE COBRA

MAKES 1 DRINK

2 oz. tequila
½ oz. blue curaçao
1½ oz. grapefruit
1 oz. lemon juice
club soda

Pour all ingredients except soda into a shaker with ice. Shake well and strain into an old-fashioned glass over ice. Top with club soda.

BLUE COCKTAIL

OLD-FASHIONED

MAKES 1 DRINK

1 oz. gin
1 oz. blue curaçao
1 lime

Squeeze juice from lime into a shaker filled with ice. Add the other ingredients and shake well. Pour into a sugar-rimmed old-fashioned glass over ice. Garnish with a lime twist.

BLUE DOLPHIN

COLLINS ▮

MAKES 1 DRINK

2 oz. vermouth
½ oz. blue curaçao
lemonade
dash grenadine

Pour vermouth and blue curaçao into an ice-filled Collins glass. Stir. Top up with lemonade and grenadine. Garnish with a lemon slice.

BLUE FIX

COLLINS ▮

MAKES 1 DRINK

½ lemon or lime
1 tsp. powdered
   sugar
1 tsp. water
2½ oz. blue curaçao

Squeeze the juice of lemon or lime into a Collins glass. Add sugar and water and stir. Fill the glass with ice. Add the blue curaçao and stir well. Garnish with a lemon slice and serve with a straw.

BLUE GRASS MARTINI

MARTINI

MAKES 1 DRINK

1½ oz. bourbon
1 oz. pineapple
   juice
1 oz. lemon juice
¼ oz. cherry liqueur

Pour ingredients into a shaker with ice. Shake well and strain into a chilled martini glass.

BLUE HAWAII

MAKES 1 DRINK

1 oz. light rum
1 oz. blue curaçao
pineapple juice
sweet-and-sour mix

Pour the rum and blue curaçao into an ice-filled Collins glass. Add the pineapple juice and sweet-and-sour mix in equal amounts to fill. Garnish with a cherry, pineapple slice, and paper parasol.

BLUE HAWAII SHAKE (NONALCOHOLIC)

COLLINS

MAKES 1 DRINK

½ cup blueberries, fresh or frozen
2 oz. coconut cream
4 oz. milk

Pour ingredients into a blender with ice. Blend thoroughly. Pour into a Collins or parfait glass. Garnish with orange slice and a cherry.

BLUE HERON

OLD-FASHIONED

MAKES 1 DRINK

2 oz. Canadian whiskey
1 oz. blueberry brandy
½ oz. cognac

Pour ingredients into a shaker with ice. Stir and strain into a chilled old-fashioned glass over ice or straight up in a martini glass.

BLUE LAGOON

HIGHBALL

MAKES 1 DRINK

1 oz. vodka
1 oz. blue curaçao
lemonade

Pour vodka and curaçao into a highball glass over ice and stir. Add lemonade to fill. Garnish with green cherry.

BLUE MARLIN

MARTINI

MAKES 1 DRINK

1 shot blue curaçao
1 shot light rum
4 oz. lemon-lime
mix

Pour ingredients into a shaker with ice. Shake and strain into a chilled martini glass.

BLUE TABOO

COLLINS

MAKES 1 DRINK

1 oz. blueberry
schnapps
½ oz. blue curaçao
½ oz. vodka
sweet-and-sour mix
7-Up

Pour the first three ingredients into a Collins glass over ice. Fill with equal amounts sweet-and-sour mix and 7-Up. Garnish with a maraschino cherry.

BLUE VELVETINI

MARTINI

MAKES 1 DRINK

1 oz. light rum
1 oz. blue curaçao
1oz. blueberry
schnapps
2 oz. white (clear)
cranberry juice
sugar
blue food coloring

Mix the sugar with just enough food coloring to make it blue, and put sugar in a saucer or small plate. Rim a martini glass with the blue sugar. Pour the first four ingredients into a shaker with ice. Shake and then strain into the glass.

BLUE WAVE

MARTINI

MAKES 1 DRINK

1 oz. light rum
½ oz. peach
schnapps
¼ oz. blue curaçao
2 oz. sweet-and-
sour mix

Pour all ingredients over ice in a large martini glass. Garnish with a lemon wedge.

BLUEBERRY MARGARITA   MARGARITA

MAKES 1 DRINK

½ cup fresh
    or frozen
    blueberries
1 oz. tequila
½ oz. blue curaçao
½ oz. Cointreau
½ oz. Chambord
2 oz. sweet-and-
    sour mix

Pour all ingredients into a blender with ice. Blend until slushy-smooth. Serve in a large margarita glass garnished with a slice of lime.

BLUSHIN' BERRY (NONALCOHOLIC)   COLLINS

MAKES 1 DRINK

½ cup fresh
    raspberries
½ cup straw-
    berry milk
1 cup lemon
    yogurt
½ cup milk

Pour the fresh raspberries, strawberry milk, lemon yogurt, and milk into a blender. Blend until smooth and pour into a Collins glass. Top with whipped cream. Garnish with strawberries, blueberries, and raspberries.

BLUSHING BRIDE (NONALCOHOLIC)   CHAMPAGNE

MAKES 1 DRINK

1 oz. raspberry
    syrup
3 oz. sparkling
    white grape
    juice
splash lemon
    juice

Pour the raspberry syrup and lemon juice into a Champagne glass and stir. Add grape juice to fill.

BLUSHING REINDEER   COLLINS

MAKES 1 DRINK

1 oz. white rum
1 oz. dark rum
½ oz. triple sec
1 squeeze lemon
    juice
1 dash grenadine
4 fresh
    strawberries

Pour all into a blender with ice. Serve in a Collins glass garnished with a strawberry.

BOA CONSTRICTOR

OLD-FASHIONED

MAKES 2 DRINKS

*2 oz. Southern
    Comfort
1 oz. bourbon
1 oz. Parfait Amour*

Pour ingredients into a shaker with ice. Shake well and strain into two chilled old-fashioned glasses over ice.

BOBBO'S BRIDE

MARTINI

MAKES 1 DRINK

*1 oz. gin
1 oz. vodka
¹/₃ oz. peach
    liqueur
¹/₆ oz. Campari*

Pour ingredients into a shaker with ice. Stir and strain into a martini glass. Garnish with a slice of fresh peach.

BOBBY BURNS

MARTINI

MAKES 1 DRINK

*1½ oz. scotch
1½ oz. sweet
    vermouth
1 tsp. Benedictine*

Pour ingredients into a shaker with ice. Stir and strain into a martini glass.

BOILERMAKER

SHOT

MAKES 1 DRINK

*1½ oz. whiskey
½ pint beer*

Down the whiskey and then sip the beer, or drop the whiskey, shot glass and all, into the mug of beer and chug it down before the foam hits the bar.

BOLERO

OLD-FASHIONED

MAKES 1 DRINK

1½ oz. light rum
¾ oz. calvados or
*   apple brandy*
1 tsp. sweet
*   vermouth*

Pour ingredients into a shaker with ice. Stir well and strain into an old-fashioned glass over ice.

BOLO

MARTINI

MAKES 1 DRINK

2 oz. light rum
1 oz. lime juice or
*   juice of ½ lime*
1 oz. orange juice
1 tsp. fine sugar

Pour ingredients into a shaker nearly filled with ice. Shake well and strain into a martini glass.

BOMBAY COCKTAIL

MARTINI

MAKES 1 DRINK

1 oz. brandy
½ oz. dry vermouth
½ oz. sweet
*   vermouth*
½ oz. triple sec

Pour ingredients into a shaker nearly filled with ice. Stir and strain into a martini glass. Garnish with a lemon twist.

BONNIE PRINCE

OLD-FASHIONED

MAKES 1 DRINK

2 oz. gin
½ oz. white wine
¼ oz. Drambuie

Pour ingredients into a shaker with ice. Shake and strain into a chilled old-fashioned glass.

BOOMERANG MARTINI

MARTINI

MAKES 1 DRINK

3 oz. gin
1 oz. dry vermouth
dash bitters
dash maraschino
*   liqueur*

Pour ingredients into a shaker with ice. Stir well and strain into a chilled martini glass. Garnish with a kiwi slice.

BOOTLEGGER

OLD-FASHIONED

MAKES 1 DRINK

1½ oz. Tennessee
*   bourbon*
1½ oz. tequila
1½ oz. Southern
*   Comfort*

Pour all ingredients into an old-fashioned glass and stir.

BORDEAUX COCKTAIL

MARTINI

MAKES 1 DRINK

1½ oz. citron vodka
½ oz. Lillet

Pour ingredients into a shaker with ice. Stir and strain into a martini glass. Garnish with a lemon twist.

BORDER CROSSING

HIGHBALL

MAKES 1 DRINK

2 oz. tequila
1 tsp. Rose's lime
*   juice*
1 tsp. lemon juice
4 oz. cola

Pour ingredients into a highball glass nearly filled with ice and stir. Garnish with a lime wedge.

BORN ON THE 4TH OF JULY

MARTINI

MAKES 1 DRINK

1½ oz. cherry-
flavored vodka
or rum
½ oz. blue curaçao
3 oz. white
cranberry juice

Pour the cherry-flavored vodka or rum and the white cranberry juice into a shaker filled with ice. Shake well and strain into a martini glass. Float the blue curaçao on top by pouring it over the back of a spoon. Garnish with a cherry.

BOSOM CARESSER

MARTINI

MAKES 1 DRINK

1½ oz. brandy
1 oz. Madeira
½ oz. triple sec

Pour ingredients into a shaker nearly filled with ice. Stir and strain into a martini glass.

BOSSA NOVA

MARTINI

MAKES 1 DRINK

¾ oz. dark rum
¼ oz. apricot
brandy
¼ oz. Galliano
5 oz. pineapple
juice
½ oz. lemon juice

Pour ingredients into a shaker with ice. Shake and strain into a martini glass over ice. Garnish with a pineapple fruit flag.

BOSTON COOLER

HIGHBALL

MAKES 1 DRINK

2 oz. rum
1 oz. lemon juice or
juice of ½ lemon
1 tsp. fine sugar
3 oz. club soda or
ginger ale

Into a highball glass, pour lemon juice, sugar, and a bit of soda. Stir. Nearly fill the glass with ice. Add rum and soda and stir. Garnish with a lemon twist.

BOSTON COOLER 2

MAKES 1 DRINK

2 oz. rum
2 oz. carbonated
    water
½ tsp. powdered
    sugar
carbonated water
    or ginger ale

Into a Collins glass, pour powdered sugar and carbonated water. Stir. Fill the glass with ice and add the rum. Top with carbonated water or ginger ale. Garnish with a spiral of orange or lemon peel (or both), dangled over the rim of the glass.

BOSTON SIDECAR

MARTINI

MAKES 1 DRINK

1 oz. light rum
½ oz. brandy
¾ oz. triple sec
1 oz. lime juice or
    juice of ½ lime

Pour ingredients into a shaker with ice. Shake and strain into a martini glass.

BOSTON SOUR

SOUR GLASS

MAKES 1 DRINK

2 oz. blended
    scotch
juice of ½ lemon
1 tsp. powdered
    sugar
1 egg white

Pour ingredients into a shaker with ice. Shake and strain into a sour glass. Garnish with a slice of lemon and a cherry.

BOSTON TEA PARTY

COLLINS

MAKES 1 DRINK

1 oz. vodka
1 oz. scotch
1 oz. triple sec
1 oz. dry vermouth
1 oz. rum
1 oz. gin
1 oz. tequila
orange juice
cola
sweet-and-sour mix

Pour alcohol and sweet-and-sour mix into a Collins glass. Fill the rest of the glass with a 50/50 mix of orange juice and cola.

BOURBON AND BRANCH

MAKES 1 DRINK

2 oz. bourbon
4 oz. mineral water

This drink is the updated version of bourbon and water, using mineral water as the "branch water." Pour bourbon and water into an old-fashioned glass nearly filled with ice. Stir. Garnish with a lemon twist.

BOURBON COBBLER

WINE

MAKES 1 DRINK

2 oz. bourbon
1 tbs. grapefruit
   juice
1 tsp. lemon juice
1 tsp. almond
   extract

Pour ingredients into a shaker half-filled with ice. Shake well and strain into a large wine glass or goblet over ice. Garnish with orange and lemon slices. Serve with a straw.

BOURBON CRUSTA

MARTINI

MAKES 1 DRINK

2 oz. bourbon
½ oz. triple sec
½ oz. maraschino
   liqueur
½ oz. lemon juice
2 dashes orange
   bitters

Pour ingredients into a shaker with ice. Shake and strain into a martini glass. Garnish with an orange twist.

BOURBON FURNACE

 IRISH COFFEE

MAKES 1 DRINK

6 oz. hot apple
   cider
3 whole cloves
1 stick cinnamon
1½ oz. bourbon

Pour all ingredients into an Irish coffee mug and serve immediately.

BOURBON HIGHBALL

MAKES 1 DRINK

2 oz. bourbon
ginger ale or club
soda

Pour the bourbon and soda into a high-ball glass nearly filled with ice. Garnish with a lemon twist.

BOURBON OLD-FASHIONED

OLD-FASHIONED

MAKES 1 DRINK

2 oz. bourbon
1 cube or ½ tsp.
sugar
1 tsp. water
dash or 2 bitters

Pour the sugar, bitters, and water into an old-fashioned glass and muddle with a spoon. Add the bourbon and stir. Add ice and a lemon twist. Garnish with a slice of orange or lemon and a cherry.

BOURBON ON THE ROCKS

OLD-FASHIONED

MAKES 1 DRINK

2 oz. bourbon

Pour bourbon into an old-fashioned glass nearly filled with ice. Stir.

BOURBON ROSE

HIGHBALL

MAKES 1 DRINK

1½ oz. bourbon
1 oz. triple sec
4 oz. orange juice
grenadine

Pour first three ingredients into a shaker with ice. Shake and strain into a highball glass over ice. Float a splash of grenadine on top.

BOURBON SATIN

MARTINI

MAKES 1 DRINK

1½ oz. bourbon
1 oz. white crème
   de menthe
1 oz. light cream

Pour ingredients into a shaker half filled with ice. Shake well. Strain into a martini glass.

BOURBON SLUSH

MARTINI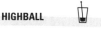

MAKES 6 DRINKS

2½ cups hot tea
12 oz. frozen
   lemonade,
   thawed
6 oz. frozen orange
   juice
2 cups bourbon
1 cup sugar
6 cups water

Let the tea cool, then pour all the ingredients into a plastic container and freeze. Scoop frozen mixture into martini glasses. Garnish with pineapple chunks, a cherry on a toothpick, and a sprig of mint.

BOXCAR

COLLINS ▮

MAKES 1 DRINK

1½ oz. gin
1 oz. triple sec
1 tsp. lemon juice
½ tsp. grenadine
1 egg white

Pour ingredients into a shaker with ice. Shake well and strain into an old-fashioned glass.

BRAIN DRAIN

HIGHBALL ⊔

MAKES 1 DRINK

1½ oz. peach
   schnapps
   (strawberry or
   butterscotch
   will also work)
1½ oz. Bailey's
   Irish cream
   liqueur
dash grenadine

Pour the schnapps into a highball glass. Pour the Bailey's in a smooth stream into the center of the schnapps. The Irish cream will form a lumpy ball suspended in the clear schnapps that resembles a brain. Top with grenadine.

BRAIN HEMORRHAGE

SHOT

MAKES 1 DRINK

¾ oz. coffee
    liqueur
¾ oz. vodka
splash Irish cream
    liqueur
splash grenadine

Pour the coffee liqueur and vodka into a shaker half-filled with ice. Shake and strain into a shot glass. "Swirl" the Irish cream and then the grenadine into the glass.

BRAINSTORM

MARTINI

MAKES 1 DRINK

2 oz. scotch
½ oz. Benedictine
1 tsp. sweet
    vermouth

Pour ingredients into a shaker with ice. Shake and strain into a martini glass.

BRANDED NIPPLE

SHOT

MAKES 1 DRINK

½ oz. butterscotch
    schnapps
½ oz. Irish cream
    liqueur
¹/₈ oz. 151 rum

Pour the butterscotch schnapps into a shot glass. Gently pour the Irish cream over the back of a spoon to layer it on top. Layer the rum on top of the Irish cream in the same way. Light the rum. Blow out the flaming liquor before drinking.

BRANDY ALEXANDER

MARTINI

MAKES 1 DRINK

1½ oz. brandy
1 oz. dark crème de
    cacao
1 oz. cream

Pour ingredients into a shaker nearly filled with ice. Strain into a martini glass. Garnish with a dash of nutmeg.

BRANDY CASSIS

MARTINI

MAKES 1 DRINK

1½ oz. brandy
¼ oz. crème de
cassis
1 oz. lemon juice or
juice of ½ lemon

Pour ingredients into a shaker nearly filled with ice. Stir and strain into a martini glass. Serve with a lemon twist.

BRANDY COBBLER

WINE

MAKES 1 DRINK

2 oz. brandy
2 oz. club soda
1 tsp. fine sugar
crushed ice

Pour club soda into a large wine glass or goblet. Add sugar and dissolve. Fill with ice. Add brandy and stir. Garnish with orange and lemon slices and a cherry, and serve with a straw.

BRANDY DAISY

OLD-FASHIONED

MAKES 1 DRINK

2 oz. brandy
1 oz. lemon juice or
juice of ½ lemon
½ tsp. fine sugar
1 tsp. grenadine

Pour the ingredients into a shaker half filled with ice. Shake well and strain into an old-fashioned glass. Garnish with orange and lemon slices and a cherry.

BRANDY DAISY 2

IRISH COFFEE

MAKES 1 DRINK

2 oz. California
brandy
juice of ½ lemon
1 tsp. raspberry
syrup or
grenadine
½ tsp. powdered
sugar

Pour ingredients into a shaker with ice. Shake well and strain into beer stein or an Irish coffee glass. Add a cube of ice and garnish with slices of orange and lemon and a cherry.

BRANDY FIX

HIGHBALL

MAKES 1 DRINK

2 oz. brandy
1 oz. lemon juice or
*   juice of ½ lemon*
1 tsp. fine sugar
2 tsp. water

Pour the sugar, lemon juice, and water into a shaker with ice. Shake and strain into a highball glass over ice. Add the brandy and stir. Garnish with lemon and serve with a straw.

BRANDY FIZZ

HIGHBALL

MAKES 1 DRINK

2 oz. brandy
1 oz. lemon juice or
*   juice of ½ lemon*
1 tsp. fine sugar
4 oz. club soda

Pour the lemon juice, sugar, and liquor into a shaker half filled with ice. Shake well and strain into a highball glass over ice. Add club soda to fill and stir. Garnish with a lemon slice.

BRANDY HOT TODDY

IRISH COFFEE

MAKES 1 DRINK

2 oz. California
*   brandy*
1 lump sugar
slice lemon
boiling water
fresh nutmeg

Put the lump of sugar into a warmed Irish coffee glass or large mug and fill two-thirds with boiling water. Add the brandy and stir. Grate the nutmeg on top. Garnish with a lemon slice.

BRANDY JULEP

WINE

MAKES 1 DRINK

1½ oz. cognac
1 tsp. powdered
*   sugar*
2 tsp. water
8–10 fresh mint
*   leaves*
dash Jamaican rum

Fill a large wine glass or goblet with crushed ice and add the cognac. In a separate glass, muddle the mint with the sugar and water, and then strain into the goblet. Add dash rum and stir. Garnish with fruit and a few sprigs of mint dipped in sugar. Serve with a straw.

BRANDY SMASH

OLD-FASHIONED

MAKES 1 DRINK

2 oz. brandy
1 tsp. fine sugar
4 sprigs of mint
1 oz. club soda

Muddle the sugar with the mint and club soda in an old-fashioned glass. Fill the glass with ice and add the brandy. Stir well. Garnish with a lemon twist.

BRANDY SOUR

SOUR GLASS

MAKES 1 DRINK

2 oz. brandy
1 oz. lemon juice or
   juice of ½ lemon
1 tsp. fine sugar
   (or 1½ oz.
   sweet-and-sour
   mix instead
   of lemon and
   sugar)

Pour ingredients into a shaker with ice. Shake and strain into a sour glass. Garnish with a lemon slice and a cherry.

BRANDY STRUDEL

IRISH COFFEE

MAKES 1 DRINK

1 oz. brandy
6 oz. hot spiced
   cider

Pour ingredients into a large mug or Irish coffee glass and stir. Garnish with a cinnamon stick and a lemon wedge.

BRANDY SWIZZLE

COLLINS

MAKES 1 DRINK

2 oz. brandy
1½ oz. lime juice or
   juice of 1 lime
1 tsp. fine sugar
2 dashes bitters
3 oz. club soda

Pour the lime juice, sugar, liquor, and bitters into a shaker half filled with ice. Shake well and strain into a Collins glass over ice. Stir. Add club soda to fill. Serve with a swizzle stick.

BRANDY VERMOUTH CLASSIC **MARTINI**

MAKES 1 DRINK

2 oz. brandy
½ oz. sweet
  vermouth
dash bitters

Pour ingredients into a shaker half filled with ice. Stir and strain into a martini glass.

BRASS MONKEY **HIGHBALL**

MAKES 1 DRINK

2 oz. rum
2 oz. vodka
orange juice

Pour ingredients into a highball glass over ice. Stir.

BRAVE BULL **OLD-FASHIONED**

MAKES 1 DRINK

2 oz. tequila
1 oz. coffee liqueur

Pour ingredients into an old-fashioned glass almost filled with ice. Stir well.

BRAVE WHITE BULL **OLD-FASHIONED**

MAKES 1 DRINK

1¼ oz. tequila
1½ oz. Kahlua
1 oz. heavy cream

Pour ingredients into a shaker about half-filled with ice. Shake well and strain into an old-fashioned glass. Sprinkle with nutmeg.

BRECKENRIDGE MUDSLIDE

MAKES 1 DRINK

½ oz. Irish cream
    liqueur
½ oz. Kahlua coffee
    liqueur
½ oz. vodka
3 oz. chocolate
    milk
crushed Oreo
    cookie

Pour all ingredients except the Oreos in a blender. Blend until smooth. Pour into a Collins glass. Top with the crushed cookie bits.

BRIDAL PARTY

MARTINI

MAKES 1 DRINK

2 oz. gin
1 oz. sweet
    vermouth
splash maraschino
    liqueur
dash orange bitters

Pour ingredients into a shaker with ice. Stir and strain into a martini glass. Garnish with a cherry.

BROKEN ANKLE

MAKES 1 DRINK

8 oz. hot spiced
    cider
1¼ oz. brandy

Pour the brandy into a warm Irish coffee glass. Add the hot cider and stir. Garnish with a cinnamon stick.

BROKEN LEG

IRISH COFFEE

MAKES 1 DRINK

8 oz. hot spiced
    cider
1¼ oz. rum

Pour the rum into a warm Irish coffee glass. Add the hot cider and stir. Serve with cinnamon stick.

BRONX

MARTINI

MAKES 1 DRINK

1½ oz. gin
¾ oz. sweet
vermouth
¾ oz. dry vermouth
¾ oz. orange juice

Pour ingredients into a shaker with ice. Shake and strain into a martini glass.

BROOKLYN

MARTINI

MAKES 1 DRINK

2 oz. rye whiskey
1 oz. dry vermouth
dash Amer Picon
dash maraschino
liqueur

Pour ingredients into a shaker half filled with ice. Shake well and strain into a martini glass.

BROWN BEAR

MARTINI

MAKES 1 DRINK

1 oz. pepper-
flavored vodka
1½ oz. coffee
liqueur

Pour ingredients into a shaker with ice. Shake and strain into a martini glass.

BROWN COW

HIGHBALL

MAKES 1 DRINK

1½ oz. Kahlua
milk

Pour the Kahlua into a highball over ice. Add the milk to fill. Stir and garnish with a dash of nutmeg.

BUBBLY MARTINI

MAKES 1 DRINK

1½ oz. gin
¾ oz. Champagne

Pour ingredients into a shaker with ice and stir gently. Strain into a martini glass. Garnish with two olives.

BUBBLY MINT

MAKES 1 DRINK

½ oz. white crème
de menthe
Champagne, chilled

Pour the crème de menthe into a Champagne glass and add the Champagne to fill.

BUCK'S FIZZ

MAKES 1 DRINK

5 oz. Champagne,
chilled
½ oz. triple sec
1 oz. orange juice
½ tsp. grenadine

Pour the Champagne, triple sec, and orange juice into a Champagne flute. Add the grenadine and stir. Garnish with an orange slice.

BUCKEYE MARTINI

MAKES 1 DRINK

3 oz. gin
½ oz. dry vermouth

Pour ingredients into a shaker with ice. Stir very gently and strain into a chilled martini glass. Garnish with a black olive.

BULL AND BEAR

MARTINI

MAKES 1 DRINK

2 oz. bourbon
1 oz. orange
* curaçao*
1 tbs. grenadine
1 oz. lime juice or
* juice of ½ lime*

Pour ingredients into a shaker half filled with ice. Shake well. Strain into a martini glass. Garnish with a cherry.

BULL SHOT

HIGHBALL

MAKES 1 DRINK

1½ oz. vodka
4 oz. chilled beef
* bouillon*
1 tsp. lemon juice
4 dashes Worcester-
* shire sauce*
Tabasco sauce to
* taste*
celery salt to taste
salt and pepper to
* taste*

Pour ingredients into a shaker half filled with ice. Shake well and strain into a highball glass over ice.

BULLDOG

HIGHBALL

MAKES 1 DRINK

1½ oz. gin
ginger ale
splash orange juice

Pour the gin into a highball glass. Add ginger ale to fill. Finish with a splash OJ.

BULLFROG

COLLINS

MAKES 1 DRINK

2 oz. vodka
4 oz. lemonade
1 tsp. Cointreau

Pour vodka and Cointreau into a Collins glass nearly filled with ice. Add lemonade to fill. Stir well. Garnish with a lemon wedge.

BULL'S EYE

MAKES 1 DRINK

1 oz. brandy
2 oz. cider
ginger ale

Pour the brandy and cider into a highball glass over ice. Add ginger ale to fill. Stir.

BURNING BUSH

MAKES 1 DRINK

*1 bottle of beer
(originally
called for Bush
beer)*
*1 oz. Southern
Comfort*
1/8 oz. 151 rum

Pour the beer into a beer glass. Pour the Southern Comfort into a shot glass. Carefully float the 151 rum on top of the Southern Comfort. Ignite the rum and let it burn for a bit so most of the rum burns away. Drop the shot into the beer and chug.

BURNT MARTINI

MAKES 1 DRINK

2 oz. dry gin
*1 oz. single malt
scotch whiskey*

Pour ingredients into a martini glass rimmed with bourbon or scotch. Stir gently.

BUSHWACKER

MAKES 1 DRINK

1 oz. rum
1 oz. vodka
1 oz. Kahlua
*1 oz. Irish cream
liqueur*
1 oz. Amaretto
1 oz. Frangelico
*1 oz. crème de
cacao*

Pour ingredients into a blender with ice. Blend until smooth. Pour into a Collins glass. Garnish with a dash of nutmeg.

BUSTIER

MAKES 1 DRINK

½ oz. apricot
    brandy
½ oz. Amaretto
3 oz. pineapple
    juice
Sprite
dash grenadine

Pour brandy and Amaretto into a shaker with ice. Shake well and strain into a Collins glass filled with ice. Add Sprite to fill. Top with a dash of grenadine. Garnish with a cherry.

BUTTER SHOTS

MAKES 1 DRINK

1 oz. butterscotch
    schnapps
1 oz. Kahlua

Pour ingredients into a shot glass and serve.

BUTTERFINGER

HURRICANE

MAKES 1 DRINK

½ oz. Kahlua
½ oz. Frangelico
½ oz. vodka
½ oz. Irish cream
    liqueur
½ oz. Butter Shots
    (see above)

Pour ingredients into a shaker with ice. Shake and strain into a hurricane glass filled with ice.

BUZZARD'S BREATH

MAKES 1 DRINK

½ oz. Amaretto
½ oz. coffee
    liqueur
½ oz. peppermint
    schnapps

Pour ingredients into a shaker with ice. Stir and strain into a shot glass.

CABARET

MARTINI

MAKES 1 DRINK

1 oz. gin
¾ oz. dry vermouth
¼ oz. Benedictine
2 dashes bitters

Pour ingredients into a shaker with ice. Stir and strain into a martini glass. Garnish with a cherry.

CABLE CAR

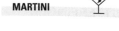

MARTINI

MAKES 1 DRINK

2 oz. spiced rum
1 oz. Cointreau
¹/₃ oz. lemon juice

Pour ingredients into a shaker about half-filled with ice. Shake well and strain into a martini glass rimmed with sugar and cinnamon. Garnish with a lemon twist and a dash of cinnamon.

CABO WABO

MARTINI

MAKES 1 DRINK

1½ oz. gold tequila
¾ oz. Grand
  Marnier
1½ oz. sweet-and-
  sour mix
3 oz. cranberry
  juice
splash Rose's lime
  juice

Pour the first 4 ingredients into a shaker with ice. Shake vigorously and strain into a martini glass. Finish with a splash of Rose's lime juice.

CACTUS BITE

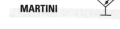

MARTINI

MAKES 1 DRINK

1½ oz. tequila
1 oz. lemon juice or
  juice of ½ lemon
2 tsp. Cointreau
2 tsp. Drambuie
½ tsp. fine sugar
dash bitters

Pour ingredients into a shaker half filled with ice. Shake well. Strain into a martini glass.

C

CADIZ

OLD-FASHIONED

MAKES 1 DRINK

¾ oz. dry sherry
¾ oz. blackberry
　brandy
½ oz. triple sec
1 tbs. light cream

Pour ingredients into a shaker with ice. Shake and strain into an old-fashioned glass.

CAESAR

HIGHBALL

MAKES 1 DRINK

1 oz. vodka
4 oz. Clamato juice
pinch of salt and
　pepper
dash Worcester-
　shire sauce
2 to 3 dashes
　horseradish

Pour ingredients into a shaker with ice. Shake and strain over ice into a highball glass rimmed with celery salt. Garnish with a celery stalk and a lemon wedge.

CAFE ROMANO

MARTINI

MAKES 1 DRINK

1 oz. white
　Sambuca
1 oz. coffee liqueur
1 oz. half-and-half

Pour ingredients into a shaker with ice. Shake and strain into a martini glass.

C

CAFE ROYAL

IRISH COFFEE

MAKES 1 DRINK

1 tsp. California
　brandy
1 cube sugar
coffee

Put the sugar cube in a teaspoon filled with brandy and hold it so that it will rest on top of an Irish coffee glass or mug filled with hot coffee. Light the brandy. When the flame burns out, dip the spoon into the coffee and stir.

CAIPIRINHA

MAKES 1 DRINK

1 lime, quartered
1 tsp. simple syrup
2 oz. cachaca

Place the lime wedges and the simple syrup into an old-fashioned glass and muddle well. Add the cachaca and stir well. Fill the glass with ice and stir again. If cachaca is not available, a good white rum or vodka may be substituted.

CAJUN MARTINI

MARTINI

MAKES 1 DRINK

3 oz. pepper-
flavored vodka
dash dry vermouth

Pour ingredients into a shaker with ice. Stir and strain into a chilled martini glass. Garnish with an olive stuffed with jalapeño pepper.

CALIFORNIA CREAMSICLE

COLLINS

MAKES 1 DRINK

1 oz. vanilla vodka
1 oz. coconut rum
½ oz. Galliano
5 oz. orange juice
2 scoops vanilla
ice cream

Pour ingredients into a blender and mix until creamy. Add more vanilla ice cream or orange juice to achieve the right consistency. Pour into a Collins glass and garnish with a paper parasol.

CALIFORNIA LEMONADE

COLLINS

MAKES 1 DRINK

2 oz. blended
whiskey
1 tbs. fine sugar
1 oz. lemon juice or
juice of ½ lemon
1 oz. lime juice or
juice of ½ lime
club soda

Pour all ingredients except the club soda into a shaker half filled with ice. Shake well and strain into a highball or Collins glass over ice. Add the club soda to fill and stir. Garnish with orange or lemon slice and a cherry.

CALIFORNIA LITE (NONALCOHOLIC) HIGHBALL

MAKES 1 DRINK

3 oz. lemonade
3 oz. limeade
club soda

Pour the lemonade and limeade into a highball glass over ice. Stir. Add the club soda to fill. Stir gently. Garnish with an orange or lemon slice and a cherry.

CALIFORNIA MARTINI

MARTINI

MAKES 1 DRINK

3 oz. vodka
½ oz. red wine
1 tbs. dark rum
4 dashes orange
    bitters

Pour ingredients into a shaker with ice. Shake and strain into a chilled martini glass. Garnish with an orange twist.

CALYPSO

MARTINI

MAKES 1 DRINK

2 oz. gold rum
1 tsp. Falernum
1 oz. pineapple
    juice
½ oz. lemon juice
dash bitters

Pour ingredients into a shaker with ice. Shake and strain into a martini glass. Sprinkle with nutmeg.

CAMPARI AND SODA

HIGHBALL

MAKES 1 DRINK

2 oz. Campari
club soda or
    sparkling water
lime wedge

Pour ingredients into a highball glass over ice. Squeeze and add the lime wedge.

CAMPARI COCKTAIL

MARTINI

MAKES 1 DRINK

1 oz. Campari
¾ oz. vodka
dash bitters

Pour ingredients into a shaker with ice. Shake well and strain into a chilled martini glass. Garnish with a lemon twist.

CAMPARI MARTINI

MARTINI

MAKES 1 DRINK

3 oz. vodka
1 oz. Campari

Pour ingredients into a shaker with ice. Shake and strain into a chilled martini glass. Garnish with a lime twist.

CAMPARI NOBILE

HIGHBALL

MAKES 1 DRINK

1 oz. vodka
1 oz. Campari
½ oz. limoncello
2 oz. orange juice
*2 oz. raspberry
   juice*

Pour all ingredients into a cocktail shaker with ice. Shake and strain into a highball glass. Garnish with raspberries, a sprig of mint, and a twist of orange on the rim. Serve with a straw and a stirrer.

CAMPARINETE

MARTINI

MAKES 1 DRINK

1½ oz. gin
*1½ oz. sweet
   vermouth*
1½ oz. Campari

Pour ingredients into a shaker with ice. Stir and strain into a martini glass. Garnish with an orange slice.

CANADIAN BREEZE

OLD-FASHIONED

MAKES 1 DRINK

1½ oz. Canadian
  whiskey
1 tsp. pineapple
  juice
1 tbs. lemon juice
½ tsp. maraschino
  liqueur

Pour ingredients into a shaker with ice. Shake and strain into an old-fashioned glass over ice cubes. Garnish with a pineapple wedge and a cherry.

CANADIAN CHERRY (NONALCOHOLIC)

OLD-FASHIONED

MAKES 1 DRINK

2 oz. cherry
  soda
1 oz. orange
  juice
1 tsp. lemon
  juice

Pour ingredients into an old-fashioned glass over ice. Stir well. Garnish with a cherry.

CANADIAN COCKTAIL

MARTINI

MAKES 1 DRINK

1½ oz. Canadian
  whisky
½ oz. Cointreau
1 tsp. fine sugar
dash bitters

Pour ingredients into a shaker half filled with ice. Shake well. Strain into a martini glass.

CANADIAN OLD-FASHIONED

OLD-FASHIONED

MAKES 1 DRINK

2 oz. Canadian
  whiskey
1 tsp. triple sec
dash bitters
dash lemon juice

Pour ingredients into a shaker with ice. Shake and strain into an old-fashioned glass. Garnish with a lemon twist and an orange twist.

CANDY APPLE

MAKES 1 DRINK

2 oz. vodka
5 oz. 7-Up
1 oz. lime juice
splash grenadine

Pour ingredients into a highball glass over ice. Stir.

CANNIBAL

OLD-FASHIONED

MAKES 1 DRINK

1 oz. tequila
2 oz. white grape juice or white cranberry grape juice
2–5 drops grenadine

Pour tequila and juice into a shaker with ice. Shake and strain into an old-fashioned glass. Top with the grenadine.

CAPE BREEZE

HIGHBALL

MAKES 1 DRINK

1½ oz. Malibu rum
2 oz. cranberry juice
1½ oz. grapefruit juice
½ tsp. superfine sugar

Pour ingredients over ice into a highball glass and stir.

CAPE CODDER

HIGHBALL

MAKES 1 DRINK

1½ oz. vodka
5 oz. cranberry juice

Pour ingredients into a highball glass over ice. Stir. Garnish with a lime wedge.

CAPTAIN COOK

MARTINI

MAKES 1 DRINK

1½ oz. gin
1½ oz. maraschino
   liqueur
1 oz. orange juice

Pour ingredients into a shaker with ice. Shake and strain into a martini glass.

CAPTAIN'S STRIPES

SHOT

MAKES 1 DRINK

¼ oz. coffee
   liqueur
¼ oz. Galliano
¼ oz. Irish cream
   liqueur
¼ oz. spiced rum

Pour the coffee liqueur into a shot glass. Gently pour the Galliano over the back of a spoon to layer it slowly on top of the coffee liqueur. Repeat with the Irish cream and the rum.

CAPTAIN'S BLOOD

MAKES 1 DRINK

1½ oz. dark rum
¼ oz. lime juice
¼ oz. simple syrup
2 dashes bitters

Pour ingredients into a shaker with ice. Shake and strain into a martini glass. Garnish with a spiral of lemon peel.

CARAMEL APPLETINI

MAKES 1 DRINK

2 oz. apple
   flavored vodka
1 oz. apple
   schnapps
1 oz. caramel
   liqueur
1 oz. half-and-half
   or milk

Pour ingredients into a shaker with ice. Shake and strain into a martini glass.

CARDINAL

MAKES 1 DRINK

1½ oz. Anejo rum
½ oz. maraschino
    liqueur
1 tsp. triple sec
1 tsp. grenadine

Pour ingredients into a shaker with ice. Shake and strain into a martini glass.

CARDINAL PUNCH (NONALCOHOLIC)   COLLINS

MAKES 1 DRINK

2 oz. cranberry
    juice
2 oz. ginger ale
½ oz. lemon
    juice
1 oz. orange
    juice

Pour the juices into a Collins glass half filled with ice. Add ginger ale to fill and stir. Garnish with orange and lemon slices.

CAREFREE KIR (NONALCOHOLIC)   WINE

MAKES 1 DRINK

1 oz. raspberry
    syrup
4 oz. white
    grape juice

Pour the syrup into a wine glass over ice. Add the grape juice to fill. Stir. Garnish with a lemon twist.

CARIBBEAN BREEZE   COLLINS

MAKES 1 DRINK

2 oz. dark rum
½ oz. Cointreau
½ oz. crème de
    banane
1 tsp. Rose's lime
    juice
1 tsp. grenadine
4 oz. pineapple
    juice

Pour all ingredients into a shaker half filled with ice. Shake well and strain into a Collins or highball glass nearly filled with ice. Garnish with orange or lemon slices and a cherry.

CARIBBEAN COFFEE

IRISH COFFEE

MAKES 1 DRINK

2 oz. dark rum
1 tsp. granulated
    sugar
4 oz. hot coffee
cream or whipped
    cream

Dissolve the sugar in the coffee into an Irish coffee glass or large mug. Add the rum and stir well. Top with whipped cream, or float the unwhipped cream on top by pouring it over the back of a spoon.

CARIBBEAN MUDSLIDE

OLD-FASHIONED

MAKES 1 DRINK

1 oz. Malibu rum
1 oz. Irish cream
    liqueur
1 oz. Kahlua

Pour into an old-fashioned glass over ice. Stir.

CARTWHEEL

SHOT

MAKES 1 DRINK

1 oz. Tuaca
1 oz. of bitters
slice of lime
powdered sugar

Pour the Tuaca into a shot glass. Thoroughly drench the lime in the bitters, and then roll it in powdered sugar to coat. Drink the shot and bite into the lime.

CARUSO

MARTINI

MAKES 1 DRINK

1 oz. gin
1 oz. dry vermouth
dash green crème
    de menthe

Pour ingredients into a chilled martini glass over ice cubes. Stir.

CASABLANCA

MARTINI

MAKES 1 DRINK

2 oz. light rum
½ oz. Cointreau
½ oz. Maraschino
   liqueur
½ oz. lime juice

Pour ingredients into a shaker half filled with ice. Shake well. Strain into a martini glass.

CASABLANCA 2

MARTINI

MAKES 1 DRINK

1 oz. vodka
½ oz. Advocaat
1 tsp. Galliano
1 tbs. lemon juice
1 tbs. orange juice

Pour ingredients into a shaker with ice. Shake and strain into a martini glass over ice. Garnish with an orange slice.

CASH OUT

MARTINI

MAKES 1 DRINK

1 oz. gin
½ oz. Grand
   Marnier

Pour ingredients into a shaker with ice. Stir and strain into a martini glass and garnish with an orange twist.

CASINO

MARTINI

MAKES 1 DRINK

2 oz. dry gin
¼ tsp. maraschino
   liqueur
¼ tsp. lemon juice
2 dashes orange
   bitters

Pour ingredients into a shaker with ice. Shake and strain into a martini glass. Garnish with a cherry.

CEDARWOOD

COLLINS

MAKES 1 DRINK

2 oz. vodka
4 oz. cranberry
    juice
1 oz. lemon juice
3 oz. ginger ale

Pour ingredients into a Collins glass over ice. Stir.

CELTIC TWILIGHT

OLD-FASHIONED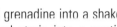

MAKES 1 DRINK

1 oz. Irish cream
    liqueur
1 oz. Irish whiskey
1 oz. Frangelico

Pour ingredients into an old-fashioned glass. Serve straight up.

CENTAURI SUNDOWN

MARTINI

MAKES 1 DRINK

½ oz. vodka
½ oz. grenadine
sweet-and-sour mix

Pour vodka and grenadine into a shaker with ice. Stir and strain into a martini glass. Top off with a splash of sweet-and-sour mix. (Can be served as a shooter.)

CHAMPAGNE BLITZ

CHAMPAGNE

MAKES 1 DRINK

4 oz. Champagne
¾ oz. white crème
    de menthe

Pour ingredients into a Champagne flute. Stir.

CHAMPAGNE CHARISMA

WINE

MAKES 1 DRINK

2 oz. Champagne,
   chilled
1 oz. vodka
½ oz. peach-flavored
   brandy
1 oz. cranberry
   juice
1–2 scoops
   raspberry sherbet

Pour all ingredients except Champagne into a blender. Blend until smooth. Pour into a wine glass or goblet. Add the Champagne and stir.

CHAMPAGNE COCKTAIL

CHAMPAGNE

MAKES 1 DRINK

1 sugar cube
2–3 dashes bitters
Champagne
1 oz. brandy

Place the sugar cube in the bottom of a Champagne flute. Saturate the cube with the bitters. Pour Champagne into the flute. Add the brandy. Garnish with an orange slice and a cherry.

CHAMPAGNE COOLER

WINE

MAKES 1 DRINK

1 oz. brandy
½ oz. triple sec
1 tsp. fine sugar
Champagne, chilled

Pour the brandy, triple sec, and sugar into a wine glass. Add the Champagne. Garnish with a sprig of mint.

CHAMPAGNE FLAMINGO

MARTINI

MAKES 1 DRINK

¾ oz. vodka
¾ oz. Campari
5 oz. chilled
   Champagne

Pour the Campari and sweet vermouth into a shaker with ice. Shake and strain into a martini glass. Top with the Champagne. Garnish with a lemon twist.

CHAMPAGNE JULEP

COLLINS

MAKES 1 DRINK

2 oz. bourbon
4 oz. Champagne
1 tsp. fine sugar
1 tsp. water
4 sprigs mint

In a mixing glass, muddle the mint, water, and sugar. Add the bourbon. Strain into a Collins glass. Fill the glass with ice. Add the Champagne to fill. Garnish with the mint.

CHAMPAGNE MINT

CHAMPAGNE

MAKES 1 DRINK

½ oz. green crème de menthe
chilled Champagne

Pour crème de menthe into a Champagne flute. Add the Champagne to fill. Stir gently.

CHAMPANSKA

CHAMPAGNE

MAKES 1 DRINK

½ cup Champagne, chilled
1 oz. black vodka
1 oz. lime cordial

Pour the vodka and lime cordial into a mixing glass. Pour the Champagne into a Champagne flute. Add the vodka and lime mixture. Garnish with the lime twist.

CHAMPINO

CHAMPAGNE

MAKES 1 DRINK

1 oz. Campari
1¼ oz. sweet vermouth
2 oz. Champagne

Shake vodka and Campari with ice. Strain into a Champagne flute and top with Champagne. Garnish with a zest of orange.

CHAMPS ELYSÉES

MARTINI

MAKES 1 DRINK

1½ oz. brandy
½ oz. sweet
    vermouth
½ oz. lemon juice
½ oz. fine sugar
dash bitters

Pour ingredients into a shaker half filled with ice. Shake well. Strain into a martini glass.

CHAPEL HILL

MARTINI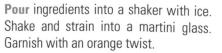

MAKES 1 DRINK

1½ oz. bourbon
½ oz. triple sec
1 tbs. lemon juice

Pour ingredients into a shaker with ice. Shake and strain into a martini glass. Garnish with an orange twist.

CHAPLIN

MARTINI

MAKES 1 DRINK

¾ oz. bourbon
    whiskey
¾ oz. dry sherry
¾ oz. Ramazotti
$1/_8$ oz. Cointreau
2 dashes orange
    bitters

Pour ingredients into a shaker with ice. Stir and strain into a martini glass. Garnish with a lemon twist.

CHARLESTON

COLLINS

MAKES 1 DRINK

1²/₃ oz. Mandarine
    Napoleon
1²/₃ oz. cherry
    brandy
lemonade

Pour the Mandarine Napoleon and cherry brandy to a Collins glass over ice. Add the lemonade to fill.

CHARLIE CHAPLIN SHOOTER SHOT

MAKES 1 DRINK

1 oz. sloe gin
1 oz. apricot-
  flavored brandy
½ oz. lemon juice

Pour ingredients into a shaker nearly filled with ice. Shake well. Strain into a shot glass.

CHARLIE'S COUSIN (NONALCOHOLIC) SHOT

MAKES 1 DRINK

1 tsp. frozen
  orange juice
  concentrate,
  thawed
2 oz. apricot
  nectar
½ oz. lemon
  juice

Pour ingredients into a shaker nearly filled with ice. Shake well. Strain into a shot glass.

CHARMER MARTINI

MAKES 1 DRINK

1½ oz. scotch
½ oz. blue curaçao
dash dry vermouth
dash orange bitters

Pour ingredients into a shaker with ice. Shake and strain into a chilled martini glass.

CHARMING PROPOSAL COLLINS

MAKES 1 DRINK

½ oz. lemon-
  flavored rum
½ oz. sour apple
  schnapps
½ oz. passion fruit
  liqueur
¼ oz. grenadine
ginger ale

Pour the first four ingredients into a Collins glass over ice. Stir. Add the ginger ale to fill and stir again.

CHAS

MAKES 1 DRINK

1¼ oz. bourbon
⅛ oz. Amaretto
⅛ oz. Benedictine
⅛ oz. Cointreau
⅛ oz. orange
    curaçao

Stir with ice. Strain into a martini glass. Garnish with an orange twist.

CHÂTEAU CARDILLO

CHAMPAGNE

MAKES 1 DRINK

1 oz. pear juice
dash black
    raspberry
    liqueur
chilled Champagne

Pour the pear juice and black raspberry liqueur into a Champagne flute. Top with the Champagne.

CHEKHOV COOLER

OLD-FASHIONED

MAKES 1 DRINK

2 oz. raspberry-
    flavored vodka
½ oz. sloe gin
4 oz. cranberry
    juice
6 raspberries

Mix all the ingredients, except the fresh raspberries, with several ice cubes in a chilled double old-fashioned glass. Add fresh raspberries and garnish with a mint sprig.

CHELSEA SIDECAR

MAKES 1 DRINK

juice of ¼ lemon
¾ oz. triple sec
¾ oz. gin

Shake with ice and strain into a martini glass.

CHERRY CHEESECAKE

HIGHBALL

MAKES 1 DRINK

1½ oz. vanilla schnapps
½ oz. cream
cranberry juice

Pour the vanilla schnapps into a highball glass over ice and mix in the cranberry juice to taste. Top with cream or half-and-half.

CHERRY COKE (NONALCOHOLIC)

HIGHBALL

MAKES 1 DRINK

2 oz. grenadine
cola

Pour the grenadine into a highball glass over ice. Add the cola to fill. Garnish with a cherry.

CHERRY DAIQUIRI

MARTINI

MAKES 1 DRINK

2 oz. light rum
½ oz. cherry liqueur
¼ tsp. Kirsch
½ oz. lime juice

Pour ingredients into a shaker with ice. Shake and strain into a chilled martini glass. Garnish with a lime twist.

CHERRY FIZZ

HIGHBALL

MAKES 1 DRINK

2 oz. cherry brandy
1 oz. lemon juice or juice of ½ lemon
4 oz. club soda

Pour the lemon juice, liquor, and soda into a shaker half filled with ice. Shake well. Pour into a highball glass over ice. Garnish with a cherry.

CHERRY KISS

CORDIAL

MAKES 1 DRINK

1 oz. Irish cream
    liqueur
1 oz. Chambord

Use a pousse-café or cordial glass. Pour in the Irish cream liqueur first. Add the Chambord by pouring it over the back of a spoon so that it floats on top.

CHICAGO COCKTAIL

OLD-FASHIONED

MAKES 1 DRINK

2 oz. brandy
dash bitters
¼ tsp. triple sec

Pour ingredients into a shaker with ice. Stir and strain into a sugar-rimmed old-fashioned glass.

CHI-CHI

WINE

MAKES 1 DRINK

1½ oz. vodka
4 oz. pineapple
    juice
1 oz. coconut
    cream
half-and-half

Pour ingredients into a blender with a cup of ice. Blend until smooth. Pour into a red wine glass. Garnish with a slice of pineapple and a cherry.

CHICKS FIX

COLLINS

MAKES 1 DRINK

juice of ½ lemon or
    lime
1 tsp. powdered
    sugar
1 tsp. water
1½ oz. coconut rum
1 oz. pineapple
    vodka

Squeeze the lemon or lime juice into a Collins glass. Add the sugar and water and stir. Fill the glass with ice. Add the rum and vodka and stir well. Garnish with a lemon slice and serve with a straw.

CHIHUAHUA

MAKES 1 DRINK

1 oz. rum
1 oz. Cointreau
1–3 sugar cubes

Pour liquor into an old-fashioned glass and add the sugar cubes to taste.

CHILLY IRISHMAN

PARFAIT

MAKES 1 DRINK

3 oz. cold espresso
1 oz. Irish whiskey
½ oz. coffee
*   liqueur*
½ oz. Irish cream
*   liqueur*
scoop of ice cream
dash simple syrup

Pour ingredients into a blender with 4 cups of crushed ice. Blend until smooth. Pour into a parfait glass. Garnish with a 3 or 4 leaf clover.

CHIMNEY FIRE

 IRISH COFFEE

MAKES 1 DRINK

1½ oz. Amaretto
4 oz. hot cider
cinnamon

Pour the Amaretto and hot cider into an Irish coffee glass or large mug. Stir. Finish with a sprinkle of cinnamon.

CHINA GIRL

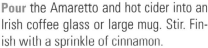

MARTINI

MAKES 1 DRINK

1½ oz. tequila
1½ oz. Frost brandy
1½ oz. tequila rose
6 oz. sweetened
*   condensed milk*

Pour ingredients into a blender. Blend with ice until smooth. Pour into a chilled martini glass.

CHIQUITA

MAKES 1 DRINK

1½ oz. vodka
½ oz. banana
   liqueur
½ oz. lime juice
¼ cup sliced
   bananas
1 tsp. orgeat syrup

Pour ingredients into a blender with ice. Blend thoroughly. Pour into a Collins or parfait glass. Serve with a straw.

CHOCO MASTERPIECE

MARTINI

MAKES 1 DRINK

1 oz. vanilla-
   flavored vodka
¾ oz. Stoli kafya
½ oz. Godiva dark
   liqueur
¼ oz. white crème
   de cocoa
1 Hershey's kiss

Pour ingredients into a shaker with ice. Shake and strain into a martini glass rimmed with cocoa. Drop the kiss into the bottom of the glass.

CHOCOLATE ALMOND CREAM

COLLINS

MAKES 1 DRINK

½ cup Amaretto
¼ cup dark crème
   de cacao
¼ cup white crème
   de cacao
1 quart vanilla ice
   cream

Pour ingredients into a blender with ice. Blend thoroughly. Pour into a Collins or parfait glass. Garnish with shaved chocolate.

CHOCOLATE BLACK RUSSIAN

WINE

MAKES 1 DRINK

1 oz. coffee liqueur
1 oz. vodka
2 scoops chocolate
   ice cream

Pour ingredients into a blender without ice. Blend thoroughly. Pour into a large wine glass. To make the drink thicker, add crushed ice while blending.

CHOCOLATE CHIP COOKIE

IRISH COFFEE

MAKES 1 DRINK

½ oz. dark crème
de cacao
½ oz. butterscotch
schnapps
½ oz. brandy
6 oz. hot chocolate

Pour ingredients into an Irish coffee glass or large mug. Top with whipped cream and chocolate sprinkles.

CHOCOLATE COVERED BERRY

WINE

MAKES 1 DRINK

1 oz. strawberry
liqueur
1 oz. white crème
de cacao
½ oz. cream

Pour ingredients into a shaker with ice. Stir and strain into a red wine glass over ice.

CHOCOLATE DAISY

OLD-FASHIONED

MAKES 1 DRINK

1 oz. California
brandy
1 oz. port wine
juice of ½ lemon
1 tsp. raspberry
syrup or
grenadine
½ tsp. powdered
sugar

Pour ingredients into a shaker with ice. Shake well and strain into an old-fashioned glass. Add a cube of ice and garnish with lemon or orange slices and a cherry.

CHOCOLATE DIP (NONALCOHOLIC)

WINE

MAKES 1 DRINK

2 oz. strawberry
soda
1 tbs. chocolate
syrup
1 oz. light
cream

Pour the chocolate syrup and cream into a shaker nearly filled with ice. Stir and strain into a wine glass over ice. Add the soda and stir again gently.

CHOCOLATE LUV

MARTINI

MAKES 1 DRINK

¾ oz. Godiva Dark
    Chocolate
    Liqueur
½ oz. Kahlua
½ oz. Irish cream
    liqueur
¼ oz. Chambord

Pour ingredients into a shaker with ice. Shake well and strain into a martini glass.

CHOCOLATE MARTINI

MARTINI

MAKES 1 DRINK

2 oz. vodka
½ oz. white crème
    de cacao

Pour ingredients into a shaker with ice. Shake vigorously and strain into a chilled martini glass. Garnish with a chocolate chip or Hershey's kiss, or coat the rim of the glass with cocoa powder.

CHOCOLATE MINT RUM

MARTINI

MAKES 1 DRINK

1 oz. light rum
½ oz. dark crème
    de cacao
½ oz. white crème
    de menthe
½ oz. light cream

Pour ingredients into a shaker half filled with ice. Shake well. Strain into a martini glass. Can be served in an old-fashioned glass over ice.

CHOCOLATE MONKEY

MARTINI

MAKES 1 DRINK

1 oz. coffee liqueur
1 oz. crème de
    banane
1 oz. light rum
1 oz. chocolate
    syrup
5 oz. half-and-half
1 banana

Pour the coffee liqueur, crème de banane, light rum, chocolate syrup, and half-and-half into a blender with the banana and a cup of ice. Blend well, adding more ice or half-and-half as needed to achieve a smooth consistency. Pour into a martini glass. Garnish with a slice of banana and a Hershey's kiss.

CHOCOLATE BERRY FONDUE

IRISH COFFEE

MAKES 1 DRINK

1½ oz. espresso
1 oz. chocolate
   syrup
1 oz. raspberry
   liquer
8 oz. steamed milk

Pour the ingredients into an Irish coffee glass or large mug. Top with whipped cream and chocolate shavings.

CHOCOLATE BERRY TRUFFLE

IRISH COFFEE

MAKES 1 DRINK

1 oz. Chambord
1 oz. Irish cream
   liqueur
hot chocolate

Pour ingredients into an Irish coffee glass or large mug. Stir. Top with unsweetened whipped cream.

CHOCOLATE VICE

IRISH COFFEE

MAKES 1 DRINK

1½ oz. light rum
½ oz. bourbon
½ oz. dark crème
   de cacao
4 oz. hot chocolate

Pour ingredients into an Irish coffee glass. Top with whipped cream.

CHOCOLATE-BANANA SUPREME

COLLINS

MAKES 1 DRINK

1½ oz. Irish cream
   liqueur
¼ oz. vanilla
   extract
½ oz. light cream
½ scoop chocolate
   ice cream
one half banana

Pour ingredients into a blender with a small amount of crushed ice. Blend until smooth. Pour into a Collins glass. Garnish with a cherry and a slice of banana.

CHRISTMAS MARTINI

MARTINI

MAKES 1 DRINK

3 oz. gin
½ oz. dry vermouth
1 tsp. peppermint
 schnapps

Pour ingredients into a shaker with ice. Shake and strain into a chilled martini glass. Garnish with a candy cane.

CHRISTMAS POUSSE-CAFÉ

CORDIAL

MAKES 1 DRINK

1 part grenadine
1 part green crème
 de menthe

Pour the grenadine into a cordial glass first. Then carefully pour crème de menthe over the back of a spoon so that it floats on the grenadine.

CHRYSANTHEMUM COCKTAIL

MARTINI

MAKES 1 DRINK

2 oz. dry vermouth
1½ oz. Benedictine
¼ tsp. Pernod

Pour the vermouth and the Benedictine into a shaker with ice. Stir and strain into a martini glass. Add the Pernod and garnish with an orange twist dropped into the glass.

CIGAR BAND

SHOT

MAKES 1 DRINK

½ oz. Amaretto
½ oz. Irish cream
 liqueur
½ oz. cognac

Pour the Amaretto into a shot glass. Gently pour the Irish cream liqueur over the back of a spoon to slowly layer it on top of the Amaretto. Then layer the cognac on the Irish cream the same way.

CINDERELLA (NONALCOHOLIC)   MARTINI

MAKES 1 DRINK

1 oz. lemon juice
1 oz. orange juice
1 oz. pineapple juice
2 oz. club soda
dash grenadine

Pour the juices into a shaker with ice and shake well. Strain into a chilled martini glass. Add club soda and grenadine. Garnish with slices of pineapple and/or orange.

CITRONELLA COOLER   COLLINS

MAKES 1 DRINK

1 oz. lemon vodka
2 oz. lemonade
2 oz. cranberry juice
splash lime juice

Pour ingredients into a highball or Collins glass over ice. Garnish with a lime wedge.

CITRONELLA FELLA (NONALCOHOLIC)   COLLINS

MAKES 1 DRINK

2 oz. lemonade
2 oz. limeade
2 oz. cranberry juice
splash club soda

Pour ingredients into a highball or Collins glass over ice. Garnish with a lime wedge.

CITRUS MARTINI   MARTINI

MAKES 1 DRINK

4 oz. lemon vodka
1 tsp. Grand Marnier
1 tsp. lime juice

Pour ingredients into a shaker with ice. Shake and strain into a chilled martini glass. Garnish with a lemon twist.

CITY SLICKER

MAKES 1 DRINK

2 oz. brandy
½ oz. triple sec
1 tbs. lemon juice

Pour ingredients into a shaker with ice. Shake and strain into a martini glass.

CLAMATO COCKTAIL ·

HIGHBALL

MAKES 1 DRINK

2 oz. vodka
3 oz. tomato juice
2 oz. clam juice
dash Worcester-
*   shire sauce*
dash Tabasco sauce

Pour all ingredients into a highball glass over ice and stir well. Garnish with a lemon wedge.

CLARET CUP

PUNCH

MAKES 15 DRINKS

2 bottles dry red
*   wine*
½ cup blackberry
*   brandy*
½ cup triple sec
½ cup lemon juice
1 cup orange juice
2 tbs. grenadine
lemon, lime, and
*   orange slices*

Pour all ingredients into a punch bowl over ice. Approximately 15 servings.

CLARET LEMONADE

COLLINS

MAKES 1 DRINK

2 oz. Claret
juice of 1 lemon
2 tsp. powdered
*   sugar*
water

Pour the lemon juice and sugar into a Collins glass over ice. Add water leaving just enough room to float the Claret. Stir well. Garnish with slices of orange and lemon, and a cherry.

CLIFFHANGER

MAKES 1 DRINK

½ oz. Amaretto
½ oz. rum
6 oz. hot chocolate

Pour ingredients into an Irish coffee glass. Top with whipped cream.

CLIMAX

MARTINI

MAKES 1 DRINK

½ oz. Amaretto
½ oz. white crème de cacao
½ oz. triple sec
½ oz. vodka
½ oz. crème de banane
1 oz. light cream

Pour ingredients into a shaker with ice. Shake well and strain into a chilled martini glass.

CLOUD 9

PARFAIT

MAKES 1 DRINK

8 oz. vanilla ice cream
1 oz. Irish cream
½ oz. black raspberry liqueur
1 oz. Amaretto

Pour ingredients into a blender. Blend until smooth. Pour into a parfait glass. Top with whipped cream and ½ a Reese's peanut butter cup.

CLOVER CLUB COCKTAIL

MARTINI

MAKES 1 DRINK

1 oz. dry gin
½ oz. grenadine
1 egg white
juice of ½ lemon or lime

Pour all ingredients into a shaker with ice. Shake vigorously and strain into a martini glass.

CLOVER LEAF

MAKES 1 DRINK

1½ oz. gin
4 dashes grenadine
juice of ½ lemon
1 egg white

Pour ingredients into a shaker with ice. Shake and strain into a wine glass. Garnish with a sprig of mint.

CLUB COOLER

COLLINS

MAKES 1 DRINK

½ tsp. grenadine
2 oz. carbonated
    water
2 oz. French
    vermouth
fill carbonated
    water or ginger
    ale

Pour the grenadine and 2 oz. carbonated water into a Collins glass. Stir. Fill the glass with ice. Add the French vermouth and the carbonated water or ginger ale to fill. Garnish with a spiral of orange or lemon peel.

COBRA

SHOT

MAKES 4 DRINKS

1 oz. vodka
1 oz. blue curaçao
1 oz. Malibu
    coconut
1 oz. pineapple
    juice

Pour ingredients into a shaker. Stir and pour tequila into four shot glasses.

COCKTAIL ALLA MELAGRANA

CHAMPAGNE

MAKES 1 DRINK

2 oz. pomegranate
    juice
4 oz. sparkling
    white wine

Pour pomegranate juice into a Champagne flute. Just before serving add sparkling wine.

COCO CHANEL

MAKES 1 DRINK

1 oz. gin
1 oz. Kahlua
1 oz. cream

Pour ingredients into a shaker with ice. Shake and strain into a martini glass. Garnish with chocolate curls.

COCO COLADA (NONALCOHOLIC) HURRICANE

MAKES 1 DRINK

4 oz. pineapple juice
2 oz. coconut cream (or 6 oz. piña colada mix)

Pour ingredients into a blender with a cup of ice. Blend until slushy. Pour into a chilled hurricane glass. Garnish with an orange slice.

COCO LOCO HIGHBALL

MAKES 1 DRINK

1 oz. dark rum
1 oz. light rum
½ oz. vodka
½ oz. crème de banane
½ oz. pineapple juice
½ oz. coconut cream
½ oz. simple syrup

Pour ingredients into a shaker with ice. Shake well and strain into a chilled highball glass. Garnish with a pineapple wedge.

COCONUT BROWNIE WITH NUTS COLLINS

MAKES 1 DRINK

1 oz. coconut rum
1 oz. vanilla vodka
½ oz. hazelnut liqueur
2 scoops chocolate ice cream
1 packet hot cocoa
1 oz. crème de coconut
half-and-half

Pour the coconut rum, vanilla vodka, hazelnut liqueur, chocolate ice cream, hot cocoa, and crème de coconut in a blender. Blend on low to medium setting and slowly add the half-and-half until a creamy smooth consistency is achieved. Pour into a Collins glass. Garnish with shredded coconut.

COCONUT COLADA

MAKES 1 DRINK

1¼ oz. coconut rum
1 oz. milk
5 oz. pineapple
   juice

Pour ingredients into a blender with ice. Blend for 10–15 seconds. Pour into a large specialty martini glass and garnish with a pineapple spear.

COCONUT CONCUBINE

COLLINS

MAKES 1 DRINK

1 oz. coconut rum
1 oz. vanilla vodka
1 oz. crème de
   coconut
pineapple juice
orange juice
grenadine

Pour the coconut rum, vanilla vodka, and crème de coconut into a Collins glass over ice. Add equal amounts of pineapple and orange juice to fill. Add a splash grenadine. Stir. Garnish with a pineapple slice and a cherry.

COCONUT KISS

MARTINI

MAKES 1 DRINK

3 oz. coconut milk
3 oz. pineapple
   juice
1½ oz. Malibu rum

Pour ingredients in a blender. Blend until smooth. Pour into a martini glass. Garnish with cherry and pineapple wedges.

COFFEE ALMOND(NONALCOHOLIC) COLLINS

MAKES 1 DRINK

¼ cup cold coffee
1 tsp. brown
   sugar
splash orgeat
   syrup
milk
1 scoop of coffee
   or chocolate
   ice cream

Dissolve the brown sugar in the coffee in a Collins glass. Add the orgeat, milk, and ice to fill. Stir well. Top with the ice cream.

COFFEE CACAO CREAM

COLLINS

MAKES 1 DRINK

½ cup crème de
   cacao
½ cup cold coffee
1 scoop coffee ice
   cream

Pour ingredients into a blender without
ice. Blend until smooth. Pour into a Collins glass. Serve with a straw.

COFFEE GRASSHOPPER

OLD-FASHIONED

MAKES 1 DRINK

1 oz. coffee liqueur
1 oz. white crème
   de menthe
1 oz. light cream

Pour ingredients into a shaker half filled
with ice. Shake well. Strain into an old-
fashioned glass over ice.

COFFEE NUDGE

IRISH COFFEE

MAKES 1 DRINK

¾ oz. dark rum
¾ oz. Kahlua
¾ oz. crème de
   cacao
6 oz. hot black
   coffee
cognac

Pour the rum, Kahlua, crème de cacao,
and coffee into an Irish coffee glass or
mug. Stir. Float the cognac and top with
whipped cream. Optional: Sprinkle with
grated chocolate.

COFFEE NUT

IRISH COFFEE

MAKES 1 DRINK

1 oz. Amaretto
1 oz. Frangelico
hot black coffee
2 oz. cream or
   whipped cream

Pour all ingredients except the cream
into an Irish coffee glass or mug. Stir. Top
with whipped cream or cream poured
over the back of a spoon to float on top.

COFFEE ROYALE

IRISH COFFEE

MAKES 1 DRINK

2 oz. brandy
4 oz. hot black coffee
1 tsp. granulated sugar
2 oz. heavy cream

Dissolve the sugar in the coffee in a mug or Irish coffee glass. Add the brandy. Stir. Add the cream by pouring it over the back of a spoon so that it floats on top.

COGNAC HIGHBALL

HIGHBALL

MAKES 1 DRINK

2 oz. cognac
carbonated water or ginger ale

Pour the cognac into a highball glass over ice. Fill with the carbonated water. Garnish with a lemon twist.

COLD COMFORT MARTINI

MARTINI

MAKES 1 DRINK

2 oz. lemon vodka
2 oz. honey vodka

Pour ingredients into a shaker with ice. Shake and strain into a chilled martini glass. Garnish with a lemon twist.

COLD KISS

HIGHBALL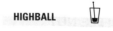

MAKES 1 DRINK

1½ oz. whiskey
½ oz. peppermint schnapps
2 tsp. white crème de cacao

Pour ingredients into a shaker with ice. Shake and strain into a highball glass.

COLONIAL

MARTINI

MAKES 1 DRINK

1½ oz. gin
1 tbs. maraschino
liqueur
½ oz. grapefruit
juice

Pour ingredients into a shaker half filled with ice. Shake well and strain into a martini glass.

COLONY CLUB MARTINI

MARTINI

MAKES 1 DRINK

3 oz. gin
1 tsp. Pernod
4 dashes orange
bitters

Pour ingredients into a shaker with ice. Shake and strain into a chilled martini glass. Garnish with an orange twist.

COMBUSTIBLE EDISON

MARTINI

MAKES 1 DRINK

1 oz. Campari
1 oz. fresh lemon
juice
2 oz. brandy

Pour the Campari and lemon juice into a shaker with ice. Shake and strain into a martini glass. Heat the brandy in a chafing dish. When the brandy is warmed, ignite it and pour it in a flaming stream into the martini glass. (If the brandy is chilled and shaken rather than ignited, the drink is known as the Edisonian.)

COME HITHER

MARTINI

MAKES 1 DRINK

1 oz. vanilla vodka
1 oz. white crème
de cacao
½ oz. Galliano
2 oz. half-and-half

Pour ingredients into a shaker with ice. Shake and strain into a martini glass.

COMFORT MOCHA

IRISH COFFEE

MAKES 1 DRINK

*1½ oz. Southern
    Comfort
1 tsp. instant cocoa
1 tsp. instant
    coffee
boiling water
whipped cream*

Pour the Southern Comfort into an Irish coffee glass. Add the dry cocoa and instant coffee. Fill the glass with boiling water. Top with whipped cream.

COMFORT SUNDAE

OLD-FASHIONED

MAKES 1 DRINK

*1½ oz. Southern
    Comfort
½ oz. Kahlua
1½ oz. cream
6 oz. root beer*

Pour ingredients into a shaker with ice. Strain into an old-fashioned glass over ice.

COMFORTABLE, FUZZY SCREW **HIGHBALL**

MAKES 1 DRINK

*1½ oz. vodka
1½ oz. Southern
    Comfort
1½ oz. peach
    schnapps
orange juice*

Pour first three ingredients into a high-ball glass over ice. Add orange juice to fill.

COMFORTABLE, FUZZY SCREW 2 **HIGHBALL**

MAKES 1 DRINK

*1½ oz. vodka
1½ oz. Southern
    Comfort
1½ oz. peach
    schnapps
orange juice
splash Galliano*

Pour first three ingredients into a high-ball glass over ice. Add orange juice to fill. Finish with a splash of Galliano.

COMFORTABLY NUMB

HIGHBALL

MAKES 1 DRINK

2 oz. Southern
   Comfort
8 oz. Mountain
   Dew

Pour ingredients into a highball glass over ice.

COMMODORE

CHAMPAGNE

MAKES 1 DRINK

2 oz. bourbon
¾ oz. white crème
   de cacao
½ oz. lemon juice
1 dash grenadine

Pour ingredients into a shaker with ice. Shake and strain into a Champagne flute.

CONFIRMED BACHELOR

MARTINI

MAKES 1 DRINK

1½ oz. gin
1 tsp. Rose's lime
   juice
1 tsp. grenadine
1 egg white

Pour ingredients into a shaker half filled with ice. Shake well and strain into a martini glass.

CONTINENTAL

MARTINI

MAKES 1 DRINK

1½ oz. light rum
½ oz. green crème
   de menthe
½ tsp. fine sugar
1 tbs. lime juice
1 tsp. lemon juice

Pour ingredients into a shaker nearly filled with ice. Shake and strain into a martini glass. Garnish with a lemon twist.

COOKIE MONSTER

MAKES 1 DRINK

*1 oz. Blue Hawaiian
    Maui schnapps
pineapple juice*

Pour the schnapps into a highball glass and add pineapple juice to fill. Serve straight up or on the rocks.

COOL AS A CUCUMBER (NONALCOHOLIC) MARTINI

MAKES 1 DRINK

*half a cucumber,
    peeled
juice from half
    a lime
2 mint leaves
half a ripe kiwi,
    peeled
2 spoons of sugar
    or Splenda*

Put the cucumber, lime juice, mint leaves, kiwi, and sugar into a blender with a cup of ice. Blend until smooth. Add water if needed to achieve smooth consistency. Pour into a large martini glass. Garnish with a sprig of mint.

COOL OPERATOR

COLLINS

MAKES 1 DRINK

*1 oz. melon liqueur
½ oz. rum
½ oz. vodka
1 oz. lime juice or
    juice of ½ lime
2 oz. grapefruit
    juice
4 oz. orange juice*

Pour ingredients into a blender and mix thoroughly. Pour into a Collins or parfait glass. Garnish with orange, lemon, and lime slices and a cherry. Serve with a straw.

COOL SUMMER BREEZE

BEER GLASS

MAKES 1 DRINK

*1 oz. vodka
1½ oz. melon
    liqueur
1 oz. blue curaçao
orange juice*

Fill a beer glass with crushed ice. Add the vodka and blue curaçao. Add orange juice to fill. Garnish with an orange slice and a cherry.

COOL YULE MARTINI

MAKES 1 DRINK

3 oz. vodka
½ oz. dry vermouth
1 tsp. peppermint
 schnapps

Pour ingredients into a shaker with ice. Shake and strain into a martini glass. Garnish with a candy cane.

COOL-AIDE

COLLINS

MAKES 1 DRINK

1 oz. blueberry
 schnapps
2 oz. cranberry
 juice
½ oz. 7-Up

Pour the blueberry schnapps cranberry juice into a Collins glass over ice. Stir and then top with the 7-Up.

COPABANANA SPLIT

COLLINS

MAKES 1 DRINK

1 oz. vanilla vodka
1 oz. strawberry-
 flavored vodka
2 oz. half-and-half
 (or to taste)
1 banana, cut in
 half lengthwise
2 scoops vanilla
 ice cream
1 oz. dark crème de
 cacao
1 oz. strawberry
 syrup

Pour the vodkas, the half-and-half, half the banana, and the ice cream into a blender. Blend until smooth, adding more half-and-half as necessary. Pour the dark crème de cacao into a Collins glass. Add the blended mixture to fill halfway. Add the strawberry syrup. Add more of the blended mixture to fill. Garnish with the remaining half a banana across the rim. Top with whipped cream, nuts, and a cherry.

COPPERHEAD

MARTINI

MAKES 2 DRINKS

2 oz. Galliano
1 oz. Amaretto

Pour ingredients into a shaker with ice. Shake and strain into two chilled martini glasses.

CORAL SNAKE BITE

SHOT

MAKES 1 DRINK

*1/3 oz. coffee
    liqueur*
1/3 oz. Galliano
*1/3 oz. cherry
    brandy*

Pour the coffee liqueur into a shot glass. Gently pour the Galliano over the back of a spoon to layer it on top of the coffee liqueur. Then layer the cherry brandy over the Galliano the same way.

CORDLESS SCREWDRIVER

SHOT

MAKES 1 DRINK

1¾ oz. vodka
sugar
orange wedge

Pour chilled vodka into a shot glass. Dip the orange wedge into the sugar. Drink the vodka and bite into the orange.

CORKSCREW

MARTINI

MAKES 1 DRINK

1½ oz. light rum
*½ oz. peach-
    flavored brandy*
½ oz. dry vermouth

Pour ingredients into a shaker nearly filled with ice. Shake and strain into a martini glass. Serve with a lemon twist.

CORONADO

OLD-FASHIONED

MAKES 1 DRINK

2 oz. gin
*½ oz. white
    curaçao*
*2 oz. pineapple
    juice*
4 dashes Kirsch

Pour ingredients into a shaker with ice. Shake and strain into an old-fashioned glass. Garnish with a cherry.

CORONATION

MAKES 1 DRINK

3 oz. dry sherry
½ oz. dry vermouth
dash maraschino
   liqueur
dash bitters

Pour ingredients into a shaker half filled with ice. Shake well and strain into a martini glass. Garnish with an olive and a lemon twist.

CORONATION COCKTAIL

MARTINI

MAKES 1 DRINK

¾ oz. dry vermouth
¾ oz. gin
¾ oz. Dubonnet

Pour ingredients into a shaker with ice. Stir and strain into a martini glass.

CORPSE REVIVER

MARTINI

MAKES 1 DRINK

¾ oz. gin
¾ oz. lemon juice
¾ oz. Cointreau
¾ oz. Lillet
dash Pernod

Pour ingredients into a shaker with ice. Shake and strain into a martini glass.

CORTÉS

SNIFTER

MAKES 1 DRINK

1 oz. Kahlua
1 oz. light rum
dash lemon juice

Pour all ingredients into a brandy snifter over ice.

COSMOPOLITAN

MARTINI

MAKES 1 DRINK

1 oz. vodka
½ oz. triple sec
½ oz. cranberry
juice
¼ oz. lime juice

Pour ingredients into a shaker half filled with ice. Shake well. Strain into a martini glass. To upgrade this popular drink, use a premium vodka and Cointreau in place of the triple sec. Flavored vodkas can be used to vary the taste.

COSMOS

MARTINI

MAKES 1 DRINK

2 oz. white rum
1 oz. lime juice
1 tsp. superfine
sugar

Pour ingredients into a shaker with ice. Shake well and strain into a martini glass.

COSMOTEQUILA

MARTINI

MAKES 1 DRINK

2 oz. tequila
1 oz. triple sec
½ oz. lime juice
splash cranberry
juice

Pour ingredients into a shaker with ice. Shake and strain into a martini glass.

COSSACK

MARTINI

MAKES 1 DRINK

½ oz. vodka
½ oz. cognac
½ oz. lime juice
1 tsp. gomme syrup

Pour ingredients into a shaker with ice. Shake and strain into a martini glass.

COSTA DEL SOL

OLD-FASHIONED

MAKES 1 DRINK

2 oz. gin
½ oz. apricot
*   brandy*
½ oz. Cointreau

Pour ingredients into a shaker half filled with ice. Shake well. Strain into an old-fashioned glass.

COTO MEXICANO

IRISH COFFEE

MAKES 1 DRINK

1 oz. gold tequila
½ oz. Grand
*   Marnier*
6 oz. hot black
*   coffee*

Pour ingredients into an Irish coffee glass or a mug. Top with whipped cream and dashes of nutmeg and cinnamon.

COTTAGE COFFEE

IRISH COFFEE

MAKES 1 DRINK

1 oz. Frangelico
*   hazelnut liqueur*
1 oz. Irish cream
1 oz. Kahlua coffee
*   liqueur*
4 oz. hot black
*   coffee*
splash Grand
*   Marnier*

Pour first four ingredients into an Irish coffee glass or mug. Finish with a splash of Grand Marnier and a dollop of whipped cream.

COTTON CANDY

BEER GLASS

MAKES 1 DRINK

3 oz. Butterscotch
*   Ripple schnapps*
1 glass of root beer

Pour ingredients into a beer mug.

COUNTRY CLUB COOLER

COLLINS

MAKES 1 DRINK

2 oz. dry vermouth
carbonated water
½ tsp. grenadine

Pour the grenadine and 2 oz. of the carbonated water into a Collins glass and stir. Add ice and dry vermouth. Fill with carbonated water and stir again. Garnish with a lemon twist and an orange spiral so that the end dangles over the rim of glass.

COUNTRY GENTLEMAN

MARTINI

MAKES 1 DRINK

1½ oz. apple
   brandy
¾ oz. curaçao
¼ oz. lemon juice
1 tsp. simple syrup

Pour ingredients into a shaker with ice. Shake and strain into a martini glass. Garnish with a lemon twist.

COURAGE

HIGHBALL

MAKES 1 DRINK

1½ oz. Amaretto
1½ oz. Southern
   Comfort
1½ oz. Malibu rum
1½ oz. blue curaçao
2 oz. orange juice
2 oz. cranberry
   juice
2 oz. pineapple
   juice

Pour the liquors into a cocktail shaker ¾ full of ice and add juices. Shake and strain into a highball glass.

COWBOY COCKTAIL

MARTINI

MAKES 1 DRINK

1½ oz. blended
   scotch whiskey
1 tbs. light cream

Pour ingredients into a shaker with ice. Shake and strain into a martini glass.

COWBOY WILL'S (NONALCOHOLIC) MARTINI

MAKES 1 DRINK

1½ oz. orange
   juice
½ oz. tonic
1 tsp. fine
   sugar

Pour all ingredients into a shaker nearly filled with ice. Shake well and strain into a martini glass.

COY COLADA (NONALCOHOLIC) COLLINS

MAKES 1 DRINK

2 oz. coconut
   cream
6 oz. pineapple
   juice
1 tsp. lime
   juice

Pour ingredients into a blender with ice. Blend thoroughly. Pour into a Collins or parfait glass. Serve with a pineapple slice, a cherry, and a straw.

CRANAPPLE   OLD-FASHIONED

MAKES 1 DRINK

1½ oz. apple
   schnapps
1½ oz. cranberry
   juice

Pour ingredients into a shaker with ice. Shake and strain into an old-fashioned glass.

CRANBERRY COOLER   PARFAIT

MAKES 1 DRINK

1½ oz. bourbon
1½ oz. cranberry
   juice
½ oz. lime juice
1 tsp. powdered
   sugar

Pour ingredients into a blender with a cup of ice and blend until smooth. Pour into a parfait glass.

CRANBERRY COSMORITA

MARTINI

MAKES 1 DRINK

1½ oz. tequila
½ oz. triple sec
juice from half a
  lime
2 oz. cranberry
  juice
2 oz. sweet-and-
  sour mix

Pour all the ingredients into a blender with a cup of ice. Blend until smooth. Pour into a salt-rimmed martini glass. Garnish with a slice of lime. May also be served on the rocks.

CRANBERRY CREAM (NONALCOHOLIC) WINE

MAKES 1 DRINK

3 oz. cranberry
  juice
2 oz. apple juice
1 oz. lime juice
1 oz. cream
dash grenadine

Pour ingredients into a blender with ice. Blend thoroughly. Pour into a large wine glass.

CRANBERRY GIN SOUR WINE

MAKES 1 DRINK

2 oz. gin
½ oz. triple sec
1 oz. lime juice or
  juice of ½ lime
1 oz. lemon juice or
  juice of ½ lemon
2 oz. light cream
1 tsp. sugar

Pour ingredients into a blender with ice. Blend thoroughly. Pour into a large wine glass.

CRANBERRY HUGS MARTINI

MAKES 1 DRINK

2 oz. cranberry
  juice
1 oz. Amaretto

Pour ingredients into a shaker with ice. Stir well and strain into a martini glass. Garnish with a lemon or lime twist. May be served on the rocks in an old-fashioned glass.

CRANBERRY KISS

HIGHBALL

MAKES 1 DRINK

¾ oz. spiced rum
½ oz. peppermint
   schnapps
2 oz. Collins mix
2 oz. cranberry
   juice

Pour the ingredients into a highball glass over ice. Garnish with a lime slice.

CRANBERRY KISSES

MARTINI

MAKES 1 DRINK

2 oz. cranberry
   juice
1 oz. Sambuca

Pour ingredients into a shaker with ice. Stir well and strain into a martini glass. Garnish with a lemon twist. May also be served on the rocks in an old-fashioned glass.

CRAPS

MARTINI

MAKES 1 DRINK

1 oz. white crème
   de cacao
¼ oz. Grand
   Marnier
½ oz. mandarin
   liqueur
¾ oz. gin
¾ oz. orange juice

Pour ingredients into a shaker with ice. Stir well and strain into a large martini glass.

CREAM CORDIAL

MARTINI

MAKES 1 DRINK

14 oz. sweetened
   milk
1¼ cups coffee
   liqueur (or
   almond, orange,
   or mint)
1 cup whipping cream
   (or light cream)
4 eggs

Pour all ingredients into a blender. Blend until smooth. Pour into a large martini glass. May be served over ice.

CREAMSICLE

MAKES 1 DRINK

1½ oz. banana
   liqueur
1½ oz. vanilla
   liqueur
1½ oz. orange juice
1 oz. heavy cream

Pour ingredients into a shaker with ice. Shake and strain into a wine glass.

CREAMSICLE 2

HIGHBALL

MAKES 1 DRINK

1½ oz. Amaretto
1½ oz. orange juice
milk or cream

Pour ingredients into a shaker with ice. Stir and strain into a highball glass over ice.

CREAMY CHERRY (NONALCOHOLIC)   COLLINS

MAKES 1 DRINK

4 oz. cherry
   soda
2 scoops
   vanilla ice
   cream

Pour ingredients into a blender without ice. Blend thoroughly. Pour into a Collins or parfait glass. Garnish with a cherry. Serve with a straw.

CREAMY MOCHA ALEXANDER   COLLINS

MAKES 1 DRINK

1 oz. coffee liqueur
1 oz. dark crème de
   cacao
1 oz. brandy
2 scoops vanilla
   ice cream

Pour all ingredients into a blender and mix without ice. Pour into a Collins or parfait glass. Serve with a straw.

CREAMY PEACH (NONALCOHOLIC) COLLINS

MAKES 1 DRINK

1 peach or 2
    oz. frozen
    peaches
1 tsp. sugar
1 oz. light cream
lemonade,
    chilled

Peel and cut up the peach, if fresh. Put it into a blender and pure. Add sugar to taste. Pour the mixture into a Collins glass and add the cream. Stir well. Add the lemonade to fill. Stir again. Garnish with a slice of peach.

CREAMY RED RUSSIAN (NONALCOHOLIC) WINE

MAKES 1 DRINK

¼ cup straw-
    berries, fresh
    or frozen
1 tbs. fine sugar
1 oz. cream

Pour ingredients into a blender with a cup of ice. Blend thoroughly. Pour into a large red wine glass. Serve with a straw.

CREAMY SCREWDRIVER COLLINS

MAKES 1 DRINK

2 oz. vodka
6 oz. orange juice
1 tsp. sugar
1 egg yolk

Pour all ingredients into a blender with ½ cup crushed ice. Blend at a low speed just until blended. Pour into a Collins glass.

CREOLE LADY MARTINI

MAKES 1 DRINK

1½ oz. bourbon
1½ oz. Madeira
1 tsp. grenadine

Pour ingredients into a shaker with ice. Stir and strain into a martini glass. Garnish with a red and a green cherry.

CRIMSON MARTINI

MARTINI

MAKES 1 DRINK

3 oz. gin
½ oz. ruby port
2 tsp. lime juice
1 tsp. grenadine

Pour ingredients into a shaker with ice. Shake and strain into a chilled martini glass. Garnish with a lime twist.

CRIMSON SUNSET

MARTINI

MAKES 1 DRINK

2 oz. gin
2 tsp. lemon juice
½ tsp. grenadine
½ oz. tawny port

Pour the gin and lemon juice into a shaker with ice. Shake well and strain into a martini glass. Drop the grenadine into the center of the drink and float the port on the top.

CROUPLER

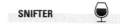 SNIFTER

MAKES 1 DRINK

1¼ oz. cognac
¾ oz. Amaretto

Pour ingredients into a shaker with ice. Stir and strain into a brandy snifter.

CROWN JEWEL

 HIGHBALL

MAKES 1 DRINK

1¼ oz. Malibu rum
1 oz. Crown Royal
pineapple juice
splash cranberry
*   juice*
splash 7-Up

Pour all the ingredients except the 7-Up into a shaker with ice. Shake and strain into a highball glass. Add a splash 7-Up to make it bubbly.

CRUEL GHOUL

OLD-FASHIONED

MAKES 1 DRINK

½ oz. Malibu rum
½ oz. peach
   schnapps
½ oz. blue curaçao
7-Up

Pour first three ingredients into a shaker with ice. Shake and strain into an old-fashioned glass over ice. Add 7-Up to fill.

CRUELLA DEVILLE

SHOT

MAKES 1 DRINK

½ oz. coffee
   liqueur
½ oz. half-and-half

Pour the coffee liqueur into a shot glass. Gently pour the half-and-half over the back of a spoon to layer it slowly on top of the coffee liqueur. Garnish with a maraschino cherry.

CRUISER

COLLINS

MAKES 1 DRINK

1¼ oz. coconut rum
3 oz. orange juice
2 oz. pineapple
   juice

Pour ingredients into a shaker with ice. Shake well and strain into a Collins glass over ice.

CRUSTA

MARTINI

MAKES 1 DRINK

2 oz. brandy
½ oz. lemon juice
1 tsp. maraschino
   liqueur
1 tsp. curaçao
2 dashes bitters

Pour ingredients into a shaker with ice. Shake and strain into a sugar-rimmed martini glass.

CRUX

MAKES 1 DRINK

¾ oz. brandy
¾ oz. Dubonnet
¾ oz. Cointreau
¾ oz. lemon juice

Pour ingredients into a shaker with ice. Stir and strain into a martini glass.

CRYSTAL SLIPPER COCKTAIL

MARTINI

MAKES 1 DRINK

1½ oz. gin
½ oz. blue curaçao
2 dashes orange
    bitters

Pour ingredients into a shaker with ice. Stir and strain into a martini glass.

CUBA LIBRE

HIGHBALL

MAKES 1 DRINK

2 oz. light rum
6 oz. any cola (but
    originally, it
    was Coca-Cola)

Pour the rum into a highball glass over ice. Add the cola to fill. Garnish with a lime wedge.

CUBACRANY

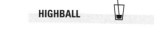

MAKES 2 DRINKS

4 oz. Puerto Rican
    white rum
6 oz. cranberry
    juice
½ lemon

Pour ingredients into a shaker with ice. Stir and strain into two highball glasses filled with ice.

D

CUBAN MARTINI

MARTINI

MAKES 1 DRINK

3 oz. light rum
½ oz. dry vermouth

Pour ingredients into a shaker with ice. Shake and strain into a chilled martini glass rimmed with sugar. Garnish with a lime twist.

CUCARACHA

OLD-FASHIONED

MAKES 1 DRINK

²/₃ oz. tequila
¹/₃ oz. Kahlua

Pour the tequila and Kahlua into an old-fashioned glass. Ignite the cocktail. Two people drink from the same glass with two plastic straws.

CUL-DE-SAC

MARTINI

MAKES 1 DRINK

2½ oz. Anejo rum
½ oz. Ricard

Pour ingredients into a shaker with ice. Stir well and strain into a martini glass.

DAIQUIRI

PARFAIT

MAKES 1 DRINK

1½ oz. light rum
1 oz. lime juice or
*   juice of ½ lime*
1 tsp. fine sugar

Pour the rum, lime juice, and sugar into a shaker half filled with ice. Shake well. Strain into a parfait glass.

D

DAMN THE WEATHER

MARTINI

MAKES 1 DRINK

1½ oz. gin
1 tbs. sweet vermouth
1 tbs. Cointreau
1 oz. orange juice

Pour ingredients into a shaker half filled with ice. Shake well. Strain into a martini glass.

DANDY

MARTINI

MAKES 1 DRINK

½ oz. rye whiskey
½ oz. Dubonnet
3 dashes Cointreau
dash bitters

Pour ingredients into a shaker with ice. Stir and strain into a martini glass. Garnish with orange and lemon twists.

DANISH MARTINI

MARTINI

MAKES 1 DRINK

3 oz. Akvavit
½ oz. dry vermouth

Pour ingredients into a shaker with ice. Shake and strain into a chilled martini glass. Garnish with an olive.

DARK & STORMY

HIGHBALL

MAKES 1 DRINK

2 oz. Gosling's Black Seal rum
3 oz. ginger beer

Pour ingredients into a highball glass over ice. Garnish with a lime wedge.

DARLING PEACHES (NONALCOHOLIC) COLLINS

MAKES 1 DRINK

3 oz. peach nectar
1 tsp. lemon juice
1 tbs. peach
　preserves
1 tsp. honey
1 wedge canned
　or fresh peach,
　cut up

Pour ingredients into a blender with ice. Blend thoroughly. Pour into a Collins or highball glass.

DAYDREAM MARTINI MARTINI

MAKES 1 DRINK

3 oz. citrus vodka
½ oz. triple sec
1 oz. orange juice
¼ tsp. sugar

Pour ingredients into a shaker with ice. Stir and strain into a chilled martini glass.

DE LA LOUISIANE MARTINI

MAKES 1 DRINK

¾ oz. rye whiskey
¾ oz. sweet
　vermouth
¾ oz. Benedictine
3 dashes pastis
3 dashes
　Peychaud's
　bitters

Pour ingredients into a shaker with ice. Stir and strain into a martini glass. Garnish with a cherry.

DEATH BY CHOCOLATE COLLINS

MAKES 1 DRINK

1 oz. vodka
½ oz. dark crème
　de cacao
½ oz. Irish cream
　liqueur
1 scoop vanilla ice
　cream

Pour ingredients into a blender with ice. Blend thoroughly. Pour into a Collins or parfait glass. Garnish with chocolate shavings.

DEATH BY CHOCOLATINI

MARTINI

MAKES 1 DRINK

½ oz. chocolate
1 strawberry
chocolate syrup
1½ oz. vanilla
   vodka
1½ oz. chocolate
   liqueur
2 oz. half-and-half

Melt the chocolate in a microwave. Dip the strawberry in the chocolate, then harden in the freezer. Swirl the chocolate syrup inside a martini glass, then put the glass in the freezer. Pour the vodka, chocolate liqueur, and half-and-half into a shaker with ice. Shake well and strain into the glass. Garnish with the chocolate-dipped strawberry.

DEATH IN THE AFTERNOON

CHAMPAGNE

MAKES 1 DRINK

1 oz. Pernod
5 oz. chilled
   Champagne

Pour Pernod into a Champagne flute. Top with Champagne.

DEATH SHOOTER

SHOT

MAKES 1 DRINK

1 oz. Jägermeister
1 oz. peppermint
   schnapps

Pour ingredients into a shaker with ice. Stir and strain into a shot glass.

DEAUVILLE COCKTAIL

MARTINI

MAKES 1 DRINK

¾ oz. brandy
¾ oz. applejack or
   calvados
¾ oz. triple sec
¾ oz. fresh lemon
   juice

Pour the ingredients into a cocktail shaker with ice. Shake well and strain into a chilled martini glass.

DEBUTANTE'S DREAM

MAKES 1 DRINK

*¹/₃ oz. bourbon
   whiskey
¹/₃ oz. brandy
¹/₃ oz. orange juice
dash lemon juice*

Pour ingredients into a shaker with ice. Shake and strain into a martini glass.

DEEP BLUE

COLLINS

MAKES 1 DRINK

*1 oz. vodka
1 oz. peach
   schnapps
1 oz. blue curaçao
1 can Red Bull
   Energy Drink*

Pour the vodka, Red Bull, and peach schnapps into a Collins glass. Add a small amount of curaçao until the mixture is a deep green. Add ice and pour the remainder of the curaçao down the side of the glass to leave a blue layer on the bottom.

DEEP FREEZE

OLD-FASHIONED

MAKES 1 DRINK

*1 oz. peppermint
   schnapps
½ oz. vodka*

Pour ingredients into a chilled shot glass or on the rocks in an old-fashioned glass.

DEEP SEA MARTINI

MARTINI

MAKES 1 DRINK

*3 oz. gin
1 oz. dry vermouth
½ tsp. Pernod
dash orange bitters*

Pour ingredients into a shaker with ice. Stir well and strain into a chilled martini glass.

DELICIOUS MARTINI

MARTINI

MAKES 1 DRINK

*3 oz. coffee-
    flavored vodka
½ oz. Grand
    Marnier*

Pour ingredients into a shaker with ice. Shake and strain into a chilled martini glass. Garnish with an orange twist.

DELILAH (OR WHITE LADY)

MARTINI

MAKES 1 DRINK

*1½ oz. gin
¾ oz. Cointreau
¾ oz. lemon juice*

Pour ingredients into a shaker with ice. Shake well and strain into a chilled martini glass.

DELMONICO

MARTINI

MAKES 1 DRINK

*1 oz. gin
½ oz. brandy
½ oz. dry vermouth
½ oz. sweet
    vermouth
1 dash orange
    bitters*

Pour ingredients into a shaker with ice. Stir and strain into a martini glass. Garnish with a lemon twist.

DEMON POSSESSION

HIGHBALL

MAKES 1 DRINK

*1 oz. citrus vodka
1 oz. light rum
¼ oz. blue curaçao
lemonade*

Pour first four ingredients into a shaker with ice. Stir and strain into a chilled highball glass filled with ice. Add the lemonade to fill. Garnish with a cherry.

DEPTH BOMB

OLD-FASHIONED

MAKES 1 DRINK

1 oz. apple brandy
1 oz. brandy
dash lemon juice
dash grenadine

Pour ingredients into a shaker with ice. Shake and strain into an old-fashioned glass over ice cubes.

DEPTH CHARGE

BEER GLASS

MAKES 1 DRINK

2 oz. peppermint
   (or any flavor)
   schnapps
1 pint beer

Pour the schnapps into a frosted mug first. Top off with beer. Stir slightly.

DEPTH CHARGE 2

MARTINI

MAKES 1 DRINK

½ oz. brandy
½ oz. calvados
4 dashes lemon
   juice
2 dashes grenadine

Pour ingredients into a shaker with ice. Shake and strain into a martini glass.

DERBY RUM FIX

COLLINS

MAKES 1 DRINK

½ lemon or lime
1 tsp. powdered
   sugar
1 tsp. water
1½ oz. rum
1 oz. triple sec

Squeeze the juice of the lemon or lime into a Collins glass. Add sugar and water and stir. Fill the glass with ice. Add the rum and triple sec. Stir well. Garnish with a slice of orange and a cherry.

DERBY SPECIAL

MARTINI

MAKES 1 DRINK

1½ oz. light rum
½ oz. Cointreau
1 oz. orange juice
½ oz. lime juice

Pour ingredients into a blender with ice. Blend thoroughly. Pour into a martini glass.

DESERT MARTINI

MARTINI

MAKES 1 DRINK

2½ oz. gin
dry vermouth

Dip a toothpick into dry vermouth. Pour the gin into a martini glass and stir it with the toothpick for the driest martini in the world.

DESPERATE MARTINI

MARTINI

MAKES 1 DRINK

3 oz. gin
½ oz. dry vermouth
½ oz. blackberry
   brandy

Pour ingredients into a shaker with ice. Shake and strain into a chilled martini glass. Garnish with fresh blackberries.

DETROIT DAISY

COLLINS

MAKES 1 DRINK

2 oz. dark rum
dash grenadine
juice of 1 lime

Pour ingredients into a shaker with ice. Shake and strain into a Collins glass. Garnish with a green cocktail cherry and a sprig of mint.

DEVIL'S COCKTAIL

MARTINI

MAKES 1 DRINK

1 1/3 oz. brandy
1 1/3 oz. green
    crème de menthe

Pour ingredients into a shaker with ice. Shake with and strain into a martini glass.

DEVIL'S TAIL

CHAMPAGNE

MAKES 1 DRINK

1½ oz. light rum
1 oz. vodka
2 tsp. apricot
    brandy
2 tsp. grenadine
½ oz. lime juice

Pour ingredients into a blender with ice. Blend thoroughly. Pour into a Champagne flute.

DIABLO

COLLINS

MAKES 1 DRINK

1½ oz. tequila
¾ oz. crème de
    cassis
½ oz. lime juice
ginger ale

Pour tequila, cassis, and lime juice into a shaker with ice. Shake and strain into a Collins glass. Top with the ginger ale. Garnish with a lime slice.

DIABLO 2

MARTINI

MAKES 1 DRINK

2 oz. rum
½ oz. Cointreau
½ oz. dry vermouth
2 dashes bitters

Pour ingredients into a shaker with ice. Stir and strain into a martini glass. Garnish with an orange twist.

163

DIAMOND FIZZ

HIGHBALL

MAKES 1 DRINK

2 oz. gin
1 oz. lemon juice or
juice of ½ lemon
1 tsp. sugar
4 oz. Champagne

Pour the gin, lemon juice, and sugar into a shaker half filled with ice. Shake well and strain into a highball glass over ice. Add the Champagne. Stir gently.

DIAMOND RING FIZZ

CHAMPAGNE

MAKES 1 DRINK

1 dash blue curaçao
1 dash amaretto
1 oz. lemon juice
4 oz. Champagne

Pour the blue curaçao, amaretto, and lemon juice into a shaker with ice. Shake and strain into a Champagen flute. Add the Champagne.

DIANA

WINE

MAKES 1 DRINK

2 oz. white crème
de menthe
3 tsp. cognac

Fill a wine glass with ice and pour in the crème de menthe. Float the brandy on top.

DIPLOMAT

COLLINS

MAKES 4 DRINKS

7 oz. red port
7 oz. Wild Turkey
bourbon
1½ oz. simple syrup
1 tbs. lemon juice
21 oz. Perrier
sparkling
natural mineral
water

In a pitcher half filled with ice, pour the simple syrup, lemon juice, red port, and bourbon. Stir. Strain into four Collins glasses filled with ice, about half to three-quarters of the way to the top. Top with the sparkling water.

DIRTY BANANA

MARTINI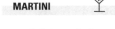

MAKES 1 DRINK

1½ oz. Tia Maria
1 banana
½–2 tsp. sugar
milk or cream

Pour first three ingredients into a blender with ice. Blend at medium speed. Add milk or cream slowly until the mixture reaches a creamy consistency. Pour into a martini glass and top with an additional splash of Tia Maria and/or chocolate shavings.

DIRTY GIRL SCOUT

OLD-FASHIONED

MAKES 1 DRINK

1 oz. vodka
1 oz. coffee liqueur
1 oz. Irish cream
  liqueur
1 tsp. green crème
  de menthe

Pour ingredients into a shaker half filled with ice. Shake well and strain into an old-fashioned glass with ice.

DIRTY MARTINI

MARTINI

MAKES 1 DRINK

2½ oz. gin
½ oz. dry vermouth
olive brine to taste

Pour gin and vermouth into a shaker with ice and stir. Slowly add the olive brine. Stir again. Strain into a chilled martini glass. Garnish with the olive. (Caution: too much brine can ruin this drink, so proceed with caution.) May be shaken instead of stirred.

DIRTY MONKEY

SNIFTER

MAKES 1 DRINK

1½ oz. Irish cream
  liqueur
1½ oz. cognac
1 oz. dark rum

Pour the Irish cream into a brandy snifter. Carefully float the cognac on the Irish cream by pouring it into the glass over the back of a spoon. Float the dark rum on the cognac in the same way. Do not stir.

DIRTY SOCK

OLD-FASHIONED

MAKES 1 DRINK

1½ oz. scotch
1½ oz. pineapple
juice

Pour ingredients into an old-fashioned glass.

DIRTY VODKA MARTINI

MARTINI

MAKES 1 DRINK

3 oz. vodka
1 oz. dry vermouth
½ oz. olive brine

Pour vodka and vermouth into a shaker with ice and stir. Slowly add the olive brine. Stir again. Strain into a chilled martini glass. Garnish with the olive. (Caution: too much brine can ruin this drink, so proceed with caution.) May be shaken instead of stirred.

DISCO LEMONADE

COLLINS

MAKES 1 DRINK

1½ oz. vodka
½ oz. blue curaçao
lemonade

Combine vodka and blue curaçao into a Collins glass over ice. Add the lemonade to fill. Garnish with a lemon slice.

DIXIE DEW

MARTINI

MAKES 1 DRINK

1½ oz. bourbon
½ tsp. white crème
de menthe
½ tsp. triple sec

Pour ingredients into a shaker with ice. Stir well and strain into a martini glass.

DIXIE STINGER

MARTINI

MAKES 1 DRINK

3 oz. bourbon
½ oz. white crème
    de menthe
½ tsp. Southern
    Comfort

Pour ingredients into a shaker with ice. Shake well and strain into a martini glass.

DIXIE WHISKEY

MARTINI

MAKES 1 DRINK

2 oz. bourbon
1 tsp. white crème
    de menthe
1 tsp. triple sec
½ oz. fine sugar
dash bitters

Pour ingredients into a shaker half filled with ice. Shake well. Strain into a martini glass.

DOROTHY'S RUBY SIPPER

IRISH COFFEE

MAKES 1 DRINK

1½ oz. cinnamon
    schnapps
hot apple cider

Pour the cinnamon schnapps into an Irish coffee glass or large mug. Add the hot cider to fill. Garnish with Red Hots candies.

DOS AMIGOS CHICORITA

MARTINI

MAKES 1 DRINK

2 oz. tequila
1 oz. Grand Marnier
1½ oz. sweet-and-
    sour mix
1½ oz. orange juice

Pour ingredients into a shaker with ice. Shake vigorously and strain over ice into a large, chilled martini glass with a salted rim. Garnish with a slice of lime. May be blended; salted rim is optional.

DOUBLE FUDGE MARTINI

MARTINI

MAKES 1 DRINK

3 oz. vodka
½ oz. chocolate
* liqueur*
½ oz. coffee
* liqueur*

Pour ingredients into a shaker with ice. Shake and strain into a chilled martini glass. Garnish with a chocolate straw.

DOUBLE MINT

IRISH COFFEE

MAKES 1 DRINK

1 oz. spearmint
* schnapps*
hot black coffee
dash green crème
* de menthe*

Pour the schnapps into an Irish coffee glass and fill with coffee. Top with whipped cream. Add a dash crème de menthe to the whipped cream for color.

DOUBLE OH 7 (007)

OLD-FASHIONED

MAKES 1 DRINK

1½ oz. orange-
* flavored vodka*
1½ oz. orange juice
splash 7-Up

Pour ingredients into an old-fashioned glass over ice. Stir.

DOUBLE STANDARD SOUR

HIGHBALL

MAKES 1 DRINK

1 oz. blended
* whiskey*
1 oz. gin
juice of ½ lemon or
* lime*
1 tsp. fine sugar
½ tsp. grenadine

Pour ingredients into a shaker with ice. Shake and strain into a highball glass. Garnish with lemon and a cherry.

DOUBLE-STUFFED OREO

COLLINS

MAKES 1 DRINK

1 oz. vodka
1 oz. coffee liqueur
milk or half-and-half
1 Oreo cookie

Pour the vodka and the coffee liqueur into a Collins glass over ice. Slowly fill with milk or half-and-half. Float the Oreo cookie on top.

DOUGLAS FAIRBANKS COCKTAIL

MARTINI

MAKES 1 DRINK

2 oz. Plymouth gin
1 oz. French vermouth

Pour ingredients into a shaker with ice. Shake well and strain into a chilled martini glass. Garnish with orange and lemon twists.

DOUGLAS MARTINI

MARTINI

MAKES 1 DRINK

4 oz. vodka
dash dry vermouth

Pour the vermouth into a martini glass. Swirl it around until the glass is coated. Put the glass in the freezer until thoroughly chilled. Shake the vodka with ice for at least 20 seconds. Pour into the chilled martini glass. Garnish two grapes.

DOWN AND DIRTY MARTINI

MARTINI

MAKES 1 DRINK

3 oz. gin
½ oz. olive brine

Pour ingredients into a shaker with ice. Shake and strain into a martini glass. Rub the rim with a lemon twist and add it to the drink. Garnish with two cocktail onions.

DOWNSIDER

MAKES 1 DRINK

1½ oz. tequila
½ oz. crème de
  banane
½ oz. Galliano
1 oz. cream
1 tsp. grenadine

Pour ingredients into a shaker half filled with ice. Shake well. Strain into a martini glass.

DOWN-UNDER

HIGHBALL

MAKES 1 DRINK

½ oz. blue curaçao
¼ oz. rum
¼ oz. tequila
¼ oz. triple sec
¼ vodka
1½ oz. club soda

Pour first four ingredients into a highball glass over ice. Add the soda to fill. Stir.

DR. PEPPER

COLLINS

MAKES 1 DRINK

1 oz. Amaretto
2 oz. Southern
  Comfort
cola

Pour Amaretto and Southern Comfort into a Collins glass over ice. Add cola to fill.

DRAGON'S BREATH

SHOT

MAKES 1 DRINK

½ oz. green crème
  de menthe
½ oz. gold tequila
¹/₈ oz. Grand
  Marnier

Pour the green crème de menthe into a shot glass. Gently pour the gold tequila over the back of a spoon to layer it on the crème de menthe. Repeat with the Grand Marnier. Ignite the drink. Be sure to blow out the flame before trying to drink it.

DRAGONFLY

MAKES 1 DRINK

1½ oz. gin
4 oz. ginger ale

Pour the ingredients into a highball glass almost filled with ice. Stir well. Garnish with a lime wedge.

DREAM COCKTAIL

MARTINI

MAKES 1 DRINK

2 oz. brandy
½ oz. triple sec
1 tsp. anisette

Pour ingredients into a shaker nearly filled with ice. Strain into a martini glass.

DREAMSICLE

OLD-FASHIONED

MAKES 1 DRINK

1½ oz. Irish cream
*   liqueur*
3½ oz. orange juice

Pour ingredients into an old-fashioned glass. Stir.

DREAMSICLE 2

MARTINI

MAKES 1 DRINK

1½ oz. Amaretto
2 oz. orange juice
2 oz. half-and-half

Pour ingredients into a blender. Blend until smooth and pour into a chilled martini glass over ice.

DRUNK MONKEY

MAKES 1 DRINK

1 oz. triple sec
1 oz. banana
*   liqueur*
1 oz. melon liqueur
cranberry juice
pineapple juice

Pour the first three ingredients into a highball glass over ice. Add equal parts of cranberry juice and pineapple juice to fill. Stir well.

DUBLIN COCKTAIL

MAKES 1 DRINK

2 oz. Irish whiskey
1 tsp. green
*   chartreuse*
3 dashes green
*   crème de*
*   menthe*

Pour ingredients into a shaker with ice. Stir and strain into a martini glass. Garnish with an olive.

DUBONNET COCKTAIL

MARTINI

MAKES 1 DRINK

1 oz. Dubonnet
1 oz. gin
dash bitters

Pour ingredients into a shaker with ice. Stir and strain into a martini glass. Garnish with a lemon twist.

DUBONNET ROUGE

MARTINI

MAKES 1 DRINK

2 oz. Dubonnet
1 oz. apple brandy

Pour ingredients into a shaker with ice. Stir and strain into a martini glass.

DURANGO

MAKES 1 DRINK

1½ oz. tequila
1½ oz. grapefruit
*   juice*
1 tsp. orgeat syrup
spring water

Pour ingredients into a shaker with ice. Shake and strain into an old-fashioned glass. Add spring water to fill. Garnish with mint sprigs.

E

DUSTY MARTINI

MAKES 1 DRINK

2 oz. gin
dash dry vermouth

Pour all ingredients into a chilled, ice-filled martini glass rimmed with scotch. Stir. Garnish with a lemon twist.

EAGER BEAVER

MAKES 1 DRINK

2 oz. rum
3 oz. Kahlua
1 oz. Cointreau

Pour ingredients into a shaker with ice. Shake and strain into a highball glass.

EAGLE COCKTAIL

MAKES 1 DRINK

1½ oz. gin
¾ oz. Parfait Amour
juice of ½ lemon
1 tsp. sugar
1 egg white

Pour ingredients into a shaker with ice. Shake and strain into a wine glass.

EARTH ANGEL SANGRIA (NONALCOHOLIC) COLLINS

MAKES 1 DRINK

¾ of a glass
of grape
juice (red or
white)
club soda

Fill a Collins glass three quarters of the way with grape juice. Add club soda to fill. Garnish with slices of orange, lime, and pineapple, and a cherry.

EARTHQUAKE SHOOTER   SHOT

MAKES 1 DRINK

¹/₃ oz. Canadian
whiskey
¹/₃ oz. Pernod
¹/₃ oz. gin

Pour ingredients into a shaker with ice. Shake well and strain into a shot glass.

EAST WING   MARTINI

MAKES 1 DRINK

3 oz. vodka
1 oz. cherry brandy
½ oz. Campari

Pour ingredients into a shaker with ice. Shake and strain into a chilled martini glass. Garnish with a lemon twist.

EASTER EGG   SHOT

MAKES 1 DRINK

¼ oz. raspberry
liqueur
¼ oz. crème de
banane
¼ oz. Parfait Amour
¼ oz. half-and-half

Pour the raspberry liqueur into a shot glass. Gently pour the crème de banane over the back of a spoon to layer it on top of the raspberry liqueur. Repeat first with the Parfait Amour and then with the half-and-half.

EASTERN SOUR

COLLINS ▮

MAKES 1 DRINK

2 oz. bourbon
1½ oz. orange juice
1 oz. fresh
*   squeezed lime*
*   juice*
¼ oz. orgeat syrup
¼ oz. simple syrup

Pour ingredients into a shaker with ice. Shake and strain into an ice-filled tumbler or Collins glass. Garnish with the spent shell of lime.

EASY ALEXANDER (NONALCOHOLIC)

MARTINI 🍸

MAKES 1 DRINK

1 tsp. instant
*   coffee*
1 oz. boiling water
1 tsp. brown sugar
1 oz. cream
nutmeg

Dissolve coffee and sugar in the water and let cool. Pour with cream into a shaker half filled with ice. Shake well and strain into a martini glass. Dust with the nutmeg.

EAT MY MARTINI

MARTINI 🍸

MAKES 1 DRINK

3 oz. honey vodka
½ oz. Amontillado
*   sherry*

Pour ingredients into a shaker with ice. Shake and strain into a chilled martini glass. Garnish with an almond-stuffed olive.

ECLIPSE

MARTINI 🍸

MAKES 1 DRINK

1½ oz. sloe gin
1 oz. gin
1 tsp. grenadine
maraschino cherry

Place the cherry in a martini glass. Cover with grenadine (more than a tsp. may be required). Pour the gins into a shaker half filled with ice. Shake well and strain into the glass over the back of a spoon so that the grenadine is not disturbed. Garnish with an orange twist.

EGG LEMONADE (NONALCOHOLIC) COLLINS

MAKES 1 DRINK

1 whole egg
juice of 1 lemon
2 tsp. powdered
    sugar
water

Pour first three ingredients into a shaker with ice. Shake well and strain into an ice-filled Collins glass. Add enough water to fill. Serve with a straw.

EGGNOG

PUNCH

MAKES 12 DRINKS

6 eggs
1 cup sugar
½ tsp. salt
1 cup rum
1½ tsp. vanilla
1 quart light cream
    or milk
nutmeg

Beat the eggs until light and foamy. Add the sugar, salt, and vanilla. Add the rum and cream. Stir well. Chill. Sprinkle with nutmeg before serving.

EGGNOG 2

PUNCH

MAKES 24 DRINKS

1 dozen eggs,
    separated
½ tsp. salt
2¼ cups sugar
2 cups bourbon
½ cup rum
1 quart milk
2 tbs. vanilla
3 pints heavy
    cream
nutmeg

Beat together the egg yolks and salt in a large mixing bowl, slowly adding 1½ cups of the sugar. Continue beating until the mixture is thick and pale. Stir in the bourbon, rum, milk, and vanilla until well mixed. Beat the egg whites until foamy, and slowly add the remaining ¾ cup sugar. Continue beating until the whites for stiff peaks and all the sugar has been incorporated. Whip the cream until stiff. Fold the egg whites into the yolk mixture, and then fold in the whipped cream. Taste and add more bourbon and/or sugar if necessary. Pour into a punch bowl and sprinkle with nutmeg before serving.

EGGNOG 3 (NONALCOHOLIC)

PUNCH

MAKES 12 DRINKS

4 eggs
¼ cup sugar
1 quart milk,
    chilled
1½ tsp. vanilla
¼ tsp. salt
nutmeg

Beat three whole eggs and a yolk until very thick and light in color. Beat in 1²/₃ tablespoons of sugar. Stir in milk, vanilla, and salt, and pour the mixture into glasses. Beat the remaining egg whites until almost stiff. Add remaining sugar and beat until peaks appear. Top each glass with a spoonful of the meringue, and sprinkle with nutmeg.

EGG SOUR

SOUR GLASS

MAKES 1 DRINK

2 oz. brandy
1 tsp. Cointreau
½ oz. lemon juice
1 egg

Pour ingredients into a shaker filled two-thirds with ice. Shake and strain into a sour glass.

EL CHICO

MARTINI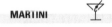

MAKES 1 DRINK

1½ oz. light rum
½ oz. sweet
    vermouth
¼ tsp. grenadine
¼ tsp. curaçao

Pour ingredients into a shaker nearly filled with ice. Shake and strain into a martini glass. Garnish with a cherry and a lemon twist.

EL CID

MARTINI

MAKES 1 DRINK

½ oz. dry gin
½ oz. melon liqueur
½ oz. Rose's lime
    juice
1 oz. orange juice

Pour ingredients into a shaker with ice. Shake and strain into a sugar-rimmed martini glass. Garnish with a cherry.

EL PRESIDENTÉ

MARTINI

MAKES 1 DRINK

1½ oz. light rum
1 oz. lime juice or
    juice of ½ lime
½ oz. pineapple
    juice
1 tsp. grenadine

Pour ingredients into a shaker nearly filled with ice. Stir and strain into a martini glass.

EL DORADO

COLLINS

MAKES 1 DRINK

1 tbs. honey
1½ oz. lemon juice
2 oz. tequila

Pour ingredients into a shaker with ice. Shake and strain into a Collins glass over ice. Garnish with an orange slice.

ELECTRIC ICE TEA

HIGHBALL

MAKES 1 DRINK

1½ oz. rum
1½ oz. vodka
1½ oz. gin
1 oz. tequila
1 oz. triple sec
splash blue curaçao
7-Up

Pour all ingredients except the 7-Up into a highball glass over ice. Top with the 7-Up. Garnish with a lemon slice.

ELEPHANT TREK

SHOT

MAKES 1 DRINK

¹/₃ oz. Jack
    Daniel's whiskey
¹/₃ oz. tequila
¹/₃ oz. 151 proof
    rum

In a shot glass, add the Jack Daniel's first, then the tequila, then the rum, so they more or less float on top of each other. Ignite the rum. Blow out the flame before drinking.

ELK MOUNTAIN HOT APPLE

MAKES 1 DRINK

1½ oz. applejack
1 packet instant
    hot apple cider
6 oz. hot water

Pour instant cider mix and water into an Irish coffee glass or large mug. Add the applejack and stir. Finish with a dash of ground cinnamon.

EMBASSY ROYAL

MARTINI

MAKES 1 DRINK

1 oz. bourbon
    whiskey
½ oz. Drambuie
½ oz. sweet
    vermouth
2 dashes orange
    syrup

Pour ingredients into a shaker with ice. Shake and strain into a martini glass.

EMERALD ISLE

MARTINI

MAKES 1 DRINK

2 oz. gin
1½ tsp. green
    crème de
    menthe
3 dashes bitters

Pour ingredients into a shaker with ice. Stir and strain into a martini glass.

EMERALD MARTINI

 MARTINI

MAKES 1 DRINK

3 oz. citrus-
    flavored vodka
1 oz. chartreuse

Pour ingredients into a shaker with ice. Stir well and strain into a chilled martini glass. Garnish with lemon and lime twists.

EMERSON

MAKES 1 DRINK

2 oz. gin
1 oz. sweet
    vermouth
½ oz. lemon juice
½ oz. maraschino
    liqueur

Pour ingredients into a shaker with ice. Shake well and strain into a chilled martini glass.

ENGLISH HIGHBALL

HIGHBALL

MAKES 1 DRINK

¾ oz. brandy
¾ oz. gin
¾ oz. sweet
    vermouth
club soda

Pour the brandy, gin, and sweet vermouth into a highball glass over ice. Add club soda to fill. Add a lemon twist and stir.

ENGLISH ROSE

MARTINI

MAKES 1 DRINK

2 oz. gin
1 oz. dry vermouth
1 oz. apricot brandy
½ oz. lemon juice
1 tsp. grenadine

Pour ingredients into a shaker with ice. Shake well and strain into a chilled martini glass. Garnish with a cherry.

ENGLISH ROSE COCKTAIL

MARTINI

MAKES 1 DRINK

¾ oz. apricot
    brandy
1½ oz. gin
¾ oz. dry vermouth
1 tsp. grenadine
¼ tsp. lemon juice

Pour ingredients into a shaker with ice. Shake and strain into a sugar-rimmed martini glass. Garnish with a cherry.

ENIGMA

COLLINS

MAKES 1 DRINK

1 oz. Malibu rum
1 oz. vodka
1 oz. triple sec
1 oz. Southern
   Comfort
1 oz. Amaretto
splash orange juice
splash cranberry
   juice
splash grenadine

Pour ingredients into a shaker with ice. Stir and strain into a Collins glass over ice.

ETHEL DUFFY COCKTAIL

MARTINI

MAKES 1 DRINK

¾ oz. apricot
   brandy
¾ oz. white crème
   de menthe
¾ oz. curaçao

Pour ingredients into a shaker with ice. Shake well and strain into a martini glass.

EVERGLADE

OLD-FASHIONED

MAKES 1 DRINK

1 oz. Everclear
1 oz. Gatorade
   (green)

Pour ingredients into an old-fashioned glass. Serve straight up.

EVERYBODY'S IRISH

MARTINI

MAKES 1 DRINK

2 oz. Irish whiskey
1 oz. green crème
   de menthe
1 oz. green
   chartreuse

Pour ingredients into a shaker with ice. Stir and strain into a martini glass. Garnish with a green olive.

EXECUTIVE SUNRISE

COLLINS

MAKES 1 DRINK

1½ oz. tequila,
    gold
4 oz. orange juice
2 tsp. crème de
    cassis

Pour the tequila and the orange juice into an ice-filled Collins glass. Stir well. Drop the cassis into the center of the drink.

EXORCIST

MARTINI

MAKES 1 DRINK

1½ oz. tequila
¾ oz. blue curaçao
¾ oz. lime juice

Pour ingredients into a shaker with ice. Shake and strain into a martini glass.

EXTERMINATOR

IRISH COFFEE

MAKES 1 DRINK

½ oz. Kahlua
½ oz. Irish cream
½ oz. 151 rum
½ oz. Grand
    Marnier
6 oz. hot black
    coffee

Pour all ingredients into an Irish coffee glass or a mug. Topped with whipped cream.

EYE OF THE HURRICANE (NONALCOHOLIC) HIGHBALL

MAKES 1 DRINK

2 oz. passion
    fruit syrup
1 oz. lime juice
club soda or
    lemon-lime
    soda

Pour syrup and lime juice into a shaker nearly filled with ice. Stir and strain into a highball or Collins glass over ice. Add the soda. Garnish with a wedge of lime.

EYEFUL (NONALCOHOLIC)

HIGHBALL

MAKES 1 DRINK

*4 oz. pink grape-
    fruit juice
1 oz. tonic water
½ oz. grenadine
1 tsp. fine sugar*

Pour ingredients into a shaker half filled with ice. Shake well and strain into a highball glass over ice.

FACE PLANT (NONALCOHOLIC)

COLLINS

MAKES 1 DRINK

*2 oz. orange
    juice
1 oz. chocolate
    syrup
4–6 strawberries
2 oz. milk
4 oz. ice*

Pour all ingredients into a blender. Blend until smooth. Pour into a Collins glass. Garnish with an orange slice.

F

FAIR AND WARMER

MARTINI

MAKES 1 DRINK

*1½ oz. light rum
½ oz. sweet
    vermouth
splash curaçao*

Pour ingredients into a shaker half filled with ice. Shake well and strain into a martini glass. Garnish with a lemon twist.

FAIRY GODFATHER

MARTINI

MAKES 1 DRINK

*1½ oz. Amaretto
1½ oz. scotch
    whiskey*

Pour the Amaretto and scotch into an ice-filled old-fashioned glass and stir. May also be served straight up: Shake with ice and strain into a martini glass.

FAIRY GODMOTHER

MAKES 1 DRINK

1½ oz. Amaretto
1½ oz. vodka

Pour the Amaretto and vodka into an ice-filled old-fashioned glass and stir. May also be served straight up: Shake with ice and strain into a martini glass.

FALLEN ANGEL

MARTINI

MAKES 1 DRINK

1½ oz. gin
½ tsp. white crème
   de menthe
juice of ½ lemon
dash bitters

Shake with ice and strain into a martini glass. Top with a cherry and serve.

FALLEN LEAVES

MARTINI

MAKES 1 DRINK

¾ oz. calvados
   (apple brandy)
¾ oz. sweet
   vermouth
¼ oz. dry vermouth
dash brandy
lemon slice

Pour ingredients into a shaker with ice. Stir and strain into a martini glass. Squeeze a lemon twist into the drink and use it as a garnish.

FALLING STAR

HIGHBALL

MAKES 1 DRINK

1¼ oz. spiced rum
¼ oz. lime juice
2 oz. orange juice
2 oz. tonic water

Pour the rum, lime juice, and orange juice into a highball glass over ice. Add the tonic to fill. Stir.

FALSE START

OLD-FASHIONED

MAKES 2 DRINKS

4 oz. apple cider
2 oz. bourbon
1 oz. apple brandy
½ lemon

Into a shaker filled with ice, squeeze the juice of the lemon. Add the other ingredients and shake well. Strain into two old-fashioned glasses over ice.

FANCY BRANDY

MARTINI

MAKES 1 DRINK

2 oz. brandy
¼ oz. Cointreau
¼ tsp. fine sugar
dash bitters

Pour ingredients into a shaker with ice. Stir and strain into a martini glass. Garnish with a lemon twist.

FANCY FIX

COLLINS

MAKES 1 DRINK

½ lemon or lime
1 tsp. powdered sugar
1 tsp. water
2½ oz. Champagne
lemon slice

Into a Collins glass, squeeze juice of the lemon or lime. Add sugar and water and stir. Fill the glass with ice. Add the Champagne and stir well. Garnish with a slice of lemon. Serve with a straw.

FANCY WHISKEY

MARTINI

MAKES 1 DRINK

2 oz. blended whiskey
½ oz. superfine sugar
½ oz. triple sec
dash bitters

Pour ingredients into a shaker with ice. Shake well and strain into a chilled martini glass. Garnish with a lemon twist.

FANCY-FREE COCKTAIL

MARTINI

MAKES 1 DRINK

*2 oz. bourbon
whiskey
½ oz. maraschino
liqueur
1 dash bitters
1 dash orange
bitters*

Pour ingredients into a shaker with ice. Stir and strain into a martini glass.

FARMER'S MARTINI

MARTINI

MAKES 1 DRINK

*3 oz. gin
½ oz. dry vermouth
½ oz. sweet
vermouth
4 dashes bitters*

Pour ingredients into a shaker with ice. Shake and strain into a chilled martini glass.

FICKLE PICKLE

HIGHBALL

MAKES 1 DRINK

*¾ oz. vodka
¾ oz. melon liqueur
¼ oz. Crown Royal
½ oz. triple sec
sweet-and-sour mix*

Pour ingredients into a shaker with ice. Shake and strain into a highball glass. Garnish with a cherry.

FIERY SUNSET TEA

COLLINS

MAKES 1 DRINK

*½ oz. vodka
½ oz. gin
½ oz. rum
½ oz. tequila
½ oz. triple sec
sweet-and-sour mix
1 oz. cranberry
juice
½ oz. 151 rum*

Pour the vodka, gin, rum, tequila, and triple sec into an ice-filled Collins glass. Add sweet-and-sour mix to nearly fill. Stir. Top first with cranberry juice and then with rum. Ignite the rum.

FIFTY-FIFTY MARTINI

MARTINI

MAKES 1 DRINK

2 oz. gin
2 oz. dry vermouth

Pour ingredients into a shaker with ice. Stir well and strain into a chilled martini glass. Garnish with an olive.

FIN DE SIECLE

MARTINI

MAKES 1 DRINK

1½ oz. gin
¾ oz. sweet
vermouth
¼ oz. Amer Picon
1 dash orange
bitters

Pour ingredients into a shaker with ice. Stir and strain into a martini glass.

FINO MARTINI

MARTINI

MAKES 1 DRINK

2½ oz. gin (or
vodka)
1½ tsp. Fino sherry

Pour ingredients into a shaker with ice. Stir well and strain into a martini glass. Garnish with a lemon twist.

FIREBALL

OLD-FASHIONED

MAKES 1 DRINK

¾ oz. cinnamon
schnapps
¾ oz. cherry brandy

Pour ingredients into an old-fashioned glass.

FIRECRACKER

OLD-FASHIONED

MAKES 1 DRINK

1½ oz. cinnamon
   schnapps
1½ oz. cherry
   brandy
dash Tabasco sauce

Pour ingredients into an old-fashioned glass.

FIREFLY

HIGHBALL

MAKES 1 DRINK

2 oz. vodka
4 oz. grapefruit
   juice
1 oz. grenadine

Pour the vodka and grapefruit juice into a shaker with ice. Stir well and strain into a highball glass. Add the grenadine and stir again.

FIREMAN'S SOUR

SOUR GLASS

MAKES 1 DRINK

2 oz. light rum
2 oz. lime juice or
   juice of 1 lime
1 tbs. grenadine
1 tsp. fine sugar
club soda

Pour all ingredients except the club soda into a shaker with ice. Shake well and strain into a sour glass. Add the club soda to fill. Garnish with a lemon slice and cherry.

FIRST AND TEN

COLLINS

MAKES 2 DRINKS

3 oz. gin
2 oz. orange juice
2 oz. pineapple juice
2 oz. grapefruit juice
2 oz. cranberry juice
2 oz. lemon juice
2 oz. lime juice
dash grenadine
splash soda water
   or seltzer
splash dark rum

Pour all the fruit juices with the gin into a large shaker half filled with ice. Strain into two Collins glasses over ice. Top with the grenadine, soda, and rum.

FISH HOUSE PUNCH

MAKES ABOUT 25 DRINKS

1 bottle peach brandy
1 bottle light rum
2 bottles dry white wine
1 quart club soda
1½ cups lemon juice
½ cup fine sugar

Dissolve sugar in lemon juice and brandy. Add rum and wine. Stir. Refrigerate. Pour into a punch bowl over ice. Add club soda just before serving.

FLAMINGO COCKTAIL

MARTINI

MAKES 1 DRINK

½ oz. apricot nectar liqueur
1¼ oz. dry gin
½ lime
1 tsp. grenadine

Pour ingredients into a shaker with ice. Shake well and strain into a martini glass.

FLORADORA COOLER

COLLINS

MAKES 1 DRINK

1 lime
½ tsp. powdered sugar
½ oz. grenadine or raspberry syrup
2 oz. club soda
2 oz. gin
ginger ale

Pour the juice of the lime, powdered sugar, grenadine, and club soda into a Collins glass. Stir. Add ice to fill. Add the gin. Add ginger ale to fill.

FLORIDA

MARTINI

MAKES 1 DRINK

1 oz. gin
1 tsp. kirschwasser
1 tsp. Cointreau
1 oz. orange juice
1 tsp. lemon juice

Pour ingredients into a shaker half filled with ice. Shake well and strain into a martini glass.

FLORIDA SUNSET

COLLINS

MAKES 1 DRINK

1½ oz. orange-
    flavored vodka
½ oz. grenadine
orange juice

Pour the orange-flavored vodka and the grenadine into an ice-filled Collins glass. Pack the glass again with ice, then slowly fill with orange juice. The result should be a red layer on the bottom blending with the orange layer. Garnish with an orange slice.

FLORIDITA DAIQUIRI

MARTINI

MAKES 1 DRINK

3 oz. Anejo rum
3 oz. fresh
    squeezed
    grapefruit juice
1 oz. fresh
    squeezed lime
    juice
1 oz. simple syrup (or
    1 tsp. of sugar)

Pour all ingredients into a blender with 2 cups of ice. Blend until smooth. Pour into a martini glass. Garnish with lime slice.

FLYING GRASSHOPPER

MARTINI

MAKES 1 DRINK

1 oz. green crème
    de menthe
1 oz. white crème
    de cacao
1 oz. vodka

Pour all ingredients into a shaker nearly filled with ice. Shake well and strain into a martini glass.

FLYING SCOTSMAN

MARTINI

MAKES 1 DRINK

1 oz. scotch
    whiskey
1 oz. sweet
    vermouth
dash bitters
¼ tsp. simple syrup

Pour ingredients into a shaker with ice. Shake well and strain into a martini glass.

FOG CUTTER

MAKES 1 DRINK

2 oz. fresh lemon
  juice
1 oz. orange juice
½ oz. orgeat syrup
2 oz. white rum
1 oz. brandy
½ oz. gin
½ oz. sweet sherry

Pour all ingredients except the sherry into a shaker with ice. Shake well and strain into an ice-filled tiki mug or hurricane glass. Float the sherry on top.

FOGGY AFTERNOON

MARTINI

MAKES 1 DRINK

1 oz. vodka
½ oz. apricot
  brandy
½ oz. triple sec
1 tsp. crème de
  banane
1 tsp. lemon juice

Pour ingredients into a shaker half filled with ice. Shake well and strain into a martini glass.

FOGHORN

HIGHBALL

MAKES 1 DRINK

2 oz. gin
ginger ale
juice of ½ lime

Pour gin and lime juice into a highball glass over ice. Add the ginger ale to fill. Put the squeezed lime in the glass as a garnish. Stir.

FOREIGN AFFAIR

MARTINI

MAKES 1 DRINK

1 oz. Sambuca
1 oz. brandy

Pour ingredients into a shaker with ice. Stir and strain into a martini glass.

FOUR WHEELER

MARTINI

MAKES 1 DRINK

1¼ oz. dark rum
1 oz. coconut
  cream
2 oz. orange juice
2 oz. pineapple
  juice

Pour all ingredients into a blender with a scoop of crushed ice. Blend until smooth. Pour into a large martini glass. Garnish with an orange slice.

FOURTH OF JULY

SHOT

MAKES 1 DRINK

1 oz. grenadine
1 oz. vodka
1 oz. blue curaçao

Pour ingredients, in order given, into a cordial or tall shot glass. Pour each over the back of a spoon so that they form separate layers.

FOX AND HOUNDS

MARTINI

MAKES 1 DRINK

1½ oz. bourbon
  whiskey
½ oz. Pernod
½ oz. lemon juice
½ tsp. superfine
  sugar
1 egg white

Pour ingredients into a shaker with ice. Shake and strain into a martini glass.

FOX TROT

MARTINI

MAKES 1 DRINK

1¼ oz. dark rum
dash curaçao
1/3 oz. lime juice
½ tsp. sugar

Pour ingredients into a shaker with ice. Shake and strain into a chilled martini glass.

FOXY LADY

MARTINI

MAKES 1 DRINK

½ oz. Amaretto
½ oz. dark crème
    de cacao
2 oz. light cream

Pour ingredients into a shaker with ice. Shake and strain into a chilled martini glass.

FRENCH 75

CHAMPAGNE

MAKES 1 DRINK

¼ oz. lemon juice
¼ oz. gin
¼ oz. Cointreau
5 oz. Champagne

Pour the lemon juice, gin, and Cointreau into a shaker with ice. Shake well and strain into a chilled Champagne flute. Add the Champagne to fill. Garnish with a lemon slice and a cherry.

FRENCH 76

CHAMPAGNE

MAKES 1 DRINK

¼ oz. lemon juice
¼ oz. vodka
¼ oz. Cointreau
5 oz. Champagne

Pour the lemon juice, vodka, and Cointreau into a shaker with ice. Shake well and strain into a chilled Champagne flute. Add the Champagne to fill. Garnish with a lemon slice and a cherry.

FRENCH BREEZE

MARTINI

MAKES 1 DRINK

2 oz. Pernod
1 oz. peppermint
    schnapps

Pour ingredients into a shaker half filled with ice. Shake well and strain into a martini glass.

FRENCH CREAM PUNCH

MAKES 15–20 DRINKS

1 cup Amaretto
*1 cup coffee
    liqueur or 1 cup
    coffee brandy*
¼ cup triple sec
*½ gallon softened
    vanilla ice
    cream*

Allow the ice cream to soften at room temperature (about 10 minutes) before adding. Blend all ingredients well in a large pitcher. Do not add ice.

FRENCH KISS

MARTINI

MAKES 1 DRINK

¾ oz. Chambord
*¾ oz. peach
    schnapps*
¾ oz. vodka
splash orange juice
*splash pineapple
    juice*
*splash cranberry
    juice*

Pour ingredients into a shaker with ice. Stir and strain into a martini glass.

FRENCH MARTINI

MARTINI

MAKES 1 DRINK

1½ oz. vodka
*1 oz. black
    raspberry
    liqueur*

Pour ingredients into a shaker with ice. Shake and strain into a martini glass.

FRENCH MARTINI 2

MARTINI

MAKES 1 DRINK

1½ oz. vodka
1 oz. Chambord
1 oz. Grand Marnier
*½ oz. sweet-
    and-sour mix
    (optional)*

Pour ingredients into a shaker with ice. Shake and strain into a chilled martini glass.

FRENCH ORGASM

SNIFTER

MAKES 1 DRINK

2½ oz. cognac
1½ oz. Irish cream
*   liqueur*

Pour ingredients in order given into a brandy glass. Pour the Irish cream liqueur over the back of a spoon to float it on the cognac in a separate layer. Do not stir.

FRENCH QUARTER

MARTINI

MAKES 1 DRINK

2½ oz. brandy
¾ oz. Lillet

Pour ingredients into a shaker with ice. Stir and strain into a martini glass. Garnish with a thin wedge of lemon.

FRENCH RIVIERA

MARTINI

MAKES 1 DRINK

1 oz. rye whiskey
½ oz. apricot
*   brandy*
1 tsp. fresh lemon
*   juice*

Pour ingredients into a shaker with ice. Shake and strain into a martini glass. Garnish with a cherry.

FRETFUL MARTINI

MARTINI

MAKES 1 DRINK

3 oz. gin
½ oz. blue curaçao
dash bitters

Pour ingredients into a shaker with ice. Shake and strain into a chilled martini glass. Garnish with an olive.

FRIENDLY FROG (NONALCOHOLIC)   COLLINS

MAKES 1 DRINK

1 oz. lemon juice
1 tsp. granulated sugar
3 oz. chilled water
2 oz. orange juice

Pour ingredients into a highball or Collins glass nearly filled with ice. Stir well. Garnish with a lemon wedge.

FRISCO SOUR   SOUR GLASS

MAKES 1 DRINK

2 oz. blended whiskey
½ oz. Benedictine
½ oz. lemon juice
½ oz. lime juice
½ tsp. fine sugar

Pour ingredients into a shaker filled two-thirds with ice. Shake and strain into a sour glass. Garnish with a lemon slice and a cherry.

FRISKY WITCH   OLD-FASHIONED

MAKES 1 DRINK

1½ oz. vodka
½ oz. Sambuca

Pour ingredients into an old-fashioned glass over ice. Garnish with a black licorice stick.

FRONT FOUR EXPRESS   COLLINS

MAKES 1 DRINK

¼ oz. melon liqueur
¼ oz. peach schnapps
¼ oz. Malibu rum
¼ oz. vodka
2 oz. orange juice
2 oz. pineapple juice
2 oz. cranberry juice

Pour ingredients into a shaker with ice. Shake and strain into a Collins glass over ice.

FROSTBITE

MAKES 1 DRINK

1 oz. tequila
*¾ oz. white crème
de cacao*
¾ oz. cream

Pour ingredients into a shaker with ice. Shake hard and strain into a martini glass. Garnish with a dash of nutmeg.

FROSTY DAWN

HIGHBALL

MAKES 1 DRINK

4 oz. white rum
*1 oz. maraschino
liqueur*
1 oz. Falerno
4 oz. orange juice

Pour all ingredients into a highball glass over ice. Stir.

FROSTY NOGGIN

PARFAIT

MAKES 1 DRINK

1½ oz. rum
*¾ oz. white crème
de cacao*
3 oz. eggnog
*3 cups of vanilla
ice cream*

Pour ingredients into a blender. Blend until smooth and pour into a parfait glass. Top with whipped cream and garnish with a few drops of green crème de menthe and a rolled cookie.

FROZEN BANANA DAIQUIRI

COLLINS

MAKES 1 DRINK

2 oz. rum
½ oz. triple sec
*1 oz. lime juice or
juice of ½ lime*
1 tsp. fine sugar
1 banana, sliced

Pour all ingredients into a blender in this order: rum, triple sec, lime juice, sugar, banana, and ice. Blend thoroughly. Pour into a Collins or parfait glass. Serve with a straw.

FROZEN COCOA MUDSLIDE COLLINS

MAKES 1 DRINK

¾ cup chocolate
  ice cream
¼ cup real cream
1½ oz. Kahlua
1 oz. Irish cream
1 oz. Absolut vodka

Pour ingredients into a blender. Blend until smooth. Serve in a Collins glass. Garnish with a cherry.

FROZEN CREAMADE (NONALCOHOLIC) COLLINS

MAKES 1 DRINK

2 oz. orange
  juice
2 oz. milk
½ cup vanilla
  ice cream

Pour milk and ice cream into a blender. Add orange juice. Blend thoroughly. Serve in a Collins glass topped with whipped cream, a cherry, and an orange slice.

FROZEN DAIQUIRI COLLINS

MAKES 1 DRINK

2 oz. light rum
1½ oz. fresh lime
  juice
¾ oz. simple syrup

Blend all ingredients with enough ice to almost fill a 12-oz. Collins glass. Garnish with the lime wedge.

FROZEN DAIQUIRI 2 COLLINS

MAKES 1 DRINK

2 oz. rum
½ oz. triple sec
1 oz. lime juice or
  juice of ½ lime
1 tsp. fine sugar

Pour ingredients into a blender with ice. Blend thoroughly. Pour into a Collins or parfait glass. Garnish with a slice of lime. Serve with a straw.

FROZEN FUZZY

MARTINI

MAKES 1 DRINK

*1 oz. peach
    schnapps
½ oz. triple sec
½ oz. lime juice
½ oz. grenadine
splash lemon-lime
    soda*

Blend all ingredients on low for five seconds with an equal amount of crushed ice. Then blend on high until firm. Pour into a martini glass. Garnish with a slice of lemon or lime.

FROZEN MARGARITA

MARGARITA

MAKES 1 DRINK

*2 oz. tequila
1 oz. triple sec
2 oz. lemon or lime
    juice
1–2 tsp. fine sugar*

Pour ingredients into a blender in this order: tequila, triple sec, lime juice, sugar, and ice. Blend thoroughly. Pour into a large margarita glass with a salted rim.

FROZEN MARTINI

MARTINI

MAKES 1 DRINK

*2½ oz. gin
½ oz. dry vermouth*

Pour the gin and vermouth into a shaker. Place the shaker, a martini glass, and 2 almond-stuffed olives in a freezer for approximately four hours. Remove the shaker from the freezer and shake the contents vigorously. Pour into a chilled martini glass. Garnish with frozen olives.

FROZEN MATADOR

COLLINS

MAKES 1 DRINK

*1½ oz. tequila
1 oz. pineapple
    juice
1 oz. orange juice
1 tbs. lime juice*

Pour ingredients into a blender with ice. Blend thoroughly. Pour into a Collins or parfait glass. Garnish with orange, lemon, or lime slices and a cherry.

FROZEN MOCHA RUSH (NONALCOHOLIC) WINE

MAKES 1 DRINK

2 oz. cold
    black coffee
2 scoops of
    chocolate
    ice cream

Pour ingredients into a blender without ice. Blend thoroughly. Pour into a large red wine glass. Top with chocolate shavings.

FROZEN PEACH DAIQUIRI COLLINS

MAKES 1 DRINK

2 oz. rum
½ oz. peach-
    flavored brandy
1 oz. lime juice or
    juice of ½ lime
1 canned peach
    half
1 tsp. fine sugar

Pour ingredients into a blender with ice. Blend thoroughly. Pour into a Collins or parfait glass. Serve with a straw.

FROZEN PIÑA COLADA HURRICANE

MAKES 1 DRINK

2 oz. light rum
½ cup pineapple
    cubes or 2 oz.
    pineapple juice
1½ oz. coconut
    cream

Blend all ingredients with approximately two cups of ice. Pour into a hurricane glass. Garnish with a cherry and a pineapple slice.

FROZEN PINEAPPLE DAIQUIRI COLLINS

MAKES 1 DRINK

2 oz. rum
½ oz. triple sec
1 oz. lime juice or
    juice of ½ lime
1 tsp. fine sugar
½ cup pineapple
    chunks

Pour ingredients into a blender in this order: rum, triple sec, lime juice, sugar, pineapple, and ice. Blend thoroughly. Pour into a Collins or parfait glass. Serve with a straw.

FROZEN PINK KISS (NONALCOHOLIC)   COLLINS

MAKES 1 DRINK

4 oz. cranberry
   juice
¼ cup rasp-
   berries, fresh
   or frozen
1 scoop vanilla
   ice cream

Put all ingredients into a blender and
mix thoroughly. Pour into a Collins or
parfait glass. Serve with a straw.

FROZEN STRAWBERRY DAIQUIRI   COLLINS

MAKES 1 DRINK

2 oz. rum
½ oz. triple sec
1 oz. lime juice or
   juice of ½ lime
1 tsp. fine sugar
½ cup strawberries,
   fresh or frozen

Pour ingredients into a blender in this
order: rum, triple sec, lime juice, sugar,
strawberries, and ice. Blend thoroughly.
Pour into a Collins or parfait glass. Serve
with a straw.

FROZEN STRAWBERRY MARGARITA   MARGARITA

MAKES 1 DRINK

2 oz. tequila
1 oz. triple sec
3 oz. lemon or lime
   juice
½ cup strawberries,
   fresh or frozen
1–2 tsp. fine sugar

Pour all ingredients into a blender in
this order: tequila, triple sec, lime juice,
strawberries, sugar, and ice. Blend thoroughly. Pour into a large margarita glass
with a sugared rim.

FUMBLE   OLD-FASHIONED

MAKES 2 DRINKS

2 oz. gin
2 oz. vodka
2 oz. grapefruit
   juice
2 oz. cranberry
   juice
club soda or seltzer

Pour all fruit juices, vodka, and gin
into a large shaker half filled with ice.
Shake and strain into two old-fashioned
glasses packed with ice. Add soda or
seltzer to fill.

FURRY PURPLE SQUIRREL

MARTINI

MAKES 1 DRINK

1 oz. light rum
1 oz. coconut rum
1 oz. blue curaçao
1 oz. grenadine
1 oz. lime juice
1 oz. club soda
splash coconut rum

Pour all ingredients except the club soda and coconut rum into a shaker with ice. Shake well. Add the club soda and pour into a martini glass over ice. Finish with a splash of coconut rum. Garnish with a slice of lime with an almond embedded in it.

FUZZY MARTINI

MARTINI

MAKES 1 DRINK

2 oz. vanilla vodka
½ oz. coffee vodka
1 tsp. peach schnapps

Pour ingredients into a shaker with ice. Stir and strain into a martini glass. Garnish with a fresh peach slice.

FUZZY NAVEL

HIGHBALL

MAKES 1 DRINK

1 oz. vodka
1 oz. peach-flavored brandy
4 oz. orange juice

Pour all ingredients into a highball glass over ice. Stir well.

FUZZY NAVEL 2

HIGHBALL

MAKES 1 DRINK

1½ oz. peach schnapps
orange juice

Pour the schnapps into a highball glass over ice. Add orange juice to fill.

G

GAELIC COFFEE

IRISH COFFEE

MAKES 1 DRINK

¾ oz. Irish whiskey
¾ oz. Irish cream
  liqueur
1½ oz. dark crème
  de cacao
2 oz. milk
1 tsp. instant
  coffee

Pour ingredients into a blender. Blend until smooth and pour into an Irish coffee mug. Top with whipped cream and sprinkle with green crème de menthe for color.

GALACTIC ALE SHOOTER

SHOT

MAKES 1 DRINK

1 oz. vodka
1 oz. blue curaçao
½ oz. crème de
  cassis
splash lime juice

Pour ingredients into a shaker half filled with ice. Shake well and strain into a shot glass.

GALE AT SEA

MARTINI

MAKES 1 DRINK

1½ oz. vodka
½ oz. dry vermouth
½ oz. Galliano
½ oz. blue curaçao

Pour ingredients into a shaker nearly filled with ice. Stir and strain into a martini glass.

G

GALLIANO STINGER

MARTINI

MAKES 1 DRINK

2 oz. Galliano
2 oz. white crème
  de menthe

Pour ingredients into a shaker nearly filled with ice. Stir and strain into a martini glass.

GANDY DANCER

MAKES 1 DRINK

1 oz. Yukon Jack
1 oz. Amaretto
1 oz. banana
   liqueur
1 oz. pineapple
   juice

Pour ingredients into a shaker with ice. Shake and strain into a chilled Collins glass.

GANGRENE ZOMBIE

OLD-FASHIONED

MAKES 1 DRINK

½ oz. vodka
½ oz. coconut rum
½ oz. blackberry
   schnapps
½ oz. blue curaçao
1 oz. orange juice
   (lots of pulp)

Pour ingredients into a shaker with ice. Shake and strain into an old-fashioned glass.

GARBO COCKTAIL

HIGHBALL

MAKES 1 DRINK

1 oz. brandy
1 oz. dry vermouth
1 oz. orange juice
¼ oz. grenadine
dash crème de
   menthe

Pour ingredients into a shaker with ice. Shake well and strain into a chilled highball glass.

GASSEY'S JACKWACKER

 IRISH COFFEE

MAKES 1 DRINK

½ shot Chambord
½ shot Irish cream
   liqueur
6 oz. hot chocolate

Pour all ingredients into an Irish coffee glass or large mug. Top with whipped cream.

GAUGUIN

MAKES 1 DRINK

2 oz. light rum
1 oz. passion fruit
  syrup
1 tsp. lime juice or
  juice of ½ lime
1 tsp. grenadine
½ tsp. fine sugar

Pour ingredients into a blender and mix thoroughly. Pour into a Collins or parfait glass. Garnish with orange, lemon, and lime slices, and a cherry. Serve with a straw.

GENTLE WAVE (NONALCOHOLIC)

COLLINS

MAKES 1 DRINK

1½ oz. pine-
  apple juice
1½ oz. cranberry
  juice
splash orange
  juice
1 tsp. grenadine
4 oz. tonic water

Pour all ingredients except tonic into a Collins glass over ice. Stir well. Add tonic. Stir again. Garnish with lemon, lime, or orange slices and a cherry.

GENTLEMAN'S CLUB

OLD-FASHIONED

MAKES 1 DRINK

1½ oz. gin
1 oz. brandy
1 oz. sweet
  vermouth
1 oz. club soda

Pour all ingredients into an old fashioned glass almost filled with ice. Stir well.

GENTLEMAN'S COCKTAIL

HIGHBALL

MAKES 1 DRINK

2 oz. bourbon
½ oz. crème de
  menthe
½ oz. brandy
4 oz. club soda

Pour first three ingredients into a highball glass filled with ice. Add club soda. Stir. Garnish with a lemon twist.

GEORGIA MINT JULEP

OLD-FASHIONED

MAKES 1 DRINK

1 oz. brandy
1 oz. peach-
flavored brandy
1 tsp. fine sugar
2 sprigs mint
splash water

Muddle the mint, sugar, and water in an old-fashioned glass. Add ice. Add the brandies. Stir.

GEORGIA PEACH

COLLINS

MAKES 1 DRINK

1½ oz. vodka
1 oz. peach-
flavored brandy
1 tsp. lemon juice
1 tsp. peach
preserves
1 peach wedge,
cut up

Pour ingredients into a blender with ice. Blend thoroughly. Pour into a Collins or highball glass.

GEORGIA PEACH 2

COLLINS

MAKES 1 DRINK

1½ oz. vodka
½ oz. peach
schnapps
dash grenadine
lemonade

Pour first three ingredients into a Collins glass filled with ice. Add lemonade to fill.

GEORGIAN SUNRISE

HIGHBALL

MAKES 1 DRINK

¾ oz. tequila
¼ oz. peach
schnapps
½ oz. strawberry
liqueur
3 oz. sweet-and-
sour mix

Pour all four ingredients a highball glass over ice. Stir well. Garnish with lime slice.

GEORGIO

PARFAIT

MAKES 1 DRINK

2 oz. coffee liqueur
2 oz. Irish cream
*   liqueur*
1 banana
½ cup light cream

Pour ingredients into a blender. Blend until smooth. Pour into a parfait glass. Top with whipped cream and a light dusting of cocoa. Garnish with mint leaves.

GERMAN CHOCOLATE CAKE SHOT

MAKES 1 DRINK

½ oz. Jägermeister
½ oz. chocolate
*   liqueur*
splash coconut rum
splash butterscotch
*   schnapps*

Pour into a shaker with ice. Shake and strain into a shot glass.

GIBSON MARTINI

MAKES 1 DRINK

2½ oz. gin
½ oz. dry vermouth

Pour ingredients into a shaker with ice. Add the vermouth first, then the gin. Stir and strain into a martini glass. Serve with cocktail onions.

GIMLET MARTINI

MAKES 1 DRINK

2 oz. gin
½ oz. Rose's lime
*   juice*

Pour ingredients into a shaker with ice. Stir well and strain into a martini glass. Garnish with a lime wedge.

GIN AND IT

MAKES 1 DRINK

¾ oz. sweet
   vermouth
1½ oz. gin

Pour the vermouth directly into a martini glass without ice. Add the gin. Garnish with the cherry.

GIN AND SIN

MARTINI

MAKES 1 DRINK

1 oz. gin
1 oz. lemon juice
1 oz. orange juice
dash grenadine

Pour the vodka and juices into a shaker with ice. Add the grenadine. Shake well and strain into a chilled martini glass.

GIN AND TONIC

HIGHBALL

MAKES 1 DRINK

2 oz. gin
5 oz. tonic water

Pour the ingredients into a highball glass over ice. Stir well. Garnish with a lime wedge.

GIN BUCK

MAKES 1 DRINK

1½ oz. gin
juice of ½ lemon
ginger ale

Pour gin and lemon juice into an old-fashioned glass over ice. Add ginger ale to fill. Stir.

GIN COBBLER

WINE

MAKES 1 DRINK

2 oz. gin
2 oz. club soda
1 tsp. fine sugar

Pour the club soda into a large wine glass or goblet. Add the sugar and dissolve. Fill with crushed ice. Add the gin and stir. Garnish with lemon, lime, or orange slices and a cherry, and serve with a straw.

GIN COOLER

COLLINS

MAKES 1 DRINK

2 oz. gin
2 oz. club soda
1 tsp. fine sugar
ginger ale

Dissolve the sugar in club soda in a Collins glass. Nearly fill the glass with ice. Add the gin. Add the ginger ale to fill. Garnish with lemon, lime, or orange slices and a cherry.

GIN COOLER 2

COLLINS

MAKES 1 DRINK

2 oz. dry gin
2 oz. carbonated
water
½ tsp. powdered
sugar
carbonated water
or ginger ale

Pour powdered sugar and carbonated water into a Collins glass. Stir. Fill glass with ice. Add the gin. Top with carbonated water or ginger ale. Garnish with a spiral of orange or lemon peel dangled over the rim of the glass.

GIN DAISY

OLD-FASHIONED

MAKES 1 DRINK

1½ oz. gin
1 oz. lemon juice or
juice of ½ lemon
½ tsp. fine sugar
1 tsp. grenadine

Pour the liquor, lemon juice, sugar, and grenadine into a shaker half filled with ice. Shake well and strain into an old-fashioned glass. Garnish with lemon, lime, or orange slices and a cherry.

GIN FIX

MAKES 1 DRINK

2 oz. gin
1 oz. lemon juice or
*   juice of ½ lemon*
1 tsp. fine sugar
2 tsp. water

Add sugar, lemon juice, and water to a shaker half filled with ice. Shake and strain into a highball glass over ice. Add gin. Stir. Garnish with lemon. Serve with a straw.

GIN MILK PUNCH

COLLINS

MAKES 1 DRINK

2 oz. gin
1 cup milk
1 tsp. powdered
*   sugar*
nutmeg

Pour all ingredients except nutmeg into a shaker with ice. Shake and strain into a Collins glass. Sprinkle nutmeg on top.

GIN OR ALABAMA FIZZ

HIGHBALL

MAKES 1 DRINK

2 oz. gin
1 oz. lemon juice or
*   juice of ½ lemon*
1 tsp. fine sugar
4 oz. club soda

Pour the lemon juice, sugar, and liquor into a shaker half filled with ice. Shake well. Pour into a highball glass partly filled with ice and add club soda to fill. Stir and garnish with lemon.

GIN SMASH

OLD-FASHIONED

MAKES 1 DRINK

2 oz. gin
1 tsp. fine sugar
4 sprigs mint
1 oz. club soda

Muddle the sugar with the mint and club soda in an old-fashioned glass. Fill the glass with ice. Add the gin. Stir well. Garnish with a lemon twist.

GIN SOUR

MAKES 1 DRINK

2 oz. gin
1 oz. lemon juice or
*   juice of ½ lemon*
1 tsp. fine sugar
*   (or 1½ oz.*
*   sweet-and-sour*
*   mix instead*
*   of lemon and*
*   sugar)*

Pour ingredients into a shaker with ice. Shake and strain into a sour glass. Garnish with a lemon slice and a cherry.

GIN SWIZZLE

COLLINS

MAKES 1 DRINK

2 oz. gin
1½ oz. lime juice or
*   juice of 1 lime*
1 tsp. fine sugar
2 dashes bitters
3 oz. club soda

Pour the lime juice, sugar, liquor, and bitters into a shaker half filled with ice. Shake well and strain into a Collins glass almost filled with ice. Add soda to fill. Stir. Serve with a swizzle stick.

GINGER BEER

BEER GLASS

MAKES 1 GALLON

1½ cups sugar
2 oz. grated ginger
*   root*
zest and juice from
*   1 lemon*
1 gallon boiling
*   water*
1 tablespoon yeast

Pour the sugar, grated ginger, and lemon zest into a large bowl. Add boiling water. Let cool until lukewarm, then strain. Add the lemon juice and the yeast and let stand overnight. Stir thoroughly, and pour into jars with tight-fitting lids or corks. Store in the refrigerator.

GINGER COLADA

MARTINI

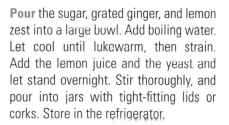

MAKES 1 DRINK

¾ oz. dark rum
½ oz. ginger brandy
4 oz. pineapple
*   juice*
1 oz. coconut
*   cream*

Pour ingredients into a blender with 2 oz. of crushed ice. Blend until the mixture is slushy. Pour into a martini glass.

GINGER ROGERS COCKTAIL

MARTINI

MAKES 1 DRINK

1 oz. dry gin
1 oz. dry vermouth
1 oz. apricot brandy
*4 dashes lemon
    juice*

Pour ingredients into a shaker with ice. Shake well and strain into a chilled martini glass.

GIN-GIN MULE

HIGHBALL

MAKES 1 DRINK

¾ oz. lime juice
1 oz. simple syrup
6–8 sprigs mint
1½ oz. gin
*1 oz. ginger beer
    (homemade)*

Pour lime juice, simple syrup, and mint in the bottom of a shaker and muddle well. Add the gin, ginger beer, and ice. Shake well. Strain into a highball glass over ice. Garnish with mint and serve with straws.

GIRL SCOUT COOKIE

OLD-FASHIONED

MAKES 1 DRINK

*1 oz. peppermint
    schnapps*
*¼ oz. crème de
    cacao*
4 oz. cream
splash club soda

Pour ingredients into a shaker with ice. Shake and strain into an old-fashioned glass over ice.

GIRL SCOUT COOKIE 2

COLLINS

MAKES 1 DRINK

*1 oz. dark crème de
    cacao*
½ oz. Frangelico
*½ oz. Irish cream
    liqueur*
*½ oz. butterscotch
    schnapps*
½ oz. vanilla vodka
*¼ oz. cinnamon
    schnapps*
*2 scoops vanilla ice
    cream*
chocolate chip cookie
whipped cream

Pour the dark crème de cacao, Frangelico, Irish cream liqueur, butterscotch schnapps, vanilla vodka, cinnamon schnapps, and ice cream into a blender. Blend until smooth. Pour into a Collins glass and place the cookie on top. Add whipped cream on top of the cookie, then stick a fat straw through the cookie into the glass.

GLASGOW

MAKES 1 DRINK

2 oz. scotch
1 tsp. dry vermouth
1 tsp. lemon juice
1 tsp. almond
    extract

OLD-FASHIONED

Pour ingredients into a shaker half filled with ice. Shake well and strain into an old-fashioned glass.

GLÖGG

MAKES ABOUT 10 DRINKS

2 bottles of dry red
    wine
1 tbs. cognac
½ cup fine sugar
5 cloves
2 sticks cinnamon
raisins
slivered almonds

IRISH COFFEE

Pour all ingredients except the raisins and almonds into a saucepan and heat. Do not boil. Serve with almonds and raisins on the side to be added to the mug or punch cup when the drink is poured.

GLUHWEIN

MAKES 1 DRINK

1 slice lemon or
    orange
4 whole cloves
1 stick cinnamon
2 dashes ground
    cinnamon
fill red dinner wine
½ tsp. sugar

IRISH COFFEE

Muddle the fruit, sugar, and spices into an Irish coffee glass. Top with well heated but not boiled wine. Stir and serve.

GOAT'S DELIGHT

MAKES 1 DRINK

1¾ oz.
    kirschwasser
1¾ oz. brandy
splash orgeat syrup
splash cream
splash pastis

MARTINI

Pour ingredients into a shaker with ice. Shake and strain into a martini glass.

GOD BLESS TEXAS

MARTINI

MAKES 1 DRINK

1 oz. gold tequila
1 oz. tequila rose
1½ oz. orange juice
*1½ oz. pineapple
  juice*

Pour ingredients into a shaker with ice. Shake and strain into a martini glass.

GODFATHER

OLD-FASHIONED

MAKES 1 DRINK

*1½ oz. scotch
  whiskey*
¾ oz. Amaretto

Pour scotch and Amaretto into an old-fashioned glass over ice. Stir.

GODMOTHER

OLD-FASHIONED

MAKES 1 DRINK

2 oz. vodka
1 oz. Amaretto

Pour vodka and Amaretto into an old-fashioned glass over ice. Stir.

GO-FOR-BROKE

MARTINI

MAKES 1 DRINK

*1 oz. extra dry
  vermouth*
*¾ oz. Bombay
  Sapphire gin*
1 dash Cointreau
1 dash bitters

Pour ingredients into a shaker with ice. Stir and strain into a martini glass and garnish with an orange twist.

GOIN' COCONUTINI

MARTINI

MAKES 1 DRINK

1 tablespoon light
    corn syrup
shredded coconut
2 oz. coconut rum
3 oz. white
    cranberry juice

Measure the corn syrup onto a saucer or small plate, and put the shredded coconut onto another. Dip the rim of a martini glass first in the corn syrup, then in the shredded coconut. Pour the next two ingredients into a shaker with ice. Shake and strain into the coconut-rimmed glass.

GOLDEN CADILLAC

MARTINI

MAKES 1 DRINK

¾ oz. cream
¾ oz. white crème
    de cacao
¾ oz. Galliano

Pour ingredients into a shaker with ice. Shake well and strain into a chilled martini glass.

GOLDEN DAWN

MARTINI

MAKES 1 DRINK

1½ oz. gin
1 oz. apricot
    liqueur
1 oz. lime juice or
    juice of ½ lime
1 oz. orange juice
dash grenadine

Pour ingredients into a shaker half filled with ice. Shake well and strain into a martini glass.

GOLDEN DREAM

MARTINI

MAKES 1 DRINK

¾ oz. cream
¾ oz. orange juice
¾ oz. Cointreau
¾ oz. Galliano

Pour ingredients into a shaker with ice. Shake well and strain into a chilled martini glass.

GOLDEN EGGNOG GROG

OLD-FASHIONED

MAKES 1 DRINK

1½ oz. dark rum
eggnog
pinch of nutmeg

Pour the rum eggnog into an old-fashioned glass. (If the eggnog is cold, you don't need to add ice.) Garnish with a pinch of nutmeg.

GOLDEN FIZZ

HIGHBALL

MAKES 1 DRINK

2 oz. gin
juice of 1 lemon or
   lime
yolk of 1 egg
2 tbs. sugar
club soda

Drop the egg yolk into a shaker with ice. Add gin, sugar, and juice. Shake 30 times. Strain into a highball glass and add club soda to fill.

GOLDEN FRIENDSHIP

COLLINS

MAKES 1 DRINK

1 oz. light rum
1 oz. sweet
   vermouth
1 oz. Amaretto
4 oz. ginger ale

Pour rum, vermouth, and Amaretto into a Collins glass over ice. Add ginger ale to fill. Garnish with a cherry.

GOLDEN LEMONADE (NONALCOHOLIC) COLLINS

MAKES 1 DRINK

1 egg yolk
juice of 1
   lemon
2 tsp.
   powdered
   sugar
6 oz. water

Pour ingredients into a shaker with ice. Shake well and strain into a Collins glass. Garnish with slices of orang and lemon and a cherry.

GOLDEN OLDIE

HIGHBALL

MAKES 1 DRINK

¾ oz. dark rum
½ oz. crème de
    banane
4 oz. pineapple
    juice

Pour all ingredients into a highball glass over ice.

GOLDEN SLIPPER

MARTINI

MAKES 1 DRINK

2 oz. apricot brandy
¾ oz. yellow
    chartreuse
1 egg yolk
    (unbroken)

Pour the brandy and Chartreuse into a shaker with ice. Stir and strain into a martini glass. Float the unbroken egg yolk on top.

GOLDILOCKS

IRISH COFFEE

MAKES 1 DRINK

1½ oz. white
    chocolate
    liqueur
hot black coffee

Pour the chocolate liqueur into an Irish coffee glass or mug and fill with the hot coffee. Top with whipped cream.

GOLF MARTINI

MARTINI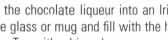

MAKES 1 DRINK

4 oz. gin
1 oz. dry vermouth
4 dashes bitters

Pour ingredients into a shaker with ice. Shake and strain into a chilled martini glass. Garnish with an olive.

GOOBER

MAKES 1 DRINK

1½ oz. vodka
1½ oz. black
   raspberry liqueur
1½ oz. melon liqueur
1 oz. triple sec
1 oz. grenadine
3 oz. pineapple
   juice
4 oz. orange juice

Pour ingredients into a shaker with ice. Shake and strain into a Collins glass filled with ice. Garnish with an orange slice and a cherry.

GOOD AND PLENTY

HIGHBALL

MAKES 1 DRINK

1 oz. Sambuca
6 oz. Dr. Pepper

Pour the Dr. Pepper down the side of a chilled highball glass and then pour the Sambuca in over the back of a spoon. Microwave on high for 3 minutes and serve.

GOOD KARMATINI

MARTINI

MAKES 1 DRINK

1 oz. light rum
1 oz. raspberry
   liqueur
1 oz. melon liqueur
1 oz. pineapple
   juice
1 oz. sweet-and-
   sour mix

Pour all ingredients into a shaker with ice. Shake well and strain into a martini glass.

GOOD SHIP LOLLIPOP (NONALCOHOLIC) COLLINS

MAKES 1 DRINK

3 small canta-
   loupe balls
3 small water-
   melon balls
1 large scoop of
   orange sherbet
cold Diet Rite
   Golden Peach
   soda or Nehi
   Peach soda

Drop a large scoop of orange sherbet into the bottom of a Collins glass. Fill with soda. Add the cantaloupe and watermelon balls.

218

GOODY-GIMLET (NONALCOHOLIC) HIGHBALL

MAKES 1 DRINK

3 oz. lime juice
  or juice
2 tsp. fine
  sugar
5 oz. ice water

Into a highball glass, dissolve the sugar in the lime juice. Fill glass with ice. Add ice water to fill. Stir. Garnish with a slice of lime.

GORDON COCKTAIL MARTINI

MAKES 1 DRINK

2 oz. gin, chilled
½ oz. dry sherry

Pour the sherry into a chilled martini glass and swirl. Add the gin. Garnish with lemon or lime curl.

GOTHAM OLD-FASHIONED

MAKES 1 DRINK

½ tsp. Pernod
3 dashes peach
  bitters
3 oz. brandy

Coat a chilled old-fashioned glass with the Pernod. Add the peach bitters and brandy. Garnish with a lemon twist.

GOTTA DRIVE (NONALCOHOLIC) OLD-FASHIONED

MAKES 1 DRINK

2 oz. cranberry
  juice
2 oz. orange
  juice
2 oz. pineapple
  juice
1 oz. whipped
  cream

In a large shaker with ice, blend until smooth. Strain into an old-fashioned glass over ice. Top with a cherry.

GRANDMA'S BERRY COBBLER WINE

MAKES 1 DRINK

1½ oz. blackberry
  brandy
½ oz. Southern
  Comfort

Pour the blackberry brandy and Southern Comfort into a large wine glass or goblet over ice. Stir.

GRAPE NEHI MARTINI

MAKES 1 DRINK

1 oz. vodka
1 oz. Chambord
1 oz. fresh lemon
  juice

Pour ingredients into a shaker with ice. Shake and strain into a martini glass.

GRAPE SODA COLLINS

MAKES 1 DRINK

½ oz. blue curaçao
½ oz. blackberry
  brandy
½ oz. Chambord
  raspberry liqueur
½ oz. vodka
2 oz. cranberry juice
1 oz. sweet-and-sour
  mix
¼ oz. Sprite

Pour first six ingredients into a shaker with ice. Shake and strain into a Collins glass over ice. Add Sprite to fill.

GRASSHOPPER MARTINI

MAKES 1 DRINK

1 oz. green crème
  de menthe
1 oz. white crème
  de cacao
1 oz. light cream

Pour all ingredients into a shaker nearly filled with ice. Shake well and strain into a martini glass.

GRASSHOPPER SHOOTER

SHOT

MAKES 1 DRINK

*½ oz. crème de
menthe, green
½ oz. light cream
½ oz. crème de
cacao*

Pour ingredients into a cocktail shaker
with ice. Shake well and strain into a
shot glass.

GRAVEYARD

BEER GLASS

MAKES 1 DRINK

*¼ oz. triple sec
¼ oz. rum
¼ oz. vodka
¼ oz. gin
¼ oz. tequila
¼ oz. bourbon
whiskey
¼ oz. scotch
pilsner-style beer
stout*

Pour the liquors into a beer mug. Top
with half the beer and half the stout.

GRAVITY

IRISH COFFEE

MAKES 1 DRINK

*¾ oz. Tia Maria
¾ oz. Irish cream
¾ oz. cognac
6 oz. hot black
coffee*

Pour into an Irish coffee glass or mug.
Top with whipped cream.

GRAVITY SHOOTER

OLD-FASHIONED

MAKES 1 DRINK

*½ shot Meyor's rum
¼ shot 151 rum
¼ shot Bacardi
light rum
1 splash sweet-
and-sour mix
1 splash orange
juice
1 splash pineapple
juice
1 dash grenadine*

Pour all ingredients into an old-
fashioned glass.

GREAT CAESAR'S MARTINI

MARTINI

MAKES 1 DRINK

3 oz. vodka
½ oz. dry vermouth

Pour ingredients into a shaker with ice. Shake and strain into a chilled martini glass. Garnish with an anchovy-stuffed olive.

GREAT ESCAPE

IRISH COFFEE

MAKES 1 DRINK

1 oz. Grand Marnier
1 oz. rumpleminz
6 oz. hot chocolate

Pour all ingredients into an Irish coffee glass.

GREEN APPLE MARTINI

MARTINI

MAKES 1 DRINK

1½ oz. vodka
1 oz. green apple
schnapps

Pour into a shaker filled with ice. Stir and strain into a martini glass. Garnish with a raisin.

GREEN DEMON SHOOTER

SHOT

MAKES 1 DRINK

½ oz. vodka
½ oz. rum
½ oz. melon liqueur
½ oz. limeade

Pour ingredients into a shaker half filled with ice. Shake well and strain into a shot glass.

GREEN DEVIL

OLD-FASHIONED

MAKES 1 DRINK

1½ oz. gin
1 oz. crème de
  menthe
½ oz. lime juice

Pour ingredients into a shaker half filled with ice. Shake well and strain into an old-fashioned glass over ice.

GREEN FIZZ

HIGHBALL

MAKES 1 DRINK

½ tsp. powdered
  sugar
1 egg white
½ lemon, juice of
2 oz. dry gin
1 tsp. green crème
  de menthe
club soda

Pour all ingredients except the club soda into a shaker with ice. Shake well and strain into a highball glass. Add soda to fill.

GREEN GHOST

HURRICANE

MAKES 1 DRINK

1 oz. blue curaçao
1 oz. gin
½ oz. peach
  schnapps
2 oz. lemonade
squeeze lime
  wedge

Pour ingredients into a shaker with ice. Shake and strain into a hurricane glass filled with ice. Garnish with the lime wedge.

GREEN GLACIER (NONALCOHOLIC) HIGHBALL

MAKES 1 DRINK

12 seedless
  green grapes
4 oz. white
  grape juice
4 oz. cold
  sparkling
  water

Freeze the grapes. Pour 10 frozen grapes and the grape juice into a blender. Blend until smooth and thick. Pour into a highball glass. Add the sparkling water. Stir gently. Garnish with the remaining 2 frozen grapes.

GREEN HORNET

MAKES 1 DRINK

½ oz. peach
  schnapps
½ oz. blue curaçao
½ oz. melon liqueur
1½ oz. pineapple
  juice
1½ oz. sweet-and-
  sour mix

Pour ingredients into a shaker with ice. Shake well and strain into an old-fashioned glass. Garnish with a pineapple wedge and a cherry.

GREEN MARTINI

MARTINI

MAKES 1 DRINK

3 oz. gin
½ oz. green
  Chartreuse

Pour ingredients into a shaker with ice. Shake and strain into a chilled martini glass. Garnish with an almond-stuffed olive.

GREEN ROOM

MARTINI

MAKES 1 DRINK

½ tsp. blue curaçao
¾ oz. brandy
1½ oz. French
  vermouth

Pour ingredients into a shaker with ice. Shake well and strain into a martini glass.

GREEN SWIZZLE

COLLINS

MAKES 1 DRINK

1 lime
1 tsp. powdered
  sugar
2 oz. carbonated
  water
2 dashes bitters
2 oz. rum
1 tbsp. green crème
  de menthe

Squeeze the juice of the lime into a Collins glass. Add sugar and carbonated water and stir. Fill the glass with ice and stir thoroughly. Add bitters, crème de menthe, and rum. Add carbonated water to fill. Serve with swizzle stick.

GREEN-EYED BLONDTINI

MARTINI

MAKES 1 DRINK

1 oz. melon liqueur
1 oz. banana
    liqueur
1 oz. Irish cream
    liqueur
2 oz. half-and-half
    or milk

Pour ingredients into a shaker with ice. Shake and strain into a martini glass.

GRETEL'S HOT TODDY

IRISH COFFEE

MAKES 1 DRINK

½ cup water
1-inch knob of
    fresh ginger,
    thinly sliced
¹/₈ cup sugar
1 oz. rum
1 cup hot apple
    cider

Pour the water and ginger into a saucepan and bring to a boil. Remove from heat, cover, and let steep 30 minutes. Add the sugar and bring to a boil again, stirring until the sugar dissolves (about 3 minutes). Strain ¼ cup into an Irish coffee glass or mug and add the rum. Fill with hot apple cider.

GREYHOUND

HIGHBALL

MAKES 1 DRINK

1½ oz. vodka
grapefruit juice

Pour the vodka into a highball glass over ice. Add grapefruit juice to fill.

GRINCH

HIGHBALL

MAKES 1 DRINK

1½ oz. lemon vodka
½ oz. sweet-and-
    sour mix
Mountain Dew

Pour first two ingredients into a highball glass over ice. Add the Mountain Dew to fill.

GRIZZLY BEAR

HIGHBALL

MAKES 1 DRINK

1 oz. Amaretto
1 oz. Jägermeister
1 oz. Kahlua
2½ oz. milk

Pour all ingredients into a highball glass over ice. Stir.

GRYPHON

SHOT

MAKES 1 DRINK

¼ oz. vodka
¼ oz. gin
¾ oz. melon liqueur
splash sweet-and-
sour mix

Pour into a shot glass in the order listed. Chase with a lemon wedge.

GUADALAJARA

MARTINI

MAKES 1 DRINK

2 oz. tequila
1 oz. dry vermouth
½ oz. Benedictine

Pour ingredients into a shaker with ice. Stir and strain into a martini glass. Garnish with a lemon twist.

GUINNESS MARTINI

MARTINI

MAKES 1 DRINK

1 oz. espresso
3 oz. vanilla vodka
½ oz. Tia Maria
½ oz. Irish cream
liqueur
½ oz. Kahlua

Pour ingredients in the order given into a shaker with ice. Shake and strain into a martini glass.

GUMDROP MARTINI

MAKES 1 DRINK

*2 oz. lemon-
    flavored rum
1 oz. vodka
½ oz. Southern
    Comfort
½ tsp. dry vermouth
½ oz. lemon juice*

Pour ingredients into a shaker with ice. Shake and strain into a sugar-rimmed, chilled martini glass. Garnish with a lemon slice and gumdrops.

GUN BARREL

IRISH COFFEE

MAKES 1 DRINK

*¾ oz. Irish cream
¾ oz. dark crème
    de cacao
6 oz. hot black
    coffee
151 rum*

Pour the Irish cream and dark crème de cacao into an Irish coffee glass or large mug. Add coffee to nearly fill, and stir. Float the rum on top.

GYPSY

MARTINI

MAKES 1 DRINK

*1 oz. vodka
½ oz. Benedictine
dash bitters*

Pour ingredients into a shaker with ice. Shake and strain into a martini glass.

GYPSY MARTINI

MARTINI

MAKES 1 DRINK

*4 oz. gin
1 oz. sweet
    vermouth*

Pour ingredients into a shaker with ice. Shake and strain into a chilled martini glass. Garnish with a maraschino cherry.

HAIRLESS REGGAE (NONALCOHOLIC) COLLINS

MAKES 1 DRINK

½ oz. banana,
  sliced
1 oz. orange juice
1 oz. pineapple
  juice
1 oz. grapefruit
  juice
1 tsp. grenadine

Mash the banana. Pour it with the juices and grenadine into a shaker half filled with ice. Shake well and strain into a Collins glass nearly filled with ice. Garnish with orange, lemon, or lime slices and a cherry.

HAIRY NAVEL HIGHBALL

MAKES 1 DRINK

1 oz. vodka
1½ oz. peach
  schnapps
orange juice

Pour the vodka and schnapps into a highball glass over ice. Add orange juice to fill.

HALLOWEEN CIDER PUNCH PUNCH

MAKES ABOUT 15 DRINKS

2 quarts hard cider
6 oz. Drambuie
6 oz. dry sherry
¼ cup sugar
2 oz. lemon juice
2 cups sparkling
  water
4 apples, sliced

Put all ingredients into a punch bowl with a block of ice. Garnish with the apple slices. (Dip the apples in lemon juice to keep them from turning brown.)

HANGMAN'S NOOSE WINE

MAKES 1 DRINK

9 oz. red wine
18 oz. hot black tea
2 cinnamon sticks
4 tsp. sugar

Brew the tea, and then add the wine and the sugar. Simmer covered with the cinnamon sticks. Serve warm in a wine glass.

HAPPY APPLE

OLD-FASHIONED

MAKES 1 DRINK

2 oz. rum
3 oz. apple cider
½ oz. lime juice

Pour ingredients into a shaker half filled with ice. Shake well and strain into an old-fashioned glass. Garnish with a lime twist.

HAPPY HOOKER

SHOT

MAKES 1 DRINK

1/3 shot Tia Maria
1/3 shot Drambuie
1/3 shot Grand
  Marnier

Pour in a tall shot glass in order given.

HAPPY YOUTH

CHAMPAGNE

MAKES 1 DRINK

1 oz. cherry brandy
2 oz. orange juice
1 tsp. fine sugar
Champagne, chilled

Dissolve the sugar in the brandy and orange juice in a Champagne glass. Add Champagne to fill.

HARRINGTON

MARTINI

MAKES 1 DRINK

1½ oz. vodka
¼ oz. Cointreau
1/8 oz. Chartreuse

Pour ingredients into a shaker with ice. Stir and strain into a martini glass. Add an orange twist.

H

229

HARVEY WALLBANGER

COLLINS

MAKES 1 DRINK

1½ oz. vodka
4 oz. orange juice
1 oz. Galliano

Pour the vodka and orange juice into a Collins glass over ice. Stir. Float Galliano on top.

HASTY MARTINI

MARTINI

MAKES 1 DRINK

3 oz. gin
½ oz. dry vermouth
4 dashes Pernod
1 tsp. grenadine

Pour ingredients into a shaker with ice. Shake and strain into a chilled martini glass.

HARVARD COOLER

COLLINS

MAKES 1 DRINK

½ tsp. powdered sugar
2 oz. carbonated water
2 oz. applejack
carbonated water or ginger ale

Pour the powdered sugar and carbonated water into a Collins glass. Stir. Fill with ice. Add applejack. Add more carbonated water or ginger ale to fill. Garnish with a spiral of orange or lemon peel (or both) dangled over rim.

HAWAIIAN COCKTAIL

MARTINI

MAKES 1 DRINK

2 oz. gin
½ oz. triple sec
½ oz. pineapple juice

Pour ingredients into a shaker with ice. Shake well and strain into a martini glass.

HAWAIIAN LEMONADE (NONALCOHOLIC)

MAKES 1 DRINK

*3 oz. pineapple
juice
4 oz. lemonade*

Pour lemonade and pineapple juice into a Collins glass over ice. Garnish with fruit.

HAWAIIAN MARGARITA

MARGARITA

MAKES 1 DRINK

*1 whole canned
Bartlett pear
1¼ oz. silver
tequila
½ oz. Amaretto
½ oz. blue curaçao
3–4 slices cored
pineapple
2 oz. sweet-and-
sour mix*

Pour ingredients into a blender with about a cup or so of ice. Blend until slushy-smooth. Pour into a margarita glass. Garnish with a lime slice.

HAWAIIAN VOLCANO

COLLINS

MAKES 1 DRINK

*2 oz. Passoa
liqueur
1 oz. dark rum
5 oz. piña colada
mix
1 oz. 151 rum*

Pour the Passoa into a Collins glass. Pour the dark rum and piña colada mix into a blender with a cup of ice. Blend until smooth. Slowly pour that mixture into the Collins glass and watch the Passoa rise like red lava up the glass. Top the drink with the 151 rum. Ignite the rum.

HAZY DAY (NONALCOHOLIC)

MARTINI

MAKES 1 DRINK

*3 slices
banana
1 oz. apricot
nectar
1 oz. orange
juice
1 tsp. lemon
juice*

Mash the banana slices. Pour them with the other ingredients into a shaker half filled with ice. Shake well and strain into a martini glass.

HEAT WAVE

HIGHBALL

MAKES 1 DRINK

1½ oz. light rum
½ oz. peach-
flavored brandy
½ oz. coconut
cream
2 oz. orange juice
2 oz. pineapple
juice
½ oz. grenadine

Pour all ingredients except grenadine into a highball or parfait glass over ice. Stir well. Top with grenadine. Garnish with a fruit slice.

HEATHER BLUSH

CHAMPAGNE

MAKES 1 DRINK

1 oz. scotch
whiskey
1 oz. crème de
cassis
3 oz. chilled
sparkling wine

Pour the scotch and crème de cassis into a Champagne glass. Add sparkling wine to fill.

HEATHER BLUSH 2

CHAMPAGNE

MAKES 1 DRINK

1 oz. scotch
whiskey
1 oz. strawberry
liqueur
3 oz. sparkling
wine (chilled)

Pour the scotch and liqueur into a Champagne flute. Add the sparkling wine to fill. Garnish with a strawberry.

HENNESSY MARTINI

MARTINI

MAKES 1 DRINK

2 oz. Hennessy
cognac
½ tsp. lemon juice

Pour ingredients into a shaker with ice. Stir gently and let stand for a few minutes. Strain into a chilled martini glass and garnish with a twist of lemon.

HIGH ROLLER

MAKES 1 DRINK

¾ oz. Grand
  Marnier
1½ oz. vodka
4 oz. orange juice
2–3 dashes
  grenadine

Pour the first three ingredients into a shaker filled with ice. Shake and strain into a highball glass over ice. Finish with a few drops of grenadine.

HIGHLAND COCKTAIL

MARTINI

MAKES 1 DRINK

1½ oz. scotch
  whiskey
1½ oz. sweet
  vermouth
1 dash orange
  bitters

Pour ingredients into a shaker with ice. Stir and strain into a martini glass.

HIGHLAND COOLER

COLLINS

MAKES 1 DRINK

2 oz. scotch
  whiskey
2 oz. carbonated
  water
½ tsp. powdered
  sugar
carbonated water
  or ginger ale

Pour the powdered sugar and 2 oz. of carbonated water into a Collins glass. Stir. Fill glass with ice. Add the scotch. Add carbonated water or ginger ale to fill. Garnish with spirals of orange and lemon.

HIGHLAND COOLER 2

 HIGHBALL

MAKES 1 DRINK

1 tsp. powdered
  sugar
juice of ½ lemon
2 dashes bitters
1 oz. scotch
  whiskey
ginger ale

Pour first four ingredients into a highball glass over ice. Add ginger ale to fill.

HIGHLAND FLING

MAKES 1 DRINK

1 oz. scotch
whiskey
1 oz. Amaretto
ginger ale

Pour scotch and Amaretto into a highball glass over ice. Add ginger ale to fill. Garnish with a twist of orange.

HOFFMAN HOUSE MARTINI

MARTINI

MAKES 1 DRINK

4 oz. gin
½ oz. dry vermouth
4 dashes orange
bitters

Pour ingredients into a shaker with ice. Stir well and strain into a chilled martini glass. Garnish with an olive.

HOLLY BERRY

MARTINI

MAKES 1 DRINK

1½ oz. raspberry
vodka
½ oz. triple sec
¼ oz. Rose's lime
juice
3 oz. cranberry
juice

Pour first four ingredients into a shaker with ice. Shake well and strain into a martini glass.

HONEY BEE

OLD-FASHIONED

MAKES 1 DRINK

1½ oz. Jamaican
rum
1 oz. lime juice
½ oz. honey

Pour ingredients into a shaker with ice. Shake well and strain into an old-fashioned glass filled with ice.

HONEYMOON

MARTINI

MAKES 1 DRINK

1 oz. apple brandy
1 oz. Benedictine
1 tsp. triple sec
1 oz. lemon juice or
juice of ½ lemon

Pour ingredients into a shaker half filled with ice. Shake well and strain into a martini glass.

HONEYMOON COCKTAIL

MARTINI

MAKES 1 DRINK

¾ oz. apple brandy
¾ oz. Benedictine
1 tsp. triple sec
juice of ½ lemon

Pour ingredients into a shaker with ice. Shake and strain into a martini glass.

HONEYMOON SUITETINI

MARTINI

MAKES 1 DRINK

1 oz. Irish cream
liqueur
1 oz. hazelnut liqueur
½ oz. coffee liqueur
½ oz. honey
2 oz. half-and-half
or milk
2 chocolate kiss
candies

Pour liquid ingredients into a shaker with ice. Shake well and strain into a martini glass. Drop the two chocolate kisses into the drink. (Be sure to unwrap first.)

HONOLULU HAMMER

SHOT

MAKES 1 DRINK

1½ oz. vodka
½ oz. Amaretto
splash pineapple
juice

Pour ingredients into a shaker with ice. Shake and strain into a shot glass.

HONOLULU PUNCH

**MAKES APPROXI-
MATELY 15 SERVINGS**

1 liter light rum
½ cup dark rum
½ cup triple sec
¼ cup fine sugar
½ cup lemon juice
2 cups orange juice
2 cups pineapple
*   juice*

Pour all ingredients into a punch bowl over ice. Garnish with tropical fruit.

HOP SKIP

MAKES 2 DRINKS

1 oz. vodka
¼ oz. peach
*   schnapps*
¼ oz. melon liqueur
½ oz. pineapple juice
½ oz. 7-Up
½ oz. cranberry juice
½ lime, fresh
*   squeezed*

Pour ingredients into a shaker with ice. Shake well and strain into two martini glasses.

HOP TOAD

MAKES 1 DRINK

¾ oz. light rum
¾ oz. apricot
*   brandy*
1 oz. lime juice or
*   juice of ½ lime*

Pour ingredients into a shaker with ice. Stir and strain into a martini glass.

HORSE'S NECK

MAKES 1 DRINK

2 oz. blended
*   whiskey*
dash bitters
ginger ale
lemon rind spiral
*   cut from the*
*   whole lemon*

Place the lemon rind into a Collins glass with one end over the rim. (That's the "horse's neck" stretching to the finish.) Fill the glass with ice. Add the whiskey and bitters, and ginger ale to fill. Stir.

HOSKINS

MAKES 1 DRINK

2 oz. gin
¾ oz. Torani Amer
½ oz. maraschino
 liqueur
¼ oz. Cointreau
1 dash orange
 bitters

Pour ingredients into a shaker with ice. Stir and strain into a martini glass. Garnish with an orange twist.

HOT AND DIRTY MARTINI

MAKES 1 DRINK

3 oz. pepper vodka
½ oz. dry vermouth
1 tsp. olive brine

Pour ingredients into a shaker with ice. Shake and strain into a chilled martini glass. Garnish with an olive stuffed with pickled jalapeño pepper.

HOT APPLE PIE

MAKES 1 DRINK

¼ oz. Apple Pucker
 schnapps
¼ oz. cinnamon
 schnapps
¼ oz. Irish cream
 liqueur
¼ oz. spiced rum
$^{1}/_{8}$ oz. 151 rum
whipped cream

Pour the schnapps, cinnamon schnapps, Irish cream liqueur, and spiced rum into a shot glass. Carefully float the 151 rum on top and ignite. Put out the flame with a dollop of whipped cream. Eat the whipped cream, then drink the shot.

HOT BLOODED

MAKES 1 DRINK

1½ oz. tequila
Tabasco sauce to
 taste
$^{1}/_{8}$ oz. 151 rum

Pour the tequila into a shot glass and add several dashes of Tabasco. Gently layer the 151 rum on top, then ignite. Let the flame die all the way down to burn off all the rum before drinking.

HOT BOOTIE

IRISH COFFEE

MAKES 1 DRINK

1 oz. Sambuca
6 oz. hot chocolate

Pour into an Irish coffee glass and serve.

HOT BRANDY FLIP

IRISH COFFEE

MAKES 1 DRINK

1½ oz. California
*   brandy*
1 tsp. powdered
*   sugar*
1 egg
hot milk

Beat the egg, sugar, and brandy together and pour into an Irish coffee glass or mug. Add the hot milk to fill. Grate nutmeg on top.

HOT BRANDY TODDY

IRISH COFFEE

MAKES 1 DRINK

1 sugar cube
boiling water
2 oz. brandy

Put the sugar cube into an Irish coffee glass or mug. Fill ²/₃ with boiling water. Add brandy and stir. Garnish with a slice of lemon and a sprinkle of nutmeg.

HOT BRICK TODDY

IRISH COFFEE

MAKES 1 DRINK

1½ oz. bourbon
*   whiskey*
*   sp. butter*
*   sp. powdered*
*   sugar*
*   inches cinnamon*
*   iling water*

Pour the butter, sugar, cinnamon, and 1 oz. of the boiling water into a stemmed mug. Add bourbon and fill with boiling water. Stir with a cinnamon stick.

HOT BUTTERED CIDER

PUNCH

MAKES 10 DRINKS

7 cups apple cider
1/3 cups brown sugar
4 cinnamon sticks
1 tsp. whole cloves
1 tsp. whole allspice
3 strips lemon peel
1½ cup dark rum
1 tbs. butter

Combine cider and brown sugar in a saucepan. Tie spices and lemon peel in a square of cheesecloth to form spice bag. Add the bag to cider mixture and bring to a boil. Reduce heat and simmer, covered, for 15 minutes. Remove the spice bag. Add rum. Pour into mugs. Float about ½ tsp. butter or margarine on each.

HOT BUTTERED COMFORT

IRISH COFFEE

MAKES 1 DRINK

1¼ oz. Southern
Comfort
4 oz. hot water
1 tsp. butter

Pour first two ingredients into an Irish coffee glass or mug. Float the butter. Garnish with a cinnamon stick and a lemon slice.

HOT BUTTERED RUM

IRISH COFFEE

MAKES 1 DRINK

2 oz. rum
1½ tsp. brown
sugar
1 tsp. cinnamon
1 tbs. butter
4 oz. milk
dash salt

Heat milk in a saucepan, but do not boil. Pour sugar, cinnamon, and salt into an Irish coffee glass or mug. Add the rum and the butter. Pour in the hot milk. Sprinkle with nutmeg.

HOT BUTTERED RUM 2

IRISH COFFEE

MAKES 1 DRINK

1 oz. light rum
½ tbs. hot buttered
rum batter (see
page 240)
6 oz. hot water

Pour rum and batter into an Irish coffee glass or large mug. Fill mug with hot water and garnish with a pat of butter and cinnamon stick.

HOT BUTTERED RUM 3

MAKES 1 DRINK

1 tsp. sugar
½ tsp. butter
1 oz. light rum
4 cloves

In an Irish coffee glass or mug, mix sugar, butter, rum, and cloves. Fill with boiling water. Stir.

HOT BUTTERED RUM BATTER

1 lb. brown sugar
¼ lb. butter
pinch of salt
¼ tsp. nutmeg
¼ tsp. cloves
½ tsp. cinnamon

Pour all ingredients into an Irish coffee glass or mug and stir together until well blended and creamy.

HOT BUTTERED SUGARPLUM

MAKES 1 DRINK

1 oz. dark rum
½ oz. plum liqueur
*2 spoonfuls of hot
    buttered rum
    batter*
hot water

Pour the dark rum, plum liqueur, and hot buttered rum batter into an Irish coffee glass or mug. Fill with hot water and stir to dissolve.

HOT BUTTERED WINE

MAKES 8 DRINKS

*6 oz. frozen
    orange juice
    concentrate*
2 cups water
2 cups muscatel
$1/_8$ tsp. cinnamon
$1/_8$ tsp. nutmeg
½ cups sugar
1 tbs. butter
*½ fresh lemon,
    sliced*

Pour all ingredients into a saucepan or chafing dish and stir until sugar dissolves. Heat until steaming hot, but do not boil. Serve in Irish coffee glasses or mugs.

HOT CIDER-CRANBERRY PUNCH ^{IRISH COFFEE}

MAKES 12 DRINKS

8 cups apple cider
4 cups cranberry
  juice
3 cinnamon sticks
4 cloves
3 strips orange
  peel
1 cup dark rum

Put the cider, cranberry juice, cinnamon, cloves, and orange peel into a large pot. Bring to a boil over medium-high heat. Reduce heat and simmer, uncovered for 25 to 35 minutes. Line a strainer with cheesecloth and strain the punch. Put 1 to 2 tablespoons of rum into each mug, then fill to the rim with hot punch.

HOT CLAMATO (NONALCOHOLIC)   HIGHBALL

MAKES 1 DRINK

6 oz. Clamato
  juice
1 oz. lime juice
dash Worcester-
  shire sauce
dash Tabasco
¼ tsp. horse-
  radish

Pour all ingredients into a highball glass over ice and stir well. Garnish with a lemon wedge.

HOT ICE   HIGHBALL

MAKES 1 DRINK

1 oz. pepper-
  flavored vodka
½ oz. blue curaçao
½ oz. pineapple
  juice
¾ oz. 7-Up

Pour all ingredients into a highball glass over ice.

HOT MULLED CIDER   PUNCH

MAKES 12 DRINKS

1 gal. fresh apple
  cider
3 cinnamon sticks
2 whole cloves
¼ tsp. whole
  allspice
peel of 1 lemon,
  no white
¼ cup brown sugar
1-2 oz. rum

In a large saucepan, slowly heat all ingredients for 15 to 20 minutes. Strain through cheesecloth or coffee filter. Served warm with 1–2 oz. of rum per cup.

HOT MULLED WINE

WINE

MAKES 1 DRINK

3 parts Zinfandel
  wine
1 part mulling
  syrup

Add Zinfandel to heated syrup. Over low heat stir occasionally. Serve in a traditional wine glass or clear stemmed mug.

HOT NOT TODDY (NONALCOHOLIC) IRISH COFFEE

MAKES 1 DRINK

6 oz. hot tea
1 tbs. honey
splash lemon
  juice
dash ground
  cloves
dash cinnamon
dash nutmeg

In an Irish coffee glass or mug, dissolve the honey and spices in 1 oz. of the tea. Stir. Add the lemon juice and the rest of the tea. Stir well.

HOT PANTS

OLD-FASHIONED

MAKES 1 DRINK

1½ oz. tequila
½ oz. peppermint
  schnapps
½ oz. grapefruit
  juice
1 tsp. fine sugar

Pour ingredients into a shaker with ice. Shake well and strain into an old-fashioned glass.

HOT RASPBERRY CIDER

IRISH COFFEE

MAKES 8 DRINKS

8 cups apple cider
1 cup frozen
  raspberry juice
  concentrate
¼ cup sugar
1 cinnamon stick
2 cups Cointreau

Pour all ingredients except brandy into a 4-quart saucepan. Heat over medium heat, stirring occasionally, until mixture starts to simmer. Reduce heat and simmer 10 minutes. Remove from heat. Remove cinnamon stick. Serve hot in stemmed mugs with 2 oz. Cointreau.

HOT SPICED WINE

MAKES 20 DRINKS

1 cup sugar
4 cups water
spiral lemon peel
18 whole cloves
2 750-ml bottles
*   red dinner wine*
2 cinnamon sticks

Dissolve sugar in water in large saucepan. Add slices of lemon peel, cloves, and cinnamon. Boil 15 minutes; then strain out the peel and spices. Add the wine and heat gently, but do not boil. Serve in stemmed mugs.

HOT SULTRY ZOË

MAKES 1 DRINK

1 oz. tequila
½ oz. Galliano
5 oz. hot chocolate
2 oz. cream

Pour tequila, Galliano, and hot chocolate into an Irish coffee glass or mug. Stir gently. Add cream by pouring it over the back of a spoon so that it floats on top.

HOT TODDY

MAKES 1 DRINK

2 oz. bourbon
4 oz. boiling water
1 tbs. fine sugar
splash lemon juice
dash ground cloves
dash cinnamon

In an Irish coffee glass, dissolve the sugar and spices in 1 oz. of the boiling water. Stir. Add the lemon juice, bourbon, and the rest of the water. Stir well.

HOT WINE LEMONADE

MAKES 1 DRINK

1½ oz. red wine
1 oz. lemon juice or
*   juice of ½ lemon*
1 tbs. fine sugar
4 oz. boiling water

Into an Irish coffee glass or mug, dissolve sugar in a splash of the hot water. Add the wine and lemon juice. Stir. Add hot water to fill. Stir well. Garnish with a lemon twist.

HOUSE COCKTAIL

MARTINI

MAKES 1 DRINK

1½ oz. gin
¾ oz. dry vermouth
2–3 dashes orange
* bitters*

Pour ingredients into a shaker with ice. Stir and strain into a martini glass. Garnish with an olive.

HULA HULA

MARTINI

MAKES 1 DRINK

2 oz. gin
1 oz. pineapple
* juice*
1 tbs. Cointreau
¼ tsp. fine sugar

Pour ingredients into a shaker half filled with ice. Shake well and strain into a martini glass.

HUMMINGBIRD

COLLINS

MAKES 1 DRINK

2 oz. vodka
1 oz. rum cream
* liqueur*
½ oz. Tia Maria
1 banana
dash strawberry
* syrup*
dash milk

Blend all the ingredients with ice until smooth. Pour into a Collins glass. Garnish with a slice of banana and a strawberry.

HUNKA HUNKA BURNING LOVE **COLLINS**

MAKES 1 DRINK

1 oz. raspberry-
* flavored vodka*
* or rum*
1 oz. hazelnut liqueur
½ oz. raspberry
* liqueur*
2 scoops banana
* ice cream*
milk
half a banana
1 oz. 151 rum

Pour the raspberry-flavored vodka or rum, hazelnut liqueur, raspberry liqueur, and banana ice cream into a blender. Blend at medium speed. Add the milk little by little to reach a smooth consistency. Pour into a Collins glass. Stick the banana straight up on top as a garnish. Pour the 151 rum all over the banana and light.

HURRICANE

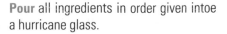

MARTINI

MAKES 1 DRINK

1 oz. light rum
1 oz. dark rum
2 tbs. passion fruit
    syrup
1 tsp. lime juice

Pour ingredients into a shaker half filled with ice. Shake well and strain into a martini glass.

HURRICANE 2

HURRICANE

MAKES 1 DRINK

8 oz. pineapple
    juice
4 oz. orange juice
1¼ oz. dark rum
splash grenadine

Pour all ingredients in order given intoe a hurricane glass.

HURRICANE CAROLYNE

OLD-FASHIONED

MAKES 1 DRINK

1 oz. Malibu rum
1 oz. spiced rum
1 oz. light rum
splash 151 rum
1 oz. orange juice
1 oz. cranberry
    juice

Pour ingredients into a shaker with ice. Shake well and strain into an old-fashioned glass over ice. Float the 151 on top. Garnish with an orange slice and a cherry.

HYPNOTIZING MARGARITA

MARGARITA

MAKES 1 DRINK

1½ oz. tequila
1 oz. Hpnotiq
juice from half a
    lime
3 oz. sweet-and-
    sour mix

Pour the tequila, the blue-colored Hpnotiq, the lime juice, and the sweet-and-sour mix into a blender with a cup of ice. Blend until smooth. Pour into a margarita glass rimmed with salt. Garnish with a lime slice.

I DREAM OF GENIE MARTINIS

MAKES 4 DRINKS

1½ cups cherry-
 flavored vodka
3 cups pink
 lemonade
1 oz. grenadine for
 color
large chunk of dry
 ice

Pour the first three ingredients into a large serving pitcher and refrigerate. When ready to serve, drop the dry ice into the pitcher to create smokey vapor. Pour into martini glasses.

I SEE NOTHING!

MARTINI

MAKES 1 DRINK

½ shot vodka
¾ shot Irish cream
 liqueur
¾ shot chocolate
 liqueur
2 shots milk
½ cup ice

Pour ingredients into a blender in this order: ice, alcohol, and milk. Blend until smooth and serve in a martini glass.

ICE BREAKER

IRISH COFFEE

MAKES 1 DRINK

½ oz. peppermint
 schnapps
½ oz. Kahlua
½ oz. dark crème
 de cacao
5 oz. hot chocolate

Pour Kahlua, crème de cacao, and hot chocolate into an Irish coffee glass or mug. Stir in peppermint schnapps and top with whipped cream.

ICE QUEEN

CHAMPAGNE

MAKES 1 DRINK

1 oz. Aquavit
1 oz. Chambord
4 oz. Champagne
1 tsp. sweetened
 lime juice

Pour the Aquavit, Chambord, and lime juice into a Champagne flute. Add the Champagne to fill. Garnish with raspberries.

IDEAL MARTINI

MAKES 1 DRINK

3 oz. gin
1 oz. dry vermouth
½ tsp. maraschino
  liqueur
1 tsp. lemon juice

Pour ingredients into a shaker with ice. Shake and strain into a chilled martini glass. Garnish with a lemon twist.

IDONIS

MAKES 1 DRINK

2 oz. vodka
½ oz. apricot
  brandy
1 oz. pineapple
  juice

Pour ingredients into a shaker with ice. Shake well and strain into a chilled martini glass.

IGUANA

MAKES 1 DRINK

1 oz. tequila
1 oz. coffee liqueur
1 oz. vodka

Pour ingredients into a shaker with ice. Stir and strain into a martini glass.

ILLUSIONS

MAKES 1 DRINK

1 oz. melon liqueur
1 oz. Galliano
1 oz. Malibu rum
1 oz. gin
1 oz. light rum
1 oz. vodka
4 oz. pineapple
  juice

Pour ingredients into a shaker with ice. Shake vigorously and serve in a chilled martini glass.

IMMACULATE COCKTAIL

MARTINI

MAKES 1 DRINK

2 oz. light rum
½ oz. Amaretto
1 oz. lime juice
1 oz. lemon juice
½ tsp. superfine
sugar

Pour ingredients into a shaker with ice. Shake well and strain into a chilled martini glass.

IMPERIAL COCKTAIL

MARTINI

MAKES 1 DRINK

1 oz. dry vermouth
1 oz. gin
1 tsp. maraschino
liqueur
lemon twist for
garnish

Pour ingredients into a shaker with ice. Stir well and strain into a chilled martini glass. Garnish with the lemon twist.

IMPERIAL FIZZ

HIGHBALL

MAKES 1 DRINK

1 oz. light rum
1 oz. blended
whiskey
1 oz. lemon juice or
juice of ½ lemon
1 tsp. fine sugar
4 oz. club soda

Pour the lemon juice, sugar, and liquor into a shaker half filled with ice. Shake well and strain into a highball glass partly filled with ice. Add club soda to fill. Stir and garnish with lemon.

IN THE MOOD

MARTINI

MAKES 1 DRINK

1 oz. dark crème de
cacao
1 oz. dark rum
3 oz. half-and-half
or milk
1 spoonful hot
cocoa mix

Pour the first three ingredients into a shaker with ice. Shake and strain into a martini glass rimmed with the hot cocoa power mix.

INCANTATIONS

MARTINI

MAKES 1 DRINK

1 oz. vodka
*½ oz. green
  curaçao*
2 oz. lemonade
*2–3 drops
  grenadine*

Pour first three ingredients into a blender with ice. Blend until slushy-smooth. Pour into a large martini glass. Add drops of grenadine. Garnish with a sugar-coated lime wedge.

INCOME TAX COCKTAIL

MARTINI

MAKES 1 DRINK

1¼ oz. gin
¾ oz. orange juice
¼ oz. dry vermouth
*¼ oz. sweet
  vermouth*
1 dash bitters

Pour ingredients into a shaker with ice. Shake well and strain into a martini glass.

INCOMPLETE PASS

SHOT

MAKES 2 DRINKS

*2 oz. bourbon
  whiskey*
*1 oz. pineapple
  juice*

Pour ingredients into a shaker with ice. Shake well and strain into two shot glasses. Garnish with pineapple chunks.

INDEPENDENCE PUNCH (NONALCOHOLIC) **PUNCH**

MAKE ABOUT 15 DRINKS

*2 quarts cran-
  berry juice*
*1 quart raspberry
  soda*
*1 pkg. frozen
  raspberries*

Chill the juice and soda. Thaw the raspberries. Pour all the ingredients into a punch bowl with ice or an ice ring.

INTERCEPTION (NONALCOHOLIC) MARTINI

MAKES 1 DRINK

*2 oz. tonic water
splash pineapple
juice*

Rub the inside of a martini glass with lime wedge. Add chilled tonic water and splash pineapple juice.

INTERNATIONAL COCKTAIL MARTINI

MAKES 1 DRINK

*2 oz. gin
¼ oz. French
    vermouth
¼ oz. Pernod*

Swirl the vermouth in a chilled martini glass. Pour the gin and Pernod into a shaker with ice. Stir gently and strain into the martini glass. Garnish with a twist of lime.

INTERNATIONAL STINGER MARTINI

MAKES 1 DRINK

*1 oz. Galliano
1 oz. white crème
    de menthe
1 oz. Metaxa*

Pour ingredients into a shaker with ice. Stir and strain into a martini glass.

IRISH CANADIAN MARTINI

MAKES 1 DRINK

*2 oz. Canadian
    whiskey
1 oz. Irish Mist*

Pour ingredients into a shaker with ice. Stir and strain into a martini glass.

IRISH CAR BOMB

IRISH COFFEE

MAKES 1 DRINK

*1 pint of Guinness
    stout*
½ oz. Irish whiskey
*½ oz. Irish cream
    liqueur*

Pour the Guinness into a pint glass. Pour the Irish whiskey into a shot glass, then gently pour the Irish cream over the back of a spoon to layer it slowly on top of the whiskey. Drop the shot into the beer, then drink.

IRISH COCKTAIL

MARTINI

MAKES 1 DRINK

2 oz. Irish whiskey
2 dashes curaçao
2 dashes Pernod
*1 dash maraschino
    liqueur*
1 dash bitters

Pour ingredients into a shaker with ice. Stir well and strain into a martini glass. Garnish with an olive and a lemon twist.

IRISH COFFEE

IRISH COFFEE

MAKES 1 DRINK

*2½ oz. strong, hot
    coffee*
*1½ oz. Irish
    whiskey*
1 tsp. brown sugar
*1 oz. whipping
    cream*

Pour the first three ingredients into an Irish coffee glass or mug. Stir well. Float the cream on top.

IRISH DREAM

COLLINS

MAKES 1 DRINK

*½ oz. Irish cream
    liqueur*
*½ oz. hazelnut
    liqueur*
*½ oz. brown crème
    de cacao*
*1 scoop vanilla ice
    cream*

Pour ingredients into a blender with ice. Blend thoroughly. Pour into a Collins or parfait glass. Serve with a straw.

IRISH FLAG SHOOTER

CORDIAL

MAKES 1 DRINK

1 oz. green crème de menthe
1 oz. Bailey's Irish cream liqueur
1 oz. Grand Marnier

Pour ingredients, in order given, into a pousse-café or cordial glass, so that they form separate layers.

IRISH GREEN-EYED BLONDE

SHOT

MAKES 1 DRINK

1/3 oz. melon liqueur
1/3 oz. crème de banane
1/3 oz. Bailey's Irish cream liqueur

Pour the melon liqueur into a shot glass. Gently pour the crème de banane over the back of a spoon to layer it on top of the melon liqueur. Layer the Irish cream liqueur on top of the crème de banane.

IRISH MARTINI

MARTINI

MAKES 1 DRINK

3 oz. Zubrowka (or any other bison grass vodka)
½ oz. dry vermouth
Irish whiskey

Pour the vodka and vermouth into a shaker with ice. Shake well and strain into a chilled martini glass rinsed with the Irish whiskey. Garnish with a lemon twist.

IRISH RICKEY

HIGHBALL

MAKES 1 DRINK

1½ oz. Irish whiskey
1 oz. lime juice or juice of ½ lime
club soda

Pour the whiskey and lime juice into a highball glass nearly filled with ice. Stir. Add club soda to fill. Garnish with a twist of lime.

IRISH SHILLELAGH

OLD-FASHIONED

MAKES 1 DRINK

1½ oz. Irish whiskey
½ oz. light rum
½ oz. sloe gin
1 tsp. powdered sugar
1 oz. lemon juice or juice
    of ½ lemon
¼ cup peaches, fresh or
    canned, diced
¼ cup raspberries, fresh
    or frozen

Pour ingredients into a blender with ice. Blend thoroughly. Pour into an old-fashioned glass. Garnish with raspberries.

IRISH SPRING

COLLINS

MAKES 1 DRINK

1 oz. Irish whiskey
½ oz. peach brandy
1 oz. orange juice
1 oz. sweet-and-
    sour mix

Pour all ingredients into a Collins glass over ice cubes. Stir. Garnish with a slice of orange and a cherry.

IRISH TOBOGGAN

IRISH COFFEE

MAKES 1 DRINK

1 shot Irish cream
6 oz. hot chocolate
splash Irish
    whiskey

Pour ingredients into an Irish coffee glass or mug.

IRISH WHISKEY HIGHBALL

HIGHBALL

MAKES 1 DRINK

2 oz. Irish whiskey
fill ginger ale

Into a highball glass place one ice cube. Add the Irish whiskey. Fill with ginger ale. Garnish with a lemon twist and stir gently.

ITALIAN SCREWDRIVER

HIGHBALL

MAKES 1 DRINK

1½ oz. citrus vodka
3 oz. orange juice
2 oz. grapefruit
 juice
splash ginger ale

Pour ingredients into a shaker with ice. Stir well and strain into a highball glass over ice. Garnish with a slice of fruit.

IT'S ONLY 10 BELOW

IRISH COFFEE

MAKES 1 DRINK

1 shot spiced rum
6 oz. hot apple
 cider
1 cinnamon stick

Pour rum and hot cider into an Irish coffee glass or mug. Stir with the cinnamon stick.

J. R.'S GODFATHER

OLD-FASHIONED

MAKES 1 DRINK

2 oz. bourbon
 whiskey
½ oz. Amaretto

Pour the bourbon and Amaretto into an old-fashioned glass nearly filled with ice. Stir well.

JACK BE NIMBLE JAVA

IRISH COFFEE

MAKES 1 DRINK

½ oz. Jack Daniel's
1 oz. Amaretto
coffee

Pour the Jack Daniel's and Amaretto into an Irish coffee glass or mug and fill with coffee. Top with whipped cream.

JACK LONDON MARTINI

MARTINI

MAKES 1 DRINK

3 oz. black currant
    vodka
1 oz. Dubonnet
    (Blanc)
½ oz. maraschino
    liqueur

Pour ingredients into a shaker with ice. Shake and strain into a chilled martini glass. Garnish with a lemon twist.

JACK ROSE

MARTINI

MAKES 1 DRINK

1½ oz. apple
    brandy
1 oz. lime juice or
    juice of ½ lime
½ oz. grenadine

Pour ingredients into a shaker nearly filled with ice. Stir well and strain into a martini glass.

J

JACK SPRAT

OLD-FASHIONED

MAKES 1 DRINK

¾ shot butterscotch
    schnapps
¾ shot crème de
    cacao
¾ shot Amaretto
¾ shot Irish cream
3 oz. milk

Pour all ingredients into an old-fashioned glass over ice.

JACKPOT

CHAMPAGNE

MAKES 1 DRINK

3 oz. Champagne
1 oz. Goldschlager
1 dash Courvoisier

Pour the Goldschlager into a Champagne flute. Add Champagne to fill. Top with Courvoisier.

JÄGER BOMB

BEER GLASS

MAKES 1 DRINK

*1 can of Red Bull
  Energy Drink
1 oz. Jägermeister*

Fill a shot glass with Jägermeister. Pour the Red Bull into a beer mug, about ¾ full. Drop the shot into the mug. Drink fast.

JAMAICAN COCKTAIL

MARTINI

MAKES 1 DRINK

*¾ oz. dark rum
½ oz. coffee
  liqueur
¾ oz. lime juice
dash bitters*

Pour ingredients into a shaker with ice. Shake and strain into a chilled martini glass.

JAMAICAN FIREFLY

HIGHBALL

MAKES 1 DRINK

*¾ oz. lime juice
1 oz. simple syrup
1½ oz. dark rum
2 oz. ginger beer*

Pour ingredients into a shaker with ice. Shake and strain into a highball glass. Garnish with a lime slice and a piece of candied ginger.

JAMAICAN MARTINI

MARTINI

MAKES 1 DRINK

*3 oz. gin
½ oz. red wine
1 tbs. dark rum
4 dashes orange
  bitters*

Pour ingredients into a shaker with ice. Shake and strain into a chilled martini glass. Garnish with cherry peppers.

JAMES BOND MARTINI

MARTINI

MAKES 1 DRINK

3 oz. gin
1 oz. vodka
½ oz. Lillet (white)

Pour ingredients into a shaker with ice. Shake and strain into a chilled martini glass. Garnish with a lemon twist.

JAPANESE COCKTAIL

MARTINI

MAKES 1 DRINK

2 oz. brandy
½ oz. orgeat
(almond syrup)
2 dashes bitters

Pour ingredients into a shaker with ice. Stir and strain into a martini glass. Garnish with a lemon twist.

JASMINE

MARTINI

MAKES 1 DRINK

1½ oz. gin
1 oz. Cointreau
¾ oz. Campari
½ oz. lemon juice

Pour ingredients into a shaker with ice. Shake and strain into a martini glass.

JEAN HARLOW COCKTAIL

MARTINI

MAKES 1 DRINK

2 oz. light rum
2 oz. sweet
vermouth
lemon peel for
garnish

Pour ingredients into a shaker with ice. Shake well and strain into a chilled martini glass. Garnish with the lemon peel.

JELL-O SHOTS

SHOT

MAKES 6 DRINKS

6 oz. vodka
6 oz. water
*3 oz. Jell-O
    gelatin, any
    flavor*

Pour vodka and water into a saucepan and bring to a boil. Stir in the gelatin. Allow to set in the refrigerator. The longer it sets, the firmer the Jell-O. "Slushy" is the preferred consistency. When ready, scoop into shot glasses.

JELLYBEAN

MARTINI

MAKES 1 DRINK

*1½ oz. blackberry
    brandy*
½ oz. anisette

Pour ingredients into a shaker with ice. Stir and strain into a martini glass.

JELLYBEAN SHOOTER

SHOT

MAKES 1 DRINK

*½ oz. blackberry
    brandy*
½ oz. anisette

Pour ingredients into a shaker with ice. Stir and strain into a shot glass.

JERICHO'S BREEZE

WINE

MAKES 1 DRINK

1 oz. vodka
¾ oz. blue curaçao
*2½ oz. sweet-and-
    sour mix*
*splash lemon-lime
    soda*
splash orange juice

Pour ingredients into a shaker with ice. Shake until frothy and strain into a wine glass or goblet. Garnish with a pineapple spear and a cherry.

JERRY LEE SPECIAL

OLD-FASHIONED

MAKES 1 DRINK

½ oz. Amaretto
½ oz. Southern
   Comfort
½ oz. orange juice
½ oz. cranberry
   juice

Pour ingredients into a shaker with ice. Shake and strain into an old-fashioned glass over ice.

JIMINY CRICKET GRASSHOPPER **MARTINI**

MAKES 1 DRINK

1 oz. green crème
   de menthe
1 oz. white crème
   de cacao
2 oz. half-and-half
grated chocolate

Pour the green crème de menthe, white crème de cacao, and half-and-half into a shaker full of ice. Shake well and strain into a martini glass. Garnish with grated chocolate. This drink can also be blended.

JOCK COLLINS

COLLINS

MAKES 1 DRINK

2 oz. scotch
   whiskey
1 oz. lemon juice or
   juice of ½ lemon
1 tsp. fine sugar
3 oz. club soda

Pour ingredients into a Collins glass over ice. Garnish with a lemon slice and a cherry.

JOCKEY CLUB

COLLINS

MAKES 1 DRINK

1½ oz. gin
½ tsp. white crème
   de cacao
splash lemon juice
3 oz. club soda

Pour the gin, crème de cacao, and lemon juice into a shaker with ice. Shake well and strain into a Collins glass almost filled with ice. Add the club soda. Stir and garnish with a cherry and an orange slice.

JOHN COLLINS

MAKES 1 DRINK

*2 oz. bourbon
  whiskey
1 oz. lemon juice
1 tsp. superfine
  sugar
3 oz. club soda*

Pour the bourbon, lemon juice, and sugar into a shaker with ice. Shake well and strain into a Collins glass almost filled with ice. Add the club soda. Stir and garnish with a cherry and an orange slice.

JOHNNIE COCKTAIL

MAKES 1 DRINK

*¾ oz. curaçao
1½ oz. sloe gin
1 tsp. anisette*

Pour ingredients into a shaker with ice. Stir well and strain into a martini glass.

JOURNALIST MARTINI

 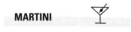

MAKES 1 DRINK

*3 oz. gin
1 tsp. dry vermouth
1 tsp. sweet
  vermouth
1 tsp. triple sec
1 tsp. lime juice
dash bitters*

Pour ingredients into a shaker with ice. Shake well and strain into a chilled martini glass.

JOY TO THE WORLD

MAKES 1 DRINK

*1½ oz. light rum
½ oz. bourbon
½ oz. dark crème
  de cacao*

Pour ingredients into a shaker with ice. Stir and strain into a martini glass.

JUBILEE FIZZ

HIGHBALL

MAKES 1 DRINK

2 oz. gin
1 oz. lemon juice or
    juice of ½ lemon
½ tsp. fine sugar
4 oz. chilled
    Champagne

Pour the lemon juice, gin, and sugar into a shaker half filled with ice. Shake well. Pour into a highball glass partly filled with ice. Stir. Add the Champagne.

JUICY JULEP (NONALCOHOLIC)

COLLINS

MAKES 1 DRINK

1 oz. lime juice
1 oz. orange juice
1 oz. pineapple juice
½ oz. raspberry syrup
club soda
4 crushed mint
    leaves

Pour all ingredients except club soda into a shaker half filled with ice. Shake well and strain into a Collins glass. Add the club soda and stir gently. Garnish with a sprig of mint.

JUMPING BEAN

MARTINI

MAKES 1 DRINK

1½ oz. tequila
½ oz. Sambuca
3 coffee beans

Pour ingredients into a shaker with ice. Stir and strain into a martini glass. Add coffee beans.

JUPITER

MARTINI

MAKES 1 DRINK

2 oz. gin
1 oz. dry vermouth
1 tsp. orange juice
1 tsp. Parfait
    Amour

Pour ingredients into a shaker with ice. Shake well and strain into a martini glass. (Measure the Parfait Amour carefully; too much will ruin the drink.)

JUST SAY NO COCOA

IRISH COFFEE

MAKES 1 DRINK

*1 packet hot cocoa
    mix
¾ cup hot water
eggnog
whipped cream*

Pour a packet of hot cocoa mix into an Irish coffee glass or mug. Fill three quarters of the way with very hot water, then stir well. Fill the rest of the way with eggnog and top with whipped cream.

KAHLUA MARTINI

OLD-FASHIONED

MAKES 1 DRINK

*1 oz. Kahlua
1 oz. vodka
splash coffee*

Pour all ingredients over ice in an old-fashioned glass.

KAHLUA SOUR

SOUR GLASS

MAKES 1 DRINK

*1 cup Kahlua
1 cup lemon juice*

Pour the ingredients into a blender with a cup of ice. Blend until slushy. Pour into a sour glass.

KAMA SUTRA

COLLINS

MAKES 1 DRINK

*½ oz. Passoa
    Passion
½ oz. Alize Red
    Passion
½ oz. Cheri-berri
    Pucker
Sprite*

Pour the Passoa Passion, Alize Red Passion, and Cheri-berri Pucker into a Collins glass over ice. Add Sprite to fill. Garnish with maraschino cherries. Do not stir; it should have a layered look.

KAMIKAZE

MARTINI

MAKES 1 DRINK

1½ oz. vodka
1 oz. lime juice
1 oz. triple sec

Pour ingredients into a shaker with ice. Shake well and strain into a chilled martini glass. Garnish with the lime wedge.

KAMIKAZE SHOOTER

SHOT

MAKES 1 DRINK

½ oz. lime juice
1.2 oz. orange
   liqueur
1 oz. vodka

Pour ingredients into a shaker with ice. Shake well and strain into a shot glass.

KANGAROO

COLLINS

MAKES 1 DRINK

1½ oz. vodka
½ oz. dry vermouth

Pour ingredients into a shaker with ice. Stir and strain into a chilled Collins glass. Garnish with a lemon twist.

K

KENO

MARTINI

MAKES 1 DRINK

1 oz. dark rum
¼ oz. white
   curaçao
¼ oz. maraschino
   liqueur
1 tbs. grenadine

Pour ingredients into a shaker with ice. Shake and strain into a martini glass. Garnish with an orange twist and a cherry.

KENTUCKY

MARTINI

MAKES 1 DRINK

*2 oz. bourbon
   whiskey
1 oz. pineapple
   juice*

Pour ingredients into a shaker with ice. Shake well and strain into a martini glass.

KENTUCKY BLACK-EYED SUSAN

MAKES 1 DRINK

*1 oz. Cointreau
1 oz. Mount Gay
   rum
1 oz. vodka
1 oz. pineapple
   juice
1 oz. orange juice
lime wedge*

Pour the Cointreau, rum, and vodka into a shaker with ice. Stir and strain into a highball glass. Top with pineapple juice and orange juice. Garnish with the lime wedge.

KENTUCKY BLIZZARD

OLD-FASHIONED

MAKES 1 DRINK

*1½ oz. bourbon
1½ oz. cranberry
   juice
½ oz. lime juice
½ oz. grenadine
1 tsp. fine sugar*

Pour ingredients into a shaker with ice. Stir and strain into an old-fashioned glass filled with ice. Garnish with an orange slice.

KENTUCKY COLONEL

MARTINI

MAKES 1 DRINK

*3 oz. bourbon
   whiskey
½ oz. Benedictine*

Pour ingredients into a shaker with ice. Shake and strain into a martini glass. Garnish with a lemon twist.

KENTUCKY MINT JULEP

COLLINS

MAKES 1 DRINK

*4 oz. bourbon
    whiskey
1 tsp. powdered
    sugar
3 tablespoons
    water
12–16 fresh mint
    leaves*

Put sprigs of mint in bowl, cover with powdered sugar and just enough water to dissolve sugar. Crush with a wooden pestle. Place half of the mixture in the bottom of a Collins glass. Fill halfway with ice. Add the rest of the mint liquid and finish filling with ice. Add the bourbon until the glass is brimming full. Refrigerate for an hour.

KEOKE COFFEE

IRISH COFFEE

MAKES 1 DRINK

*1 oz. brandy
½ oz. Kahlua
6 oz. coffee*

Pour ingredients into an Irish coffee glass or mug. Top with whipped cream.

KEY LIME PIE MARGARITA

MARGARITA

MAKES 1 DRINK

*1½ oz. tequila
½ oz. key lime
    crème liqueur
3 oz. key lime
    yogurt
juice from ½ a lime
lime wedge, crushed
    graham cracker,
    and kosher salt*

Rub the lime around the rim of a margarita glass. Dip half the rim in kosher salt, half in the graham crackers. Pour the tequila, key lime crème liqueur, key lime yogurt, and lime juice into a blender with a cup of ice. Blend until smooth. Pour into the glass and garnish with the lime slice.

KING KENNETH

COLLINS

MAKES 1 DRINK

*2 oz. Campari
1 oz. peach
    schnapps
1 oz. orange juice
1 tsp. lemon juice
4 oz. tonic water*

Pour all ingredients except tonic into a shaker half filled with ice. Shake well and strain into a Collins glass over ice. Add the tonic to fill. Stir. Garnish with a lemon twist.

KING OF DENMARK

MARTINI

MAKES 1 DRINK

8 oz. Pernod
6 oz. black currant
   cordial
20 oz. water

Blend all ingredients in a pitcher, adding several large ice cubes. Serve in martini glasses.

KINGSTON

MARTINI

MAKES 1 DRINK

¾ oz. spiced rum
½ oz. gin
½ oz. lime juice
3 dashes grenadine

Pour ingredients into a shaker with ice. Shake and strain into a chilled martini glass.

KIR

WINE

MAKES 1 DRINK

½ oz. crème de
   cassis
4 oz. dry white
   wine

Pour the cassis into a large wine glass. Add the wine. Do not stir. The cassis is meant to drift to the bottom so the drink gets sweeter as you drink it. Garnish with a lemon twist.

KIR ROYAL

CHAMPAGNE

MAKES 1 DRINK

¼ oz. crème de
   cassis
2¼ oz. Champagne

Pour the crème de cassis into a Champagne flute. Slowly add the Champagne. Do not stir. The cassis is meant to drift to the bottom so the drink gets sweeter as you drink it. Garnish with a lemon twist.

KIRSCH RICKEY

HIGHBALL

MAKES 1 DRINK

2 oz. kirschwasser
1 tbs. lime juice
club soda

Pour kirschwasser and lime juice into a highball glass nearly filled with ice. Add the club soda to fill. Stir gently. Garnish with a cherry.

KISS FROM A ROSARITA

MAKES 1 DRINK

1½ oz. gold tequila
1 oz. tequila rose
3 strawberries
3 oz. sweet-and-
*   sour mix*

Pour ingredients into a blender with a cup of ice. Blend until smooth. Pour into a margarita glass rimmed with salt. Garnish with a lime slice.

KISS IN THE DARK

MAKES 1 DRINK

1 oz. gin
½ oz. cherry brandy
½ oz. dry vermouth

Pour ingredients into a shaker with ice. Stir and strain into a martini glass.

KISS OF AN ANGEL

HIGHBALL

MAKES 1 DRINK

1 oz. Kahlua
1 oz. vodka
1 oz. Irish cream
*   liquour*
milk

Pour first three ingredients into a highball glass over ice. Add milk to fill.

KISS ON THE CHEEK (NONALCOHOLIC) HIGHBALL

MAKES 1 DRINK

*2 oz. apricot
 nectar
1 oz. lemon
 juice or
 juice of ½
 lemon
club soda*

Pour the apricot nectar and lemon juice into a shaker with ice. Stir well and strain into a highball glass over ice. Add the club soda to fill. Garnish with a lemon twist.

KISS ON THE LIPS COLLINS

MAKES 1 DRINK

*1½ oz. bourbon
 whiskey
5 oz. apricot nectar*

Pour into a Collins glass nearly filled with ice. Stir gently. Serve with a straw.

KISS THE BOYS GOODBYE MARTINI

MAKES 1 DRINK

*1½ oz. brandy
½ oz. sloe gin
1 oz. lemon juice or
 juice of ½ lemon
1 egg white*

Pour ingredients into a shaker with ice. Shake well and strain into a martini glass.

KISSIN' CANDY MARTINI

MAKES 1 DRINK

*½ oz. Amaretto
½ oz. cherry brandy
½ oz. dark crème
 de cacao
1 oz. cream*

Pour ingredients into a shaker with ice. Shake and strain into a martini glass. Top with whipped cream and a cherry.

KISSIN' COUSIN

MARTINI

MAKES 1 DRINK

¾ oz. cherry brandy
¾ oz. dry vermouth
¾ oz. gin

Pour ingredients into a shaker with ice. Stir and strain into a martini glass.

KITCHEN WALL

IRISH COFFEE

MAKES 1 DRINK

½ oz. butterscotch
    schnapps
½ oz. Irish cream
    liqueur
5 oz. hot black
    coffee
whipped cream
splash Kahlua

Pour first three ingredients into an Irish coffee glass or mug. Top with the whipped cream and drizzle with Kahlua.

KLONDIKE COOLER

COLLINS

MAKES 1 DRINK

2 oz. rye or
    bourbon whiskey
2 oz. club soda
½ tsp. powdered
    sugar
carbonated water
    or ginger ale
spiral of orange or
    lemon peel

Pour the powdered sugar and club soda into a Collins glass. Stir. Fill the glass with ice and add the whiskey. Top with more club soda or ginger ale. Garnish with a spiral of orange or lemon.

KNICKERBOCKER

MARTINI

MAKES 1 DRINK

3 oz. gin
1 oz. dry vermouth
½ tsp. sweet
    vermouth

Pour ingredients into a shaker with ice. Stir and strain into a chilled martini glass. Garnish with a lemon twist.

KNOCKOUT

MARTINI

MAKES 1 DRINK

1 oz. gin
1 oz. scotch
whiskey
½ oz. French
vermouth
½ oz. Italian
vermouth
1 tbs. grenadine

Pour ingredients into a shaker with ice. Stir well and strain into a martini glass.

KOKOMO JOE

HIGHBALL

MAKES 1 DRINK

1 oz. white rum
1 oz. banana
liqueur
5 oz. orange juice
3 oz. piña colada
mix
½ banana

Pour ingredients into a blender. Blend with a cup of ice until smooth. Pour into a highball glass. Garnish with a slice of orange.

KON TIKI

HIGHBALL

MAKES 1 DRINK

2 oz. scotch
1 oz. dark rum
1 oz. Cointreau

Pour all ingredients into a highball glass over ice and stir. Garnish with a lemon peel.

KYOTO

MARTINI

MAKES 1 DRINK

3 oz. gin
1 oz. melon liqueur
½ oz. dry vermouth
¼ tsp. lemon juice

Pour ingredients into a shaker with ice. Stir and strain into a chilled martini glass. Garnish with a small melon ball.

L

LA BAMBA MARGARITA

MARGARITA

MAKES 1 DRINK

1¼ oz. Sauza
   Commemorativo
   tequila
½ oz. triple sec
¼ oz. grenadine
¼ oz. pineapple
   juice
1½ oz. orange juice

Pour ingredients into a shaker with ice. Shake and strain into a margarita glass. Garnish with a pineapple spear.

LA BOMBA

MARTINI

MAKES 1 DRINK

1½ oz. tequila
½ oz. Cointreau
1½ oz. pineapple
   juice
1½ oz. orange juice
splash grenadine

Pour ingredients into a shaker with ice. Shake well and strain into a martini glass.

LA BOOM (NONALCOHOLIC)

COLLINS

MAKES 1 DRINK

4 oz. orange
   juice
4 oz. pineapple
   juice
splash
   grenadine
squeeze lime

Pour ingredients into a shaker with ice. Shake well and strain into a Collins glass. Garnish with fruit. Serve with a straw.

LA HABANA

MARTINI

MAKES 1 DRINK

1 oz. gin
1 oz. apricot brandy
juice of ½ lime

Pour the gin and apricot brandy into a shaker with ice. Add a few drops of lime juice. Shake well and strain into a chilled martini glass ¾ full of ice.

L

LA HOYA (NONALCOHOLIC)

MARTINI

MAKES 1 DRINK

2 slices banana
2 oz. orange juice
1 oz. grapefruit juice
1 tsp. lemon juice

Pour ingredients into a blender without ice. Blend thoroughly. Pour into a martini glass.

LA JOLLA

MARTINI

MAKES 1 DRINK

1½ oz. brandy
½ oz. crème de banane
2 tsp. orange juice
1 tsp. lemon juice

Pour ingredients into a shaker nearly filled with ice. Shake and strain into a martini glass.

LADYFINGER

MARTINI

MAKES 1 DRINK

1 oz. cherry brandy
1 oz. gin
½ oz. Kirsch

Pour ingredients into a shaker with ice. Shake and strain into a martini glass.

LADY GODIVA

HIGHBALL

MAKES 1 DRINK

1 tsp. sugar
2 dashes triple sec
juice of ¼ lemon
juice of ½ lime
brandy

Pour all ingredients except brandy into a shaker with ice. Shake and strain into a highball glass. Add brandy to fill.

LADY'S COCKTAIL

MARTINI

MAKES 1 DRINK

1½ oz. blended
    whiskey
½ tsp. anisette
dash bitters

Pour ingredients into a shaker with ice.
Stir and strain into a martini glass.

LANDED GENTRY

MARTINI

MAKES 1 DRINK

1½ oz. dark rum
½ oz. Tia Maria
1 oz. heavy cream

Pour ingredients into a shaker with ice.
Shake and strain into a martini glass.

LAST WORD

MARTINI

MAKES 1 DRINK

½ oz. gin
½ oz. maraschino
½ oz. Chartreuse
½ oz. lime juice

Pour ingredients into a shaker with ice.
Shake and strain into a martini glass.

LATITUDE ATTITUDE ADJUSTER

BEER GLASS

MAKES 1 DRINK

beer (any kind)
orange juice
½ oz. 151 rum
½ oz. Amaretto

Fill just about half of a beer mug with
the beer and half with the orange juice,
leaving some room at the top. Pour the
151 rum and Amaretto into a shot glass.
Drop the shot into the glass.

LAUGHING AT THE WAVES

MARTINI

MAKES 1 DRINK

1½ oz. vodka
½ oz. dry vermouth
½ oz. Campari

Pour ingredients into a shaker with ice. Stir and strain into a martini glass.

LAURENTIS LATTE (NONALCOHOLIC) IRISH COFFEE

MAKES 1 DRINK

1½ oz. espresso
½ oz. almond syrup
½ oz. hazelnut syrup or Frangelico
8 oz. milk

In an Irish coffee glass or large mug, pour steamed milk, followed by the syrups and espresso. Top with whipped cream, chocolate shavings, and toasted almond shavings.

LAVA FLOW (NONALCOHOLIC) COLLINS

MAKES 1 DRINK

3 oz. milk
½ oz. coconut cream
3 oz. pineapple juice
½ banana
½ cup straw-berries, fresh or frozen

Pour all ingredients into a blender in this order: milk, coconut cream, pineapple juice, banana, strawberries, and ice. Blend thoroughly. Pour into a Collins or parfait glass. Serve with a straw.

LE FEMME NIKITA RITA MARGARITA

MAKES 1 DRINK

1½ oz. gold tequila
1 oz. limoncello
juice from half a lemon
3 oz. sweet-and-sour mix

Pour the tequila, limoncello, lemon juice, and sweet-and-sour mix into a blender with a cup of ice. Blend until smooth. Pour into a margarita glass with a salted rim. Garnish with the lemon slice. (Can also be served on the rocks.)

LEANING TOWER

MARTINI

MAKES 1 DRINK

*2 dashes orange
    bitters
2 oz. gin
1 tsp. dry vermouth*

Pour ingredients into a shaker with ice.
Stir well and strain into a martini glass.

LEAPFROG

HIGHBALL

MAKES 1 DRINK

*2 oz. gin
1 oz. lemon juice or
    juice of ½ lemon
ginger ale*

Pour gin and lemon juice into a highball
glass nearly filled with ice. Add ginger
ale. Stir.

LEAP YEAR MARTINI

MARTINI

MAKES 1 DRINK

*2 oz. gin
½ oz. sweet
    vermouth
½ oz. Grand
    Marnier
dash lemon juice*

Pour ingredients into a shaker with ice.
Shake well and strain into a martini
glass.

LEAP YEAR VODKA MARTINI

MARTINI

MAKES 1 DRINK

*3 oz. citrus vodka
½ oz. sweet
    vermouth
½ oz. Grand
    Marnier
½ tsp. lemon juice*

Pour ingredients into a shaker with ice.
Shake well and strain into a martini
glass.

LEAVE IT TO ME

MARTINI

MAKES 1 DRINK

1½ oz. dry gin
1 tsp. lemon juice
¼ tsp. maraschino
1 tsp. raspberry
  syrup

Pour ingredients into a shaker with ice. Stir and strain into a martini glass.

LEE'S COOLER (NONALCOHOLIC)

COLLINS

MAKES 1 DRINK

2 oz. white
  grape juice
2 oz. club soda
½ tsp. fine
  sugar
1 oz. lime juice
ginger ale

Pour lime juice, sugar, and club soda into a Collins glass. Stir. Fill with ice. Add grape juice and ginger ale. Stir well and serve with a slice of fruit.

LEMON DAISY (NONALCOHOLIC)

OLD-FASHIONED

MAKES 1 DRINK

2 oz. lemon
  juice
1 oz. grenadine
1 oz. lemon and
  lime soda
1 oz. sparkling
  water

Pour lemon juice and grenadine over ice in an old-fashioned glass. Stir well. Add equal parts lemon and lime soda and sparkling water. Stir gently. Add a lemon twist.

LEMON DROP

MARTINI

MAKES 1 DRINK

1½ oz. vodka
¾ oz. lemon juice
1 tsp. simple syrup

Pour ingredients into a shaker with ice. Shake well and strain into a chilled martini glass. Garnish with the lemon twist.

LEMON DROP MARTINI

MARTINI

MAKES 1 DRINK

*3 oz. lemon-
    flavored vodka
½ oz. dry vermouth*

Pour ingredients into a shaker with ice. Shake well and strain into a chilled martini glass, rimmed with sugar. Garnish with a lemon twist.

LEMON DROP SHOOTER

SHOT

MAKES 1 DRINK

*1½ oz. vodka
sugar
lemon wedge*

Pour the chilled vodka into a shot glass. Coat the lemon with sugar. To drink: down the shot; suck on the lemon.

LEMON LOVE SHACK SHAKE

MARTINI

MAKES 1 DRINK

*1 oz. lemon-
    flavored vodka
1 oz. Cointreau
2 oz. half-and-half
1 big scoop lemon
    Italian ice*

Put all the ingredients into a blender. Blend until smooth. Add more Italian lemon ice for more of a lemony taste. To make it creamier, add more half-and-half. Pour into a martini glass.

LEMON RASPBERRY RITA

MARGARITA

MAKES 1 DRINK

*1½ oz. gold tequila
½ oz. Chambord
juice from half a
    lemon
lemonade*

Fill a salt-rimmed margarita glass with ice. Add the tequila, Chambord, and lemon juice. Add lemonade to fill. Garnish with a lemon slice.

LEMON TWIST

MARTINI

MAKES 1 DRINK

3 oz. lemon-
  flavored vodka
½ oz. dry vermouth

Pour ingredients into a shaker with ice. Shake and strain into a chilled martini glass. Garnish with a lemon twist.

LEMONY APPLE (NONALCOHOLIC) COLLINS

MAKES 1 DRINK

3 oz. apple
  juice
1 oz. lemon
  juice
1 oz. grenadine
8 oz. ginger ale

Pour apple and lemon juice into a Collins or highball glass. Stir. Add the ginger ale. Drizzle in the grenadine.

LEPRECHAUN

MARTINI

MAKES 1 DRINK

1 1/3 oz. Irish
  whiskey
2/3 oz. white rum
1/3 oz. sloe gin
2/3 oz. lime juice
½ tsp. powdered
  sugar
¼ peach
a few strawberries

Pour all ingredients into a blender. Blend until smooth. Pour into a martini glass.

LEVIATHAN

MARTINI

MAKES 1 DRINK

1 oz. brandy
½ oz. sweet
  vermouth
½ oz. orange juice

Pour ingredients into a shaker with ice. Shake and strain into a martini glass.

LIBERAL

MARTINI

MAKES 1 DRINK

1½ oz. rye whiskey
½ oz. sweet
   vermouth
¼ oz. Amer Picon
1 dash orange
   bitters

Pour ingredients into a shaker with ice. Stir and train into a martini glass. Garnish with an orange twist.

LIBERTY COCKTAIL

MARTINI

MAKES 1 DRINK

¾ oz. white rum
1½ oz. apple
   brandy
¼ tsp. simple syrup

Pour ingredients into a shaker with ice. Stir and strain into a martini glass.

LICORICE STICK

MARTINI

MAKES 1 DRINK

1 oz. Sambuca
   (black)
1 oz. vodka
½ oz. crème de
   cacao

Pour ingredients into a shaker with ice. Shake and strain into a martini glass.

LIKE A VIRGIN (NONALCOHOLIC)

COLLINS

MAKES 1 DRINK

handful of
   blackberries
spoon of sugar
lemonade
lemon and
   blackberries
   for garnish

Put the blackberries and sugar into a blender. Blend until smooth, then pour into a Collins glass. Pack the glass with ice, and add lemonade to fill. Garnish with a lemon slice and some blackberries.

LIME COLA (NONALCOHOLIC)

MAKES 1 DRINK

1 oz. lime juice
  or juice of ½
  lime
cola to fill

Pour into a highball glass over ice. Garnish with a lime wedge.

LIME RICKEY

HIGHBALL

MAKES 1 DRINK

1½ oz. gin
1½ oz. Rose's lime
  juice
4 oz. club soda

Pour the gin and lime juice into a highball glass nearly filled with ice. Stir gently. Add club soda. Garnish with a twist of lime.

LINCHBURG LEMONADE

HIGHBALL

MAKES 1 DRINK

1 oz. Jack Daniel's
  Country Cocktail
  (Downhome
  Punch)
1 oz. triple sec
1 oz. sweet-and-
  sour mix
1 oz. Squirt

Pour into a highball glass over ice.

LIQUID VIAGRA

MAKES 1 DRINK

1 oz. vodka
½ oz. blue curaçao
½ oz. apricot
  brandy
½ oz. lime juice

Pour all the ingredients into an old-fashioned glass over ice.

LITTLE BASTARD

HIGHBALL

MAKES 1 DRINK

1 oz. rum
1 oz. orange juice
½ oz. pineapple juice
7-Up

Pour all ingredients except the 7-Up into a shaker with ice. Shake and strain into a highball glass and fill with 7-Up.

LITTLE PRINCE (NONALCOHOLIC)

OLD-FASHIONED

MAKES 1 DRINK

2 oz. sparkling cider
1 oz. apricot nectar
1 oz. lemon juice or juice of ½ lemon

Pour ingredients into a shaker with ice. Stir and strain into an old-fashioned glass. Add a lemon twist.

LITTLE PRINCESS

MARTINI

MAKES 1 DRINK

2 oz. light rum
1 oz. sweet vermouth

Pour ingredients into a shaker half filled with ice. Shake well and strain into a martini glass.

LITTLE RED TEDDY SHOOTER

SHOT

MAKES 4 DRINKS

4 oz. vodka
1 oz. Chambord
1 oz. white crème de cacao

Pour ingredients into a shaker with ice. Shake well and strain into four shot glasses.

LOCH LOMOND

MAKES 1 DRINK

*1 oz. scotch
    whiskey
1 oz. blue curaçao
½ oz. peach-
    flavored brandy
3 oz. grapefruit
    juice
½ oz. lemon juice*

Pour all ingredients into a shaker half filled with ice. Shake well and strain into a Collins or parfait glass over ice. Garnish with an orange, lemon, or lime slice.

LOCH NESS MONSTER

OLD-FASHIONED

MAKES 1 DRINK

*1½ oz. scotch
    whiskey
1 tsp. peppermint
    schnapps
3 oz. club soda*

Pour ingredients into a shaker with ice. Stir and strain into an old-fashioned glass.

LOLITA

WINE

MAKES 1 DRINK

*4 oz. Burgundy
    wine
4 oz. sweet-and-
    sour mix*

Pour ingredients into a wine glass and stir. Garnish with a lemon slice and a cherry.

LOMOND CRUSH (NONALCOHOLIC) COLLINS

MAKES 1 DRINK

*¼ cup blue-
    berries, fresh
    or frozen
1 oz. peach nectar
2 oz. grapefruit
    juice
½ oz. lemon juice*

Pour all ingredients into a blender with ice. Blend until smooth. Pour into a Collins or parfait glass. Garnish with an orange, lemon, or lime slice, and a cherry. Serve with a straw.

LONDON BUCK

MAKES 1 DRINK

2 oz. gin
½ tsp. maraschino
    liqueur
2 dashes orange
    bitters
½ tsp. simple syrup

Pour ingredients into a shaker with ice. Stir and strain into a highball glass. Garnish with a lemon twist.

LONDON FOG

MARTINI

MAKES 1 DRINK

1 oz. white crème
    de menthe
1 oz. anisette
1 dash bitters

Pour ingredients into a shaker with ice. Shake and strain into a martini glass. Serve with a thin strip of toast spread with Welsh Rarebit (or other spread).

LONDON FOG 2

HIGHBALL

MAKES 1 DRINK

1½ oz. gin
¼ oz. Pernod

Pour ingredients into a blender. Mix until smooth. Pour into a highball glass.

LONDON MARTINI

MARTINI

MAKES 1 DRINK

3 oz. gin
½ tsp. maraschino
    liqueur
4 dashes orange
    bitters
½ tsp. sugar

Pour ingredients into a shaker with ice. Shake well and strain into a chilled martini glass. Garnish with a lemon twist.

LONDON TOWN

MARTINI

MAKES 1 DRINK

1½ oz. gin
½ oz. maraschino
  liqueur
2 dashes orange
  bitters

Pour ingredients into a shaker with ice. Shake and strain into a martini glass.

LONE TREE COOLER

COLLINS

MAKES 1 DRINK

2 oz. gin
½ oz. French
  vermouth
2 oz. carbonated
  water
½ tsp. powdered
  sugar
ginger ale

Pour powdered sugar and 2 oz. carbonated water into a Collins glass. Stir. Fill the glass with ice. Add the gin and vermouth. Add carbonated water or ginger ale to fill. Garnish with a spiral of orange or lemon (or both).

LONG BEACH ICED TEA

HIGHBALL

MAKES 1 DRINK

1 oz. vodka
1 oz. light rum
1 oz. tequila
1 oz. gin
1 oz. triple sec
½ oz. cranberry
  juice

Pour all ingredients except the cranberry juice into a highball glass over ice. Add cranberry juice to fill. Stir gently. Garnish with a lemon wedge.

LONG ISLAND ICED TEA

COLLINS

MAKES 1 DRINK

½ oz. vodka
½ oz. gin
½ oz. light rum
½ oz. triple sec
1 oz. lemon juice
cola

Pour all ingredients except the cola into a tumbler or Collins glass over ice. Add cola to fill. Garnish with a lemon wedge.

LONG ISLAND ICED TEA 2

COLLINS

MAKES 1 DRINK

½ oz. tequila
½ oz. gin
½ oz. light rum
½ oz. vodka
1 oz. lemon juice
1 tsp. fine sugar
cola

Pour all ingredients except cola into a shaker half filled with ice. Shake well and strain into a Collins glass over ice. Add the cola to fill and stir.

LONG ISLAND SUNSET

COLLINS

MAKES 1 DRINK

3 oz. spiced rum
3 oz. peach
    schnapps
3 oz. sweet-and-
    sour mix
3 oz. cranberry
    juice

Pour ingredients into a shaker with ice. Shake and strain into a tumbler or Collins glass. Garnish with a cherry and a slice of orange.

LORD AND LADY

OLD-FASHIONED

MAKES 1 DRINK

1½ oz. dark rum
½ oz. Tia Maria

Pour the rum and Tia Maria into an old-fashioned glass almost filled with ice. Stir well.

LOS ANGELES COCKTAIL

OLD-FASHIONED

MAKES 1 DRINK

1½ oz. blended
    scotch whiskey
¼ oz. sweet
    vermouth
juice of ½ lemon
1 tsp. powdered
    sugar
1 egg

Pour ingredients into a shaker with ice. Shake and strain into an old-fashioned glass.

LOTUS CLUB COCKTAIL

OLD-FASHIONED

MAKES 1 DRINK

2 oz. bourbon
  whiskey
2–3 drops bitters
1 dash Pernod
1 lump sugar

Muddle the lump of sugar with bitters in the bottom of a mixing glass. Add the Pernod and whiskey. Stir and pour into an old-fashioned glass over ice. Garnish with a lemon twist.

LOUISE COFFEE

IRISH COFFEE

MAKES 1 DRINK

½ oz. Grand
  Marnier
½ oz. Irish cream
  liqueur
½ oz. Kahlua
6 oz. hot black
  coffee

Pour all ingredients into an Irish coffee glass or mug. Stir well. Top with whipped cream and a cherry.

LOUISIANA LULLABY

MARTINI

MAKES 1 DRINK

1½ oz. dark rum
2 tsp. Dubonnet
  (Rouge)
3 drops Grand
  Marnier

Pour ingredients into a shaker with ice. Stir and strain into a martini glass. Garnish with a sliver of lemon.

LOUISVILLE COOLER

OLD-FASHIONED

MAKES 1 DRINK

1½ oz. bourbon
  whiskey
1 oz. orange juice
1 tbs. lime juice
1 tsp. fine sugar

Pour ingredients into a shaker half filled with ice. Stir and strain into an old-fashioned glass over ice. Garnish with an orange slice.

LOUISVILLE-STYLE MINT JULEP HIGHBALL

MAKES 1 DRINK

2 oz. bourbon
  whiskey
1 cup sugar
1 cup water
1 bunch fresh mint

Combine sugar and water in a saucepan. Boil for 5 minutes, without stirring. Cool. Pour over a handful of mint leaves. Refrigerate overnight in a closed jar. Remove the mint and continue to refrigerate. Combine a tablespoon of this mixture with a tablespoon of water in a high-ball glass. Add ice and bourbon. Stir gently until the glass is frosted.

LOVE POTION #9 COLLINS

MAKES 1 DRINK

1 oz. Parfait Amour
1 oz. mandarin
  vodka
white cranberry
  juice
sprig of purple
  seedless grapes

Pour the Parfait Amour and mandarin vodka into a Collins glass over ice. Add white cranberry juice to fill. Break off a sprig of the grapes for a garnish.

LOVER'S KISS PARFAIT

MAKES 1 DRINK

½ oz. Amaretto
½ oz. cherry brandy
½ oz. dark crème
  de cacao
1 oz. cream

Pour ingredients into a shaker with ice. Shake and strain into a parfait glass. Garnish with whipped cream, a sprinkle of chocolate shavings, and a cherry.

LOW TIDE MARTINI MARTINI

MAKES 1 DRINK

3 oz. vodka
½ oz. dry vermouth
1 tsp. clam juice

Pour ingredients into a shaker with ice. Shake and strain into a chilled martini glass. Garnish with an olive stuffed with smoked clam and a lemon twist.

LUCKY CHARMARTINI

MARTINI

MAKES 1 DRINK

1 oz. tequila rose
1 oz. white crème
    de menthe
3 oz. milk
marshmallows from
    Lucky Charms
    cereal

Pour the first three ingredients into a shaker with ice. Swirl to chill. Strain into a martini glass, then sprinkle Lucky Charms marshmallows on top.

LULU

COLLINS

MAKES 1 DRINK

½ oz. vodka
½ oz. triple sec
½ oz. white rum
½ oz. Amaretto
½ oz. peach schnapps
1 oz. sweet-and-sour
    mix
splash pineapple juice
splash grenadine

Shake with ice and strain into a Collins glass. Add splash grenadine. Serve with a straw.

LULU OF A LUAU

COLLINS

MAKES 1 DRINK

1 oz. cranberry juice
1 oz. raspberry
    vodka
1 oz. peach
    schnapps
1 oz. blue curaçao
2 scoops rainbow
    sherbet
1 oz. Champagne

Pour the cranberry juice into a Collins glass. Pour the vodka, schnapps, curaçao, and rainbow sherbet into a blender. Blend until smooth. Pour that mixture into the Collins glass, leaving room to add the Champagne on top. Garnish with an orange, lemon, or lime slice, and a cherry. Finish with a paper parasol.

LYNCHBURG LEMONADE

COLLINS

MAKES 1 DRINK

1 oz. Jack Daniel's
    whiskey
1 oz. triple sec
1 oz. sweet-and-
    sour mix
2–4 oz. Sprite

Pour ingredients over ice in a tumbler or Collins glass.

M&M SHOOTER

SHOT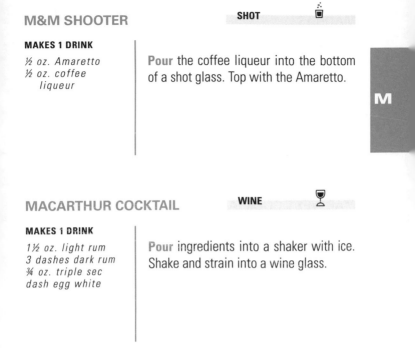

MAKES 1 DRINK

½ oz. Amaretto
½ oz. coffee
    liqueur

Pour the coffee liqueur into the bottom of a shot glass. Top with the Amaretto.

M

MACARTHUR COCKTAIL

WINE

MAKES 1 DRINK

1½ oz. light rum
3 dashes dark rum
¾ oz. triple sec
dash egg white

Pour ingredients into a shaker with ice. Shake and strain into a wine glass.

MACINTOSH ROUGE (NONALCOHOLIC) **MARTINI**

MAKES 1 DRINK

2 oz. apple
    juice
2 oz. grapefruit
    juice
½ tsp.
    grenadine

Pour ingredients into a shaker half filled with ice. Shake well. Strain into a martini glass.

MAD COW

SHOT

MAKES 1 DRINK

½ oz. Kahlua
½ oz. cream
½ oz. 151 proof
    rum

Pour ingredients into a blender with ice. Blend until smooth. Pour into a large shot glass.

MADRAS

HIGHBALL

MAKES 1 DRINK

1½ oz. vodka
3 oz. cranberry
*   juice*
1 oz. orange juice

Pour the vodka and cranberry juice into a highball glass. Stir well. Top off with orange juice.

MAE WEST COCKTAIL

HIGHBALL

MAKES 1 DRINK

3–4 oz. brandy
1 egg yolk
1 tsp. powdered
*   sugar*
dash cayenne
*   pepper*

Pour ingredients into a shaker with ice. Shake very vigorously to mix the egg yolk well with the other ingredients. Strain into a highball glass over ice. Top with cayenne pepper.

MAESTRO

COLLINS

MAKES 1 DRINK

1½ oz. Anejo rum
½ oz. cream sherry
½ oz. lime juice
4 oz. ginger ale

Pour the rum, sherry, and lime juice into a shaker half-filled with ice. Shake well and strain into a Collins glass almost filled with ice. Top off with the ginger ale. Garnish with a lemon twist.

MAGIC WAND ESPRESSO

ESPRESSO CUP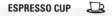

MAKES 1 DRINK

1½ oz. Sambuca
1 cup hot espresso
star fruit slice
bamboo skewer
2 heaping spoons
*   of confectioners'*
*   sugar*

Moisten the star fruit in water and dip it in the powdered sugar to coat. Stick the skewer into the fruit so that it looks like a star at the end of a wand. Pour the Sambuca into an espresso cup and fill with espresso. Tap the magic wand on the rim to sprinkle the drink with sugar.

MAGNOLIA MAIDEN

OLD-FASHIONED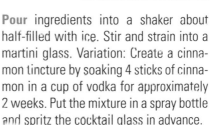

MAKES 1 DRINK

1½ oz. bourbon
whiskey
1 oz. Grand Marnier
½ tsp. fine sugar
splash lemon juice
splash club soda

Pour the bourbon, Grand Marnier, sugar, and lemon juice into a shaker half filled with ice. Shake well and strain into an old-fashioned glass over ice. Add the club soda. Stir gently.

MAGNOLIA PUNCH (NONALCOHOLIC)

PUNCH

MAKES ABOUT 25 DRINKS

15 sprigs of mint
1 cup granulated sugar
1 quart boiling water
1 cup lemon juice
1 quart orange juice
1 quart pineapple
juice
1 quart ginger ale

Pour the mint, sugar, and water into a saucepan. Simmer for 10 minutes. Refrigerate. To assemble punch, strain the mint syrup and add to the punch bowl with all the other ingredients except the ginger ale. Mix well. Just before serving, add the ginger ale.

MAHOGANY

MARTINI

MAKES 1 DRINK

1½ oz. dry
vermouth
¾ oz. Jägermeister
¾ oz. Benedictine

Pour ingredients into a shaker about half-filled with ice. Stir and strain into a martini glass. Variation: Create a cinnamon tincture by soaking 4 sticks of cinnamon in a cup of vodka for approximately 2 weeks. Put the mixture in a spray bottle and spritz the cocktail glass in advance.

MAI TAI

OLD-FASHIONED

MAKES 1 DRINK

2 oz. light rum
1 oz. triple sec
1 tbs. orgeat syrup
½ oz. grenadine
1 oz. lime juice or
juice of ½ lime

Pour all of the ingredients into a shaker half filled with ice. Shake well and strain into an old-fashioned glass over ice. Garnish with slices of fruit (pineapple preferred) and a paper umbrella.

MAI TAI ME UP

MAKES 1 DRINK

1 oz. dark rum
½ oz. light rum
½ oz. 151 rum
1½ oz. pineapple
*   juice*
1½ oz. sweet-and-
*   sour mix*

Pour all the liquid ingredients into a shaker with ice. Shake well and strain into a martini glass. (Can be made for an oversized glass by adding more sweet-and-sour.) Garnish with a canned pineapple slice with a cherry in the center.

MAIDEN NO MORE

MARTINI

MAKES 1 DRINK

1½ oz. gin
½ oz. Cointreau
1 tbs. brandy
1 tsp. fine sugar
1 oz. lemon juice or
*   juice of ½ lemon*

Pour ingredients into a shaker half filled with ice. Shake well. Strain into a martini glass.

MAIDEN'S BLUSH

MARTINI

MAKES 1 DRINK

1½ oz. dark rum
1 oz. ruby red
*   grapefruit*
3 tsp. powdered
*   sugar*
1 dash bitters
juice of one lime

Squeeze juice of the lime into a shaker filled with ice. Add the other ingredients and shake well. Strain into a martini glass.

MAIDEN'S BLUSH 2

MARTINI

MAKES 1 DRINK

1½ oz. gin
½ oz. triple sec
1 tsp. cherry
*   brandy*
1 oz. lemon juice

Pour the gin, triple sec, cherry brandy, and lemon juice into a shaker half filled with ice. Shake well. Strain into a martini glass. Garnish with a cherry.

MAIDEN'S DREAM

HIGHBALL

MAKES 1 DRINK

3 oz. gin
3 oz. Pernod
1 oz. grenadine

Pour ingredients into a highball glass. Stir.

MAJOR BAILEY JULEP

HIGHBALL

MAKES 1 DRINK

1½ jiggers dry gin
1 tsp. powdered
    sugar
½ lemon
4–6 fresh mint
    leaves

Put the mint leaves into a bowl and cover them with powdered sugar. Squeeze the juice of the lemon over them. Muddle. Add the muddled mixture to a highball glass. Add the gin and fill glass with crushed ice. Stir until the glass is frosted. Garnish with more mint sprigs. Serve with a straw.

MALIBU BAY BREEZE

COLLINS

MAKES 1 DRINK

1½ oz. Malibu rum
2 oz. cranberry
    juice
2 oz. pineapple
    juice

Pour ingredients into a Collins glass over ice. Stir.

MALIBU PUNCH

MARTINI

MAKES 1 DRINK

¹/₃ oz. blue curaçao
¹/₃ oz. crème de
    banane
¹/₃ oz. Malibu rum
pineapple juice (to
    taste)
lime juice (to taste)

Pour ingredients into a shaker with ice. Shake and strain into a martini glass. Garnish with a slice of lemon or lime.

293

MAMA'S MARTINI

MARTINI

MAKES 1 DRINK

3 oz. vanilla-
   flavored vodka
½ oz. apricot
   brandy
4 dashes bitters
4 dashes lemon
   juice

Pour ingredients into a shaker with ice. Shake and strain into a chilled martini glass.

MANGO HEAT WAVE

COLLINS

MAKES 1 DRINK

2 oz. mandarin
   vodka
1 oz. Passoa
   liqueur
3 oz. mango nectar
2 oz. sweet-and-
   sour mix

Pour the vodka, Passoa liqueur, mango nectar, and sweet-and-sour mix into a blender with a cup of ice. Blend until smooth. Pour into a Collins glass. Garnish with an orange, lemon, or lime slice, and a cherry. (A slice of mango would be appropriate, when available.) Finish with a paper parasol.

MANGO MARGARITA

MARGARITA

MAKES 1 DRINK

½ cup peeled sliced
   mango
1¼ oz. tequila
½ oz. Cointreau
¼ juice of one lime
splash Chambord

Into blender, squeeze the juice of the lime. Add the mango and blend. Add the tequila and Cointreau and continue to blend. Pour into a margarita glass over ice. Add the splash Chambord. Garnish with a lime slice.

MANGO VIRGO (NONALCOHOLIC)

MARTINI

MAKES 1 DRINK

3 oz. mango
   nectar
juice of ½ lime
2 oz. half-and-
   half
star fruit

Pour the mango nectar, lime juice, and half-and-half into a shaker with ice. Shake and strain into a chilled martini glass. Garnish with a slice of star fruit.

MANGORITA

MARGARITA

MAKES 1 DRINK

½ cup peeled sliced
    mango
1¼ oz. tequila
½ oz. Cointreau
½ oz. Rose's lime
    juice

Pour ingredients into a blender with ice. Blend until slushy-smooth. Pour into a margarita glass. Garnish with a lime wedge.

MANHASSET

MARTINI

MAKES 1 DRINK

1½ oz. blended
    scotch whiskey
1½ tsp. sweet
    vermouth
1½ tsp. dry
    vermouth
1 tbs. lemon juice

Pour ingredients into a shaker with ice. Shake and strain into a martini glass.

MANHATTAN

MARTINI

MAKES 1 DRINK

2 oz. bourbon
    whiskey
1 oz. sweet
    vermouth
2 dashes bitters

Pour ingredients into a shaker with ice. Shake and strain into a martini glass to serve straight up, or into an old-fashioned glass over ice. Garnish with a cherry.

MANHATTAN COMFORT

MARTINI

MAKES 1 DRINK

2 oz. Southern
    Comfort
¾ oz. sweet
    vermouth
maraschino cherry

Pour Southern Comfort and vermouth into a shaker half filled with ice. Stir and then strain into a martini glass. Garnish with a cherry.

MANHATTAN, DRY

MAKES 1 DRINK

*2 oz. blended
  whiskey
¾ oz. dry vermouth
dash bitters*

Pour ingredients into a shaker with ice. Shake and strain into a martini glass to serve straight up, or into an old-fashioned glass over ice. Garnish with a cherry.

MANHATTAN, LATIN

MARTINI

MAKES 1 DRINK

*1 oz. rum
1 oz. dry vermouth
1 oz. sweet
  vermouth*

Pour ingredients into a shaker with ice. Shake and strain into a martini glass to serve straight up, or into an old-fashioned glass over ice. Garnish with a cherry.

MANHATTAN, MOCK (NONALCOHOLIC) MARTINI

MAKES 1 DRINK

*2 oz. orange juice
2 oz. cranberry
  juice
splash lemon
  juice
splash maraschino
  cherry juice
dash orange bitters*

Pour ingredients into a shaker with ice. Shake and strain into a martini glass to serve straight up, or into an old-fashioned glass over ice. Garnish with a cherry.

MANHATTAN, PERFECT

MARTINI

MAKES 1 DRINK

*2½ oz. blended
  whiskey
½ oz. dry vermouth
½ oz. sweet
  vermouth
dash bitters*

Pour ingredients into a shaker with ice. Shake and strain into a martini glass to serve straight up, or into an old-fashioned glass over ice. Garnish with a cherry.

MANHATTAN, SMOOTH

MARTINI

MAKES 1 DRINK

*1½ oz. Southern
   Comfort
¾ oz. dry vermouth
2 dashes bitters*

Pour ingredients into a shaker with ice. Stir and strain into a martini glass. Garnish with a cherry or a lemon twist.

MANHATTAN, SWEET

MARTINI

MAKES 1 DRINK

*2 oz. bourbon
   whiskey
1 oz. sweet
   vermouth
2 dashes bitters
maraschino cherry
   juice*

Pour ingredients into a shaker with ice. Shake and strain into a martini glass to serve straight up, or into an old-fashioned glass over ice. Finish with a splash of cherry juice. Garnish with a cherry.

MANHATTAN, TEQUILA

MARTINI

MAKES 1 DRINK

*2 oz. tequila
¾ oz. sweet
   vermouth*

Pour ingredients into a shaker with ice. Shake and strain into a martini glass to serve straight up, or into an old-fashioned glass over ice. Garnish with a cherry.

MANILA FIZZ

HIGHBALL

MAKES 1 DRINK

*2 oz. gin
2 oz. root beer
juice of ½ lemon
1 egg
1 tsp. powdered
   sugar*

Pour ingredients into a shaker with ice. Shake very well to blend egg, and strain into a highball glass over two ice cubes.

MAPLE LEAF

MARTINI

MAKES 1 DRINK

*1 oz. bourbon
    whiskey
½ oz. lemon juice
1 tsp. maple syrup*

Pour ingredients into a shaker with ice. Shake and strain into a martini glass.

MAPLE LEAF MARTINI

MARTINI

MAKES 1 DRINK

*1 oz. orange-
    flavored vodka
½ oz. vanilla-
    flavored vodka
½ oz. Cointreau
splash orange juice
splash cream*

Pour ingredients into a shaker with ice. Shake and strain into a chilled martini glass. Garnish with an orange slice.

MAPLECCINO (NONALCOHOLIC)

IRISH COFFEE

MAKES 1 DRINK

*1 oz. hot
    espresso
1 oz. maple
    syrup
3 oz. hot
    chocolate
2 oz. steamed
    milk*

Pour ingredients into an Irish coffee glass or mug. Top with whipped cream and toasted sliced almonds.

MARGARITA

MARGARITA

MAKES 1 DRINK

*1½ oz. tequila
½ oz. triple sec
1 oz. lime juice
    or the juice of
    ½ lime*

Pour ingredients into a shaker half filled with ice. Shake well and strain into a salt-rimmed margarita glass or serve on the rocks in an old-fashioned glass. Garnish with a lime wedge.

MARGARITA BLUE

MARGARITA

MAKES 1 DRINK

1½ oz. tequila
½ oz. blue curaçao
1 tsp. triple sec
1 oz. lime juice or
    juice of ½ lime

Pour ingredients into a shaker half filled with ice. Shake well and strain into a salt-rimmed margarita glass. Garnish with a lime wedge.

MARGARITA JELL-O SHOT

SHOT

MAKES 4 DRINKS

1 oz. fresh lime
    juice
1 oz. simple syrup
1 oz. water
1 package
    unflavored
    gelatin (¼ oz.)
3 oz. white tequila
2 oz. triple sec

Pour the lime juice, simple syrup, and water into a glass mixing bowl and add the gelatin. Let sit for one minute. Microwave on high for thirty seconds. Stir thoroughly, ensuring the gelatin is dissolved. Add the tequila and triple sec. Stir thoroughly. Pour into shot glasses. Refrigerate until the liquid sets. Serve cold.

MARGARITA PEACH

MARGARITA

MAKES 1 DRINK

1½ oz. tequila
1 oz. peach liqueur
1 tsp. triple sec
1 oz. lime juice or
    juice of ½ lime

Pour ingredients into a shaker half filled with ice. Shake well. Strain into a salt-rimmed margarita glass. Garnish with a lime wedge.

MARGUERITE COCKTAIL

MARTINI

MAKES 1 DRINK

1½ oz. dry gin
¾ oz. French
    vermouth
¼ tsp. curaçao
1 dash orange
    bitters

Pour ingredients into a shaker with ice. Stir well and strain into a martini glass. Garnish with an olive.

MARIONETTE

OLD-FASHIONED

MAKES 1 DRINK

1 oz. white rum
1 oz. Cherry
    Heering
1 oz. apricot brandy
1 oz. dry sake

Pour all ingredients into an old-fashioned glass. Stir gently.

MARLENE DIETRICH COCKTAIL

WINE

MAKES 1 DRINK

3 oz. rye or
    Canadian
    whiskey
2 dashes bitters
2 dashes curaçao
orange and lemon
    peels

Pour ingredients into a shaker with ice. Shake well and strain into a wine glass. Squeeze orange and lemon peels on top, and then use them as the garnish.

MARMALADE

HIGHBALL

MAKES 1 DRINK

1½ oz. curaçao
tonic water to fill

Pour ingredients into a highball glass over ice. Garnish with an orange slice.

MARTINEZ

MARTINI

MAKES 1 DRINK

1 oz. gin
¾ oz. dry vermouth
¼ oz. triple sec
1 dash orange
    bitters

Pour ingredients into a shaker with ice. Stir well and strain into a chilled martini glass. Twist the lemon peel over the drink and drop it into the glass.

MARTINI

MARTINI

MAKES 1 DRINK

2 oz. gin
¹/₈ oz. dry vermouth
*2 big pimento-
   stuffed green
   olives*

Chill the gin and dry vermouth ahead of time in a refrigerator or freezer. Pour the gin and vermouth into a shaker with ice. Shake or stir, and strain into a chilled martini glass. For a drier martini, use less vermouth (to taste). Drop the olives into the drink.

MARTINI MILANO

MARTINI

MAKES 1 DRINK

2 oz. gin
½ oz. dry vermouth
*½ oz. dry white
   wine*
1 tsp. Campari

Pour ingredients into a shaker with ice. Shake and strain into a chilled martini glass. Garnish with a lime twist.

MARTINI, CLASSIC

MARTINI

MAKES 1 DRINK

1½ oz. gin
½ oz. dry vermouth
*1 dash orange
   bitters*

Pour ingredients into a shaker with ice. Stir and strain into a martini glass. Garnish with a lemon twist.

MARTINI, JAMES BOND

MARTINI

MAKES 1 DRINK

3 oz. gin
1 oz. vodka
½ oz. Lillet

Pour ingredients into a shaker with ice. Shake and strain into a martini glass. Garnish with a lemon twist.

MARTINI, LEMON VODKA

MARTINI

MAKES 1 DRINK

2 oz. lemon vodka
3 drops Cointreau

Pour ingredients into a shaker with ice. Shake and strain into a martini glass. Garnish with a lemon twist.

MARTINI, MARITIME

MARTINI

MAKES 1 DRINK

3 oz. gin
1 oz. dry vermouth

Pour ingredients into a shaker with ice. Shake and strain into a chilled martini glass. Garnish with an anchovy-stuffed olive.

MARTINI, TEQUILA

MARTINI

MAKES 1 DRINK

2½ oz. tequila
½ oz. dry vermouth

Pour ingredients into a shaker with ice. Shake and strain into a martini glass. Garnish with an olive and a twist of lemon.

MARTINI, VODKA

MARTINI

MAKES 1 DRINK

2½ oz. vodka
½ oz. dry vermouth

Pour ingredients into a shaker with ice. Shake and strain into a martini glass. Garnish with one or two olives or a twist of lemon.

MARY PICKFORD COCKTAIL

MARTINI

MAKES 1 DRINK

1 oz. light rum
1 oz. pineapple
   juice
½ tsp. grenadine
½ tsp. maraschino
   cherry juice

Pour ingredients into a shaker half filled with ice. Shake well. Strain into a martini glass and garnish with a cherry.

MARY'S SISTER (NONALCOHOLIC)

MARTINI

MAKES 1 DRINK

1 oz. white
   grape juice
1 oz. pineapple
   juice

Pour ingredients into a shaker half filled with ice. Shake well. Strain into a martini glass and garnish with a cherry.

MARYLAND COMPROMISE JULEP

COLLINS

MAKES 1 DRINK

2 oz. rye whiskey
1½ tbs. powdered
   sugar
2 tbs. water
4–6 fresh mint
   leaves

Bruise but do not crush mint leaves. Put all ingredients into a Collins glass filled with ice. Stir until frosted and garnish with some more mint.

MASSACRE

HIGHBALL

MAKES 1 DRINK

2 oz. tequila
½ oz. Campari
4 oz. ginger ale

Pour all ingredients into a highball glass over ice. Stir well.

MAUI BREEZE

COLLINS

MAKES 1 DRINK

½ oz. Amaretto
½ oz. triple sec
½ oz. brandy
1 oz. lemon juice or
    juice of ½ lemon
1 tsp. fine sugar
2 oz. pineapple
    juice
2 oz. guava juice

Pour all ingredients into a blender with ice. Blend thoroughly. Pour into a Collins or parfait glass. Garnish with an orange, lemon, or lime slice, and a cherry.

MAUI BREEZE 2

COLLINS

MAKES 1 DRINK

½ oz. Amaretto
½ oz. triple sec
½ oz. brandy
1 oz. sweet-and-
    sour mix
2 oz. orange juice
1 oz. guava juice

Blend all ingredients with a cup of ice until smooth. Pour into a Collins or parfait glass. Garnish with a pineapple spear, a cherry, and an orchid.

MAYFLOWER COCKTAIL

MARTINI

MAKES 1 DRINK

1½ oz. sweet
    vermouth
½ oz. dry vermouth
½ oz. brandy
1 tsp. Pernod
1 tsp. triple sec
dash orange bitters

Pour ingredients into a shaker half filled with ice. Shake well and strain into a martini glass.

MCDUFF

MARTINI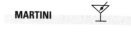

MAKES 1 DRINK

1½ oz. scotch
½ oz. triple sec
2 dashes bitters

Pour ingredients into a shaker with ice. Stir well and strain into a martini glass. Garnish with an orange slice.

MELON BALL

HIGHBALL

MAKES 1 DRINK

1 oz. vodka
2 oz. melon liqueur
4 oz. pineapple
  juice

Pour ingredients into a shaker with ice. Stir and strain into a highball or Collins glass over ice. Garnish with fruit.

MELON BALL 2

HIGHBALL

MAKES 1 DRINK

2 oz. melon liqueur
1 oz. vodka
grapefruit juice

Pour ingredients into a shaker with ice. Stir and strain into a highball glass over ice.

MELON MARVEL (NONALCOHOLIC) **COLLINS**

MAKES 1 DRINK

1 wedge
  cantaloupe,
  cubed (6 oz.)
½ cup orange
  juice
½ oz. lime juice
splash club
  soda

Pour first three ingredients into a blender without ice. Blend thoroughly. Pour into a Collins or parfait glass. Add the splash club soda. Stir well.

MELON PATCH

HIGHBALL

MAKES 1 DRINK

1 oz. melon liqueur
½ oz. triple sec
½ oz. vodka
4 oz. club soda
orange slice for
  garnish

Pour the first three ingredients into a shaker with ice. Shake well and strain into a highball glass over ice. Add the club soda. Garnish with the orange slice.

MELONLISCIOUS MISTRESS

COLLINS

MAKES 1 DRINK

1 oz. melon liqueur
1 oz. lemon-
flavored vodka
or rum
7-Up
maraschino cherry

Pour the melon liqueur and lemon-flavored vodka or rum into a Collins glass over ice. Add 7-Up to fill. Stir. Garnish with a maraschino cherry.

MELONTINI

MARTINI

MAKES 1 DRINK

½ oz. dark
chocolate
2 oz. Southern
Comfort
1 oz. crème de
noyaux
2 oz. orange juice

Melt the chocolate in a microwave. After it has cooled, dip the tip of your finger into the chocolate and make polka dots on the inside of a martini glass. Set the glass in the freezer for a minute to harden the chocolate. Pour the rest of the ingredients into a shaker with ice. Shake and strain into the polka dot martini glass.

MENAGE À TROIS

MARTINI

MAKES 1 DRINK

1 oz. light rum
1 oz. Cointreau
1 oz. light cream

Pour ingredients into a shaker half filled with ice. Shake well and strain into a martini glass.

METEORITE

IRISH COFFEE

MAKES 1 DRINK

1 oz. Sambuca
(divided into
two equal parts)
½ oz. coffee
liqueur
hot black coffee
2 spoons of sugar
lemon slice

Rub the lemon over the rim and all over the inside of an Irish coffee glass or other clear mug. Coat with the sugar. Pour half of the Sambuca into the glass and light it to caramelize the sugar. Carefully pour the rest of the Sambuca and the coffee liqueur into the glass. Add coffee to fill. Top with whipped cream.

METROPOLE

MARTINI

MAKES 1 DRINK

1½ oz. brandy
1½ oz. dry
   vermouth
2 dashes orange
   bitters
1 dash Peychaud's
   bitters

Pour ingredients into a shaker with ice. Stir and strain into a martini glass. Garnish with a cherry.

METROPOLITAN

MARTINI

MAKES 1 DRINK

1½ oz. brandy
1 oz. sweet
   vermouth
½ tsp. simple syrup
2 dashes bitters

Pour ingredients into a shaker with ice. Shake well and strain into a chilled martini glass.

METROPOLITAN 2

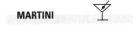
MARTINI

MAKES 1 DRINK

3 oz. black currant
   vodka (or any
   other currant
   vodka)
½ oz. Lillet (white)
½ tsp. lime juice

Pour ingredients into a shaker with ice. Shake and strain into a chilled martini glass. Garnish with a lemon twist.

MEXICAN COFFEE

IRISH COFFEE

MAKES 1 DRINK

½ oz. tequila
1 oz. coffee liqueur
1 oz. hot black
   coffee
1 oz. heavy cream

Pour coffee into an Irish Coffee glass or mug. Add the tequila and coffee liqueur. Stir well. Float the cream on top by pouring it over the back of a spoon.

MEXICAN DINGLE BERRY

SHOT

MAKES 1 DRINK

½ shot tequila rose
½ shot Chambord

Pour ingredients into a shot glass.

MEXICAN FLAG

SHOT

MAKES 1 DRINK

¹/₃ oz. green crème
de menthe
¹/₃ oz. peppermint
schnapps
¹/₃ oz. sloe gin

Pour the ingredients into a shot glass in the following order: crème de menthe, schnapps, slow gin. Layer the last two ingredients by pouring them very slowly over the back of a spoon. The result should be green, white, and red stripes, the colors of the Mexican flag.

MEXICAN FLAG 2

SHOT

MAKES 1 DRINK

½ oz. melon liqueur
½ oz. white tequila
½ oz. grenadine

Pour the ingredients into a chilled shot glass in the following order: melon liqueur, tequila, grenadine. Layer the last two ingredients by pouring them very slowly over the back of a spoon. The result should be green, white, and red stripes, the colors of the Mexican flag.

MEXICAN MADRAS

OLD-FASHIONED

MAKES 1 DRINK

1 oz. gold tequila
1 oz. orange juice
3 oz. cranberry
juice
splash lime juice

Pour ingredients into a shaker with ice. Shake well and strain into an old-fashioned glass over ice.

MEXICAN SCREW

HIGHBALL

MAKES 1 DRINK

1½ oz. tequila
orange juice

Pour ingredients into a shaker with ice. Shake and strain into a highball glass over ice. Add orange juice to fill.

MEXICANA

MARTINI

MAKES 1 DRINK

2 oz. tequila
1 oz. pineapple
  juice
½ oz. lemon juice
1 tsp. grenadine

Pour ingredients into a shaker half filled with ice. Shake well. Strain into a martini glass.

MEXICOLA

COLLINS

MAKES 1 DRINK

2 oz. tequila
cola
juice of ½ lime

Pour the tequila and cola into a Collins glass over ice. Squeeze the lime juice into the drink and stir. Garnish with a lime wedge.

MIAMI BEACH

OLD-FASHIONED

MAKES 1 DRINK

1½ oz. scotch
1 oz. dry vermouth
1½ oz. grapefruit
  juice

Pour ingredients into a shaker half filled with ice. Shake well. Strain into an old-fashioned glass over ice.

MIAMI ICE

HIGHBALL

MAKES 1 DRINK

½ oz. vodka
½ oz. peach
   schnapps
½ oz. gin
½ oz. rum
2 oz. sweet-and-
   sour mix
orange juice

Pour first five ingredients into a highball glass over ice. Add orange juice to fill. Garnish with a mint leaf and an orange slice.

MIAMI SPECIAL

MARTINI

MAKES 1 DRINK

½ oz. gin
½ oz. orange juice
½ oz. French
   vermouth
3 tsp. orange
   marmalade
2 dashes bitters

Pour ingredients into a shaker with ice. Shake 25 times or more and strain into a martini glass.

MIDNIGHT COWBOY

MARTINI

MAKES 1 DRINK

2 oz. bourbon
   whiskey
1 oz. dark rum
½ oz. heavy cream

Pour ingredients into a shaker with ice. Shake and strain into a martini glass.

MIDNIGHT EXPRESS

OLD-FASHIONED

MAKES 1 DRINK

1½ oz. dark rum
½ oz. Cointreau
¾ oz. lime juice
splash sweet-and-
   sour mix

Pour ingredients into a shaker with ice. Shake and strain into an old-fashioned glass over ice.

MIDNIGHT MARTINI

HIGHBALL

MAKES 1 DRINK

1 oz. gin
1 oz. dry vermouth

Pour ingredients into a shaker with ice. Stir and strain into a highball glass. Garnish with a black olive.

MIDORI COCKTAIL

CHAMPAGNE

MAKES 1 DRINK

3 oz. Champagne
1 oz. Midori Melon
Liqueur

Pour ingredients into a Champagne glass.

MIDORI COLADA

COLLINS

MAKES 1 DRINK

1 oz. Midori Melon
Liqueur
1 oz. light rum
2 oz. coconut
cream
4 oz. pineapple
juice

Pour all ingredients into a blender in this order: Midori, rum, coconut cream, pineapple juice, and a cup of ice. Blend thoroughly. Pour into a Collins or parfait glass. Serve with a pineapple or melon slice, a cherry, and a straw.

MIDORI MIMOSA

CHAMPAGNE

MAKES 1 DRINK

2 oz. Midori Melon
Liqueur
1 tsp. Rose's lime
juice
4 oz. Champagne,
chilled

Pour all ingredients into a Champagne flute or white wine glass. Stir gently.

MIKADO

OLD-FASHIONED

MAKES 1 DRINK

1½ oz. brandy
½ oz. triple sec
1 tsp. crème de noyaux
1 tsp. grenadine
dash bitters

Pour ingredients into an old-fashioned glass almost filled with ice cubes. Stir well.

MIKHAIL'S MARTINI

MARTINI

MAKES 1 DRINK

2 oz. coffee-flavored vodka
¼ oz. vanilla-flavored vodka

Pour ingredients into a shaker with ice. Stir and strain into a martini glass. Garnish with coffee beans.

MILD MADRAS (NONALCOHOLIC)

HIGHBALL

MAKES 1 DRINK

4 oz. cranberry juice
4 oz. orange juice
squeeze lime

Pour juices into a shaker with ice. Stir and strain into a highball glass over ice. Finish with a squeeze of lime.

MILK PUNCH

COLLINS

MAKES 1 DRINK

4 oz. bourbon whiskey
oz. milk
tsp. dark rum
tablespoon simple syrup

Pour ingredients into a shaker with ice. Shake and strain into a chilled Collins glass. Dust with nutmeg.

MILLENNIUM COCKTAIL

MARTINI

MAKES 1 DRINK

2 oz. gin
1 oz. cherry brandy
3 oz. orange juice
splash ginger ale

Pour ingredients into a shaker with ice. Shake and strain into a well-chilled martini glass.

MILLENNIUM MARTINI

MARTINI

MAKES 1 DRINK

1 oz. vodka
1 sugar cube
blue curaçao
Champagne

Soak the sugar cube in some blue curaçao. In the glass side of a shaker, pour the champagne and count to 4. Add all the other ingredients, except the sugar, and stir. Strain into a chilled martini glass. Drop in the sugar cube.

MILLION DOLLAR COCKTAIL

HIGHBALL

MAKES 1 DRINK

1 oz. gin
1 tsp. sweet
  vermouth
1 tsp. dry vermouth
½ cup pineapple
  juice
dash egg white
dash bitters

Pour ingredients into a shaker with ice. Shake vigorously to froth up the egg white. Strain into a chilled highball glass.

MILLIONAIRE

MARTINI

MAKES 1 DRINK

1¼ oz. gin
1¼ oz. Italian
  vermouth
3 tsp. grenadine
3 tsp. lime juice

Pour ingredients into a shaker with ice. Shake 20 times. Strain into a martini glass.

MIMI'S MIMOSA (NONALCOHOLIC) CHAMPAGNE

MAKES 1 DRINK

3 oz. sparkling
    white grape
    juice, chilled
3 oz. orange
    juice

Pour the orange juice into a Champagne flute until half full. Add the grape juice. Stir gently.

MIMOSA

CHAMPAGNE

MAKES 1 DRINK

fresh-squeezed
    orange juice
Champagne
strawberry half

Fill about a quarter of a Champagne glass with orange juice. Top off with Champagne. Garnish the rim with a strawberry. (Don't add the strawberry until the end, or the glass will tip over.)

MINT JULEP

COLLINS

MAKES 1 DRINK

2½ oz. bourbon
    whiskey
1 tsp. fine sugar
1 tsp. water
4 sprigs mint

Into a Collins glass, muddle the mint leaves, sugar, and water. Fill the glass with ice and add the bourbon. Garnish with mint and serve with a straw.

MINT JULEP PUNCH

PUNCH

MAKES 25 DRINKS

1 cup mint jelly
4 cups water
3½ cups bourbon
    whiskey
6 cups pineapple
    juice
¼ cup lime juice
6 cups lemon and
    lime soda

Heat the mint jelly in a saucepan with two cups of the water until the jelly melts. Let cool. Add the rest of the ingredients except the soda. Pour mixture into a punch bowl over a block of ice. Add soda and stir gently.

MINT RUSSK

MARTINI

MAKES 1 DRINK

3 oz. vodka
5 mint leaves

Prepare the vodka by storing it in the freezer overnight. Place 3 to 6 crushed fresh mint leaves into a martini glass. Add 2 to 3 oz. of the frozen vodka. Stir lightly.

MINTY-FRESH TOOTHPASTE

SHOT

MAKES 1 DRINK

¼ oz. butterscotch
schnapps
¼ oz. green crème
de menthe
¼ oz. Irish cream
liqueur
¼ oz. half-and-half

Pour the butterscotch schnapps into a shot glass. Gently pour the green crème de menthe over the back of a spoon to layer on top. Layer the Irish cream liqueur and half-and-half the same way.

MISS BELLE

MARTINI

MAKES 1 DRINK

1½ oz. dark rum
½ oz. Grand
Marnier
2 tsp. dark crème
de cacao

Pour ingredients into a shaker with ice. Shake and strain into a martini glass.

MISSION BELL

PUNCH

MAKES 30 DRINKS

16 oz. orange juice,
no pulp
2 750 ml bottles
pink Champagne
2 750 ml bottles
white dinner
wine
12 oz. brandy
1 lemon
orange slices

In a large punch bowl or pitcher, squeeze the juice of the lemon. Add the white wine, brandy, and orange juice. Stir well. When ready to serve, add the Champagne and stir gently. Float several orange slices to garnish.

MISSISSIPPI MUD

MARTINI

MAKES 1 DRINK

1½ oz. Southern
    Comfort
1½ oz. coffee
    liqueur
2 scoops of vanilla
    ice cream

Pour ingredients into a blender. Blend until smooth and pour into a martini glass. Garnish with shaved chocolate.

MOCHA MINT

MARTINI

MAKES 1 DRINK

1 oz. coffee brandy
1 oz. white crème
    de cacao
1 oz. crème de
    menthe

Pour ingredients into a shaker half filled with ice. Shake well. Strain into a martini glass.

MODERN COCKTAIL

MARTINI

MAKES 1 DRINK

1½ oz. scotch
    whiskey
1 tsp. dark rum
½ tsp. anisette
½ tsp. lemon juice
2 dashes orange
    bitters

Pour ingredients into a shaker with ice. Shake well. Strain into a martini glass.

MODEST MUDSLIDE (NONALCOHOLIC) COLLINS

MAKES 1 DRINK

1 scoop chocolate
    ice cream
1 scoop vanilla ice
    cream
1 oz. black coffee
2 spoons of Café Vienna
    (GF International
    Coffee)
1 oz. chocolate syrup
milk or half-and-
    half to blend

Put the chocolate ice cream, vanilla ice cream, coffee, Café Vienna, and chocolate syrup into a blender. Blend, adding milk or half-and-half little by little until smooth. Pour into a Collins glass.

MOJITO

MAKES 1 DRINK

2 tsp. sugar
6–8 mint leaves
club soda
1 lime, cut in half
2 oz. light rum

HIGHBALL

Pour the sugar, mint leaves, and a little club soda into a highball glass. Muddle well to dissolve the sugar and to release the mint flavor. Squeeze the juice from both halves of the lime into the glass. Drop one half of the lime into the glass. Add the rum. Stir. Fill the glass with ice. Add club soda to fill. Garnish with a mint sprig.

MOJO

MAKES 1 DRINK

3 oz. ale
1 oz. rum
1 oz. cherry brandy
2 oz. orange juice
2 oz. pineapple juice
2 oz. cola
2 oz. lemon lime soda

COLLINS

Pour all ingredients into a Collins glass filled with ice. Stir.

MOLL FLANDERS

MAKES 1 DRINK

2 oz. gin
1 oz. sloe gin
1 oz. dry vermouth
4 dashes bitters

MARTINI

Pour ingredients into a shaker with ice. Stir and strain into a chilled martini glass.

MOLLY'S MILK

MAKES 1 DRINK

1 oz. Kahlua
1 oz. brandy
4 oz. hot black coffee
2 oz. half-and-half

IRISH COFFEE

Pour into an Irish coffee glass or mug. Top with whipped cream.

MOLOTOV COCKTAIL

IRISH COFFEE

MAKES 1 DRINK

*1 quart of vanilla
 ice cream
2 cups of coffee
1 quart of vodka
½ oz. 151 proof
 rum*

Pour first three ingredients into a blender. Blend until smooth and pour a portion into an Irish coffee glass or mug. For each serving add the rum. Garnish with cinnamon or nutmeg.

MOM'S MILK

IRISH COFFEE

MAKES 1 DRINK

*½ oz. vodka
½ oz. hazelnut
 liqueur
½ oz. crème de
 cacao
6 oz. hot
 cappuccino*

Pour the liqueurs into an Irish coffee glass or mug. Add the cappuccino. Top with whipped cream.

MONACO

PINT

MAKES 1 DRINK

*½ pint of 7-Up
½ pint of lager
dash grenadine*

Pour the ingredients into a pint beer glass in this order: grenadine, 7-Up, lager.

MONK

MARTINI

MAKES 1 DRINK

*2 oz. Irish cream
 liqueur
1 oz. Frangelico
2 scoops of vanilla
 ice cream*

Pour ingredients into a blender. Blend until smooth and pour into a martini glass. Serve with a straw.

MONK'S COFFEE

IRISH COFFEE

MAKES 1 DRINK

1½ oz. Frangelico
½ oz. dark crème
   de cacao
4 oz. hot black
   coffee
2 oz. heavy cream

Pour all ingredients except the cream into a mug or Irish Coffee glass. Stir. Add the cream by pouring it over the back of a spoon so that it floats on top.

MONKEY GLAND

MARTINI

MAKES 1 DRINK

2 oz. gin
1 oz. orange juice
¼ oz. grenadine
1 dash Pernod

Pour ingredients into a shaker with ice. Shake well and strain into a chilled martini glass. Garnish with an orange slice.

MONKEY SHINE SHOOTER

SHOT

MAKES 1 DRINK

½ oz. bourbon
   liqueur
½ oz. crème de
   banane
½ oz. Irish cream
   liqueur

Pour ingredients into a shaker half filled with ice. Shake well. Strain into a shot glass.

MONKEY WRENCH

OLD-FASHIONED

MAKES 1 DRINK

1½ oz. white rum
3 oz. grapefruit
   juice
dash bitters

Combine all ingredients in an old-fashioned glass almost filled with ice cubes. Stir well.

MONONGAHELA COBBLER

COLLINS

MAKES 1 DRINK

1 tsp. icing sugar
2 oz. bourbon
*   whiskey*
orange and lemon
*   peels*

Put the sugar in a tumbler or Collins glass with some thin parings of orange and lemon peels. Fill 1/3 of the glass with ice and add bourbon. Stir.

MONT BLANC

WINE

MAKES 1 DRINK

1 oz. black
*   raspberry*
*   liqueur*
1 oz. vodka
1 oz. light cream
1 scoop of vanilla
*   ice cream*

Pour ingredients into a blender. Blend until smooth and serve in a large red wine glass.

MONTANA

OLD-FASHIONED

MAKES 1 DRINK

2 oz. brandy
1½ oz. port
½ oz. dry vermouth

Pour ingredients into an old-fashioned glass over ice. Stir.

MONTE CARLO

MARTINI

MAKES 1 DRINK

2 oz. rye whiskey
½ oz. Benedictine
2 dashes bitters

Pour ingredients into a shaker with ice. Stir and strain into a martini glass.

MONTEZUMA

CHAMPAGNE

MAKES 1 DRINK

1½ oz. tequila
1 oz. madeira
1 egg yolk

Pour ingredients into a blender with ½ cup of ice. Blend at a low speed for a few moments. Pour into a Champagne flute.

MONTMARTRE COCKTAIL

MARTINI

MAKES 1 DRINK

1¼ oz. dry gin
½ oz. sweet
  vermouth
½ oz. triple sec

Pour ingredients into a shaker with ice. Stir and strain into a martini glass. Garnish with a cherry.

MORNING COCKTAIL

MARTINI

MAKES 1 DRINK

¾ oz. brandy
¾ oz. dry vermouth
2 dashes orange
  curaçao
2 dashes maraschino
  liqueur
2 dashes orange
  bitters
2 dashes Pernod

Pour ingredients into a shaker with ice. Stir and strain into a martini glass. Garnish with a cherry and lemon twist.

MORNING GLORY

MARTINI

MAKES 1 DRINK

1 oz. brandy
½ oz. orange
  curaçao
½ oz. lemon juice
dash bitters
dash Pernod

Pour ingredients into a shaker with ice. Shake and strain into a martini glass. Garnish with a lemon twist.

MOSCOW MULE

MAKES 1 DRINK

1¾ oz. vodka
½ oz. lime juice
ginger beer

Pour the vodka and lime juice into a highball glass over ice. Add ginger beer to fill. Garnish with a lime wedge.

MOTHER TERESA (NONALCOHOLIC) COLLINS

MAKES 1 DRINK

5 oz. chai tea mix
2 scoops vanilla ice cream
milk or half-and-half

Put the chai tea mix and the vanilla ice cream into a blender. Blend on a low speed and slowly add the milk or half-and-half to reach a smooth consistency. Pour into a Collins glass and garnish with a cinnamon stick.

MOTHER-IN-LAW

MARTINI

MAKES 1 DRINK

2½ oz. bourbon
1 tsp. Cointreau
1 tsp. maraschino liqueur
1 tsp. simple syrup
2 dashes Peychaud's bitters
2 dashes bitters
2 dashes Amer Picon

Pour ingredients into a shaker with ice. Stir and strain into a martini glass. Garnish with a cherry.

MOUNT CREEK COFFEE

IRISH COFFEE

MAKES 1 DRINK

½ oz. Kahlua
½ oz. Irish cream liqueur
½ oz. Frangelico
½ oz. vodka
½ oz. cream
6 oz. hot black coffee

Pour first five ingredients into an Irish coffee glass or mug. Fill with the coffee. Top with whipped cream.

MOUNTAIN GROG

IRISH COFFEE

MAKES 1 DRINK

6 oz. hot apple cider
½ oz. brandy
½ oz. apricot brandy

Into an Irish coffee glass or large mug, pour the hot cider and brandy. Stir in the apricot brandy and top with a dash of cinnamon.

MOUNTAIN MADNESS

IRISH COFFEE

MAKES 1 DRINK

1 oz. 151 rum
1 oz. Kahlua
6 oz. hot chocolate

Pour ingredients into an Irish coffee glass or mug. Top with whipped cream.

MOUSETRAP

BEER GLASS

MAKES 1 DRINK

6 oz. Southern Comfort
2 oz. grenadine
10 oz. orange juice
sparkling wine

Pour first three ingredients into a shaker with ice. Shake and strain into a beer mug and fill with the sparkling wine.

MUDSLIDE

MARTINI

MAKES 1 DRINK

1 oz. vodka
1 oz. Irish cream liqueur
1 oz. coffee brandy

Pour ingredients into a shaker nearly filled with ice. Stir well. Strain into a martini glass.

MULLED CIDER (NONALCOHOLIC) PUNCH

MAKES 20 DRINKS

2 gallons apple
  cider
2 lemons, sliced
2 oranges, sliced
5 cinnamon sticks
1 tbs. cinnamon
1 tbs. nutmeg
6 cloves

Pour all ingredients into a large pot. Heat just to boiling. Serve hot.

MULLED CRANBERRY (NONALCOHOLIC) IRISH COFFEE

MAKES 1 DRINK

6 oz. cranberry
  juice
splash lemon
  juice
1 tsp. honey
  or more to
  taste
2 whole cloves

Pour ingredients into a saucepan and heat to a simmer. Do not boil. Stir well. Pour into an Irish coffee glass or mug. Finish with a dash of nutmeg.

MULLED WINE

IRISH COFFEE

MAKES 10 DRINKS

12 oz. port
750 ml red dinner
  wine
¼ cup lemon juice
½ cup sugar
1 tbs. cinnamon
½ tsp. ground cloves
¼ tsp. nutmeg
lemon slices

Pour all ingredients except lemon slices into the top of a double boiler. Heat for 30 minutes. Stir occasionally. Serve in warmed mugs. Add a lemon slice to each mug.

MULLED WINE 2

IRISH COFFEE

MAKES 8 DRINKS

2 bottles red wine
2 oz. sugar
2 tsp. honey
2 sliced lemons
pinch ground cloves
1 stick cinnamon
2 pinches grated
  nutmeg
1 cup water

Bring the water and sugar to a boil, then remove from heat. Add the wine, honey, cloves, and cinnamon. Reheat without boiling for 5 minutes. Pour over the sliced lemon, and top with the grated nutmeg. Serve warm.

MULLED WINE FOR ONE

IRISH COFFEE

MAKES 1 DRINK

6 oz. red wine
splash brandy
1 tbs. fine sugar
splash lemon juice
2 whole cloves
1 dash cinnamon

Pour ingredients into a saucepan and heat to a simmer. Do not boil. Stir well and pour into an Irish coffee glass or mug.

MULLIGAN'S DOWNFALL

IRISH COFFEE

MAKES 1 DRINK

1 oz. Drambuie
1 oz. Irish cream
    liqueur
6 oz. hot black
    coffee

Pour Drambuie and Irish cream into an Irish coffee glass or mug. Add coffee and stir. Top with whipped cream.

MUMBO JUMBO

OLD-FASHIONED

MAKES 1 DRINK

1½ oz. dark rum
½ oz. applejack
½ oz. lemon juice
½ tsp. superfine
    sugar
$^1/_8$ tsp. cinnamon
    (ground)
$^1/_8$ tsp. nutmeg
    (grated)

Pour ingredients into a shaker with ice. Shake well and strain into an old-fashioned glass over ice.

MUSCOVY MARTINI

MARTINI

MAKES 1 DRINK

1 oz. cinnamon
    vodka
1 oz. orange vodka
½ oz. triple sec
½ oz. orange juice

Pour ingredients into a shaker with ice. Stir and strain into a chilled martini glass. Garnish with an orange twist. Finish with a sprinkling of powdered cinnamon.

MUY BONITA RITA

MAKES 1 DRINK

½ oz. tequila
1½ oz. Licor 43
1 oz. sweet-and-sour mix
1 oz. half-and-half
lime slice and a crushed graham cracker

Rub the lime around the rim of a margarita glass, then dip the rim into a pile of the crushed graham cracker crumbs. Pour the tequila, Licor 43, sweet-and-sour mix, and half-and-half into a shaker of ice. Shake and strain into the glass. Garnish with a lime slice.

MY TYPE (NONALCOHOLIC)

OLD-FASHIONED

MAKES 1 DRINK

3 oz. orange juice
1 oz. lime juice or juice
1 tsp. fine sugar
1 tbs. orgeat syrup
½ oz. grenadine

Pour all ingredients into a shaker half filled with ice. Shake well. Strain into an old-fashioned glass half filled with ice. Garnish with an orange, lemon, or lime slice.

NADA COLADA

COLLINS

MAKES 1 DRINK

¼ oz. of rum extract
¼ oz. of vanilla extract
3 oz. pineapple juice
3 oz. coconut cream
milk or half-and-half

Pour the rum extract, vanilla extract, pineapple juice, and coconut cream into a blender with a cup of ice. Add milk or half-and-half and blend until smooth. Pour into a Collins glass. Garnish with a pineapple slice and a cherry.

NAKED LADY

HIGHBALL

MAKES 1 DRINK

1 oz. white rum
1 oz. sweet vermouth
4 dashes apricot brandy
2 dashes grenadine
4 dashes lemon juice

Pour ingredients into a shaker with ice. Shake and strain into a highball glass.

NAKED MARTINI

MARTINI

MAKES 1 DRINK

3 oz. gin

Pour the gin into a chilled martini glass and leave in the freezer until well-chilled. Garnish with an olive and serve immediately.

NANTUCKET

HIGHBALL

MAKES 1 DRINK

2 oz. white brandy
1 oz. cranberry juice
1 oz. grapefruit juice

Pour ingredients into a highball glass and garnish with a lime slice.

NAPOLEON

WINE

MAKES 1 DRINK

2 oz. gin
2 dashes Dubonnet
2 dashes curaçao
2 dashes Fernet Branca

Pour ingredients into a shaker with ice. Shake and strain into a wine glass. Garnish with a lemon twist.

NAPOLEON 2

MARTINI

MAKES 1 DRINK

2 oz. gin
½ oz. Dubonnet Rouge
½ oz. Grand Marnier

Pour ingredients into a shaker with ice. Stir and strain into a martini glass.

NARRAGANSETT

OLD-FASHIONED

MAKES 1 DRINK

2 oz. bourbon
1 oz. sweet
* vermouth*
dash anisette

Pour ingredients into an old-fashioned glass nearly filled with ice. Stir. Add a lemon twist.

NASHVILLE EGGNOG

PUNCH

MAKES ABOUT 10 DRINKS

4 cups of eggnog
6 oz. bourbon
* whiskey*
3 oz. brandy
3 oz. Jamaican rum

Pour ingredients into a punch bowl and stir. Serve in punch cups; sprinkle each cup with nutmeg.

NEAPOLITAN SHOOTER SUNDAE

SHOT

MAKES 1 DRINK

1/3 dark crème de
* cacao*
1/3 vanilla
* schnapps*
1/3 strawberry-
* flavored vodka*
drop of red food
* coloring*

Pour the dark crème de cacao into a shot glass. Gently add the vanilla schnapps over the back of a spoon to form a layer. Stir the red food coloring into the strawberry-flavored vodka, then layer it next. Top with whipped cream and a cherry.

NEGRONI

MARTINI

MAKES 1 DRINK

1½ oz. gin
1½ oz. sweet
* vermouth*
1½ oz. Campari

Pour ingredients into a shaker with ice. Stir and strain into a martini glass. Garnish with an orange slice.

NETHERLAND

MAKES 1 DRINK

1 oz. triple sec
1 oz. brandy
dash bitters

Pour all ingredients into an old-fashioned glass over ice cubes. Stir well.

NEVA

MARTINI

MAKES 1 DRINK

1½ oz. pepper
   vodka
½ oz. tomato juice
½ oz. orange juice

Pour ingredients into a shaker with ice. Shake and strain over ice into a martini glass.

NEVADA COCKTAIL

MARTINI

MAKES 1 DRINK

1½ oz. light rum
1½ oz. grapefruit
   juice
1 oz. lime juice or
   juice of ½ lime
3 tsp. fine sugar
dash bitters

Pour ingredients into a shaker with ice. Shake and strain into a martini glass.

NEVINS

MARTINI

MAKES 1 DRINK

2 oz. bourbon
½ oz. apricot
   brandy
½ oz. grapefruit
   juice
1 tsp. lemon juice
dash bitters

Pour ingredients into a shaker with ice. Shake well and strain into a martini glass.

NEW ORLEANS

OLD-FASHIONED

MAKES 1 DRINK

2 oz. bourbon
*   whiskey*
½ oz. Pernod
dash anisette
dash bitters
dash orange bitters
1 tsp. fine sugar

Pour ingredients into a shaker half filled with ice. Shake well. Strain into an old-fashioned glass over ice. Serve with a lemon twist.

NEW ORLEANS FIZZ

COLLINS

MAKES 1 DRINK

juice of ½ lime
juice of ½ lemon
2 dashes orange
*   flower water*
1 tsp. sugar
1 oz. sweetened
*   cream*
2 oz. gin
1 egg white

Pour ingredients into a shaker with ice. Shake very well and strain into a Collins glass.

NEW YORK

MARTINI

MAKES 1 DRINK

1½ oz. blended
*   whiskey*
1 oz. lemon juice or
*   juice of ½ lemon*
1 tsp. fine sugar
½ tsp. grenadine

Pour ingredients into a shaker half filled with ice. Shake well. Strain into a martini glass. Garnish with a lemon twist.

NEW YORK COCKTAIL

MARTINI

MAKES 1 DRINK

2 oz. blended
*   whiskey*
1 oz. lemon juice
1 tsp. superfine
*   sugar*
½ tsp. grenadine

Pour ingredients into a shaker with ice. Shake well and strain into a chilled martini glass. Garnish with the lemon twist.

NEW YORK SOUR

MAKES 1 DRINK

2 oz. blended
   scotch whiskey
juice of ½ lemon
1 tsp. sugar
claret

Pour the scotch, lemon juice, and powdered sugar into a shaker with ice. Shake and strain into a sour glass. Float claret on top. Garnish with a half-slice of lemon and a cherry.

NEWBURY

MARTINI

MAKES 1 DRINK

3 oz. gin
1 oz. sweet
   vermouth
½ oz. triple sec

Pour ingredients into a shaker with ice. Shake and strain into a chilled martini glass. Garnish with a lemon twist.

NIAGARA FALLS

HIGHBALL

MAKES 1 DRINK

2 oz. vodka
2 oz. Mandarine
   Napoleon
1½ oz. sweet-and-
   sour mix
splash ginger ale

Pour ingredients into a highball glass.

NICKY FINN

MARTINI

MAKES 1 DRINK

1 oz. brandy
1 oz. Cointreau
1 oz. lemon juice or
   juice of ½ lemon
dash Pernod

Pour ingredients into a shaker with i
Stir and strain into a martini glass.

NIGHT CAP

MAKES 1 DRINK

2 oz. light rum
1 tsp. fine sugar
warm milk

Pour ingredients into an Irish coffee glass or mug. Stir. Sprinkle with nutmeg.

NIGHT LIGHT

MARTINI

MAKES 1 DRINK

1 oz. white rum
½ oz. orange
*   curaçao*
1 egg yolk

Pour ingredients into a shaker with ice. Shake and strain into a martini glass.

NIGHT OF PASSION (NONALCOHOLIC)   WINE

MAKES 1 DRINK

2 oz. passion fruit
*   juice*
1 oz. orange juice
1 oz. pineapple
*   juice*
2 tbs. cream
1 egg yolk
dash club soda

Pour ingredients into a shaker half filled with ice. Shake well. Strain into a wine glass over ice. Serve with a straw.

NIGHTMARE

MARTINI

MAKES 1 DRINK

2 oz. gin
1 oz. Madeira
½ oz. cherry brandy
1 tbs. orange juice

Pour ingredients into a shaker half filled with ice. Shake well. Strain into a martini glass.

NINETEENTH HOLE

MAKES 1 DRINK

1½ oz. gin
1 oz. dry vermouth
1 tsp. sweet
  vermouth
dash bitters

Pour ingredients into a shaker with ice. Stir and strain into a martini glass. Garnish with an olive.

NINOTCHKA

MARTINI

MAKES 1 DRINK

3 oz. vanilla vodka
1 oz. chocolate
  liqueur
½ oz. lemon juice

Pour ingredients into a shaker with ice. Shake and strain into a chilled martini glass.

NINOTCHKA COCKTAIL

MARTINI

MAKES 1 DRINK

2 oz. vodka
½ oz. lemon juice
½ oz. crème de
  cacao

Pour ingredients into a shaker with ice. Shake well and strain into a chilled martini glass.

NON EGGNOG (NONALCOHOLIC)

HIGHBALL

MAKES 1 DRINK

1 egg
¼ tsp. almond
  extract
¼ tsp. vanilla
  extract
1 tbs. fine
  sugar
6 oz. milk

Pour ingredients into a shaker with ice. Shake well and strain into a highball glass without ice. Sprinkle with nutmeg.

NORTHERN LIGHTS

MAKES 30 DRINKS

46 oz. white
    grapefruit juice
2 750 ml bottles
    brut Champagne
12 oz. blue curaçao
lemon sherbet
1 orange, sliced

Pour grapefruit juice and curaçao into a large pitcher or punch bowl. Stir well. When ready to serve, add the sherbet, fruit, and Champagne.

NOT CHAMPAGNE PUNCH (NONALCOHOLIC)

MAKES ABOUT 20 DRINKS

1 cup fine sugar
1 cup water
2 cups grapefruit
    juice
juice of 1 lemon
1½ quarts ginger
    ale

In a punch bowl, dissolve the sugar in the water. Add the grapefruit and lemon juices. Add the ginger ale just before serving.

NUTCRACKER

HIGHBALL

MAKES 1 DRINK

2 oz. vodka
2 oz. Kahlua
2 oz. Irish cream
    liqueur
2 oz. Amaretto

Pour ingredients into a shaker with ice. Shake and strain into a highball glass.

NUTTY COLADA

COLLINS

MAKES 1 DRINK

3 oz. Amaretto
2 oz. coconut
    cream
3 oz. pineapple
    juice

Pour ingredients into a blender with ice. Blend thoroughly. Pour into a Collins or parfait glass. Serve with a straw.

NUTTY IRISHMAN

IRISH COFFEE 📫

MAKES 1 DRINK

1 oz. Irish cream
1 oz. Frangelico
6 oz. hot black
  coffee

Pour liqueur into an Irish coffee glass or mug. Add coffee and stir.

NUTTY MARTINI

MARTINI 🍸

MAKES 1 DRINK

3 oz. vodka
½ oz. Frangelico

Pour ingredients into a shaker with ice. Shake and strain into a chilled martini glass. Garnish with a lemon twist.

NUTTY NEW GIRL IN SCHOOL   **MARTINI** 🍸

MAKES 1 DRINK

3 oz. Coco Lopez
juice from 1 lime
spoonful of honey
shredded coconut

Prep a martini glass by dipping the rim into honey then into the shredded coconut to create a fun coconut rim. Pour the Coco Lopez and lime juice into a shaker tin of ice. Shake, then strain into a martini glass. Chill the glass in the freezer to add a nice touch.

NYQUIL

MAKES 1 DRINK

3 oz. triple sec
1½ oz. Sambuca
1½ oz. grenadine

Pour ingredients into an old-fashioned glass. Stir.

OAKLAND COCKTAIL

MARTINI

MAKES 1 DRINK

2 oz. vodka
1 oz. dry vermouth
1 oz. orange juice

Pour ingredients into a shaker with ice. Shake and strain into a chilled martini glass.

OBITUARY COCKTAIL

MARTINI

MAKES 1 DRINK

2 oz. gin
¼ oz. dry vermouth
¼ oz. pastis

Pour ingredients into a shaker with ice. Stir and strain into a martini glass.

OCTOPUS

SNIFTER

MAKES 1 DRINK

1 shot light rum
    151
1 shot orange juice
1 shot passion fruit
    nectar
dash bitters
club soda

Pour all ingredients except the club soda into a large snifter. Fill with finely crushed ice. Top with soda and stir.

OL' DIRTY BASTARD

OLD-FASHIONED

MAKES 1 DRINK

2 oz. Southern
    Comfort
2 oz. Captain
    Morgan's spiced
    rum
1 oz. Absolut vodka
½ oz. Coca-Cola

Pour ingredients over ice into an old-fashioned glass. Stir.

OLD COUNTRY MARTINI

MARTINI

MAKES 1 DRINK

3 oz. vodka
1 oz. Madeira
1 oz. cherry brandy

Pour ingredients into a shaker with ice. Stir and strain into a chilled martini glass. Garnish with an orange twist.

OLD CUBAN

MARTINI

MAKES 1 DRINK

¾ oz. fresh lime juice
1 oz. simple syrup
1½ oz. rum
2 dashes bitters
6 mint leaves
2 oz. Champagne

Muddle lime juice, syrup, and mint in the bottom of a glass shaker. Add rum, bitters, and ice. Shake well and strain into a martini glass. Top with the Champagne. Garnish with a sugar-coated vanilla bean.

OLD PAL

MARTINI

MAKES 1 DRINK

1 oz. rye or bourbon whiskey
¾ oz. dry vermouth
¾ oz. Campari

Pour ingredients into a shaker with ice. Stir and strain into a martini glass. Garnish with a lemon twist.

O

OLD-FASHIONED

OLD-FASHIONED

MAKES 1 DRINK

1 sugar cube
2–3 dashes bitters
2 orange slices
2 oz. bourbon
½ oz. club soda

Place the sugar cube at the bottom of an old-fashioned glass. Saturate the cube with the bitters. Add one orange slice. Muddle these ingredients. Fill the glass with ice. Add the bourbon and the club soda. Stir well. Garnish with the second orange slice.

OLYMPIA

MARTINI

MAKES 1 DRINK

2½ oz. dark rum
½ oz. cherry brandy
½ oz. lime juice

Pour ingredients into a shaker with ice. Shake and strain into a martini glass.

OLYMPIC COCKTAIL

MARTINI

MAKES 1 DRINK

¾ oz. brandy
¾ oz. triple sec
¾ oz. orange juice

Pour ingredients into a shaker with ice. Shake and strain into a martini glass.

ONE-ARMED BANDIT

COLLINS

MAKES 6 TO 8 DRINKS

750 ml dry white wine
6 oz. Cointreau
2 oranges
½ lime
½ lemon
4–5 dashes grenadine

Pour the white wine with the Cointreau into a large pitcher. Squeeze the juice of the oranges, lime, and lemon into the pitcher. Add grenadine for color. Garnish with cherries and sliced citrus. Serve in Collins glasses filled with ice.

OPAL MARTINI

MARTINI

MAKES 1 DRINK

3 oz. gin
½ oz. triple sec
1 oz. orange juice
¼ tsp. sugar

Pour ingredients into a shaker with ice. Shake and strain into a chilled martini glass.

OPERA MARTINI

MAKES 1 DRINK

2 oz. gin
½ oz. Dubonnet
¼ oz. maraschino
liqueur
1 dash orange
bitters

Pour ingredients into a shaker with ice. Stir and strain into a martini glass. Garnish with a lemon twist.

ORANGE BLOSSOM

MAKES 1 DRINK

1½ oz. gin
½ oz. orange juice
2 dashes lime juice
2 dashes simple
syrup

Pour ingredients into a shaker with ice. Shake and strain into a martini glass. Garnish with a small twist of orange peel.

ORANGE BLOSSOM SPECIAL

MAKES 1 DRINK

1 oz. peach
schnapps
2½ oz. lemon lime
soda
3 oz. sherbet
(orange)
1½ oz. vanilla ice
cream
2½ oz. light cream

Pour ingredients into a blender. Blend with 6 ice cubes until smooth. Pour into a parfait glass. Garnish with a cherry and an orange slice.

ORANGE BUCK

MAKES 1 DRINK

1½ oz. gin
2 oz. orange juice
1 oz. lime juice or
juice of ½ lime
ginger ale

Pour all ingredients except ginger ale into a shaker half filled with ice. Shake well. Strain into a Collins or highball glass over ice. Garnish with a lime slice.

ORANGE CRUSH SHOOTER

SHOT

MAKES 1 DRINK

¾ oz. vodka
¾ oz. triple sec
splash club soda

Pour ingredients into a shaker with ice. Stir and strain into a shot glass.

ORANGE DROP

SHOT

MAKES 1 DRINK

1 shot orange
    vodka
1 orange slice
Pixie Stix

Add the vodka to a shaker of ice and swirl to chill. Strain into a shot glass. Empty the Pixie Stix stick onto an orange slice. Down the shot and bite the orange.

ORANGE FIZZ (NONALCOHOLIC)

WINE

MAKES 1 DRINK

2 oz. orange
    juice
2 oz. sparkling
    white grape
    juice
lime wedge

Pour all ingredients except the lime into a large wine glass over ice. Squeeze the lime wedge over the drink and drop it in.

ORANGE MARTINI

MARTINI

MAKES 1 DRINK

3 oz. vodka
½ oz. triple sec
dash orange bitters

Pour ingredients into a shaker with ice. Shake and strain into a chilled martini glass. Garnish with an orange twist.

ORANGE REVOLUTION

COLLINS

MAKES 1 DRINK

2 cups ice
½ oz. Grand Marnier
½ oz. white curaçao
½ oz. triple sec
1 oz. gin
1½ oz. orange juice

Pour ingredients into a blender. Blend until smooth. Pour into a Collins glass. Garnish with an orange slice.

ORGASM

HIGHBALL

MAKES 1 DRINK

1½ oz. vodka
1½ oz. triple sec
splash lime juice
½ tsp. fine sugar
club soda or 7-Up

In a highball glass, dissolve the sugar in the lime juice. Nearly fill glass with ice. Add the vodka, triple sec, and soda. Stir.

ORGASM SHOOTER

SHOT

MAKES 1 DRINK

½ oz. Irish cream
½ oz. peppermint schnapps

Layer ingredients in a shot glass.

OVER THE RAINBOW

PARFAIT

MAKES 1 DRINK

2 oz. spiced rum
1 oz. orange curaçao
2 scoops of sherbet (rainbow)
4 slices of peach (peeled)
2 strawberries

Pour ingredients into a blender. Blend with a cup of ice until smooth. Pour into a parfait glass. Garnish with a strawberry and a slice of peach.

OYSTER MARTINI

MAKES 1 DRINK

3 oz. vodka
½ oz. dry vermouth

Pour ingredients into a shaker with ice. Shake and strain into a chilled martini glass. Garnish with a smoked oyster on a toothpick.

PADDY COCKTAIL

MARTINI

MAKES 1 DRINK

1¼ oz. Irish
  whiskey
1¼ oz. Italian
  vermouth
1 dash bitters

Pour ingredients into a shaker with ice. Stir well and strain into a martini glass.

PAINKILLER

COLLINS

MAKES 1 DRINK

1 oz. coconut
  cream
1 oz. orange juice
4 oz. pineapple
  juice
2 oz. rum

Combine all ingredients into a Collins glass over ice. Top with fresh nutmeg.

PALACE PATRIA

MAKES 1 DRINK

1½ oz. Bacardi
  Limon rum
2 tablespoons
  sugar cane syrup
3 sprigs mint
2 tablespoons fresh
  squeezed lemon-
  lime juice
splash club soda

Place sugar, mint, and lemon-lime juice into a highball glass. Muddle lightly. Add the rum and stir. Add ice to fill. Top with a splash club soda. Garnish with a spear of sugar cane.

P

PALL MALL

OLD-FASHIONED

MAKES 1 DRINK

1½ oz. gin
½ oz. sweet
   vermouth
½ oz. dry vermouth
½ oz. white crème
   de cacao

Pour all ingredients into an old-fashioned glass over ice. Stir.

PALL MALL MARTINI

MARTINI

MAKES 1 DRINK

2 oz. gin
½ oz. dry vermouth
½ oz. sweet
   vermouth
1 tsp. white crème
   de menthe
dash orange bitters

Pour ingredients into a shaker with ice. Stir and strain into a chilled martini glass.

PALM BEACH COCKTAIL

MARTINI

MAKES 1 DRINK

1½ oz. gin
1 tsp. sweet
   vermouth
2 oz. grapefruit
   juice

Pour ingredients into a shaker half filled with ice. Shake well. Strain into a martini glass.

PALM BEACH MARTINI

MARTINI

MAKES 1 DRINK

3 oz. gin
1 tsp. sweet
   vermouth
2 oz. grapefruit
   juice

Pour ingredients into a shaker with ice. Shake and strain into a chilled martini glass.

P

PALM BREEZE

MAKES 1 DRINK

1 oz. vodka
1½ oz. peach
*   schnapps*
orange juice
Blue Hawaiian
*   Punch*

Pour vodka and schnapps into a highball glass. Fill with equal amounts of orange juice and Hawaiian Punch.

PANZERWAGEN

MARTINI

MAKES 1 DRINK

½ oz. vodka
½ oz. gin
½ oz. Cointreau

Pour ingredients into a shaker with ice. Stir and strain into a martini glass. Serve with almonds and green olives.

PAPA BEAR'S BLACK HONEY

IRISH COFFEE

MAKES 1 DRINK

1½ oz. Drambuie
honey
hot black coffee

Pour the Drambuie into an Irish coffee glass or mug and fill with coffee. Stir in a spoonful of honey to taste. Top with whipped cream.

PARADISE SHOOTER

SHOT

MAKES 1 DRINK

½ oz. apricot
*   brandy*
½ oz. orange juice
½ oz. Plymouth gin

Pour ingredients into a shaker with ice. Shake well and strain into a shot glass.

PARADISE UNDER A COCONUT TREE TIKI

MAKES 1 DRINK

2 oz. coconut rum
1 oz. light rum
3 oz. coconut cream
3 oz. pineapple
  juice
2 oz. half-and-half
¼ oz. vanilla extract
coconut

Pour ingredients into a blender. Blend until smooth. Pour into a tiki glass. You can also make a coconut cup by cutting the top off a coconut. (You'll need a hacksaw or an electric band saw.)

PARISIAN

MARTINI

MAKES 1 DRINK

1½ oz. gin
1½ oz. dry
  vermouth
½ oz. crème de
  cassis

Pour ingredients into a shaker with ice. Stir and strain into a martini glass. Garnish with a lemon twist.

PARISIAN BLONDE SHOOTER SHOT

MAKES 1 DRINK

½ oz. light rum
½ oz. triple sec
½ oz. dark rum

Pour ingredients into a shaker half filled with ice. Shake well. Strain into a shot glass.

PARK AVENUE

MARTINI

MAKES 1 DRINK

1½ oz. gin
¼ oz. dry vermouth
¼ oz. sweet
  vermouth
¼ oz. unsweetened
  pineapple juice

Pour ingredients into a shaker with ice. Stir well and strain into a chilled martini glass.

PARK AVENUE MARTINI

MARTINI

MAKES 1 DRINK

3 oz. gin
½ oz. sweet vermouth
½ oz. dry vermouth

Shake with cracked ice and strain into a chilled martini glass.

PARTY GIRL

HIGHBALL

MAKES 1 DRINK

1½ oz. dry vermouth
1 tbs. gin
½ oz. crème de cassis

Pour ingredients into a highball glass. Stir.

PASSION COCKTAIL

MARTINI

MAKES 1 DRINK

2 oz. gold tequila
3 oz. cranberry juice
1 oz. lime juice
2 oz. Grand Marnier

Pour first three ingredients into a shaker with ice. Shake well and strain into a chilled martini glass. Add the Grand Marnier. Garnish with a slice of lime.

PASSION CUP

WINE

MAKES 1 DRINK

2 oz. vodka
2 oz. orange juice
1 oz. passion fruit juice
½ oz. coconut cream

Pour ingredients into a shaker with ice. Shake well and strain into a large wine glass. Garnish with a cherry.

PASSION PUNCH

HIGHBALL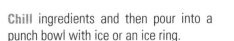

MAKES 1 DRINK

1 oz. spiced rum
1 oz. passion fruit
*   liqueur*
2 oz. pineapple
*   juice*
2 oz. orange juice
dash grenadine

Pour rum, juice, and grenadine into a highball glass. Stir well. Top with the passion fruit liqueur.

PASSIONATE MARTINI

MARTINI

MAKES 1 DRINK

1½ oz. light rum
1 oz. lime juice or
*   juice of ½ lime*
½ oz. passion fruit
*   syrup*

Pour ingredients into a shaker half filled with ice. Shake well. Strain into a martini glass.

PASSIONATE SCREW

MARTINI

MAKES 1 DRINK

4 oz. vodka
4 oz. passion fruit
*   juice*
5 oz. orange juice
2 dashes bitters

Pour ingredients into a shaker with ice. Shake and strain into a martini glass.

PATRIOTIC PUNCH

PUNCH

MAKES ABOUT 25 DRINKS

1 liter vodka
2 quarts grapefruit
*   juice*
2 quarts cranberry
*   juice*

Chill ingredients and then pour into a punch bowl with ice or an ice ring.

PAUL BUNYAN BUTTERBALL

OLD-FASHIONED

MAKES 1 DRINK

1½ oz. Irish cream
1½ oz. butterscotch
schnapps

Pour simultaneously over ice into an old-fashioned glass. Serve with a wrapped butterscotch candy on the side.

PAUL BUNYAN COCOA

IRISH COFFEE

MAKES 1 DRINK

6 oz. hot chocolate
1½ oz. butterscotch
schnapps

Pour ingredients into an Irish coffee glass or mug. Top with whipped cream and sprinkle with crushed bits of a Butterfinger candy bar. (The candy bits simulate wood chips.)

PEACH BUNNY

CORDIAL

MAKES 1 DRINK

1 oz. peach-
flavored brandy
¾ oz. white crème
de cacao
¾ oz. light cream

Pour ingredients into a shaker half filled with ice. Shake well. Strain into a cordial glass.

PEACH COBBLER

IRISH COFFEE

MAKES 1 DRINK

1¼ oz. peach
schnapps
6 oz. hot apple
cider

Pour ingredients into an Irish coffee glass or mug. Top with whipped cream.

PEACH FUZZ

OLD-FASHIONED

MAKES 1 DRINK

*1½ oz. peach
   schnapps
1½ oz. cranberry
   juice*

Pour ingredients into a shaker with ice. Shake and strain into an old-fashioned glass.

PEACHES AND CREAM

OLD-FASHIONED

MAKES 1 DRINK

*2 oz. peach liqueur
2 oz. light cream*

Pour ingredients into a shaker half filled with ice. Shake well. Strain into an old-fashioned glass over ice.

PEACHES AND CREAM 2

MARTINI

MAKES 1 DRINK

*¾ oz. Amaretto
¾ oz. peach
   schnapps
1 cup crushed ice
1 scoop vanilla ice
   cream*

Pour ingredients into a blender. Blend until smooth and frothy. Pour into a large martini glass.

PEACHES AND CREAMTINI

MARTINI

MAKES 1 DRINK

*1½ oz. orange-
   flavored vodka
1½ oz. peach
   schnapps
2 oz. orange juice
splash half-and-
   half*

Pour ingredients into a shaker with ice. Shake and strain into a martini glass. (Mandarin-flavored vodka works, too.)

PEACHES AT THE BEACHES COLLINS

MAKES 1 DRINK

*2 oz. peach
  schnapps
1 oz. light rum
5 oz. orange juice
½ oz. grenadine
1 peach*

Pour the peach schnapps, light rum, orange juice, grenadine, and half of the peach into a blender with a cup of ice. Blend until smooth. Add more orange juice if needed. Pour into a Collins glass. Garnish with slices of remaining peach half and a paper parasol.

PEACHY MARTINI MARTINI

MAKES 1 DRINK

*3 oz. strawberry-
  flavored vodka
1 oz. peach brandy*

Pour ingredients into a shaker with ice. Shake and strain into a chilled martini glass. Garnish with a lemon twist.

PEAK'S PEACH SNIFTER

MAKES 1 DRINK

*¾ oz. vodka
¾ oz. peach
  schnapps
¾ oz. Amaretto
4 oz. club soda
splash orange juice*

Put ¼ cup crushed ice into a snifter. Add the liqueurs and fill with the club soda. Finish with a splash of orange juice. Garnish with a peach slice.

PEANUT BUTTER & JELLY SHOOTER SHOT

MAKES 1 DRINK

*¾ oz. Frangelico
¾ oz. Chambord*

Pour ingredients into a shot glass.

PEANUT BUTTER CUP

HURRICANE

MAKES 1 DRINK

1 oz. Kahlua
1 oz. Frangelico
1 oz. Irish cream
　liqueur
milk

Pour ingredients into a shaker with ice. Shake and strain into a hurricane glass over ice.

PEAR MARGARITA

MARGARITA

MAKES 1 DRINK

1 whole canned
　Bartlett pear
1 oz. silver tequila
½ oz. triple sec
½ oz. Rose's lime
　juice
1½ oz. sweet-and-
　sour mix

Pour ingredients into a blender with ice. Blend until smooth. Pour into a margarita glass. Garnish with a lime slice.

PEAR PHERO MOAN

CHAMPAGNE

MAKES 1 DRINK

1 oz. pear schnapps
½ oz. pear nectar
dry Champagne

Pour the pear schnapps and pear nectar into a Champagne flute. Add the Champagne to fill. Stir gently. Garnish with a strawberry.

PEGU

MARTINI

MAKES 1 DRINK

2 oz. gin
1 oz. orange
　curaçao
1 tsp. lime juice
1 dash bitters
1 dash orange
　bitters

Pour ingredients into a shaker with ice. Stir and strain into a martini glass.

PEPPERMINT MOJITO FRAPPE

MAKES 1 DRINK

2 oz. white rum
4 oz. brut
 Champagne
½ lime, cut into
 wedges
3 sprigs fresh mint
1 tbs. sugar

Muddle the sugar, mint, and lime with two or three ice cubes in a cocktail shaker until everything is well crushed. Add the rum. Shake well (until frothy) and strain into a flute, making sure to get some of the crushed mint leaves in the cocktail. Top with the Champagne.

PEPPERMINT PATTY

MAKES 1 DRINK

1½ oz. white crème
 de menthe
1½ oz. white crème
 de cacao

Pour ingredients into a shaker with ice. Shake and strain into an old-fashioned glass.

PEPPERMINT PATTY 2 IRISH COFFEE

MAKES 1 DRINK

1 oz. peppermint
 schnapps
6 oz. hot chocolate

Pour the hot chocolate and peppermint schnapps into an Irish coffee glass or mug. Top with whipped cream and a cherry.

PEPPERMINT PATTY SHOOTER SHOT

MAKES 1 DRINK

½ oz. crème de
 cacao
½ oz. peppermint
 schnapps
1 oz. cream

Pour ingredients into a shaker with ice. Stir well and strain into a shot glass.

PEPPERMINT STICK

CHAMPAGNE

MAKES 1 DRINK

1 oz. peppermint
    schnapps
1½ oz. white crème
    de cacao
1 oz. light cream

Pour ingredients into a shaker with ice.
Shake and strain into a Champagne flute.

PEPPERTINI

OLD-FASHIONED

MAKES 1 DRINK

1½ oz. pepper
    vodka
½ oz. dry vermouth

Pour ingredients into a shaker with ice.
Shake and strain into an old-fashioned
glass. Garnish with an olive.

PERSONAL PUNCH (NONALCOHOLIC)   **PUNCH**

MAKES 20 DRINKS

10 oz. frozen
    strawberries
2 cups orange juice
2 cups pineapple
    juice
1 12-oz. can of frozen
    juice concentrate
3 cups water
2 bottles sparkling
    water

Thaw the strawberries and purée
them in a blender. Pour all ingredients except the sparkling water into
a punch bowl over ice. Add the sparkling water just before serving. Garnish with fruit.

PETER'S PLUNGE

OLD-FASHIONED

MAKES 1 DRINK

1 shot Southern
    Comfort
½ shot cherry
    brandy
½ shot apricot
    brandy
2 oz. pineapple
    juice
2 oz. cranberry juice

Pour ingredients into a shaker with ice.
Shake and strain into an old-fashioned
glass over ice.

PETIT ZINC

MAKES 1 DRINK

1 oz. vodka
½ oz. Cointreau
½ oz. sweet
vermouth
½ oz. orange juice
(fresh-squeezed
Seville oranges;
if not available,
add ¼ oz. lemon
juice)

Pour ingredients into a shaker with ice. Shake and strain into a martini glass. Garnish with a wedge of orange.

PICADILLY MARTINI

MAKES 1 DRINK

3 oz. gin
1 oz. dry vermouth
½ tsp. Pernod
dash grenadine

Pour ingredients into a shaker with ice. Stir and strain into a chilled martini glass.

PICON CREMAILLERE

MAKES 1 DRINK

1½ oz. gin
¾ oz. Amer Picon
¾ oz. Dubonnet
1 dash orange
bitters

Pour ingredients into a shaker with ice. Stir and strain into a martini glass.

PIKE'S PEAK COOLER

MAKES 1 DRINK

½ lemon
1 tsp. powdered
sugar
1 egg
hard cider

Pour lemon juice, powdered sugar, and egg into a shaker with ice. Shake well and strain into a Collins glass. Add hard cider to fill. Garnish with orange and lemon twists.

PIMM'S COCKTAIL

COLLINS

MAKES 1 DRINK

2 oz. Pimm's No.1
*3 oz. lemon-lime
soda*

Pour the Pimm's and the soda into a Collins glass over ice. Garnish with a lemon twist and a cucumber slice.

PIMM'S RANGOON

COLLINS

MAKES 1 DRINK

2 oz. Pimm's No. 1
3 oz. ginger ale

Pour the Pimm's and the ginger ale into a Collins glass over ice. Garnish with a lemon twist and a cucumber slice.

PIMM'S ROYAL

COLLINS

MAKES 1 DRINK

2 oz. Pimm's No.1
3 oz. Champagne

Pour the Pimm's and Champagne into a Collins glass over ice. Garnish with a lemon twist and a cucumber slice.

PIÑA COLADA

PARFAIT

MAKES 1 DRINK

2 oz. light rum
*2 oz. coconut
cream*
*4 oz. pineapple
juice*

Pour these ingredients into a blender in this order: rum, coconut cream, juice, and about a cup of ice. Blend thoroughly. Pour into a parfait glass. Serve with a pineapple slice, a cherry, and a straw.

PIÑA COLADA ROYAL

PARFAIT

MAKES 1 DRINK

3 oz. white rum
2 oz. coconut rum
3 oz. pineapple
  (crushed)
1 scoop of vanilla
  ice cream

Pour ingredients into a blender with about a cup of ice. Blend until thick and smooth. (Add additional ice if necessary.) Pour into a parfait glass. Garnish with a cherry on top.

PINEAPPLE CONNECTION

COLLINS

MAKES 1 DRINK

¾ oz. rum
½ oz. crème de
  banane
¾ oz. Grand
  Marnier
4 oz. pineapple
  juice
4 oz. cranberry
  juice

Pour ingredients into a shaker with ice. Shake and strain and serve in a Collins glass over lots of ice.

PINEAPPLE COOLER

COLLINS

MAKES 1 DRINK

½ tsp. powdered
  sugar
2 oz. club soda
2 oz. dry white
  wine
ginger ale

Pour sugar and 2 oz. of club soda into a Collins glass. Fill with ice. Add the wine. Fill with ginger ale. Garnish with a lemon peel spiral.

PINEAPPLE FIZZ

HIGHBALL

MAKES 1 DRINK

2 oz. light rum
1 oz. pineapple
  juice
1 tsp. fine sugar
club soda

Pour rum, juice, and sugar into a shaker with ice. Shake well and strain into a highball glass over ice. Add the club soda to fill. Garnish with a lemon twist.

PINEAPPLE GRANDE

OLD-FASHIONED

MAKES 1 DRINK

1½ oz. bourbon
whiskey
½ oz. Amaretto
splash pineapple
juice

Pour ingredients into an old-fashioned glass over ice.

PINEAPPLE LEAP

COLLINS

MAKES 1 DRINK

1¼ oz. tequila
2 oz. pineapple
juice
juice of ¼ lemon
¼ oz. grenadine

Pour ingredients into a shaker with ice. Shake well and strain into a Collins glass over ice.

PINEAPPLE MARGARITA

MARGARITA

MAKES 1 DRINK

½ cup fresh
pineapple
1¼ oz. tequila
½ oz. triple sec
½ oz. orange juice

Pour ingredients into a blender with ice. Blend until smooth. Pour into a margarita glass with salted or sugared rim. Garnish with a lime wedge.

PINEAPPLE MIST

MARTINI

MAKES 1 DRINK

2 oz. light rum
3 oz. pineapple
juice

Pour ingredients into a blender. Blend thoroughly and pour into a martini glass. Garnish with a cherry.

PINEAPPLE SPARKLER (NONALCOHOLIC) WINE

MAKES 1 DRINK

4 oz. pineapple
juice
1 tsp. fine sugar
club soda or
sparkling
water

Pour juice and sugar into a shaker half filled with ice. Shake well. Strain into a wine glass. Add soda to fill. Garnish with a lemon or lime wedge.

PINEAPPLE TWIST (NONALCOHOLIC) MARTINI

MAKES 1 DRINK

4 oz. pineapple
juice
1 oz. lemon
juice or juice
of ½ lemon
2 oz. orange
juice or juice
of ½ orange

Pour juices into a blender with ice and blend thoroughly. Pour into a martini glass and garnish with a cherry.

PINK CADILLACTINI MARTINI

MAKES 1 DRINK

1 oz. vanilla vodka
½ oz. Galliano
½ oz. white crème
de cacao
$^1/_8$ oz. grenadine
3 oz. half-and-half
or milk

Pour ingredients into a shaker with ice. Shake until cold and frothy, then strain into a martini glass.

PINK CREOLE MARTINI

MAKES 1 DRINK

1½ oz. white rum
1 tbs. lime juice
1 tsp. grenadine
1 tsp. light cream

Pour ingredients into a shaker with ice. Shake and strain into a martini glass. Garnish with a black cherry soaked in rum.

PINK DAIQUIRI

CHAMPAGNE

MAKES 1 DRINK

3 oz. white label rum
1 oz. lime juice
½ oz. grenadine

Pour ingredients into a shaker with crushed ice. Shake vigorously. Pour without straining into a Champagne glass. Serve with a short straw.

PINK GIN

MARTINI

MAKES 1 DRINK

1½ oz. gin
3–4 dashes bitters

Pour ingredients into a shaker with ice. Shake well and strain into a chilled martini glass.

PINK GIN MARTINI

MARTINI

MAKES 1 DRINK

4 oz. gin
1 tsp. bitters

Pour the bitters into a martini glass and swirl it around until the inside of the glass is completely coated. Add the gin and serve. (Do not chill.)

PINK LADY

MARTINI

MAKES 1 DRINK

2 oz. gin
1 tsp. cherry brandy
1 tsp. grenadine
1 tsp. light cream
1 egg white

Pour ingredients into a shaker half filled with ice. Shake well. Strain into a martini glass.

PINK LADY 2

MARTINI

MAKES 2 DRINKS

2 oz. gin
1 oz. apple brandy
1 oz. lemon or lime juice
½ oz. grenadine
1 egg white (for each 2 drinks)

Pour the juice, grenadine, and egg white into a shaker with ice. Shake thoroughly. Add half the liquor, and shake again. Add the remaining liquor, and shake once more. Strain into two martini glasses.

PINK LEMONADE

OLD-FASHIONED

MAKES 1 DRINK

1½ oz. citrus vodka
½ oz. Chambord Raspberry Liqueur
2 oz. sweet-and-sour mix

Pour ingredients into a shaker with ice. Shake and pour over ice in an old-fashioned glass.

PINK MONKEY

PARFAIT

MAKES 1 DRINK

¾ oz. strawberry liqueur
¾ oz. banana liqueur
¾ cup fresh strawberries
½ banana
1 cup crushed ice
1 scoop strawberry ice cream

Pour ingredients into a blender. Blend until smooth. Serve in a parfait glass topped with whipped cream and a strawberry.

PINK PANTHER

COLLINS

MAKES 1 DRINK

1 cup crushed ice
1 oz. Amaretto
1 oz. vodka
8 oz. pineapple juice
1 tsp. grenadine

Pour ingredients into a blender. Blend well and pour into a chilled Collins glass. Garnish with an umbrella, a pineapple slice, and a cherry.

PINK PINEAPPLE (NONALCOHOLIC) COLLINS

MAKES 1 DRINK

4 oz. pineapple
   juice
3 oz. cherry
   soda

Pour ingredients into a highball or Collins glass over ice. Mix slightly. Garnish with an orange, lemon, or lime slice, and a cherry.

PINK SQUIRREL MARTINI

MAKES 1 DRINK

1½ oz. crème de
   noyaux
1 oz. white crème
   de cacao
1 oz. light cream

Pour ingredients into a shaker half filled with ice. Shake well. Strain into a martini glass.

PINK SWEET CHAMPAGNE

MAKES 10 DRINKS

5 oz. pink
   grapefruit juice
10 oz. grapefruit
   vodka
750 ml chilled
   sparkling wine

Pour the grapefruit juice and vodka into a punch bowl. Add the sparkling wine. Serve in Champagne flutes.

PINK VALENTINE PUNCH CHAMPAGNE

MAKES ABOUT 15 DRINKS

1 bottle
   Champagne,
   chilled
1 bottle rosé wine
10 oz. frozen
   strawberries,
   thawed
¼ cup fine sugar

Pour sugar and strawberries (with their juice) into a punch bowl. Stir to dissolve the sugar. Add the wine and Champagne. Serve in glasses or Champagne flutes.

PIRATE'S FLOAT

COLLINS

MAKES 1 DRINK

1½ oz. spiced rum
1½ oz. root beer
    schnapps
cola

Pour rum and root beer into a Collins glass over ice. Add the cola to taste.

PISCO SOUR

CHAMPAGNE

MAKES 1 DRINK

2 oz. Pisco
1 oz. lime juice
¼ oz. simple syrup
½ egg white
1 dash bitters

Pour ingredients into a shaker with ice. Shake and strain into a Champagne flute. Top with a dash bitters.

PISTON BULLY

IRISH COFFEE

MAKES 1 DRINK

6 oz. hot black
    coffee
1 oz. Kahlua
1 oz. Grand Marnier

Pour ingredients into an Irish coffee glass or mug. Top with whipped cream.

PLANTER'S PUNCH

HIGHBALL

MAKES 1 DRINK

2 oz. light rum
1 oz. dark rum
1 oz. lime juice
1 oz. lemon juice
2 oz. orange juice
1 oz. pineapple
    juice
1 dash triple sec
1 dash grenadine

Pour all ingredients except the triple sec and grenadine into a shaker half filled with ice. Shake well. Pour into a highball glass nearly filled with ice. Top with the triple sec and grenadine. Garnish with slices of orange and pineapple, wedges of lemon and lime, and a cherry.

PLANTER'S PUNCH (NONALCOHOLIC) HIGHBALL

MAKES 1 DRINK

1 tsp. Rose's lime
   juice
1 tsp. lemon juice
3 oz. orange juice
2 oz. pineapple juice
1 oz. grapefruit juice
1 tsp. powdered
   sugar
1 dash grenadine

Pour all ingredients except grenadine into a shaker half filled with ice. Shake well. Pour into a highball glass nearly filled with ice. Top with grenadine. Garnish with slices of orange and pineapple, wedges of lemon and lime, and a cherry.

PLAYMATE MARTINI

MAKES 1 DRINK

½ oz. apricot
   brandy
½ oz. brandy
½ oz. Grand
   Marnier
½ oz. orange juice
1 egg white
dash bitters

Pour ingredients into a shaker with ice. Shake and strain into a martini glass.

PLAZA MARTINI MARTINI

MAKES 1 DRINK

1 oz. gin
1 oz. dry vermouth
1 oz. sweet
   vermouth

Pour ingredients into a shaker with ice. Shake and strain into a chilled martini glass.

POCAHONTAS NUTS & BERRIES OLD-FASHIONED

MAKES 1 DRINK

1 oz. Frangelico
1 oz. Chambord
half-and-half or
   milk

Pour the Frangelico and Chambord in an old-fashioned glass over ice. Add half-and-half or milk to fill. (May also be shaken with ice and strained into a martini glass.)

POET'S DREAM

MAKES 1 DRINK

¾ oz. gin
¾ oz. dry vermouth
¾ oz. Benedictine

Pour ingredients into a shaker with ice. Stir and strain into a martini glass. Garnish with a lemon twist.

POINSETTIA

CHAMPAGNE

MAKES 1 DRINK

3 oz. Champagne
   (chilled)
1 oz. triple sec
3 oz. cranberry
   juice

Pour ingredients into a Champagne glass and stir well.

POISON ARROW

HIGHBALL

MAKES 1 DRINK

1 oz. vodka
1 oz. light rum
¼ oz. melon liqueur
¼ oz. blue curaçao
splash pineapple
   juice

Pour ingredients into a shaker with ice. Stir and strain into a chilled highball glass filled with crushed ice.

POKER COCKTAIL

MARTINI

MAKES 1 DRINK

1 oz. sweet
   vermouth
½ oz. light rum

Pour ingredients into a shaker with ice. Stir and strain into a chilled martini glass. Garnish with a lime slice.

POLAR BEAR

MARTINI

MAKES 1 DRINK

1 oz. vodka
1 oz. lime juice
2 oz. Sprite

Pour ingredients over ice into a martini glass. Stir.

POLYNESIAN PEPPER POT

HIGHBALL

MAKES 1 DRINK

1½ oz. vodka
1 oz. dark rum
4 oz. pineapple
*   juice*
½ oz. orgeat syrup
4 dashes Tabasco
*   sauce*
dash curry powder

Pour ingredients except curry powder into a shaker half filled with ice. Shake well. Strain into a highball glass. Sprinkle curry powder on top. Serve with a straw.

POMME FIZZ

CHAMPAGNE

MAKES 1 DRINK

1½ oz. vermouth
½ oz. apple juice
*   concentrate*
2 oz. Champagne
apple chips

Put the vermouth and apple syrup into a shaker half-filled with ice and shake vigorously. Strain the mixture into a Champagne glass. Add Champagne to fill. Garnish with an apple chip.

POMPANO

MARTINI

MAKES 1 DRINK

1 oz. gin
½ oz. dry vermouth
1 oz. grapefruit
*   juice*

Pour ingredients into a shaker with ice. Shake and strain into a martini glass.

PORT WINE COCKTAIL

MAKES 1 DRINK

2 oz. ruby port
dash brandy

Pour ingredients into a shaker with ice. Stir and strain into a martini glass. Garnish with a lemon twist.

POUSSE-CAFÉ

MAKES 1 DRINK

anisette (50 proof):
17.8
crème de noyaux
(50 proof): 17.7
crème de menthe
(60 proof): 15.9
crème de banane
(50 proof): 15.0
coffee liqueur
(50 proof): 14.2
cherry liqueur
(48 proof): 12.7
parfait amour
(50 proof): 12.7
blue curaçao
(60 proof): 11.7
blackberry liqueur
(50 proof): 11.2
apricot liqueur
(58 proof): 10.0
orange curaçao
(60 proof): 9.8
triple sec (60 proof):
9.8
coffee-flavored brandy
(70 proof): 9.0
peach-flavored brandy
(70 proof): 7.0
cherry-flavored brandy
(70 proof): 6.8
apricot-flavored brandy
(70 proof): 6.6
Rock & Rye liqueur
(60 proof): 6.5
ginger-flavored brandy
(70 proof): 6.4
peppermint schnapps
(60 proof): 5.2
Kummel (78 proof): 4.2
peach liqueur
(60 proof): 4.1
sloe gin (60 proof): 4.0

This rainbow cocktail is a dazzling combination of colored liqueurs layered in a tall glass. The trick to making it properly is to know the specific gravity or weight of each liqueur (listed for each, after the proof), and to pour them carefully, from heaviest to lightest, over the back of a spoon. When you do it right, the liqueurs will float on top of each other and form distinct layers. You can use virtually any combination of the liqueurs listed to achieve this result.

POWDER HOUND

IRISH COFFEE

MAKES 1 DRINK

1 oz. Irish cream
1 oz. Grand Marnier
6 oz. hot black
coffee

Serve in an Irish coffee glass or mug. Top with whipped cream.

POWDER HOUSE COCKTAIL

SNIFTER

MAKES 1 DRINK

2½ oz. half-and-
half
1¼ oz. Frangelico

Pour ingredients into an espresso frothing pitcher and steam until foamy. Pour into a snifter. Garnish with a sprinkle of nutmeg and chocolate.

POWDER PIG

OLD-FASHIONED

MAKES 1 DRINK

1 shot butterscotch
schnapps
1 shot Irish cream
2–4 oz. half-and-
half

Pour into an old-fashioned glass over ice. Top with a sprinkle of nutmeg.

PRAIRIE FIRE SHOOTER

SHOT

MAKES 1 DRINK

1½ oz. tequila
Tabasco sauce to
taste

Pour ingredients into a shaker with ice. Stir and strain into a shot glass.

PREAKNESS

MAKES 1 DRINK

1½ oz. blended
whiskey
½ oz. Benedictine
1 tsp. brandy
dash bitters

Pour ingredients into a shaker half filled with ice. Shake well. Strain into a martini glass. Garnish with a lemon twist.

PRETTY MARTINI

MARTINI

MAKES 1 DRINK

2 oz. vodka
½ oz. Grand
Marnier
½ oz. Amaretto
½ oz. dry vermouth

Pour ingredients into a shaker with ice. Shake and strain into a chilled martini glass. Garnish with an orange twist.

PRINCE EDWARD

MAKES 1 DRINK

1½ oz. scotch
whiskey
½ oz. Lillet
½ oz. Drambuie

Pour ingredients into a shaker half filled with ice. Shake well. Strain into an old-fashioned glass. Garnish with an orange slice.

PRINCE EDWARD MARTINI

MARTINI

MAKES 1 DRINK

3 oz. gin
½ oz. Drambuie

Pour ingredients into a shaker with ice. Shake and strain into a chilled martini glass. Garnish with a lemon twist.

PRINCE'S SMILE

MARTINI

MAKES 1 DRINK

1½ oz. gin
1 oz. apple brandy
1 oz. apricot brandy
1 tsp. lemon juice

Pour ingredients into a shaker half filled with ice. Shake well. Strain into a martini glass.

PROPER LADY (NONALCOHOLIC)

HIGHBALL

MAKES 1 DRINK

¼ cup melon, cut up
5 oz. grapefruit juice
1 tsp. lemon juice

Pour the melon, lemon juice, and 1 oz. of the grapefruit juice into a blender without ice. Blend well. Pour into a highball glass over ice. Add grapefruit juice and stir thoroughly.

PROSERPINE'S REVENGE

MARTINI

MAKES 1 DRINK

1 oz. white crème de menthe
1 oz. cognac

Pour the crème de menthe into a martini glass. Float cognac on the liqueur by pouring it slowly over the back of a spoon. Serve with a short straw.

PROSPECTOR'S TODDY

SNIFTER

MAKES 1 DRINK

¾ oz. Cruzan rum
¾ oz. macadamia nut liqueur
dash honey
5 oz. hot water

Pour all ingredients into a brandy snifter and stir gently. Garnish with a lemon slice.

PSYCHO TSUNAMI

SHOT

MAKES 1 DRINK

½ oz. blue curaçao
½ oz. fresh lime
* juice*
½ oz. tequila
2 dashes Tabasco
* sauce*

Pour ingredients into a shot glass. Allow Tabasco to settle before drinking.

PUCCINI

WINE

MAKES 1 DRINK

2 oz. mandarin
* orange juice,*
* fresh squeezed*
4 oz. sparkling
* white wine*

Run the mandarin juice through a sieve to strain out the pulp. Pour the strained juice with the wine into a wine glass.

PUMPKIN PIE

MARTINI

MAKES 1 DRINK

½ oz. Irish cream
* liqueur*
½ oz. butterscotch
* schnapps*
scoop vanilla ice
* cream*
dash hot damn
* schnapps*

Pour ingredients into a blender. Blend until smooth and pour into a large martini glass.

PUNT

SHOT

MAKES 2 DRINKS

2 oz. tequila
2 oz. vodka
2 tsp. sugar
juice of 1 lemon
soda water or
* seltzer*
hard lemon candy

Pour the lemon juice, sugar vodka, and tequila into a shaker with ice. Stir and strain into two sugar-rimmed shot glasses. Top with seltzer. Drinkers sit up straight and try to drop candy from their mouth into the shooter.

PURE POLYNESIAN (NONALCOHOLIC) HIGHBALL

MAKES 1 DRINK

4 oz. pineapple
   juice
½ oz. orgeat syrup
1 oz. lemon juice
4 dashes Tabasco
   sauce
dash curry powder

Pour ingredients except the curry powder into a shaker half filled with ice. Shake well and strain into a highball glass. Sprinkle curry on top. Serve with a straw.

PURPLE HOOTER   MARTINI

MAKES 1 DRINK

1½ oz. vodka
1 oz. raspberry
   liqueur
1 oz. pineapple
   juice
1 oz. sweet-and-
   sour mix

Pour ingredients into a shaker with ice. Shake and strain into a martini glass.

PURPLE JESUS   PUNCH

VARYING

1 part ginger ale
1 part grape juice
1 part vodka
1 part grain alcohol
   (188 proof)

Pour all ingredients into a punch bowl. Stir.

PURPLE PANTIES   COLLINS

MAKES 1 DRINK

2 oz. vodka
1 oz. triple sec
1 oz. pineapple
   juice
1 oz. grape juice
seltzer

Pour the first four ingredients into a shaker with ice. Shake and strain into a Collins glass over ice. Add seltzer to fill. Garnish with a lime slice.

PURPLE PYTHON SHOOTER
SHOT

MAKES 1 DRINK

½ oz. sloe gin
½ oz. vodka
½ oz. raspberry
    liqueur

Pour ingredients into a shaker with ice. Shake and strain into a shot glass.

PUSH
COLLINS

MAKES 1 DRINK

½ oz. apricot
    brandy
½ oz. Amaretto
3 oz. pineapple
    juice
Champagne

Pour brandy, Amaretto, and pineapple juice into a shaker with ice. Shake and strain into Collins glass over ice. Add Champagne to fill. Garnish with a lime slice and a cherry.

PUSSER'S PAINKILLER
TIKI

MAKES 1 DRINK

2 oz. Pusser's rum
    (95 proof)
4 oz. unsweetened
    pineapple juice
1 oz. orange juice
1 oz. coconut
    cream

Pour ingredients into a shaker with ice. Shake and strain into an ice-filled tiki mug. Garnish with ground nutmeg, cinnamon, a pineapple stick, and an orange slice.

PUSSYFOOT (NONALCOHOLIC)
COLLINS

MAKES 1 DRINK

1 tbs. lemon
    juice
2 tbs. lime juice
6 tbs. orange
    juice
1 egg yolk
cold sparkling
    water

Pour juices, powdered sugar, and egg yolk in a cocktail shaker with ice. Shake vigorously to thoroughly blend the yolk. Strain into a chilled Collins glass. Add the sparkling water to fill. Stir gently. Garnish with the orange slice.

PYTHON

SHOT

MAKES 1 DRINK

½ shot Jack
  Daniel's whiskey
½ shot tequila
Tabasco

Put 10 to 15 dashes of Tabasco sauce into a chilled shot glass. Top with the tequila and whiskey.

Q

QUAKER'S COCKTAIL

MARTINI

MAKES 1 DRINK

¾ oz. white rum
¾ oz. brandy
juice of ¼ lemon
2 tsp. raspberry
  syrup

Pour ingredients into a shaker with ice. Shake and strain into a martini glass.

QUARTERBACK SACK

SHOT

MAKES 4 DRINKS

2 oz. gin
2 oz. vodka
1 oz. triple sec
4 oz. Bloody Mary
  mix
splash tonic water

Pour all ingredients except tonic water into a shaker with ice. Strain into four shot glasses. Add tonic water to fill.

QUARTERDECK MARTINI

MARTINI

MAKES 1 DRINK

3 oz. berry vodka
½ oz. maraschino
  liqueur
½ oz. grapefruit
  juice

Pour ingredients into a shaker with ice. Stir and strain into a chilled martini glass. Garnish with a mint sprig.

QUEBEC

MARTINI

MAKES 1 DRINK

*1½ oz. Canadian
  whiskey
½ oz. dry vermouth
1½ tsp. Amer Picon
1½ tsp. maraschino
  liqueur*

Pour ingredients into a shaker half filled with ice. Shake well. Strain into a martini glass.

QUEEN BEE

MARTINI

MAKES 1 DRINK

*1 oz. coffee brandy
1½ oz. lime vodka
½ oz. cream sherry*

Pour ingredients into a shaker with ice. Shake and strain into a martini glass.

QUEEN ELIZABETH

MARTINI

MAKES 1 DRINK

*1 oz. Benedictine
2 oz. sweet
  vermouth*

Pour ingredients into a shaker half filled with ice. Shake well and strain into a martini glass.

QUEEN ELIZABETH MARTINI

MARTINI

MAKES 1 DRINK

*3 oz. gin
½ oz. dry vermouth
2 tsp. Benedictine*

Pour ingredients into a shaker with ice. Shake and strain into a chilled martini glass.

QUEEN OF SCOTS

MARTINI 🍸

MAKES 1 DRINK

1 tsp. sugar
2 tsp. water
1 tsp. lemon juice
2 oz. scotch
½ tsp. green
  Chartreuse
½ tsp. blue curaçao

Pour ingredients into a shaker with ice. Shake and strain into a martini glass.

QUEEN'S COUSIN

WINE 🍷

MAKES 1 DRINK

1 oz. vodka
1 oz. Grand Marnier
½ oz. Cointreau
splash lime juice
dash bitters
3 oz. sparkling
  white wine

Pour ingredients except wine into a shaker half filled with ice. Shake well. Strain into a large wine glass. Add wine and stir.

QUEENS

MARTINI 🍸

MAKES 1 DRINK

½ oz. gin
½ oz. dry vermouth
½ oz. sweet
  vermouth
½ oz: pineapple
  juice

Pour ingredients into a shaker with ice. Shake and strain into a martini glass.

QUICK FIX

COLLINS ▯

MAKES 1 DRINK

½ lemon or lime
1 tsp. powdered
  sugar
1 tsp. water
2½ oz.
  Jägermeister

Squeeze the lemon or lime into a Collins glass. Add the sugar and water and stir. Fill glass with ice. Add the Jägermeister and stir well. Serve with a slice of lemon and a straw.

QUICKIE

MAKES 1 DRINK

1 oz. bourbon
1 oz. rum
dash triple sec

Pour ingredients into a shaker with ice. Shake and strain into an old-fashioned glass over ice, or straight.

QUIET PASSION (NONALCOHOLIC) COLLINS

MAKES 1 DRINK

3 oz. white
   grape juice
3 oz. grapefruit
   juice
1 oz. passion
   fruit juice

Pour ingredients into a shaker half filled with ice. Shake well and strain into a Collins or highball glass over ice.

RAGIN' CAJUN MARDI GRAS PUNCH PUNCH

MAKES 20 DRINKS

1 bottle (750ml)
   chilled citrus-
   flavored vodka
2 40-oz. bottles
   chilled grape juice
2 48-oz. cans chilled
   pineapple juice
1 2-liter bottle
   chilled ginger ale
green seedless
   grapes, frozen

First, make an ice ring by doing the following: fill half a ring mold with some of the grape juice, freeze, fill with pineapple juice, and freeze again. Now, string the grapes on the fishing line to make "beads." Pour the vodka, remaining grape and pineapple juice, and ginger ale into a punch bowl. Place the ice ring and the string of grapes in the bowl.

RAGTIME

MARTINI

MAKES 1 DRINK

1 oz. coffee liqueur
1 oz. brandy
1 oz. half-and-half

Pour ingredients into a shaker with ice. Shake and strain into a martini glass. Garnish with coffee beans.

RAMOS FIZZ

COLLINS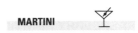

MAKES 1 DRINK

*2 dashes orange
    flower water
juice of ½ lemon
2 oz. gin
1 oz. cream
1 egg white
seltzer*

Pour ingredients into a shaker with ice. Shake well and strain into a Collins glass over ice. Add seltzer to fill.

RAMOS GIN FIZZ

WINE

MAKES 1 DRINK

*1½ oz. dry gin
½ oz. lemon juice
½ oz. lime juice
2 tbs. cream
1 egg white
¼ oz. seltzer
1 tbs. powdered sugar
3 to 4 dashes orange
    flower water*

Pour ingredients into a shaker with ice. Shake well for at least one minute to create a foamy consistency. Strain into a wine glass and top with the club soda.

R

RANGER COCKTAIL

MARTINI

MAKES 1 DRINK

*¹/₃ oz. white rum
¹/₃ oz. gin
¹/₃ oz. lemon juice
1 tsp. sugar*

Pour ingredients into a shaker with ice. Shake and strain into a martini glass.

RASPBERRY CHEESECAKE

PARFAIT

MAKES 1 DRINK

*1 tbs. cream cheese
    (softened)
1 oz. white crème
    de cacao
1 oz. black
    raspberry liqueur
2 scoops of vanilla
    ice cream*

Pour ingredients into a blender. Blend with ½ cup of ice until smooth. Pour into a parfait glass.

RASPBERRY CLOUD (NONALCOHOLIC) WINE

MAKES 1 DRINK

¼ cup rasp-
berries, fresh
or frozen
1 oz. milk
1 tbs. honey

Put the berries into a blender and blend well. Add milk, honey, and 2 ice cubes. Blend until smooth. Pour into a large wine glass.

RASPBERRY MARGARITA MARGARITA

MAKES 1 DRINK

½ cup fresh
raspberries
1¼ oz. tequila
½ oz. Cointreau
½ oz. orange juice
1½ oz. sweet-and-
sour mix

Pour ingredients into a blender with ice. Blend until smooth and pour into a margarita glass. Garnish with a slice of lime.

RASPBERRY MARTINI MARTINI

MAKES 1 DRINK

1½ oz. raspberry
vodka
¾ oz. Chambord
Raspberry
Liqueur
splash cranberry
juice
splash sweet-and-
sour mix

Shake or stir ingredients in a shaker with ice until well chilled. Strain into a martini glass. Garnish with a raspberry.

RASPBERRY PUNCH (NONALCOHOLIC) PUNCH

MAKES 20 DRINKS

2 qts. cranberry-
raspberry drink
1 qt. raspberry
soda, chilled
10 oz. frozen rasp-
berries, thawed,
with juice
1 qt. raspberry
sherbet

Pour all ingredients except soda into a punch bowl over ice. Stir well. Add a block of ice or ice ring to chill. Add soda just before serving.

RASPBERRY ROMANCE

COLLINS

MAKES 1 DRINK

1 oz. black
raspberry
liqueur
1 oz. coffee liqueur
1½ oz. Irish cream
liqueur
club soda

Pour liqueurs into a Collins or parfait glass over ice. Stir. Add club soda to fill. Stir again gently.

RASPBERRY TRUFFLE

MARTINI

MAKES 1 DRINK

2 oz. Irish cream
½ oz. coffee liqueur
½ oz. crème de
cacao
½ oz. raspberry
liqueur
½ oz. Grand Marnier
milk (to taste)

Pour ingredients into a shaker with ice. Shake and strain into a martini glass over ice.

RATTLER

MARTINI

MAKES 1 DRINK

1½ oz. gold tequila
3 oz. grapefruit
juice
splash triple sec
juice of ¼ lime

Pour ingredients into a shaker with ice. Shake and strain into a martini glass. Garnish with a lime wedge.

RATTLESNAKE

MARTINI

MAKES 1 DRINK

2 oz. blended
whiskey
1 tsp. Pernod
½ oz. lemon juice
1 tsp. fine sugar

Pour ingredients into a shaker half filled with ice. Shake well. Strain into a martini glass.

RATTLESNAKE COCKTAIL

MARTINI

MAKES 1 DRINK

1½ oz. blended
    scotch whiskey
1 tsp. lemon juice
¼ tsp. Anis
½ tsp. powdered
    sugar
1 egg white

Pour ingredients into a shaker with ice. Shake and strain into a martini glass.

REBEL PUNCH

PUNCH

MAKES 25 DRINKS

1 pint brandy
1 pint bourbon whiskey
1 quart club soda
1 12-oz. can pineapple
    juice concentrate
¼ cup fresh lemon
    juice
2 oz. grenadine
2 bottles sparkling rosé

Pour all ingredients except the sparkling rosé and chill. Pour over ice into a punch bowl. Add the wine just before serving.

REBEL YELL

OLD-FASHIONED

MAKES 1 DRINK

2 oz. bourbon
    whiskey
½ oz. triple sec
1 oz. lemon juice
1 egg white

Pour ingredients into a shaker with ice. Shake well and strain into an old-fashioned glass. Garnish with an orange slice.

RED APPLE SUNSET (NONALCOHOLIC)

MARTINI

MAKES 1 DRINK

3 oz. apple juice
1 oz. grapefruit
    juice
4 dashes
    grenadine

Pour ingredients into a shaker half filled with ice. Shake well. Strain into a martini glass.

RED CLOUD

MARTINI

MAKES 1 DRINK

1½ oz. gin
½ oz. apricot
brandy
1 tbs. lemon juice
1 tsp. grenadine

Pour ingredients into a shaker with ice. Shake and strain into a martini glass.

RED DEATH

MARTINI

MAKES 1 DRINK

½ oz. vodka
½ oz. Southern
Comfort
½ oz. Amaretto
½ oz. sloe gin
½ oz. triple sec
orange juice

Pour ingredients into a shaker with ice. Shake and strain into a martini glass. Serve cold.

RED DOG MARTINI

MARTINI

MAKES 1 DRINK

3 oz. vodka
½ oz. ruby port
2 tsp. lime juice
1 tsp. grenadine

Pour ingredients into a shaker with ice. Shake and strain into a chilled martini glass. Garnish with a lime twist.

RED HEADED TART

OLD-FASHIONED

MAKES 1 DRINK

¾ oz. Jägermeister
¾ oz. peach
schnapps
1½ oz. cranberry
juice

Pour ingredients into a shaker with ice. Shake and strain into an old-fashioned glass.

RED RUSSIAN

OLD-FASHIONED

MAKES 1 DRINK

*1 oz. strawberry
    liqueur
1 oz. vodka
½ oz. cream*

Pour ingredients into a shaker half filled with ice. Shake well. Strain into an old-fashioned glass over ice.

RED SNAPPER

MARTINI

MAKES 1 DRINK

*1 oz. light rum
1 oz. cream
¾ oz. Galliano
1 dash grenadine*

Pour ingredients into a shaker with ice. Shake well and strain into a chilled martini glass.

RED SNAPPER 2

COLLINS

MAKES 1 DRINK

*1 oz. Amaretto
1 oz. Crown Royal
cranberry juice*

Pour the Amaretto and Crown Royal into a Collins glass over ice. Add cranberry juice to fill.

RED SWIZZLE

COLLINS

MAKES 1 DRINK

*1 lime
1 tsp. powdered sugar
2 oz. carbonated
    water
2 dashes bitters
2 oz. bourbon whiskey
1 tbs. grenadine
fill carbonated water*

Squeeze the juice of the lime into a Collins glass. Add sugar and 2 oz. of carbonated water and stir. Fill the glass with ice and stir thoroughly. Add the bitters, grenadine, and bourbon. Fill with carbonated water. Serve with a swizzle stick in glass.

RED, WHITE, AND BLUE SHOOTER   SHOT

MAKES 1 DRINK

¹/₃ oz. blue curaçao
¹/₃ oz. grenadine
¹/₃ oz. peach
   schnapps

Pour the grenadine into a shot glass. Float the peach schnapps on top of the grenadine and the blue curaçao on top of the peach schnapps by pouring them slowly over the back of a spoon.

REDCOAT   MARTINI

MAKES 1 DRINK

1½ oz. light rum
½ oz. vodka
½ oz. apricot
   brandy
½ oz. lime juice
1 tsp. grenadine

Pour ingredients into a shaker with ice. Shake and strain into a martini glass.

REESE'S PEANUT BUTTER CUP   MARTINI

MAKES 1 DRINK

1½ oz. vodka
1½ oz. Cocoribe
2 scoops of vanilla
   ice cream
2 tbs. peanut
   butter (chunky)
2 tbs. chocolate
   syrup

Pour ingredients into a blender. Blend until smooth and pour into a martini glass. Drink with a straw.

REGGAE   COLLINS

MAKES 1 DRINK

2 oz. vodka
½ oz. crème de
   banane
1 oz. orange juice
1 oz. pineapple juice
1 oz. grapefruit juice
1 tsp. grenadine
dash bitters

Pour all ingredients into a shaker half filled with ice. Shake well. Strain into a Collins or highball glass nearly filled with ice. Garnish with an orange, lemon, or lime slice, and a cherry.

REHYDRATOR

COLLINS

MAKES 1 DRINK

2 oz. lime mix
2 oz. lemon mix
2 oz. club soda or
*   seltzer*
splash orange juice
splash grapefruit
*   juice*
1–3 drops bitters

Pour ingredients into a shaker with ice. Shake well and strain into a Collins glass over ice. Garnish with an orange.

REISEN

OLD-FASHIONED

MAKES 1 DRINK

1 oz. Butter Shots
1 oz. Godiva
*   liqueur*
1 oz. Bailey's Irish
*   cream liqueur*

Pour ingredients into an old-fashioned glass.

REMSEN COOLER

COLLINS

MAKES 1 DRINK

2 oz. scotch
½ tsp. fine sugar
4 oz. club soda
lemon twist

Dissolve sugar in a splash of club soda in a Collins or highball glass. Fill with ice. Add scotch and club soda. Add a lemon twist.

REMSEN COOLER 2

COLLINS

MAKES 1 DRINK

2 oz. gin
2 oz. carbonated
*   water*
½ tsp. powdered
*   sugar*
fill carbonated water
*   or ginger ale*
spiral of orange peel
spiral of lemon peel

Pour powdered sugar and 2 oz. carbonated water into a Collins glass. Stir. Fill glass with ice. Add gin. Top with carbonated water or ginger ale. Garnish with a spiral of orange or lemon.

RENAISSANCE

MAKES 1 DRINK

2 oz. brandy
1 1/3 oz. sweet
*   vermouth*
1/3 oz. limoncello
2 dashes peach
*   bitters*

Pour ingredients into a shaker with ice. Stir and strain into a martini glass. Garnish with a lemon twist.

RENAISSANCE MARTINI

MARTINI

MAKES 1 DRINK

3 oz. gin
1/2 oz. Fino sherry

Pour ingredients into a shaker with ice. Shake and strain into a chilled martini glass. Garnish with grated nutmeg.

RENDEZVOUS PUNCH

IRISH COFFEE

MAKES 1 DRINK

3/4 oz. Chambord
*   Raspberry*
*   Liqueur*
3/4 oz. dark rum
6 oz. hot spiced
*   cider*

Pour ingredients into an Irish coffee glass or mug. Garnish with a cinnamon stick.

RENO COCKTAIL (NONALCOHOLIC) MARTINI

MAKES 1 DRINK

2 oz. grapefruit
*   juice*
1 oz. lime juice
*   or juice of*
*   1/2 lime*
1/2 oz. grenadine
1 tsp. fine sugar

Pour ingredients into a shaker nearly filled with ice. Strain into a martini glass.

RESOLUTION MARTINI

MARTINI

MAKES 1 DRINK

3 oz. gin
1 oz. apricot brandy
½ oz. lemon juice

Pour ingredients into a shaker with ice. Shake and strain into a chilled martini glass.

RHINE WINE PUNCH

PUNCH

MAKES ABOUT 15 DRINKS

1 bottle Rhine wine
½ cup brandy
½ cup Cointreau
1 cup orange juice
1 bottle sparkling white wine, chilled

Pour all ingredients except sparkling wine into a punch bowl over ice. Stir well. Add sparkling wine just before serving.

RHINESTONE COWBOY SHOOTER

SHOT

MAKES 1 DRINK

½ oz. Goldschlager
½ oz. blue curaçao

Shake up the Goldschlager bottle so that the gold is mixed well, then pour into a shot glass. Gently pour the blue curaçao over the back of a spoon to layer it on top of the Goldschlager.

RIMMED BROTHERS GRIMM COCOA

IRISH COFFEE

MAKES 1 DRINK

1 oz. kirschwasser
1 packet hot cocoa
hot water
1 spoonful grenadine
1 spoonful sugar
pinch of cinnamon

Mix the sugar and cinnamon together on a saucer. Dip the rim of a mug into the grenadine then into the cinnamon sugar. Pour the kirschwasser and the packet of cocoa into the mug. Fill with hot water and stir. Garnish with whipped cream or miniature marshmallows.

RING OF FIRE

IRISH COFFEE

MAKES 1 DRINK

½ oz. Frangelico
½ oz. Irish cream
    liqueur
hot black coffee
½ oz. Grand
    Marnier
glazed donut

Pour the Frangelico, Irish cream liqueur, and hot coffee into an Irish coffee mug. Set the glazed donut on the rim of the mug and pour the Grand Marnier over it. Light the donut to create the ring of fire. Wait for the flame to die down.

RISING SUN

COLLINS

MAKES 1 DRINK

2 oz. sake
½ oz. grenadine
orange juice

Pour ingredients into a shaker with ice. Shake and strain into a Collins glass over ice. Fill with orange juice. Garnish with a lemon slice and a cherry.

ROAD RAGE AT THE TRAFFIC LIGHT

COLLINS

MAKES 1 DRINK

1 oz. crème de
    noyaux
1 oz. coconut rum
½ oz. melon liqueur
¼ oz. 151 rum
3 oz. pineapple
    juice
3 oz. orange juice

Fill a Collins glass with ice, and pour in the coconut rum and crème de noyaux to create a red layer. Pack the glass again with ice, then slowly fill the glass with the orange juice and the pineapple juice (for the yellow layer). Gently top the drink with the melon liqueur and 151 rum (for the green).

ROAD RUNNER MARTINI

MARTINI

MAKES 1 DRINK

3 oz. pepper vodka
½ oz. dry vermouth
½ oz. gold tequila

Pour ingredients into a shaker with ice. Shake and strain into a chilled martini glass. Garnish with a jalapeño-stuffed olive.

ROB ROY

MARKET MARTINI

MAKES 1 DRINK

2 oz. scotch
¾ oz. sweet
vermouth
dash bitters

Pour ingredients into a shaker about half-filled with ice. Stir and strain into a martini glass. Add the bitters. Garnish with a cherry.

ROB ROY, PERFECT

MARTINI

MAKES 1 DRINK

2 oz. scotch
1 tsp. sweet
vermouth
1 tsp. dry vermouth

Pour ingredients into a shaker with ice. Stir and strain into a martini glass. Garnish with a lemon twist.

ROBERT E. LEE COOLER

COLLINS

MAKES 1 DRINK

2 oz. gin
2 oz. club soda
¼ tsp. anisette
½ tsp. fine sugar
1 oz. lime juice or
juice of ½ lime
ginger ale

Pour lime juice, sugar, and club soda into a Collins glass. Stir. Add ice to fill, anisette, and gin. Stir. Fill with ginger ale. Stir well. Garnish with a lemon slice.

ROCKY MOUNTAIN COOLER

COLLINS

MAKES 1 DRINK

1½ oz. peach
schnapps
4 oz. pineapple
juice
2 oz. lemon lime
soda

Pour ingredients into a Collins glass over ice. Stir.

ROCKY MOUNTAIN SHOOTER SHOT

MAKES 1 DRINK

1 oz. Southern
   Comfort
1 oz. Amaretto
½ oz. lime juice

Pour ingredients into a shaker with ice.
Shake well and strain into a shot glass.

ROCOCO MARTINI

MAKES 1 DRINK

1 oz. cherry vodka
½ oz. triple sec
1 oz. orange juice

Pour ingredients into a shaker with ice.
Shake and strain into a martini glass.

ROLLS-ROYCE MARTINI

MAKES 1 DRINK

1½ oz. gin
½ oz. sweet
   vermouth
½ oz. dry vermouth
1 tsp. Benedictine

Pour ingredients into a shaker with ice.
Shake and strain into a martini glass.

ROMA CHAMPAGNE

MAKES 1 DRINK

1 oz. dry gin
¼ oz. Amaro Italian
   bitter liqueur
¼ oz. Strega Italian
   liqueur

Pour ingredients into a shaker with ice.
Stir well and strain into a Champagne
glass. Float a narrow strip of orange peel
on top.

ROMAN CANDLE

SHOT

MAKES 1 DRINK

1½ oz. Sambuca
    Romana

Pour the Sambuca Romana into a shot glass. Light the Sambuca. Grab the lit shot, hold it straight up in the air and say, "Hail Caesar"! Blow it out and then drink.

ROMULAN ALE

COLLINS

MAKES 1 DRINK

1½ oz. white rum
1 oz. blue curaçao
7-Up
6 drops of Tabasco
    sauce
salt

Pour the rum and curaçao into a Collins glass. Fill 7-Up. Add Tabasco and a dash of salt.

ROOT BEER FLOAT

COLLINS

MAKES 1 DRINK

1 oz. Galliano
1 oz. vanilla vodka
1 oz. half-and-half
cola
whipped cream

Pour Galliano, vanilla vodka, and half-and-half into a Collins glass. Add cola to fill. Garnish with whipped cream.

RORY O'MORE

MARTINI

MAKES 1 DRINK

¾ oz. Italian
    vermouth
1½ oz. Irish
    whiskey
1 dash orange
    bitters

Pour ingredients into a shaker with ice. Stir and strain into a martini glass.

ROSALIND RUSSELL

COLLINS

MAKES 1 DRINK

1 oz. Aquavit
½ oz. vermouth

Pour ingredients into a Collins glass over ice.

ROSE COCKTAIL

HIGHBALL

MAKES 1 DRINK

2 oz. French vermouth
½ oz. Kirsch
¼ oz. grenadine

Pour ingredients into a highball glass over ice.

ROSE OF WARSAW

MARTINI

MAKES 1 DRINK

1½ oz. Wyborowa Polish vodka
1 oz. cherry liqueur
½ oz. Cointreau
dash bitters

Pour ingredients into a shaker with ice. Stir and pour into a martini glass.

ROSITA

OLD-FASHIONED

MAKES 1 DRINK

1½ oz. tequila
1 oz. Campari
½ oz. dry vermouth
½ oz. sweet vermouth

Pour ingredients into an old-fashioned glass nearly filled with ice. Stir well. Serve with a lemon twist.

ROSY DAWN (NONALCOHOLIC)　　WINE

MAKES 1 DRINK

1 oz. lemon juice
1 oz. lime juice
2 oz. orange juice
1 oz. coconut
　cream
1 tsp. grenadine
1 tsp. orgeat
　syrup

Pour ingredients into a blender with ice. Blend thoroughly. Pour into a large wine glass.

ROSY RUM COSMO

MAKES 1 DRINK

1½ oz. Bacardi
　Limon
½ oz. triple sec
1 tbs. lime juice
½ tbs. cranberry
　juice

Pour the rum, triple sec, lime juice and cranberry juice into a cocktail shaker with ice. Shake well. Strain into a chilled martini glass. Garnish with a mint leaf.

ROUGE MARTINI　　MARTINI

MAKES 1 DRINK

2 oz. gin
1 tsp. Chambord
　Raspberry
　Liqueur

Pour ingredients into a shaker with ice. Stir well and strain into a martini glass.

ROULETTE

MAKES 1 DRINK

1 oz. blue curaçao
Champagne

Pour the blue curaçao into a Champagne flute. Top with Champagne and garnish with a sprig of mint.

ROUND ROBIN

WINE

MAKES 1 DRINK

1 egg white
1 tsp. sugar
1 oz. Pernod
1 oz. brandy

Pour ingredients into a shaker with ice. Shake and strain into a wine glass.

ROY ROGERS (NONALCOHOLIC)

COLLINS

MAKES 1 DRINK

6–8 oz. cola
¼ oz. grenadine

Pour ingredients into a Collins glass filled with ice. Stir well. Garnish with a cherry.

ROYAL FIZZ

HIGHBALL

MAKES 1 DRINK

2 oz. gin
1 oz. orange juice
1 oz. lemon juice or
    juice of ½ lemon
1 tsp. fine sugar
1 tsp. Cointreau
2 tsp. light cream
club soda

Pour all ingredients into a shaker half filled with ice. Shake well. Pour into a highball glass partly filled with ice. Add club soda to fill. Stir. Garnish with an orange, lemon, or lime slice, and a cherry.

ROYAL FIZZ 2

COLLINS

MAKES 1 DRINK

1 oz. gin
2 oz. sweet-and-
    sour mix
1 egg
cola

Pour all ingredients except cola into a shaker with ice. Shake and strain into a chilled Collins glass. Add cola to fill.

ROYAL FLUSH

OLD-FASHIONED

MAKES 1 DRINK

1 oz. Crown Royal
1½ oz. triple sec
2 oz. peach
schnapps
fill cranberry
1 splash orange
juice

Pour ingredients into a shaker with ice. Shake and strain into an old-fashioned glass over ice. Garnish with a twist of orange.

RUBY RED WINE PUNCH

PUNCH

MAKES 20 DRINKS

1 bottle red wine
1 cup lemon juice
¾ cup fine sugar
1 cup raspberry
syrup
1 quart club soda

Pour all ingredients except club soda into a bowl. Stir to dissolve sugar. Pour into a punch bowl over ice. Stir well. Add soda just before serving.

RUBY SLIPPER (NONALCOHOLIC)

COLLINS

MAKES 1 DRINK

2 oz. fresh
strawberries
or raspberries
2 oz. orange juice
2 oz. pineapple
juice
2 oz. cranberry
juice

Pour ingredients into a blender. Blend until smooth. Pour into a Collins glass. Top with whipped cream.

RUM COBBLER

WINE

MAKES 1 DRINK

2 oz. dark rum
2 oz. club soda
1 tsp. fine sugar

Pour club soda into a large wine glass or goblet. Add sugar and dissolve. Fill with ice. Add rum and stir. Garnish with an orange, lemon, or lime slice, and a cherry.

RUM COLLINS

COLLINS

MAKES 1 DRINK

2 oz. light rum
1 oz. lemon juice or
*   juice of ½ lemon*
1 tsp. fine sugar
3 oz. club soda

Pour ingredients into a Collins glass over ice. Stir well. Garnish with the orange and cherry.

RUM COOLER

COLLINS

MAKES 1 DRINK

2 oz. light rum
2 oz. club soda
1 tsp. fine sugar
ginger ale

Dissolve sugar in club soda in a Collins glass. Nearly fill the glass with ice. Add the rum. Fill with ginger ale. Garnish with an orange, lemon, or lime slice, and a cherry.

RUM DAISY

OLD-FASHIONED

MAKES 1 DRINK

2 oz. rum
1 oz. lemon juice or
*   juice of ½ lemon*
½ tsp. fine sugar
1 tsp. grenadine

Pour the liquor, lemon juice, sugar, and grenadine into a shaker half filled with ice. Shake well. Pour into an old-fashioned glass. Garnish with a cherry and fruit.

RUM FIX

HIGHBALL

MAKES 1 DRINK

2 oz. light rum
1 oz. lemon juice or
*   juice of ½ lemon*
1 tsp. fine sugar
2 tsp. water

Add sugar, lemon juice, and water to a shaker half filled with ice. Shake and strain into a highball glass over ice. Add rum and stir. Garnish with a lemon and serve with a straw.

RUM FRUIT PUNCH

MAKES 35 DRINKS

1 liter rum
2 cups pineapple juice
½ cup lemon juice
1 cup fine sugar
½ cup water
one half pineapple, sliced
1 pint strawberries, sliced

In a saucepan, heat water and sugar until boiling. Cool. Pour all ingredients except fruit into a punch bowl over ice. Add fruit just before serving.

RUM GIMLET

MARTINI

MAKES 1 DRINK

2 oz. rum
½ oz. Rose's lime juice

Pour ingredients into a shaker with ice. Stir and strain into a martini glass. Garnish with a lime wedge.

RUM MARTINI

MARTINI

MAKES 1 DRINK

3 oz. light rum
1 oz. dry vermouth
dash orange bitters

Pour ingredients into a shaker with ice. Shake and strain into a chilled martini glass. Garnish with an almond-stuffed olive.

RUM MILK PUNCH

COLLINS

MAKES 1 DRINK

2 oz. white rum
1 cup milk
1 tsp. powdered sugar

Shake all ingredients with ice and strain into a Collins glass. Sprinkle nutmeg on top and serve.

RUM OLD-FASHIONED

MAKES 1 DRINK

1½ oz. white rum
1 tsp. 151 proof
   rum
½ tsp. powdered
   sugar
dash bitters
1 tsp. water

Stir powdered sugar, water, and bitters in an old-fashioned glass. When sugar has dissolved, add ice and white rum. Float 151 proof rum on top. Garnish with a twist of lime.

RUM RICKEY

HIGHBALL

MAKES 1 DRINK

1½ oz. light rum
1 oz. lime juice or
   juice of ½ lime
club soda

Pour the rum and lime juice into a highball glass nearly filled with ice. Stir gently. Add club soda. Garnish with a twist of lime.

RUM RUNNER

MARTINI

MAKES 1 DRINK

1½ oz. white rum
¼ oz. banana
   liqueur
¼ oz. blackberry
   brandy
½ tsp. grenadine
5 oz. sweet-and-
   sour mix

Pour ingredients into a shaker with ice. Shake and strain into a martini glass.

RUM SOUR

SOUR GLASS

MAKES 1 DRINK

2 oz. rum
1 oz. lemon juice or
   juice of ½ lemon
1 tsp. fine sugar
(or 1½ oz. sweet-
   and-sour mix
   instead of lemon
   and sugar)

Fill shaker two-thirds with ice. Add ingredients. Shake and strain into a sour glass. Garnish with lemon and a cherry.

RUM SWIZZLE

COLLINS

MAKES 1 DRINK

1 lime
1 tsp. powdered sugar
2 oz. carbonated water
2 dashes bitters
2 oz. rum
carbonated water

Squeeze juice of one lime into a Collins glass. Add sugar and carbonated water and stir. Fill glass with ice and stir thoroughly. Add the bitters and rum. Add carbonated water to fill. Serve with a swizzle stick in the glass.

RUMMY MOULIN ROUGE

COLLINS

MAKES 1 DRINK

½ oz. light rum
½ oz. dark rum
½ oz. 151 rum
½ oz. coconut rum
½ oz. spiced rum
½ oz. grenadine

Pour the first six ingredients into a Collins glass packed with ice. Add the pineapple juice to fill and stir. Garnish with a slice of pineapple and a maraschino cherry.

RUPTURED DUCK

HIGHBALL

MAKES 1 DRINK

2 oz. crème de noyaux
2 oz. banana liqueur
2 oz. light cream

Pour ingredients into a shaker with ice. Shake and strain into a highball glass.

RUSSIAN

MARTINI

MAKES 1 DRINK

1 oz. brandy
½ oz. orange juice
dash Pernod
dash orange bitters

Pour ingredients into a shaker with ice. Shake and strain into a martini glass.

RUSSIAN APPLE

SHOT

MAKES 1 DRINK

1 oz. vodka
*¼ oz. cranberry
  juice*
*¼ oz. pineapple
  juice*

Pour the vodka into the bottom of a chilled shot glass. Gently pour the cranberry juice over the back of a spoon to layer it on top. Do the same with the pineapple juice.

RUSSIAN BEAR

OLD-FASHIONED

MAKES 1 DRINK

1 oz. vodka
*1 oz. dark crème de
  cacao*
½ oz. cream

Pour ingredients into a shaker half filled with ice. Shake well. Strain into an old-fashioned glass over ice.

RUSSIAN BRUNCH

CHAMPAGNE

MAKES 1 DRINK

1 oz. vodka
1 oz. orange juice
2 oz. Champagne

Pour the vodka and orange juice into a shaker with ice. Shake and strain into a Champagne flute. Top with the Champagne.

RUSSIAN COCKTAIL

MARTINI

MAKES 1 DRINK

¾ oz. vodka
*¾ oz. crème de
  cacao*
¾ oz. dry gin

Pour ingredients into a shaker with ice. Shake and strain into a martini glass.

RUSSIAN COCKTAIL 2

MARTINI

MAKES 1 DRINK

¾ oz. vodka
¾ oz. gin
¾ oz. white crème
de cacao

Pour ingredients into a shaker with ice. Shake and strain into a martini glass.

RUSSIAN COFFEE

IRISH COFFEE

MAKES 1 DRINK

½ oz. vodka
½ oz. coffee
liqueur
½ oz. hazelnut
liqueur
4 oz. hot black
coffee
whipped cream or
heavy cream

Pour the vodka and liqueurs into an Irish Coffee glass or mug. Stir. Add the coffee and stir. Top with whipped cream or cream poured over the back of a spoon so it floats on top.

RUSSIAN KAMIKAZE

HIGHBALL

MAKES 1 DRINK

3 oz. vodka
1 tsp. Chambord
Raspberry
Liqueur

Pour ingredients into a shaker with ice. Stir and strain into a highball glass.

RUSSIAN MARTINI

MARTINI

MAKES 1 DRINK

2 oz. vodka
2 oz. gin
½ oz. white
chocolate
liqueur

Pour ingredients into a shaker with ice. Shake and strain into a chilled martini glass.

RUSSIAN ROSE

MARTINI

MAKES 1 DRINK

3 oz. strawberry-
flavored vodka
½ oz. dry vermouth
½ oz. grenadine
dash orange bitters

Pour ingredients into a shaker with ice. Stir and strain into a chilled martini glass. Garnish with a rose.

RUSSIAN SUNRISE

COLLINS

MAKES 1 DRINK

1 oz. Jägermeister
dash grenadine
orange juice

Pour ingredients into a Collins glass over ice in this order: Jäger, orange juice, grenadine. Add a straw.

RUSTY NAIL

OLD-FASHIONED

MAKES 1 DRINK

2 oz. scotch
1 oz. Drambuie

Pour scotch and Drambuie into an old-fashioned glass over ice. Stir.

RYE AND GINGER

HIGHBALL

MAKES 1 DRINK

2 oz. rye whiskey
ginger ale
lemon twist

Fill a highball glass with ice. Add the whiskey. Fill with the ginger ale. Garnish with a lemon twist.

S'MORES

MAKES 1 DRINK

½ oz. dark crème de
  cacao
¼ oz. butterscotch
  schnapps
¼ oz. Irish cream liqueur
$1/_8$ oz. 151 rum
1 miniature marsh-
  mallow on a
  toothpick

Pour the dark crème de cacao into a shot glass. Gently layer the butterscotch schnapps on the crème de cacao. Repeat the layering process with the Irish cream and the 151 rum. Light the rum. Roast the marshmallow in the flame. Wait until the fire has died down to drink the shot.

SACRIFICE TO THE GODS

MAKES 1 DRINK

1½ oz. dark crème
  de cacao
milk or half-
  and-half
1½ oz. brandy
pinch of nutmeg

Half-fill a Collins glass with ice, and add the dark crème de cacao. Fill with milk or half-and-half. Sprinkle with the nutmeg on top. Pour the brandy into a shot glass, light. Add the shot to the drink to make your sacrifice.

SAFE SEX ON THE BEACH (NONALCOHOLIC)

S

MAKES 1 DRINK

2 oz. peach
  nectar
3 oz. cranberry
  juice
3 oz. orange
  juice

Pour all ingredients into a highball or Collins glass nearly filled with ice. Stir. Garnish with a cherry.

SALOON COFFEE

MAKES 1 DRINK

½ oz. Irish cream
1 oz. Amaretto
6 oz. hot black
  coffee

Pour the ingredients into an Irish coffee glass or mug and stir. Top with whipped cream.

SALTY CHIHUAHUA

HIGHBALL

MAKES 1 DRINK

2 oz. Sauza Blanco
4 oz. fresh
   grapefruit juice
wedge of lime

Combine the tequila and juice in a salt-rimmed highball glass filled ¾ with ice. Stir, and squeeze the lime wedge into the drink.

SALTY DOG

HIGHBALL

MAKES 1 DRINK

1½ oz. vodka
4–5 oz. grapefruit
   juice
salt and lime to rim
   glass

Rim a highball glass with salt. Almost fill the glass with ice. Pour the vodka and grapefruit juice and stir well.

SALTY PUPPY (NONALCOHOLIC)

OLD-FASHIONED

MAKES 1 DRINK

4–5 oz.
   grapefruit
   juice
coarse salt
fine sugar
lime wedge

Rub the rim of an old-fashioned glass with lime. Pour salt and sugar into a dish and dip the rim into the mixture. Pour grapefruit juice over ice.

S

SAMBUCA STRAIGHT

SNIFTER

MAKES 1 DRINK

2 oz. Sambuca
3 coffee beans

Pour the Sambuca into a brandy snifter and add coffee beans.

SAN DIEGO SUNRISE

COLLINS

MAKES 1 DRINK

1 cup orange juice
1 cup pineapple
    and papaya ice
    cream
½ cup tequila
¼ cup Amaretto
1 tbs. vanilla

Pour the tequila, orange juice, and Amaretto into a blender with two cups of ice. Blend briefly. Add the ice cream and vanilla and blend on medium until slushy. Serve in a Collins glass.

SAN FRANCISCO COCKTAIL

MARTINI

MAKES 1 DRINK

¾ oz. sweet
    vermouth
¾ oz. dry vermouth
¾ oz. sloe gin
dash orange bitters
dash bitters

Pour ingredients into a shaker with ice. Shake and strain into a martini glass. Garnish with a cherry.

SAN JUAN CAPISTRANO (NONALCOHOLIC) WINE

MAKES 1 DRINK

2 oz. grapefruit
    juice
2 oz. coconut
    cream
1 oz. lime juice
    or juice of
    ½ lime

Pour ingredients into a blender with ice. Blend thoroughly. Pour into a large wine glass.

SANGRIA

WINE

MAKES 8 DRINKS

2 bottles red wine
2 tablespoons sugar
2 oz. brandy
1 cup orange juice
½ cup pineapple juice
½ cup cherry juice
3 cups maraschino
    cherries
1 orange, thinly sliced
1 lemon, thinly sliced
1 lime, thinly sliced

Pour the first seven ingredients and half of the sliced fruit into a pitcher. Store in the refrigerator. When ready to serve, add the rest of the sliced fruit, reserving some for garnish. If you plan to present sangria in a bowl, freeze some of the mix in ice cube trays. Use the frozen cubes to prevent dilution. Serve in wine glasses.

SANGRIA 2

MAKES 10 DRINKS

1 bottle dry red wine
2 oz. triple sec
1 oz. brandy
2 oz. orange juice
1 oz. lemon juice
¼ cup fine sugar
10 oz. club soda, chilled
orange and lemon
    slices

Chill all ingredients together except the club soda for at least one hour. Before serving, pour into a pitcher or punch bowl over ice, and then add club soda.

SANGRIA BIANCA

PUNCH

MAKES 10 DRINKS

1 pineapple
1 orange, sliced
1 lemon, sliced
100 ml limoncello
750 ml white
    dinner wine

Peel the pineapple and slice into pieces. Put the pieces into a large carafe and add the sugar and limoncello. Stir and let the mixture rest in a cool place for about 2 hours. Add the orange and lemon slices and pour in the white wine. Stir and keep in the refrigerator for 12 hours.

SANGRIA BIANCA 2

PUNCH

MAKES 10 DRINKS

4 nectarines
1 orange, sliced
1 lemon, sliced
100 ml vodka
6 tbs. sugar
750 ml white
    sparkling wine

Peel and core the nectarines and cut into pieces. Put the pieces into a large carafe and add the sugar and vodka. Stir and let the mixture rest in a cool place for about 2 hours. Add the orange and lemon slices and pour in the white wine. Stir and keep in the refrigerator for 12 hours.

SANTA BARBARA FIX

COLLINS

MAKES 1 DRINK

½ lemon or lime
1 tsp. powdered
    sugar
1 tsp. water
1½ oz. red dinner
    wine
1 oz. triple sec

Squeeze the lemon or lime into a Collins glass. Add the sugar and water and stir. Fill the glass with ice. Add the wine and triple sec. Stir well. Garnish with a slice of orange, a cherry, and a straw.

SANTA BARBARA ICE TEA

HIGHBALL

MAKES 1 DRINK

1 oz. vodka
1 oz. rum
1 oz. gin
1 oz. triple sec
1 oz. melon liqueur
1 oz. orange juice
1 oz. pineapple juice
1 oz. cranberry juice
splash 7-Up

Layer in order into a highball glass (vodka at the bottom). To create a layered effect the juices must be poured lightly over the back of a spoon. Add the 7-Up last. Garnish with a cherry and an orange slice. It should look green on the bottom, with orange, yellow, and streaming cranberry colors throughout the middle and top.

SARATOGA

MARTINI

MAKES 1 DRINK

2 oz. brandy
½ tsp. maraschino
*   liqueur*
1 tsp. lemon juice
1 tbs. pineapple
*   juice*
dash bitters

Pour ingredients into a shaker with ice. Shake well and strain into a martini glass.

SATAN'S CURLED WHISKERS

MARTINI

MAKES 1 DRINK

¾ oz. gin
¾ oz. dry vermouth
¾ oz. sweet
*   vermouth*
½ oz. orange juice
½ oz. orange
*   curaçao*
1 dash orange
*   bitters*

Pour ingredients into a shaker with ice. Shake and strain into a martini glass.

SATAN'S WHISKERS

MARTINI

MAKES 1 DRINK

¾ oz. gin
¾ oz. dry vermouth
¾ oz. sweet
*   vermouth*
½ oz. orange juice
½ oz. Grand
*   Marnier*
1 dash orange
*   bitters*

Pour ingredients into a shaker with ice. Shake and strain into a martini glass. Using orange curaçao instead of Grand Marnier turns this into a "curled" version.

SATIN SHEETS

MARTINI

MAKES 1 DRINK

1½ oz. light rum
1½ oz. brandy
splash Cointreau
splash Rose's lime
     juice

Pour ingredients into a shaker with ice. Shake well and strain into a martini glass.

SAVANNAH ICED TEA

COLLINS

MAKES 1 DRINK

½ oz. rum
½ oz. vodka
½ oz. triple sec
½ oz. Southern Comfort
½ oz. peach schnapps
¾ oz. sweet-and-
     sour mix
¾ oz. cranberry juice
splash 7-Up

Pour ingredients in order into a Collins glass over ice. Stir. Garnish with mint leaves.

SAZERAC

OLD-FASHIONED

MAKES 1 DRINK

1 sugar cube
1 dash Peychaud's
     bitters
2 oz. rye whiskey
½ tsp. Pernod
water or club soda

Place the sugar cube at the bottom of an old-fashioned glass. Saturate the cube with the bitters. Muddle. Add the whiskey and the Pernod. Mix well. Top off with the water or the club soda.

SCARLET FEVER

PINT

MAKES 2 DRINKS

14 oz. vodka
14 oz. white rum
8 oz. dry gin
6 oz. cranberry
     juice

Pour ingredients into a shaker with ice. Shake and strain into a draft beer glass. Add 3 ice cubes and garnish with a lemon slice.

SCARLETT O'HARA

MARTINI

MAKES 1 DRINK

*2 oz. Southern
  Comfort
2 oz. cranberry
  juice
1 oz. lime juice or
  juice of ½ lime*

Pour ingredients into a shaker with ice. Shake and strain into a martini glass.

SCOFFLAW

MARTINI

MAKES 1 DRINK

*1 oz. Canadian
  whiskey
1 oz. dry vermouth
¼ oz. lemon juice
dash grenadine
dash orange bitters*

Pour ingredients into a shaker with ice. Stir and strain into a martini glass. Garnish with a lemon wedge.

SCOOTER

COLLINS

MAKES 1 DRINK

*2 oz. Malibu
  coconut rum
3 oz. cranberry
  juice
3 oz. orange juice
151 proof rum*

Pour first three ingredients into a shaker with ice. Shake well and strain into a Collins glass over ice. Float the rum on top.

SCOOTER SHOOTER

CORDIAL

MAKES 1 DRINK

*1 oz. brandy
1 oz. Amaretto
1 oz. light cream*

Pour ingredients into a shaker with ice. Shake and strain into a cordial glass.

SCORPION

COLLINS

MAKES 1 DRINK

2 oz. light rum
½ oz. brandy
1 oz. lemon juice
2 oz. orange juice
½ oz. orgeat syrup

Pour ingredients into a blender in this order: rum, brandy, orgeat, juices, and ice. Blend thoroughly. Pour into a highball or Collins glass. Garnish with an orange, lemon, or lime slice, and a cherry. Serve with a straw.

SCORPION 2

HIGHBALL

MAKES 1 DRINK

juice of ½ lime
1½ oz. orange juice
¾ oz. brandy
¾ oz. light rum
¾ oz. dark rum
¼ oz. triple sec

Squeeze the lime juice into a shaker of ice. Add all the other ingredients. Shake well and strain into a highball glass over ice. Garnish with a lime wedge.

SCOTCH BOUNTY

PARFAIT

MAKES 1 DRINK

1 oz. scotch
1 oz. coconut rum
*1 oz. white crème
   de cacao*
½ oz. grenadine
4 oz. orange juice

Pour ingredients into a shaker with ice. Shake and strain into a parfait glass. Garnish with a pineapple wedge and a cherry.

SCOTCH COBBLER

WINE

MAKES 1 DRINK

2 oz. scotch
2 oz. club soda
1 tsp. fine sugar

Pour the club soda into a large wine glass or goblet. Add the sugar and dissolve. Fill with ice. Add the scotch and stir. Garnish with an orange, lemon, or lime slice, and a cherry. Serve with a straw.

SCOTCH COOLER

HIGHBALL

MAKES 1 DRINK

2 oz. scotch
splash white crème
de menthe
3 oz. club soda

Pour the scotch and crème de menthe into a highball glass over ice. Add soda to fill. Stir. Garnish with mint.

SCOTCH DAISY

OLD-FASHIONED

MAKES 1 DRINK

2 oz. scotch
whiskey
1 oz. lemon juice or
juice of ½ lemon
½ tsp. fine sugar
1 tsp. grenadine

Pour the liquor, lemon juice, sugar, and grenadine into a shaker half filled with ice. Shake well. Pour into an old-fashioned glass. Garnish with a cherry and fruit.

SCOTCH HOLIDAY SOUR

SOUR GLASS

MAKES 1 DRINK

1½ oz. scotch
1 oz. cherry brandy
½ oz. sweet
vermouth
1 oz. lemon juice or
juice of ½ lemon

Pour ingredients into a shaker half filled with ice. Shake well. Strain into a sour glass over ice, serve straight up in a martini glass. Garnish with a lemon and a cherry.

SCOTCH MIST

OLD-FASHIONED

MAKES 1 DRINK

2 oz. scotch
whiskey

Fill an old-fashioned glass with crushed ice. Add scotch and serve with a straw.

SCOTCH OLD-FASHIONED

OLD-FASHIONED

MAKES 1 DRINK

*2 oz. scotch
   whiskey
1 tsp. water
1 cube or ½ tsp.
   sugar
dash or 2 bitters*

Pour the sugar, bitters, and water into an old-fashioned glass and muddle with a spoon. Add the scotch and stir. Add ice and a lemon twist. Garnish with a slice of orange or lemon and a cherry.

SCOTCH ON THE ROCKS

OLD-FASHIONED

MAKES 1 DRINK

*2 oz. scotch
   whiskey*

Pour scotch into an old-fashioned glass over ice.

SCOTCH RICKEY

HIGHBALL

MAKES 1 DRINK

*1½ oz. scotch
   whiskey
1 oz. lime juice or
   juice of ½ lime
club soda*

Pour the scotch and lime juice into a highball glass nearly filled with ice. Stir. Add club soda. Garnish with a twist of lime.

SCOTCH ROYALE

CHAMPAGNE

MAKES 1 DRINK

*1½ oz. scotch
   whiskey
1 tsp. fine sugar
dash bitters
chilled Champagne
   to fill*

Dissolve sugar in bitters and scotch in a Champagne flute. Fill with Champagne. Stir gently.

SCOTCH SOUR

SOUR GLASS

MAKES 1 DRINK

2 oz. scotch
whiskey
1 oz. lime juice or
juice of ½ lime
1 tsp. fine sugar

Pour ingredients into a shaker with ice. Shake and strain into a sour glass. Garnish with an orange slice and cherry.

SCOTCH STINGER

MARTINI

MAKES 1 DRINK

2 oz. scotch
whiskey
2 oz. white crème
de menthe

Pour ingredients into a shaker with ice. Stir and strain into a martini glass.

SCOTTISH GUARD

MARTINI

MAKES 1 DRINK

1½ oz. bourbon
whiskey
½ oz. lemon juice
½ oz. orange juice
1 tsp. grenadine

Shake with ice. Strain into a martini glass.

SCREAMING ORGASM

SHOT

MAKES 1 DRINK

½ oz. Grand
Marnier
½ oz. Irish cream
liqueur
½ oz. coffee
liqueur

Pour ingredients into a shaker half filled with ice. Shake well. Strain into a shot glass.

SCREW BY THE SEA

MARTINI

MAKES 1 DRINK

5 oz. vodka
5 oz. cranberry-
strawberry juice
7 oz. orange juice

Pour ingredients into a shaker with ice.
Shake and strain into a martini glass.

SCREWDRIVER

HIGHBALL

MAKES 1 DRINK

1½ oz. vodka
orange juice

Pour orange juice and vodka into a highball glass nearly filled with ice. Stir well.

SCREWLESS DRIVER (NONALCOHOLIC)

HIGHBALL

MAKES 1 DRINK

1½ oz. tonic
water
5 oz. orange
juice

Pour orange juice and tonic into a
highball glass nearly filled with ice.
Stir well.

SEA BREEZE

HIGHBALL

MAKES 1 DRINK

1¾ oz. vodka
3 oz. cranberry
juice
1 oz. grapefruit
juice

Pour the vodka and cranberry juice into a
highball glass over ice. Stir well. Top off
with the grapefruit juice. Garnish with a
grapefruit slice.

SEA BREEZE 2

MAKES 1 DRINK

1½ oz. vodka
1 oz. grapefruit
*   juice*
4 oz. cranberry
*   juice*

Pour ingredients into a blender. Flash blend and pour into a highball glass over ice. Garnish with a lime slice.

SEA BREEZE "DOWNEAST"

COLLINS

MAKES 1 DRINK

1½ oz. vodka
1 oz. cranberry
*   juice*
1 oz. pineapple
*   juice*
splash lime
grapefruit juice

Pour the first four ingredients into a Collins glass with ice and fill with grapefruit juice. Stir and garnish with a slice of lime.

SEA HORSE

COLLINS

MAKES 1 DRINK

1½ oz. vodka
¼ oz. Pernod
1 oz. apple juice
1 oz. cranberry
*   juice*
¼ lime, squeezed

Pour all ingredients into a Collins glass filled with cracked ice. Garnish with mint.

SECRET MARTINI

MARTINI

MAKES 1 DRINK

3 oz. gin
1 oz. Lillet (white)
2 dashes bitters

Pour ingredients into a shaker with ice. Stir and strain into a chilled martini glass.

SEETHING JEALOUSY

MARTINI

MAKES 1 DRINK

*1 oz. sweet
    vermouth
1 oz. scotch
    whiskey
½ oz. cherry brandy
½ oz. orange juice*

Pour ingredients into a shaker half filled with ice. Shake well. Strain into a martini glass.

SEVEN AND SEVEN

HIGHBALL

MAKES 1 DRINK

*2 oz. Seagram's 7
5 oz. 7-Up*

Pour the Seagram's into a highball glass nearly filled with ice. Add the soda to fill. Garnish with a lemon twist.

SEVILLA

WINE

MAKES 1 DRINK

*1½ oz. light rum
1½ oz. tawny port
1 tsp. fine sugar
1 egg*

Pour ingredients into a shaker half filled with ice. Shake well. Strain into a wine glass.

SEX IN FRONT OF THE FIREPLACE

COLLINS

MAKES 1 DRINK

*1 oz. raspberry
    liqueur
1 oz. orange-flavored
    vodka
1 oz. peach schnapps
white cranberry juice
orange juice
3 miniature Tootsie
    Rolls
½ oz. Grand Marnier*

Pour the raspberry liqueur into the bottom of a Collins glass, then fill with ice. Pour in the vodka and peach schnapps and slowly fill with equal parts white cranberry and orange juice. Garnish the top of the drink with the Tootsie Rolls (the logs). Pour the Grand Marnier on top, and light.

SEX ON THE BEACH

HIGHBALL

MAKES 1 DRINK

1½ oz. vodka
*1 oz. peach-
  flavored brandy*
2 oz. orange juice
*2 oz. cranberry
  juice*

Pour all ingredients into a highball glass almost filled with ice. Stir.

SEX ON THE SLOPES

COLLINS

MAKES 1 DRINK

*½ oz. Southern
  Comfort*
½ oz. dark rum
8 oz. iced tea
splash lemon juice

Pour all ingredients into a Collins glass almost filled with ice. Stir. Garnish with a lemon slice.

SEX WITH THE CAPTAIN

COLLINS

MAKES 1 DRINK

*2 oz. Captain Morgan
  Spiced rum*
*½ oz. peach
  schnapps*
cranberry juice
orange juice

Fill a Collins glass with ice. Pour in the rum and peach schnapps. Fill with equal parts cranberry and orange juice. Stir. Garnish with a paper parasol.

SHADY LADY

HIGHBALL

MAKES 1 DRINK

1 oz. tequila
1 oz. melon liqueur
*4 oz. grapefruit
  juice*

Pour ingredients into a shaker with ice. Stir and strain into a highball glass over ice. Garnish with an orange, lemon, or lime slice, and a cherry.

SHAKER

MAKES 1 DRINK

*2 oz. Southern
  Comfort
2 oz. banana
  liqueur
big dash milk*

Pour ingredients into a shaker with ice. Shake and strain into shot glasses. (Tastes like a bubblegum milkshake.)

SHAMROCK

MARTINI

MAKES 1 DRINK

*1½ oz. Irish
  whiskey
½ oz. dry vermouth
½ oz. green crème
  de menthe
1 tsp. green
  Chartreuse*

Pour ingredients into a shaker with ice. Stir and strain into a martini glass. Garnish with an olive.

SHANDY GAFF

HIGHBALL

MAKES 1 DRINK

*6 oz. beer
6 oz. ginger ale*

Ingredients should be chilled. Pour both into a highball glass at the same time in equal parts. Do not stir.

SHARK ATTACK

COLLINS

MAKES 1 DRINK

*2 oz. vodka
4 oz. lemonade
2 dashes grenadine*

Pour ingredients in a Collins or highball glass over ice. Stir well. Serve with a straw.

SHARK BITE

HIGHBALL

MAKES 1 DRINK

1 shot dark rum
*2 shots orange
    juice*
*splash sweet-and-
    sour mix*
splash grenadine

Pour all ingredients except grenadine into a blender. Blend with ice. Pour into a highball glass. Add grenadine and stir.

SHARK REPELLENT

COLLINS

MAKES 1 DRINK

*½ oz. Bacardi light
    rum*
½ oz. Bacardi dark rum
*½ oz. Malibu coconut
    rum*
½ oz. melon liqueur
½ oz. crème de banane
4 oz. pineapple juice

Pour ingredients into a shaker with ice. Shake strain and serve in a Collins glass with ice.

SHIRLEY TEMPLE (NONALCOHOLIC) OLD-FASHIONED

MAKES 1 DRINK

7 oz. ginger ale
½ tsp. grenadine

Pour ginger ale into an old-fashioned glass over ice. Add grenadine and stir gently. Garnish with a cherry and orange slice.

SHOTGUN

SNIFTER

MAKES 1 DRINK

1 oz. citrus vodka
1 oz. Grand Marnier
*1 oz. Rose's lime
    juice*

Pour ingredients into a brandy snifter. Stir.

SIBERIAN EXPRESS MARTINI   MARTINI

MAKES 1 DRINK

2 oz. vanilla vodka
1 oz. Chambord
  Raspberry
  Liqueur
1 oz. Godiva
  Liqueur

Pour ingredients into a shaker with ice. Shake and strain into a chilled martini glass. Garnish with a raspberry.

SIBERIAN SLEIGHRIDE   SNIFTER

MAKES 1 DRINK

1¼ oz. vodka
¾ oz. white crème
  de cacao
½ oz. white crème
  de cacao
3 oz. light cream

Shake with ice and strain into a brandy snifter. Garnish with chocolate shavings.

SIBERIAN SUNRISE   HIGHBALL

MAKES 1 DRINK

1½ oz. vodka
½ oz. triple sec
4 oz. grapefruit
  juice

Pour ingredients into a shaker with ice. Shake and strain into a highball glass.

SICILIAN KISS   OLD-FASHIONED

MAKES 1 DRINK

1 oz. Amaretto
7-Up

Pour Amaretto into an old-fashioned glass over ice. Add 7-Up to fill.

SIDEBAR

COLLINS

MAKES 1 DRINK

1¼ oz. vodka
¾ oz. Chambord
*   Raspberry*
*   Liqueur*
¾ oz. triple sec
2 oz. sweet-and-
*   sour mix*
splash 7-Up

Pour all ingredients except the 7-Up into a shaker with ice. Shake and strain into a Collins glass. Finish with a splash of the soda.

SIDECAR

MARTINI

MAKES 1 DRINK

1 oz. brandy
½ oz. Cointreau
1 oz. lemon juice or
*   juice of ½ lemon*

Pour ingredients into a shaker nearly filled with ice. Stir and strain into a martini glass.

SILK PANTIES

SHOT

MAKES 4 DRINKS

3 oz. vodka
3 oz. peach
*   schnapps*

Pour ingredients into a shaker with ice. Shake and strain into four shot glasses.

SILK STOCKINGS

MARTINI

MAKES 1 DRINK

1½ oz. tequila
1 oz. crème de
*   cacao*
1 oz. cream
dash grenadine

Pour ingredients into a shaker nearly filled with ice. Shake well. Strain into a martini glass.

SILVER FIZZ

HIGHBALL

MAKES 1 DRINK

2 oz. gin
1 tsp. lime juice
1 tsp. lemon juice
2 tbs. powdered
*   sugar*
1 egg, white only
carbonated water

Into a shaker filled with ice, pour the sugar, egg white, and juices. Add gin and shake very well. Strain into a highball glass. Add carbonated water to fill.

SILVER SPIDER SHOOTER

SHOT

MAKES 1 DRINK

½ oz. vodka
½ oz. rum
½ oz. triple sec
½ oz. white crème
*   de menthe*

Pour ingredients into a shaker with ice. Stir and strain into a shot glass.

SILVERADO

OLD-FASHIONED

MAKES 1 DRINK

1½ oz. vodka
1½ oz. Campari
1 oz. orange juice

Pour ingredients into an old-fashioned glass over ice. Stir.

SIMPLE CRANBERRY MARGARITA

MARGARITA

MAKES 1 DRINK

1¼ oz. silver
*   tequila*
½ oz. Cointreau
2 oz. cranberry
*   syrup*
splash orange juice

Pour ingredients into blender with ice. Blend until smooth. Pour into a margarita glass. Garnish with a lime wedge.

SINGAPORE SLING

COLLINS

MAKES 1 DRINK

½ oz. cherry brandy
½ oz. grenadine
1 oz. gin
2 oz. sweet-and-
    sour mix
club soda

Pour the grenadine, gin, and sweet-and-sour into a Collins glass over ice. Stir well. Fill with soda. Float cherry brandy on top. Garnish with a cherry.

SINGAPORE SLING 2

COLLINS

MAKES 1 DRINK

1 oz. gin
1 oz. Benedictine
1 oz. cherry brandy
4 oz. club soda

Pour the gin, Benedictine, and cherry brandy into a shaker with ice. Stir well and strain into a Collins glass over ice. Top with the club soda and stir well.

SINGLE EGGNOG

HIGHBALL

MAKES 1 DRINK

1 egg
1½ oz. rum or
    brandy
6 oz. milk nutmeg

Pour ingredients into a shaker half filled with ice. Shake well. Strain into a high-ball glass without ice. Sprinkle with nutmeg.

SIP AND GO NAKED

PUNCH

MAKES 12 DRINKS

48 oz. beer
1 cup gin
12 oz. lemonade
    (concentrate)
24 oz. water

Mix all ingredients in a pitcher. Tastes and smells nonalcoholic, but packs a wallop.

SIREN'S SOUR APPLE KISS

MARTINI

MAKES 1 DRINK

1½ oz. Gentleman
   Jack Rare
   Tennessee
   whiskey
½ oz. sweet-and-
   sour mix
½ oz. apple
   schnapps

Pour all ingredients into a shaker with ice. Shake and strain into a chilled martini glass. Garnish with a slice of green apple.

SKELETON

OLD-FASHIONED

MAKES 1 DRINK

½ oz. white rum
½ oz. sour apple
   vodka
lemon-lime soda

Pour the rum and vodka into an old-fashioned glass filled with ice. Add soda to fill.

SKI APEACHE

IRISH COFFEE

MAKES 1 DRINK

1 oz. peach
   schnapps
6 oz. hot cider

Pour into an Irish coffee glass or mug. Top with whipped cream and garnish with a cinnamon stick.

SKI SLOPE STUMBLE

COLLINS

MAKES 1 DRINK

½ oz. Yukon Jack
½ oz. Southern
   Comfort
1 oz. vodka
1½ oz. melon liqueur
½ oz. pineapple juice
½ oz. orange juice
½ oz. sours
1 cup crushed ice

Pour ingredients into a blender. Blend until smooth. Serve in a Collins glass with a slice of lime or lemon.

SKI TIP COFFEE

MAKES 1 DRINK

1 oz. Irish cream
1 oz. dark crème de cacao
½ oz. Grand Marnier
4 oz. hot, black French roast vanilla bean coffee

Pour ingredients into an Irish coffee glass or mug. Top with whipped cream.

SKIP, RUN, AND GO NAKED

HIGHBALL

MAKES 1 DRINK

2 oz. tequila
dash bitters
beer

Pour the tequila and bitters into a high-ball glass. Add the beer to fill.

SLAMMER ROYALE

SHOT

MAKES 2 DRINKS

6 oz. tequila
4 oz. Champagne

Pour ingredients into a shaker with ice. Stir and strain into shot glasses, leaving about a fifth of each glass unfilled. Grab a glass, covering the top with your bare palm, and slam it down on the table. (Don't break the glass!) The slam will mix the two ingredients, and create a big fizz in the glass. Now down it in one gulp.

SLEAZY SEX ON THE BEACH

HIGHBALL

MAKES 1 DRINK

1½ oz. vodka
1 oz. Grand Marnier
2 oz. orange juice
2 oz. cranberry juice

Pour all ingredients into a highball glass almost filled with ice. Stir.

SLEEPING BEAUTY

MAKES 1 DRINK

*1 oz. butterscotch
    schnapps
½ oz. Frangelico
hot black coffee
½ oz. cream*

Pour the butterscotch schnapps and the Frangelico into an Irish coffee glass or mug. Add coffee to fill. Finish with the cream. For variety, add the hazelnut creamer instead of cream, and stir.

SLIPPERY NIPPLE

SHOT

MAKES 1 DRINK

*½ oz. Sambuca
1 oz. Irish cream
    liqueur*

Pour the Irish cream liqueur into a shot glass. Top with the Sambuca.

SLOE GIN FIZZ

HIGHBALL

MAKES 1 DRINK

*2 oz. sloe gin
1 oz. lemon juice or
    juice of ½ lemon
1 tsp. fine sugar
4 oz. club soda*

Pour the lemon juice, sugar, and liquor into a shaker half filled with ice. Shake well. Pour into a highball glass partly filled with ice and add the club soda. Stir and garnish with lemon.

SLOE SCREW

COLLINS

MAKES 1 DRINK

*1 oz. vodka
1 oz. sloe gin
orange juice*

Pour all ingredients into a Collins glass over ice and stir.

SLOE SCREW AGAINST THE WALL HIGHBALL

MAKES 1 DRINK

¼ shot sloe gin
¼ shot Southern
  Comfort
¼ shot Galliano
¼ shot tequila
¼ shot brown rum
orange juice
cola

Pour all the liquors into a highball glass over ice. Add orange juice to fill. Top with a splash of cola.

SLOW COMFORTABLE SCREW HIGHBALL

MAKES 1 DRINK

1½ oz. vodka
½ oz. sloe gin
½ oz. Southern
  Comfort
4 oz. orange juice

Pour all ingredients into a highball glass nearly filled with ice. Stir well.

SLOW COMFORTABLE SCREW 2 COLLINS

MAKES 1 DRINK

½ oz. sloe gin
½ oz. Southern
  Comfort
½ oz. vodka
½ oz. triple sec
orange juice

Pour first four ingredients into a Collins glass over ice. Add orange juice to fill.

SLOW COMFORTABLE SCREW 3 COLLINS

MAKES 1 DRINK

1½ oz. vodka
1 oz. sloe gin
1 oz. Southern
  Comfort
4 oz. orange juice
1 oz. Galliano

Pour all ingredients except the Galliano into a Collins glass nearly filled with ice. Stir well. Float Galliano on top.

SLOW KISSER

MAKES 1 DRINK

1 oz. vodka
1 oz. peach
   schnapps
1 oz. crème de
   banane
dash grenadine
orange juice

Combine first four ingredients into a highball glass over ice. Add orange juice to fill.

SLOW OPERATOR (NONALCOHOLIC) COLLINS

MAKES 1 DRINK

1 oz. lime juice
   or juice of
   ½ lime
3 oz. grapefruit
   juice
4 oz. orange
   juice
1 tsp. fine sugar

Pour ingredients into a blender with ice and blend thoroughly. Pour into a Collins or parfait glass. Garnish with an orange, lemon, or lime slice, and a cherry. Serve with a straw.

SLUMBERING BULL (NONALCOHOLIC) HIGHBALL

MAKES 1 DRINK

5 oz. V-8 juice
2 oz. beef bouillon
dash Tabasco
dash Worcestershire
   sauce
dash celery salt

Pour all ingredients into a highball glass over ice and stir well. Garnish with a lime wedge.

SLURRICANE

COLLINS

MAKES 1 DRINK

½ oz. Bacardi dark
   rum
½ oz. Bacardi white
   rum
½ oz. triple sec
½ oz. pineapple
   juice
splash grenadine

Pour into a Collins glass over ice. Garnish with a cherry.

SMILING TIGER

 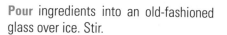

MAKES 1 DRINK

1 oz. Blavod black vodka
½ oz. black Sambuca
½ oz. vanilla vodka
¼ oz. vanilla extract
orange juice
half-and-half

Pour the Blavod, black Sambuca, vanilla vodka, and vanilla extract in a Collins glass to create the black layer. Fill glass with ice. Add orange juice slowly until the glass is three-quarters full. To make the white stripe, slowly fill the rest of the way with half-and-half. Do not stir.

SMOKY MARTINI

MAKES 1 DRINK

3 oz. gin
½ oz. dry vermouth
1 tsp. scotch whiskey

Pour ingredients into a shaker with ice. Stir and strain into a chilled martini glass. Garnish with a lemon twist.

SNAKE BITE

MAKES 1 DRINK

2 oz. Yukon Jack
1 oz. lime juice or juice of ½ lime
1 oz. club soda (or 7-Up)

Pour ingredients into an old-fashioned glass over ice. Stir.

SNAKE BITE 2

MAKES 1 DRINK

1½ oz. Jack Daniel's whiskey
1½ oz. tequila
1½ oz. Southern Comfort

Shake with ice and strain into an old-fashioned glass.

SNAKE BITE SHOOTER

SHOT

MAKES 1 DRINK

1½ oz. Yukon Jack
1 oz. lime juice or
juice of ½ lime

Pour ingredients into a shaker half filled with ice. Shake well. Strain into a shot glass.

SNAKE CHARMER

HURRICANE

MAKES 1 DRINK

3 oz. peach
schnapps
2 oz. cranberry
juice
2 oz. milk

Pour all ingredients into a blender with ice and blend. Pour into a hurricane glass and garnish with a cherry.

SNAKE EYES

MARTINI

MAKES 2 DRINKS

3 oz. Kahlua
3 oz. cream
¼ oz. Frangelico

Pour equal parts Kahlua and cream into a shaker with ice. Stir well. Pour the mixture into two martini glasses. Then using a stirrer or narrow spoon, pour Frangelico into the center of each drink to create the "eye." Always serve in pairs.

SNAKE IN THE PANTS

MARTINI

MAKES 1 DRINK

½ oz. sweet
vermouth
½ oz. brandy
½ oz. lemon juice
1 tsp. sugar
1 oz. white rum

Pour ingredients into a shaker with ice. Shake well and strain into a martini glass. Garnish with a twist of lemon.

SNAKE OIL

MAKES 1 DRINK

1 oz. rye whiskey
½ oz. white crème
de menthe

Pour ingredients into a shaker with ice. Shake and strain into a chilled shot glass. Chase with a beer.

SNEAKY PETE

OLD-FASHIONED

MAKES 1 DRINK

1 oz. Kahlua
1 oz. rye whiskey
4 oz. milk

Pour the Kahlua into an old-fashioned glass with ice cubes. Add the milk and rye. Stir well.

SNOW BUNNY

IRISH COFFEE

MAKES 1 DRINK

1½ oz. triple sec
hot chocolate

Pour into an Irish coffee glass or mug. Garnish with a stick of cinnamon.

SNOW QUEEN (NONALCOHOLIC) HIGHBALL

MAKES 1 DRINK

2 oz. ruby red
grapefruit
juice
4 oz. 7-Up
½ oz. grenadine

Pour ingredients into a highball glass with a salt-and-sugared rim. Add ice to fill. Garnish with a lemon slice.

SNOW WHITE CARAMEL APPLE IRISH COFFEE

MAKES 1 DRINK

1 oz. Dooley's
toffee liqueur
½ oz. Tuaca
hot apple cider
whipped cream

Pour the Dooley's and Tuaca into an Irish coffee glass or mug. Add hot apple cider to fill. Top with whipped cream if you desire.

SNOWBALL MARTINI

MAKES 1 DRINK

1½ oz. gin
½ oz. anisette
1 tbs. light cream

Pour ingredients into a shaker with ice. Shake and strain into a martini glass.

SNOWBALL FIGHT COLLINS

MAKES 1 DRINK

1½ oz. vanilla
vodka
½ tsp. vanilla
extract
2 spoons sugar
or Splenda
half-and-half
or milk

Pour the vanilla vodka, vanilla extract, and sugar or Splenda, into a Collins glass over ice. Add half-and-half or milk to fill. Add more sugar or Splenda to taste. Garnish with a sprinkle of cinnamon.

SNOWCAP MARTINI

MAKES 1 DRINK

1 oz. Kamora
French vanilla
liqueur
1 oz. Skyy vodka
6 oz. cream or
whole milk

Pour ingredients into a shaker with ice. Shake and strain into a martini glass.

SNOWSHOE

IRISH COFFEE

MAKES 1 DRINK

*½ oz. banana
    liqueur
½ oz. Irish cream
    liqueur
6 oz. hot black
    coffee*

Pour the liqueurs into an Irish coffee glass or mug. Add coffee to fill. Stir well and top with whipped cream and a cherry.

SNUGGLE UPPER

IRISH COFFEE

MAKES 1 DRINK

*1 oz. raspberry
    schnapps
6 oz. hot chocolate*

Pour the schnapps into an Irish coffee glass or mug. Add the hot chocolate to fill. Top with whipped cream.

SNUGGLER

IRISH COFFEE

MAKES 1 DRINK

*1 oz. butterscotch
    schnapps
6 oz. hot chocolate*

Pour the schnapps into an Irish coffee glass or mug. Add the hot chocolate to fill. Top with whipped cream.

SNUGGLER 2

IRISH COFFEE

MAKES 1 DRINK

*1 oz. peppermint
    schnapps
6 oz. hot chocolate*

Pour the schnapps into an Irish coffee glass or mug. Add the hot chocolate to fill. Top with whipped cream.

SOFT BREEZE (NONALCOHOLIC)

MAKES 1 DRINK

3 oz. cranberry
   juice
3 oz. grapefruit
   juice
splash lime
   juice

Pour ingredients into a highball glass over ice. Garnish with a lime wedge.

SOMBRERO

OLD-FASHIONED

MAKES 1 DRINK

2 oz. coffee liqueur
2 oz. light cream

Pour liqueur into an old-fashioned glass over ice. Float cream on top.

SOMEWHERE OVER THE RAINBOW

COLLINS

MAKES 1 DRINK

1 oz. melon liqueur
1 oz. strawberry-
   flavored vodka
3 oz. sweet-and-
   sour mix
3 oz. pineapple juice
1 oz. Parfait Amour
1 oz. Goldschlager
   (optional)

Pour the melon liqueur in a Collins glass, then fill with ice. Pour the vodka, sweet-and-sour, and pineapple juice into a shaker with ice. Shake and strain on top of the melon liqueur. Float the Parfait Amour on top of that. Swirl the Goldschlager bottle to mix up the gold flakes and pour a shot. Serve the shot on the side as the gold at the end of the rainbow.

SONIC BOOM

OLD-FASHIONED

MAKES 1 DRINK

1½ oz. Malibu rum
1 oz. blue curaçao
1½ oz. orange juice
dash grenadine

Pour all ingredients into an old-fashioned glass over ice.

SONNY GETS KISSED

MARTINI

MAKES 1 DRINK

1½ oz. light rum
½ oz. apricot
  brandy
1 tsp. lime juice
1 tsp. lemon juice
½ tsp. fine sugar

Pour ingredients into a shaker half filled with ice. Shake well. Strain into a martini glass.

SOUL KISS

MARTINI

MAKES 1 DRINK

1 oz. bourbon
½ oz. dry vermouth
½ oz. Dubonnet
  rouge
½ oz. orange juice

Pour ingredients into a shaker half filled with ice. Shake well. Strain into a martini glass.

SOUR SWIZZLE

COLLINS

MAKES 1 DRINK

1 lime
1 tsp. powdered
  sugar
2 oz. carbonated
  water
2 dashes bitters
2 oz. Grand Marnier
1 tbs. grenadine
carbonated water

Squeeze the juice of the lime into a Collins glass. Add sugar and carbonated water and stir. Fill the glass with ice and stir thoroughly. Add bitters, grenadine, and Grand Marnier. Fill with carbonated water and serve with a swizzle stick in the glass.

SOUTH BRONX

HIGHBALL

MAKES 1 DRINK

½ oz. sloe gin
½ oz. Amaretto
½ oz. Southern
  Comfort
6 oz. lemon-lime
  soda

Pour ingredients into a highball glass over ice. Stir.

SOUTH OF THE BORDER

OLD-FASHIONED

MAKES 1 DRINK

1 oz. tequila
¾ oz. coffee brandy
juice of ½ lime

Pour ingredients into a shaker with ice. Shake and strain into an old-fashioned glass. Garnish with a lime slice.

SOUTH OF THE PEACHY RITA

MARGARITA

MAKES 1 DRINK

1½ oz. tequila
1 oz. peach
*   schnapps*
¹/₈ oz. grenadine
3 oz. sweet-and-
*   sour mix*

Pour the tequila, schnapps, grenadine, and sweet-and-sour mix into a blender with a cup of ice. Blend until smooth. Pour into a margarita glass rimmed with salt. Garnish with a lemon slice. (May be served shaken on the rocks.)

SOUTH PACIFIC (NONALCOHOLIC)

HIGHBALL

MAKES 1 DRINK

2 oz. orange juice concentrate
½ oz. lemonade concentrate
1½ oz. cranberry juice
2 tsp. fine sugar
2½ oz. water
1½ oz. Hawaiian Punch
¼ banana, sliced
¼ cup strawberries

Pour banana, strawberries, juice concentrates, sugar, and water into a blender. Blend until smooth. Pour into a highball or Collins glass. Add cranberry juice and Hawaiian Punch. Stir well. Garnish with an orange, lemon, or lime slice, and a cherry.

SOUTHERN BEAUTY

MARTINI

MAKES 1 DRINK

1¼ oz. brandy
1¼ oz. Southern
*   Comfort*

Pour ingredients into a shaker with ice. Stir and strain into a martini glass. Garnish with lightly beaten cream, spooned onto the top as a layer.

SOUTHERN BRIDE

MARTINI

MAKES 1 DRINK

1½ oz. gin
1 tsp. maraschino
*   liqueur*
1 oz. grapefruit
*   juice*

Pour ingredients into a shaker with ice. Shake well and strain into a martini glass.

SOUTHERN COMFORT COCKTAIL **MARTINI**

MAKES 1 DRINK

1¾ oz. Southern
*   Comfort*
juice of ½ lime
¾ oz. orange
*   liqueur*

Pour ingredients into a shaker with ice. Shake and strain into a martini glass.

SOUTHERN HOSPITALITY MARTINI **MARTINI**

MAKES 1 DRINK

2 oz. Southern
*   Comfort*
2 oz. peach
*   schnapps*

Pour ingredients into a shaker with ice. Shake for about 20 seconds, then strain into a martini glass.

SOUTHERN KISS

MARTINI

MAKES 1 DRINK

1¼ oz. Southern
*   Comfort*
¾ oz. Amaretto

Pour ingredients into a shaker with ice. Shake and strain into a martini glass.

SOUTHERN LADY

COLLINS

MAKES 1 DRINK

2 oz. bourbon
1 oz. Southern Comfort
1 oz. Amaretto
3 oz. pineapple juice
2 oz. lemon and lime club soda

Pour the bourbon, Southern Comfort, Amaretto, and pineapple juice into a shaker half filled with ice. Shake and strain into a Collins or parfait glass. Add soda. Garnish with fruit and a cherry.

SOUTHERN MARTINI

MARTINI

MAKES 1 DRINK

3 oz. gin
½ oz. triple sec
4 dashes bitters

Pour ingredients into a shaker with ice. Stir and strain into a chilled martini glass. Garnish with a lemon twist.

SOUTHERN SISTER (NONALCOHOLIC)

COLLINS

MAKES 1 DRINK

¼ cup crushed pineapple
3 oz. pineapple juice
3 oz. club soda

Pour pineapple and juice into a blender without ice. Blend well. Pour into a Collins glass. Add ice. Add soda and stir. Garnish with an orange, lemon, or lime slice, and a cherry.

SOUTHSIDE

MARTINI

MAKES 1 DRINK

2 oz. gin
1 oz. fresh lemon juice
2 sprigs mint
½ oz. simple syrup

Pour ingredients into a shaker with ice. Shake and strain into a martini glass. Garnish with mint sprigs.

SOUTHSIDE ROYALE

MARTINI

MAKES 1 DRINK

2 oz. gin
*1 oz. fresh lemon
  juice*
2 sprigs mint
½ oz. simple syrup
splash Champagne

Pour all ingredients except the Champagne into a shaker with ice. Shake and strain into a martini glass. Finish with a splash of bubbly. Garnish with mint sprigs.

SOVIET COSMOPOLITAN

MARTINI

MAKES 1 DRINK

1 oz. vodka
*¼ oz. apricot
  schnapps*
*¼ oz. cranberry
  juice*
*squeeze of lime
  juice*

Pour ingredients into a shaker with ice. Shake and strain into a chilled martini glass. Serve with a sugar-coated lime wedge.

SOVIET MARTINI

MARTINI

MAKES 1 DRINK

*3 oz. black currant
  vodka (or any
  other currant
  vodka)*
½ oz. dry vermouth
½ oz. Fino sherry

Pour ingredients into a shaker with ice. Stir and strain into a chilled martini glass. Garnish with a lemon twist.

SOYLENT GREEN

COLLINS

MAKES 1 DRINK

2 oz. vodka
2 oz. melon liqueur
*Kiwi lime soda
  water*

Pour ingredients into a shaker with ice. Strain into a Collins glass over ice.

SPANISH MOSS

OLD-FASHIONED

MAKES 1 DRINK

1 oz. tequila
1 oz. coffee liqueur
1 oz. crème de
menthe

Pour ingredients into a shaker with ice. Stir and strain into an old-fashioned glass over ice.

SPANISH MOSS 2

MARTINI

MAKES 1 DRINK

1 oz. coffee liqueur
1 oz. tequila
1 oz. green crème
de menthe

Pour ingredients into a shaker with ice. Stir and strain into a martini glass.

SPARKLE

PUNCH

MAKES 35 DRINKS

46 oz. pink
grapefruit juice
1 cup strawberries
1 cup raspberries
2 750-ml bottles
brut Champagne
1 750-ml bottle
burgundy wine
½ lemon

Squeeze the juice of the lemon into a large pitcher or punch bowl. Add grapefruit juice and Burgundy. Stir well. When ready to serve, the add fruit and top with the Champagne.

SPARKLING NEW YEAR CHEER

CHAMPAGNE

MAKES 1 DRINK

1 sugar cube
6 dashes bitters
chilled Champagne
twist of lemon

Soak the sugar cube with bitters and drop it into the bottom of a Champagne flute. Fill with Champagne. Twist the strip of lemon rind to release the oils. Rub around the rim of the glass and drop it into the drink.

SPEARMINT LIFESAVER

COLLINS

MAKES 1 DRINK

*1 oz. Jack Daniel's
  whiskey
½ oz. peppermint
  schnapps
Mountain Dew*

Pour whiskey and schnapps into a Collins glass. Add ice. Fill with Mountain Dew.

SPICED CIDER (NONALCOHOLIC)

IRISH COFFEE

MAKES 12 DRINKS

*1 gallon apple
  cider
1 tsp. allspice
½ tsp. ground
  cinnamon
½ tsp. ground
  cloves
1 cinnamon stick*

Pour all the ingredients into a pot and simmer for one hour. A Crock-Pot works well for this; set it on warm and leave it a bit longer. Change the recipe by adding ¼ cup of any of these other ingredients: real maple syrup, honey, white wine, or white grape juice. Serve warm.

SPICED FORBIDDEN FRUIT

COLLINS

MAKES 1 DRINK

*1 oz. spiced rum
1 oz. apple
  schnapps
¼ oz. cinnamon
  schnapps
7-Up*

Pour the spiced rum, apple schnapps, and cinnamon schnapps into a shaker with ice. Shake and strain into a Collins glass over ice. Add 7-Up to fill.

SPICY MARY

PILSNER

MAKES 1 DRINK

*1¼ oz. Absolut Peppar
1 lime wedge,
  squeezed
3 dashes Tabasco
  pepper sauce
2 dashes Worcester-
  shire sauce
½ tsp. hot horseradish
Bloody Mary mix*

Pour Absolut Peppar, lime, pepper sauce, Worcestershire sauce, and hot horseradish over ice into a large pilsner glass. Fill to the top with Bloody Mary mix. Garnish with a pickled asparagus spear.

SPREAD EAGLE

IRISH COFFEE

MAKES 1 DRINK

½ oz. Irish cream
½ oz. Frangelico
½ oz. Remy Martin
cognac
4 oz. hot black
coffee
2 oz. hot chocolate

Pour ingredients into an Irish coffee glass or mug. Top with whipped cream.

SPRIGHTLY SMASH (NONALCOHOLIC) **COLLINS**

MAKES 1 DRINK

3 oz. grapefruit
juice
1 tsp. Rose's
lime juice
1 tbs. fine sugar
4 sprigs mint,
chopped
club soda

Pour juices and sugar into a saucepan and bring to a boil. Add mint leaves and cool. Strain into a highball or Collins glass over ice. Add soda to fill. Garnish with mint.

SPRINGTIME MARTINI **MARTINI**

MAKES 1 DRINK

3 oz. Zubrowka
1 oz. Lillet (white)

Pour ingredients into a shaker with ice. Shake and strain into a chilled martini glass. Garnish with a pickled asparagus spear.

SPY CATCHER SHOOTER **SHOT**

MAKES 1 DRINK

1 oz. Canadian
whiskey
½ oz. Sambuca

Pour ingredients into a shaker with ice. Stir and strain into a shot glass.

ST. PATRICK'S DAY COCKTAIL

MARTINI

MAKES 1 DRINK

¾ oz. green crème
  de menthe
¾ oz. green
  Chartreuse
¾ oz. Irish whiskey
1 dash bitters

Pour ingredients into a shaker with ice. Stir well and strain into a martini glass.

STAR DAISY

BEER

MAKES 1 DRINK

1 oz. dry gin
1 oz. applejack
juice of ½ lemon
1 tsp. raspberry
  syrup or
  grenadine
½ tsp. powdered
  sugar

Pour ingredients into a shaker with ice. Shake well and strain into a beer stein or 8 oz. metal cup. Add a cube of ice. Garnish with an orange, lemon, or lime slice, and a cherry.

STARS AND STRIPES

CORDIAL

MAKES 1 DRINK

¾ oz. cherry
  Heering
¾ oz. cream
¾ oz. blue curaçao

Layer ingredients in a cordial glass in the order given by pouring slowing over the back of a spoon.

STATEN ISLAND MARTINI

MARTINI

MAKES 1 DRINK

3 oz. coffee-
  flavored vodka
½ oz. dry vermouth
1 oz. lime juice

Pour ingredients into a shaker with ice. Shake and strain into a chilled martini glass. Garnish with a maraschino cherry.

STATUE OF LIBERTY

SHOT

MAKES 1 DRINK

1/3 oz. grenadine
1/3 oz. white crème de cacao
1/3 oz. blue curaçao
1/8 oz. 151 rum

Pour the grenadine into the bottom of a shot glass. Gently layer the white crème de cacao on top of the grenadine by pouring it slowly over the back of a spoon. Repeat with the blue curaçao and rum. Light. Hold the burning red, white, and blue shot/torch high, like the Statue of Liberty. Wait until the flame burns out to drink it.

STEAMING BULL

IRISH COFFEE

MAKES 1 DRINK

2 oz. tequila
2 oz. beef bouillon
4 oz. tomato juice
splash lime juice
dash Worcestershire sauce

Heat all the ingredients except the tequila in a saucepan. Do not boil. Pour the warm mixture into an Irish coffee glass or mug and add the tequila.

STELLA'S GROOVE

MARTINI

MAKES 1 DRINK

1 oz. Bacardi Limon
1 oz. Absolut Citron vodka
1 oz. melon liqueur
3 oz. pineapple juice

Pour ingredients into a shaker with ice. Shake and strain into a martini glass.

STINGER

MARTINI

MAKES 1 DRINK

2 oz. B&B or five-star brandy
2 oz. white crème de menthe

Pour ingredients into a shaker with ice. Stir and strain into a martini glass. A Stinger on the Rocks is served in an old-fashioned glass with ice.

STIRRUP CUP

OLD-FASHIONED

MAKES 1 DRINK

1 oz. brandy
1 oz. cherry-
   flavored brandy
1 oz. lemon juice or
   juice of ½ lemon
1 tsp. sugar

Pour ingredients into a shaker half filled with ice. Shake well. Strain into an old-fashioned glass over ice.

STONE COLD DEAD

SHOT

MAKES 1 DRINK

½ oz. Jägermeister
½ oz. Bacardi white
   rum
½ oz. Rumple Minze

Pour into a shot glass and serve at room temperature.

STORM WARNING

IRISH COFFEE

MAKES 1 DRINK

6 oz. hot cider
1 oz. cinnamon
   schnapps

Serve in an Irish coffee glass or large mug with cinnamon stick.

STRAITS SLING

COLLINS

MAKES 1 DRINK

2 oz. gin
½ oz. dry cherry
   brandy
½ oz. Benedictine
1 oz. lemon juice
2 dashes orange
   bitters
2 dashes bitters

Shake with ice. Strain into an ice-filled tumbler or Collins glass. Fill with soda water.

STRAWBERRY COLADA

PARFAIT

MAKES 1 DRINK

2 oz. rum
1 oz. coconut
  cream
½ cup strawberries,
  fresh or frozen
4 oz. pineapple
  juice

Pour all ingredients into a blender in this order: rum, coconut cream, strawberries, pineapple juice, and ice. Blend thoroughly. Pour into a Collins or parfait glass. Garnish with a pineapple slice or strawberry and a straw.

STRAWBERRY DAIQUIRI

COLLINS

MAKES 1 DRINK

2 oz. light rum
½ oz. triple sec
1 oz. lime juice
½ tsp. sugar
1 cup ice
5 strawberries

Pour all the ingredients into a blender. Blend well at high speed. Pour into a Collins glass. Serve with a straw.

STRAWBERRY DAWN (NONALCOHOLIC)

WINE

MAKES 1 DRINK

¼ cup straw-
  berries
1 oz. orange juice
1 tsp. sugar
orange-flavored
  sparkling
  water
orange twist

Pour berries, juice, and sugar into a blender without ice. Blend well. Pour into a large wine glass. Add sparkling water to fill. Garnish with an orange twist.

STRAWBERRY FLAPPER

CHAMPAGNE

MAKES 2 DRINKS

8 fresh
  strawberries,
  hulled
4 dashes crème de
  cassis
10 ice cubes
chilled Champagne

Put the strawberries into a blender and pulse a couple of times. Add the crème de cassis and ice cubes and blend until smooth. Fill two Champagne flutes halfway with the strawberry blend. Add Champagne to fill.

STRAWBERRY KISS

MAKES 1 DRINK

1 oz. tequila rose
½ oz. light rum
1 oz. chocolate
    liqueur
1 oz. half-and-half

MARTINI

Pour ingredients into a shaker with ice. Shake well and strain into a chilled martini glass.

STRAWBERRY MARGARITA

MAKES 1 DRINK

½ cup fresh
    or frozen
    strawberries
1 oz. tequila
½ oz. Cointreau
1 oz. Stoli strasberi
    vodka
2 oz. sweet-and-
    sour mix

MARGARITA

Pour ingredients into a blender with ice. Blend until smooth. Pour into a margarita glass rimmed with sugar. Garnish with a slice of lime and a strawberry.

STRAWBERRY MOJITORITA

MAKES 1 DRINK

juice from half a
    lime
5 large mint leaves
4 large
    strawberries
1½ oz. tequila
½ oz. triple sec
sweet-and-sour mix

MARGARITA

Reserve one small mint leaf and half a strawberry; muddle the lime juice and the rest of the mint and strawberries. Pour that mixture into a salt-rimmed margarita glass and fill with ice. Add the tequila and triple sec, then fill with sweet-and-sour mix. Garnish with a slice of lime, strawberry half, and mint leaf.

STRAWBERRY SEXUAL HEALING 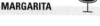 MARTINI

MAKES 1 DRINK

6 fresh
    strawberries
small handful
    of fresh mint
    leaves
juice of half a lime
1 oz. water
1 spoon sugar
1½ oz. light rum

Put all the ingredients except the rum into a shaker and mash together with a fork. Add a scoop of ice and the rum. Shake long and hard. Strain through cheesecloth or strainer into a martini glass.

STRAWBERRY SUNRISE

HIGHBALL

MAKES 1 DRINK

2 oz. strawberry
   liqueur
1 oz. grenadine
3 oz. orange juice

Pour ingredients into a highball glass over ice. Stir well. Garnish with an orange, lemon, or lime slice, and a cherry.

STRIP AND GO NAKED

COLLINS

MAKES 6–8 DRINKS

6 cans of beer
12 oz. vodka
12 oz. lemonade
   (concentrate)

Into a large pitcher, pour 3 cans of beer, then the vodka and lemonade, then the last 3 beers. Mix gently and serve in Collins glasses over ice.

STRIP, SKIP, AND GO NAKED

COLLINS

MAKES 1 DRINK

2 oz. lime-flavored
   gin
5 oz. limeade
½ oz. grenadine
beer
lime or a cherry

Pour the lime-flavored gin, limeade, and grenadine into a Collins glass with ice. Add beer to fill. Garnish with a lime or a cherry.

STROGANOFF SLING

COLLINS

MAKES 1 DRINK

1½ oz. raspberry
   vodka
½ oz. gin
½ oz. maraschino
   liqueur
1 oz. lemon juice
1 tsp. superfine
   sugar
club soda

Mix all ingredients except club soda in a tall, chilled Collins glass. Add several ice cubes and fill with cold club soda. Stir gently and garnish with a cherry and orange slice.

STUPID CUPID

MAKES 1 DRINK

1½ oz. vodka
½ oz. sloe gin
1 oz. lemon juice or
  juice of ½ lemon

Pour ingredients into a shaker with ice. Stir and strain into a martini glass. Garnish with a cherry.

SUGAR, SPICE, & EVERYTHING NICE BEER

MAKES 1 DRINK

12 oz. of Guinness
  stout
¼ cup sweetened
  condensed milk
pinch of cinnamon
pinch of nutmeg
1 packet hot cocoa
  mix

Chill the Guinness and the condensed milk. Pour the Guinness into a pitcher. Add the condensed milk, cinnamon, nutmeg, and cocoa mix, then stir until blended. Pour into a tall beer glass.

SUGAR DADDY

MARTINI

MAKES 1 DRINK

2 oz. gin
2 tsp. maraschino
  liqueur
1 oz. pineapple
  juice
dash bitters

Pour ingredients into a shaker with ice. Shake and strain into a martini glass.

SUICIDE

MAKES 1 DRINK

½ oz. 151 proof
  rum
½ oz. light rum
½ oz. Myer's rum
½ oz. triple sec
2 oz. strawberry
  mix
splash orange juice

Pour ingredients into a blender. Blend with ice until smooth and serve in a martini glass.

SUMMERTIME SLUSHIES

COLLINS

MAKES 25 DRINKS

*1 bottle (750ml)
   vanilla vodka
1 bottle (750ml) of
   coconut rum
1 gallon orange juice
1 gallon pineapple
   juice
2 2-liter bottles of
   citrus soda*

Pour the vanilla vodka, coconut rum, orange juice, and pineapple juice into a big bowl or pot. Stir. Set in the freezer for at least twenty-four hours or until frozen. When frozen, place two scoops in a Collins glass, then fill with the citrus soda.

SUMMIT EXPRESS

ESPRESSO

MAKES 1 DRINK

*1/3 shot Chambord
1/3 shot vodka
1/3 shot Godiva
   chocolate
   liqueur
2 oz. hot espresso*

Pour the liqueur into a small coffee cup. Add the espresso and stir. Top with whipped cream and chocolate sprinkles.

SUNBURN

COLLINS

MAKES 1 DRINK

*1 oz. tequila
1 oz. triple sec
cranberry juice*

Pour tequila and triple sec into a Collins glass filled with ice. Add the cranberry juice to fill.

SUNDOWNER

MARTINI

MAKES 1 DRINK

*1½ oz. brandy
¾ oz. Van Der Hum
   Liqueur
4 dashes lemon
   juice
4 dashes orange
   juice*

Pour ingredients into a shaker with ice. Shake and strain into a martini glass.

449

SUNDOWNER (NONALCOHOLIC) WINE

MAKES 1 DRINK

4 oz. white
grape juice
2½ oz. cold
sparkling
water
fresh mint sprig
for garnish

Pour the ingredients into a white wine glass with ice. Stir. Garnish with the mint sprigs.

SUNLIGHT SUNDROP SHOT

MAKES 1 DRINK

1 shot Tuaca
dash triple sec
dash sweet-and-
sour mix

Pour ingredients into a shaker with ice. Shake and strain into a shot glass.

SUNNY LAGOON (NONALCOHOLIC) COLLINS

MAKES 1 DRINK

2 oz. lemon juice
2 tsp. granulated
sugar
5 oz. chilled
water

Dissolve the sugar in the lemon juice in a Collins glass. Stir well. Add ice. Add water. Garnish with lemon.

SUNNY SOUR SOUR GLASS

MAKES 1 DRINK

1¼ oz. dark rum
¼ oz. lemon juice
½ tsp. superfine
sugar

Pour rum, lemon juice, and sugar into a shaker with ice. Shake well and strain into a sour glass. Garnish with a lemon wedge and a cherry.

SUNNY SWIZZLE (NONALCOHOLIC) COLLINS

MAKES 1 DRINK

3 oz. mixed juice
  like banana-
  strawberry
1½ oz. lime juice
1 tsp. fine sugar
1 dash orange
  bitters
3 oz. club soda

Pour the juices, sugar, and bitters into a shaker half filled with ice. Shake well. Strain into a Collins glass almost filled with crushed ice. Stir. Fill with soda. Serve with a swizzle stick.

SUNSHINE STATE (NONALCOHOLIC) COLLINS

MAKES 1 DRINK

4 oz. cherry
  soda
½ cup orange
  sherbet
1 tsp. lemon
  juice

Pour ingredients into a blender with ice. Blend well. Pour into a Collins or highball glass. Serve with a straw.

SURF'S UP
COLLINS

MAKES 1 DRINK

½ oz. crème de
  banane
½ oz. white crème
  de cacao
5 oz. pineapple
  juice
1 oz. light cream

Pour ingredients into a blender with ice. Blend thoroughly. Pour into a Collins or parfait glass. Garnish with a fruit slice and cherry.

SWEET & INNOCENT COOLER COLLINS

MAKES 1 DRINK

4 oz. white wine of
  your choice
Diet Rite white
  grape soda
Sprig of grapes

Pour the wine into a Collins glass of ice. Fill with Diet Rite white grape soda and stir. If preferred, substitute the soda with ginger ale, Sprite, or 7-Up.

SWEET & SOUR APPLE (NONALCOHOLIC) SOUR

MAKES 1 DRINK

2 oz. apple
    juice
½ oz. lemon
    juice
1 tsp. fine
    sugar
1 egg white

Pour ingredients into a shaker with ice. Shake well and strain into a sour glass. Garnish with an orange slice and a cherry.

SWEET BIRD (NONALCOHOLIC)   HIGHBALL

MAKES 1 DRINK

2 oz. pineapple
    juice
2 oz. orange
    juice
1 oz. lemonade
1 tbs. crushed
    pineapple

Spoon crushed pineapple into a highball glass. Add lemonade and stir well. Add ice. Add juices and stir. Garnish with a fruit slice and cherry.

SWEET CITY   HIGHBALL

MAKES 1 DRINK

1 oz. Bois premium
    genever
1 oz. red vermouth
1 oz. apricot brandy

Pour the ingredients into a highball glass with ice. Stir well. Garnish with a strip of orange zest.

SWEET KISSES   MARTINI

MAKES 1 DRINK

1¼ oz. Amaretto
3 oz. fresh chopped
    strawberries
¾ tsp. sugar
¼ oz. lime juice
1 oz. vanilla ice
    cream
splash spiced rum

Pour all ingredients except the spiced rum into a blender with 10 oz. of ice. Blend until smooth. Pour into a martini glass. Finish with a splash of spiced rum.

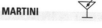

SWEET MARTINI

MARTINI

MAKES 1 DRINK

3 oz. gin
1 oz. sweet
  vermouth
dash orange bitters

Pour ingredients into a shaker with ice. Stir, then strain into a chilled martini glass. Garnish with an orange twist.

SWEET SUNRISE (NONALCOHOLIC) COLLINS

MAKES 1 DRINK

orange juice
½ oz. grenadine

Fill a Collins glass with ice. Add orange juice to fill. Slowly pour the grenadine into the drink; it will sink to the bottom of the glass, making a sunrise effect. Garnish with an orange or peach slice.

SWEET TEQUILA

SNIFTER

MAKES 1 DRINK

2 oz. tequila
1 oz. Pernod

Pour ingredients into a shaker with ice. Stir gently and strain into a brandy snifter.

SWEETHEART'S KISS

COLLINS

MAKES 1 DRINK

1 oz. bourbon
6 oz. apricot nectar

Pour into a Collins glass over ice.

SWEETIE MARTINI

MARTINI

MAKES 1 DRINK

3 oz. gin
½ oz. dry vermouth
½ oz. sweet
   vermouth

Pour ingredients into a shaker with ice. Shake and strain into a chilled martini glass. Garnish with a lemon twist.

SWIRL FROM IPANEMA

COLLINS

MAKES 1 DRINK

1 oz. dark rum
1 oz. coffee liqueur
3 oz. pineapple
   juice
2 oz. coconut
   cream
half-and-half
chocolate syrup

Pour the dark rum, coffee liqueur, and piña colada mix into a blender with a cup of ice. Blend, slowly adding the half-and-half until a smooth consistency is achieved. Swirl the chocolate syrup around the inside of a Collins glass, then pour in the blended mixture.

T-BIRD

HIGHBALL

MAKES 1 DRINK

1¹/₈ oz. Canadian
   whiskey
¾ oz. Amaretto
2 oz. pineapple
   juice
1 oz. orange juice
2 dashes grenadine

Shake with ice and strain into a highball glass. Garnish with an orange slice and a cherry.

T.N.T.

MARTINI

MAKES 1 DRINK

1½ oz. blended
   whiskey
1 oz. anisette

Pour ingredients into a shaker half filled with ice. Shake well. Strain into a martini glass.

T

TADISMS MARTINI

MARTINI

MAKES 1 DRINK

1¼ oz. Absolut
   currant vodka
¾ oz. Apple Pucker
½ oz. Cointreau
1 oz. sweet-and-
   sour mix
½ oz. cranberry
   juice
splash 7-Up

Pour all ingredients except 7-Up into a shaker about half-filled with ice. Shake and strain into a chilled martini glass. Add the splash 7-Up. Garnish with a cherry and a rimmed lime wedge.

TAHITI CLUB

OLD-FASHIONED

MAKES 1 DRINK

1 oz. light rum
1 oz. dark rum
2 oz. pineapple juice
1 tsp. lemon juice or
   juice of ½ lemon
1 tsp. lime juice or
   juice of ½ lime
1 tsp. maraschino
   liqueur

Pour all ingredients into a shaker half filled with ice. Shake well. Strain into an old-fashioned glass nearly filled with ice. Garnish with an orange, lemon, or lime slice, and a cherry.

TAHOE TOMAKAZE

MARTINI

MAKES 1 DRINK

1 shot peach
   schnapps
1 shot vodka
1 shot Rose's lime
   juice
½ shot sweet-and-
   sour mix

Pour ingredients into a shaker with ice. Shake and strain into a martini glass.

TAILSPIN

MARTINI

MAKES 1 DRINK

¾ oz. gin
¾ oz. sweet
   vermouth
¾ oz. green
   Chartreuse
1 dash Campari

Pour ingredients into a shaker with ice. Stir and strain into a martini glass. Garnish with a lemon twist and a cherry.

TALL AND DIZZY

MAKES 1 DRINK

*1 oz. Southern
  Comfort*
½ oz. Malibu rum
*3 oz. pineapple
  juice*
*2 oz. cranberry
  juice*
2 oz. orange juice
whipped cream

Pour all the ingredients with ice into a shaker. Fill with whipped cream and shake vigorously. Pour into a highball glass, add a squeeze of lime, and garnish with a cherry.

TALL SHIP

MAKES 1 DRINK

1½ oz. Kahlua
*1½ oz. Irish cream
  liqueur*
1½ oz. Drambuie

Pour all ingredients into an old-fashioned glass. Stir.

TANGERINE DREAMS

MAKES 1 DRINK

*1 oz. Isolabella
  (or Mandarine
  Napoleon)*
1 oz. vodka
orange juice

Pour liqueur and vodka into a sugar-rimmed highball glass over ice. Add orange juice and garnish with a slice of orange.

TANGO

MARTINI

MAKES 1 DRINK

½ oz. rum
*½ oz. sweet
  vermouth*
½ oz. dry vermouth
½ oz. Benedictine
½ oz. orange juice

Pour ingredients into a shaker with ice. Shake and strain into a martini glass. Garnish with an orange twist.

TARANTULA

MAKES 1 DRINK

1½ oz. scotch
  whiskey
1 oz. sweet
  vermouth
½ oz. Benedictine

Pour ingredients into a shaker with ice. Stir and strain into a martini glass. Garnish with a lemon twist.

TARTAN SWIZZLE

COLLINS

MAKES 1 DRINK

1½ oz. lime juice
1 tsp. superfine
  sugar
2 oz. scotch
  whiskey
dash bitters
3 oz. club soda

Pour lime juice, sugar, scotch, and bitters into a shaker with ice. Shake well. Almost fill a Collins glass with ice. Stir until glass is frosted. Strain the shaken mixture into the glass and add the club soda.

TASTING AWAY IN MARGARITAVILLE MARGARITA

MAKES 1 DRINK

1½ oz. tequila
½ oz. triple sec
2 oz. mango nectar
1 oz. sweet-and-
  sour mix

Pour the tequila, triple sec, mango nectar, and sweet-and-sour mix into a blender with a cup of ice. Blend until smooth. Pour into a salt-rimmed margarita glass. Add a slice of lime.

TEA TINI

MARTINI

MAKES 1 DRINK

1¾ oz. vodka
1 oz. sweet iced
  tea
¼ oz. fresh lemon
  juice

Pour ingredients into a shaker with ice. Shake well and strain into a chilled martini glass rimmed with sugar. Garnish with the lemon wedge.

TEMPTATION COCKTAIL

MARTINI

MAKES 1 DRINK

*1½ oz. scotch
    whiskey
½ tsp. Dubonnet
½ tsp. triple sec
½ tsp. Anis*

Pour scotch, Dubonnet, triple sec, and Anis into a shaker with ice. Shake and strain into a martini glass. Garnish with twists of orange and lemon peels.

TENNESSEE MUD

IRISH COFFEE

MAKES 1 DRINK

*1 oz. Amaretto
½ oz. Jack Daniel's
    Tennessee
    whiskey
6 oz. hot black
    coffee*

Pour ingredients into an Irish coffee glass or mug. Top with whipped cream.

TEQUILA CANYON

COLLINS

MAKES 1 DRINK

*1½ oz. tequila
¼ oz. triple sec
3 oz. cranberry
    juice
½ oz. pineapple
    juice
½ oz. orange juice*

Pour tequila, triple sec, and cranberry juice into a Collins or highball glass with ice. Add pineapple and orange juices. Stir. Serve with a straw.

TEQUILA COCKTAIL

MARTINI

MAKES 1 DRINK

*1½ oz. tequila
½ oz. dry vermouth
1 dash bitters*

Pour ingredients into a shaker with ice. Stir well and strain into a martini glass. Garnish with a twist of lemon and an olive.

TEQUILA COLLINS

COLLINS

MAKES 1 DRINK

2 oz. tequila
juice of ½ lemon
1 tsp. powdered
*   sugar*
carbonated water

Pour ingredients into a shaker with ice. Shake well and strain into a Collins glass over ice. Fill with carbonated water and stir. Garnish with slices of lemon and orange and a cherry. Serve with a straw.

TEQUILA DRY

OLD-FASHIONED

MAKES 1 DRINK

1½ oz. tequila
½ oz. dry vermouth
¼ oz. grenadine

Pour ingredients into a shaker with ice. Stir and strain into an old-fashioned glass over ice. Garnish with lime or orange slices.

TEQUILA FROST

PARFAIT

MAKES 1 DRINK

1¼ oz. tequila
1¼ oz. pineapple
*   juice*
1¼ oz. grapefruit
*   juice*
½ oz. honey
½ oz. grenadine
2 oz. vanilla ice
*   cream*

Pour ingredients into a blender. Blend until smooth and pour into a parfait glass. Garnish with an orange slice and a cherry.

TEQUILA FURNACE

SHOT

MAKES 1 DRINK

1 shot tequila
5–10 drops Tabasco
*   hot pepper*
*   sauce*
salt
lime wedge

Pour the Tabasco into a chilled shot glass. Add the tequila. Chase with the salt and a lime.

TEQUILA GIMLET

MAKES 1 DRINK

2 oz. tequila
½ oz. Rose's lime
  juice (or 1 oz.
  lime juice and 1
  tsp. fine sugar)

Pour ingredients into a shaker with ice. Stir and strain into a martini glass. Garnish with a lime wedge.

TEQUILA MEADOW (NONALCOHOLIC) COLLINS

MAKES 1 DRINK

2 oz. orange juice
2 oz. pineapple
  juice
½ oz. cranberry
  juice
2 oz. lemon and
  lime soda
¼ oz. grenadine

Pour all ingredients except soda into a shaker half filled with ice. Shake well. Strain into a Collins glass over ice. Add soda. Stir gently. Garnish with an orange, lemon, or lime slice, and a cherry.

TEQUILA MOCKINGBIRD

MARTINI

MAKES 1 DRINK

1½ oz. tequila
1 oz. white crème
  de menthe
1 oz. lime juice or
  juice of ½ lime

Pour ingredients into a shaker half filled with ice. Shake well. Strain into a martini glass.

TEQUILA OLD-FASHIONED

MAKES 1 DRINK

2 oz. tequila
1 tsp. water
1 cube or ½ tsp.
  sugar
dash or 2 bitters
lemon twist

Pour the sugar, bitters, and water into an old-fashioned glass and muddle with a spoon. Add tequila and stir. Add ice and a lemon twist. Garnish with a slice of orange or lemon and a cherry.

TEQUILA PUNCH

MAKES ABOUT 40 DRINKS

1 liter tequila
4 bottles chilled sauterne
1 bottle chilled Champagne
8 cups diced fruit
fine sugar to taste

Pour tequila, wine, and fruit into a punch bowl. Add ice and Champagne just before serving.

TEQUILA SOUR

SOUR GLASS

MAKES 1 DRINK

2 oz. tequila
1 oz. lemon juice or juice of ½ lemon
1 tsp. fine sugar (or 1½ oz. sweet-and-sour mix instead of lemon and sugar)

Pour ingredients into a shaker with ice. Shake and strain into a sour glass. Garnish with lemon and a cherry.

TEQUILA STINGER

MARTINI

MAKES 1 DRINK

1½ oz. white tequila
¾ oz. white crème de menthe

Pour ingredients into a shaker with ice. Shake well and strain into a martini glass.

TEQUILA STRAIGHT

SHOT

MAKES 1 DRINK

1½ oz. tequila
pinch salt
lemon wedge

Pour tequila into a shot glass. To drink: Sprinkle salt on the back of your left hand, hold the glass in that hand and the lemon wedge in the other. Lick the salt, drink the tequila, and suck the lemon.

TEQUILA SUBMARINE

PINT

MAKES 1 DRINK

2 oz. tequila
Corona or other
   light Mexican
   beer

Pour chilled tequila into a pint glass. Top with ice cold beer. Serve immediately.

TEQUILA SUNRISE

COLLINS

MAKES 1 DRINK

1½ oz. tequila
½ oz. grenadine
orange juice

Fill a Collins glass with ice. Add the tequila, and fill with the orange juice. Now pour the grenadine into the center of the drink. The grenadine is very heavy and will fall to the bottom of the glass, creating a sunrise effect. Garnish with an orange, lemon, or lime slice, and a cherry.

TEQUILA SUNRISE MARGARITA MARGARITA

MAKES 1 DRINK

1½ oz. tequila
½ oz. triple sec
1 oz. orange juice
1 oz. sweet-and-
   sour mix
½ oz. grenadine

Pour the tequila, triple sec, orange juice, and sweet-and-sour mix into a blender with a cup of ice. Blend until smooth. Pour the grenadine into a salt-rimmed margarita glass. Add the blended mixture to fill. Garnish with a lime slice.

TEQUILA SUNSET

COLLINS

MAKES 1 DRINK

1 oz. tequila
orange juice
½ oz. blackberry
   brandy

Fill a Collins glass with ice. Add the tequila, and fill with the orange juice. Top with blackberry brandy and stir lightly. Garnish with a cherry.

TEQUILA TODDY

 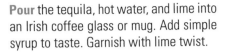

MAKES 1 DRINK

1½ oz. tequila
½ oz. simple syrup
4 oz. hot water
1 twist lime

Pour the tequila, hot water, and lime into an Irish coffee glass or mug. Add simple syrup to taste. Garnish with lime twist.

TEQUONIC

OLD-FASHIONED

MAKES 1 DRINK

2 oz. tequila
juice of ½ lemon
    or lime
tonic water

Pour tequila into an old-fashioned glass over ice. Add the juice, and fill with tonic water and stir.

TERMINATOR SHOOTER

SHOT

MAKES 1 DRINK

½ oz. Jägermeister
½ oz. Irish cream
    liqueur
½ oz. peppermint
    schnapps
½ oz. bourbon

Pour ingredients into a shaker with ice. Stir and strain into a shot glass.

TEXAS ROSE

MARTINI

MAKES 1 DRINK

1 oz. rum
2 oz. orange juice
1 oz. crème de
    banane
1 oz. pineapple
    juice

Pour ingredients into a shaker with ice. Shake well and strain into a martini glass over ice.

TEXAS TEA

MARTINI

MAKES 1 DRINK

¾ oz. vodka
¾ oz. rum
¾ oz. gin
¾ oz. triple sec
¾ oz. tequila
1½ oz. sweet-and-
    sour mix
splash orange juice
splash cola

Pour ingredients into a shaker with ice. Shake and strain into a martini glass. Garnish with a lemon wedge.

THANK GOD I'M TWENTY-ONE!   SHOT

MAKES 1 DRINK

½ oz. coffee
    liqueur
½ oz. Irish cream
    liqueur
whipped cream

Layer the coffee liqueur over the Irish cream liqueur in a shot glass by pouring over the back of a spoon. Top with a dollop of whipped cream. To drink properly: Put your hands behind your back, suck out the cream, wrap your lips around the shot glass, tilt back your head, and swallow the liquor, then put the shot glass back down with your mouth.

THANKSGIVING SPECIAL

MARTINI

MAKES 1 DRINK

1 oz. gin
¾ oz. apricot-
    flavored brandy
¾ oz. dry vermouth
splash lemon juice

Pour ingredients into a shaker with ice. Shake well and strain into a martini glass.

THANKSGIVING TURKEY

COLLINS

MAKES 1 DRINK

1½ oz. bourbon
    whiskey
4 oz. orange juice
1 tsp. frozen
    lemonade
    concentrate
1 tsp. frozen limeade
    concentrate
3 oz. ginger ale

Pour the bourbon, orange juice, lemonade concentrate, and limeade concentrate into a Collins glass. Stir. Add ice. Fill with ginger ale. Stir again.

THANKSGIVING TURKEY COSMO   MARTINI

MAKES 1 DRINK

1½ oz. Wild Turkey
½ oz. triple sec
¼ oz. lime juice
2 oz. cranberry
    juice

Pour ingredients into a shaker with ice. Shake and strain into a martini glass.

THIN MINT   OLD-FASHIONED

MAKES 1 DRINK

1 oz. green crème
    de menthe
1 oz. Godiva
    Liqueur
1 oz. chocolate
    liqueur
1 oz. Irish cream
    liqueur
1 oz. cream

Pour ingredients into an old-fashioned glass.

THIRD DEGREE MARTINI   MARTINI

MAKES 1 DRINK

3 oz. gin
1 oz. dry vermouth
½ oz. Pernod

Pour ingredients into a shaker with ice. Shake and strain into a chilled martini glass. Garnish with a star anise.

THIRD RAIL   MARTINI

MAKES 1 DRINK

¾ oz. white rum
¾ oz. brandy
¾ oz. apple brandy
¼ tsp. Anis

Pour ingredients into a shaker with ice. Shake and strain into a martini glass.

THISTLE COCKTAIL

MAKES 1 DRINK

1½ oz. sweet
    vermouth
1½ oz. scotch
    whiskey
2 dashes bitters

Pour ingredients into a shaker with ice. Shake and strain into a martini glass.

THREE MILE ISLAND ICED TEA

MAKES 1 DRINK

½ oz. gin
½ oz. vodka
½ oz. tequila
½ oz. white rum
½ oz. triple sec
½ oz. lemon juice
½ oz. lime juice
cola

Pour all ingredients except cola into a shaker with ice. Shake well and pour into a hurricane glass. Add cola as you pour to nearly fill. Garnish with lemon and lime slices.

THREE SEÑORITAS MARGARITA

MAKES 1 DRINK

1½ oz. triple sec
juice from ½ lime
5 oz. sweet-and-
    sour mix
1 oz. brandy
1 oz. tequila rose
1 oz. sherry
3 plastic test tubes

Pour the triple sec, lime juice, and sweet-and-sour into a blender with a cup of ice. Blend until smooth, then pour into a margarita glass. Fill the first test tube with brandy, the next with tequila rose, and the third with sherry. Stick all three tubes so they stand up in the margarita. Drink the "ladies" at your leisure.

THRILLER

MAKES 1 DRINK

1½ oz. scotch
    whiskey
1 oz. green ginger
    wine
1 oz. orange juice

Pour ingredients into a shaker with ice. Shake and strain into a martini glass.

THUNDERCLAP

MARTINI

MAKES 1 DRINK

1½ oz. bourbon
whiskey
½ oz. gin
½ oz. brandy

Pour ingredients into a shaker with ice.
Stir and strain into a martini glass.

THUNDERCLAP 2

MARTINI

MAKES 1 DRINK

¾ oz. scotch
whiskey
¾ oz. brandy
¾ oz. gin

Pour ingredients into a shaker with ice.
Shake and strain into a martini glass.

TIDAL WAVE

OLD-FASHIONED

MAKES 1 DRINK

1 oz. rum
1 oz. vodka
1 oz. brandy
1 oz. bourbon
dash orgeat syrup
½ lime, squeezed
½ oz. sweet and-
sour mix
splash 151 rum

Pour in order given into a double old-
fashioned glass over ice.

TIDAL WAVE OF PASSION

COLLINS

MAKES 1 DRINK

2 oz. passion fruit
liqueur
3 oz. orange juice
1 oz. grapefruit
juice

Pour ingredients into a Collins glass over
ice. Garnish with an orange, lemon, or
lime slice, and a cherry.

TIE ME TO THE BEDPOST NAKED HIGHBALL

MAKES 1 DRINK

½ oz. vodka
½ oz. Jack Daniel's
  whiskey
½ oz. Southern Comfort
½ oz. peach schnapps
½ oz. Amaretto
splash grenadine
splash 7-Up
splash pineapple juice

Pour over ice into a highball glass. Stir.

TIGER'S MILK OLD-FASHIONED

MAKES 1 DRINK

1 oz. dark rum
1 oz. brandy
4 oz. milk
2 tsp. fine sugar

Pour ingredients into a shaker half filled with ice. Shake well. Strain into an old-fashioned glass over ice.

TIGHT SWEATER IRISH COFFEE

MAKES 1 DRINK

1 oz. Kahlua
¼ oz. Frangelico
  hazelnut liqueur
¼ oz. Amaretto
¼ oz. Irish cream
6 oz. hot black
  coffee

Pour into an Irish coffee glass or mug. Top with whipped cream.

TIJUANA SLING COLLINS

MAKES 1 DRINK

1¼ oz. tequila
¾ oz. crème de
  cassis
¾ oz. fresh lime
  juice
2 dashes
  Peychaud's
  bitters
club soda

Pour all ingredients except the club soda into a shaker with ice. Shake and strain over ice into a Collins glass. Top with soda. Garnish with a lime slice.

TIJUANA TAXI

MAKES 1 DRINK

1½ oz. gold tequila
1 oz. blue curaçao
1 oz. passion fruit
  liqueur
4 oz. lemon and
  lime
club soda

Pour liquors into a highball glass over ice. Stir. Add soda to fill. Garnish with an orange slice and a cherry.

TIJUANA TAXI 2

HIGHBALL

MAKES 1 DRINK

2 oz. gold tequila
1 oz. blue curaçao
1 oz. tropical fruit
  schnapps
lemon-lime soda

Pour liquors into a highball glass over ice. Stir. Add soda to fill. Garnish with an orange slice and a cherry.

TIKI TORCH

TIKI

MAKES 1 DRINK

1 oz. dark rum
1 oz. coconut rum
½ oz. grenadine
pineapple juice
orange juice
sweet-and-sour mix
1 oz. 151 proof rum

Pour the dark rum, coconut rum, and grenadine into a tall, ice-filled tiki glass. Fill with equal parts pineapple juice, orange juice, and sweet-and-sour mix. Stir. Top the drink with the rum and light. Wait until the fire has died down to drink.

TIKI DREAM

HIGHBALL

MAKES 1 DRINK

¾ oz. melon liqueur
4¼ oz. cranberry
  juice

Pour ingredients into a sugar-rimmed highball glass over ice. Garnish with a wedge of watermelon.

TILLICUM

MAKES 1 DRINK

2¼ oz. gin
¾ oz. dry vermouth
2 dashes
   Peychaud's
   bitters

Pour ingredients into a shaker with ice. Stir and strain into a martini glass. Garnish with a slice of smoked salmon skewered flat on a pick.

TILT THE KILT

MAKES 1 DRINK

1 tsp. powdered
   sugar
2 tsp. water
2 oz. scotch
   whiskey
1 tsp. lemon juice
splash triple sec

Pour all ingredients except triple sec into a shaker with ice. Stir and strain into a martini glass. Float the triple sec on top.

TIME OUT

 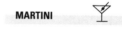

MAKES 2 DRINKS

3 oz. Jägermeister
1 oz. anisette

Pour ingredients into a shaker with ice. Shake well and strain into two sugar-rimmed martini glasses.

TIP TOP

MAKES 1 DRINK

2 oz. dry vermouth
1 splash
   Benedictine
2 dashes bitters

Pour ingredients into a shaker with ice. Stir and strain into a martini glass. Garnish with a lemon twist.

TIPPERARY COCKTAIL

MARTINI

MAKES 1 DRINK

¾ oz. sweet
  vermouth
¾ oz. Irish whiskey
¾ oz. green
  Chartreuse

Pour ingredients into a shaker with ice.
Stir and strain into a martini glass.

TITTY TWISTER

HIGHBALL

MAKES 1 DRINK

3 oz. coconut rum
5 oz. orange juice
2 oz. pineapple
  juice

Pour into a highball glass over ice.

TOAD IN A BLENDER

MARTINI

MAKES 1 DRINK

1½ oz. coffee
  liqueur
½ oz. green crème
  de menthe
½ oz. cinnamon
  schnapps

Pour the coffee liqueur, green crème de
menthe, and cinnamon schnapps into
a blender with a cup of ice. Blend until
smooth, then pour into a martini glass.
May also be served straight up in an
old-fashioned glass. Instead of blending,
shake and strain.

TOASTED ALMOND

OLD-FASHIONED

MAKES 1 DRINK

1½ oz. Amaretto
1½ oz. Kahlua
1 oz. cream or milk

Pour ingredients into a shaker with ice.
Shake well and strain into an ice-filled
old-fashioned glass.

TOBLERONE

MAKES 1 DRINK

1 oz. Irish cream
    liqueur
1 oz. Kahlua
1 oz. Frangelico
2 oz. cream
dash chocolate
    syrup

Pour ingredients into a blender with a scoop of ice. Blend until smooth. Pour into a large, honey-rimmed martini glass. Garnish with chocolate powder and syrup.

TOKYO TEA

MAKES 1 DRINK

¾ oz. vodka
¾ oz. rum
¾ oz. gin
¾ oz. triple sec
¾ oz. melon liqueur
1½ oz. sweet-and-
    sour mix
splash orange juice
splash cola

Pour ingredients into a shaker with ice. Shake and strain into a Collins glass. Garnish with a lemon wedge.

TOM AND JERRY

MAKES 1 DRINK

2 oz. light rum
1 oz. brandy
2 tsp. sugar
1 egg white
1 egg yolk
6 oz. hot milk

Beat the egg white and yolk separately. Mix them together into an Irish coffee glass or mug. Add the sugar and mix vigorously. Pour in the rum and brandy. Fill with milk. Stir gently. Garnish with a dash nutmeg.

TOM AND JERRY 2

MAKES 1 DRINK

1½ oz. rum
1 tbs. Tom and
    Jerry batter
hot milk
½ oz. California
    brandy

Into an Irish coffee glass or mug, dissolve the batter in three tablespoons hot milk. Add rum, then fill with hot milk to within ¼ inch of the top of the mug and stir gently. Top with the brandy. Garnish with a dash nutmeg. The secret of this version is to have a stiff batter and a warm mug.

TOM AND JERRY BATTER MIX

1 lb. sugar
3 eggs (whites and yolks separated)
2 oz. rum
1 tsp. cinnamon
½ tsp. cloves
½ tsp. allspice
½ tsp. crème de tartar

Beat the egg whites to a stiff froth, and the yolks until they are as thin as water. Mix yolks and whites together and add the rum and spices. Thicken with sugar until the mixture attains the consistency of a light batter.

TOM COLLINS

COLLINS

MAKES 1 DRINK

1½ oz. gin
2 oz. sweet-and-sour mix
club soda or Sprite

Fill a Collins glass with ice. Add the gin, sweet-and-sour mix, and the club soda or Sprite. Stir vigorously to work up a bit of a froth. Garnish with an orange slice and a cherry.

TOMOKO KOKO

IRISH COFFEE

MAKES 1 DRINK

½ oz. Irish cream
½ oz. Frangelico hazelnut liqueur
½ oz. cinnamon schnapps
5 oz. hot chocolate

Pour into an Irish coffee glass or mug. Top with whipped cream.

TOOTSIE ROLL

HIGHBALL

MAKES 1 DRINK

1½ oz. coffee liqueur
1½ oz. dark crème de cacao
3 oz. milk

Pour ingredients into a shaker half filled with ice. Shake well and strain into a highball glass over ice.

TOOTSIE ROLL MARTINI

MARTINI

MAKES 1 DRINK

3 oz. vodka
½ oz. chocolate
liqueur
½ oz. Grand
Marnier

Pour ingredients into a shaker with ice. Shake and strain into a chilled martini glass. Garnish with an orange twist.

TOOTSIE ROLL SHOOTER

SHOT

MAKES 1 DRINK

½ oz. coffee
liqueur
½ oz. orange juice
½ oz. vodka

Pour all ingredients into a shot glass.

TOOTSIE ROLLTINI

MARTINI

MAKES 1 DRINK

1 oz. coffee liqueur
1 oz. dark crème de
cacao
3 oz. orange juice

Pour ingredients into a shaker with ice. Shake and strain into a martini glass.

TOP BANANA

OLD-FASHIONED

MAKES 1 DRINK

1 oz. crème de
banane
1 oz. vodka
juice of ½ orange

Pour ingredients into a shaker with ice. Shake and strain into an old-fashioned glass over ice cubes, and serve.

TOP OF THE MORNING

MARTINI

MAKES 1 DRINK

1 oz. brandy
½ oz. apple brandy
½ oz. Italian
*   vermouth*
1 dash lemon juice

Pour ingredients into a shaker with ice. Stir well and strain into martini glass. Garnish with an olive.

TORANI DREAM (NONALCOHOLIC) COLLINS

MAKES 1 DRINK

6 oz. soda water
1 oz. orange
*   syrup*
1 oz. cream
*   syrup*

Pour all ingredients into a Collins glass over ice. Stir well.

TOREADOR

MARTINI

MAKES 1 DRINK

1½ oz. tequila
½ oz. crème de
*   cacao*
1 tbs. cream

Pour ingredients into a shaker with ice. Shake well and strain into a martini glass.

TOTEMOFF SPECIAL

IRISH COFFEE

MAKES 1 DRINK

1 oz. Kahlua
1 oz. Myer's rum
6 oz. hot chocolate
Wild Turkey
*   bourbon*

Into an Irish coffee glass or large mug, pour the rum and Kahlua. Add the hot chocolate and mix. Float Wild Turkey on top.

TOUCHDOWN

HURRICANE

MAKES 2 DRINKS

4 oz. bourbon
8 oz. lemonade
8 oz. iced tea
   (unsweetened)

Pour ingredients into a shaker with ice. Strain equal parts into two hurricane glasses filled with ice. Top with the lemonade.

TOUCHED BY A FUZZY ANGEL

COLLINS

MAKES 1 DRINK

1 oz. Torani peach
   syrup
orange juice

Pour the peach syrup into a Collins glass over ice. Add orange juice to fill. Garnish with an orange or peach slice.

TREE FROG

MARTINI

MAKES 1 DRINK

1 oz. dark rum
¼ oz. blue curaçao
dash white crème
   de menthe
4 oz. orange juice

Pour ingredients into a blender. Blend with 12 oz. of ice until slushy. Pour into a martini glass. Garnish with an orange, lemon, or lime slice, and a cherry.

TRIDENT

MARTINI

MAKES 1 DRINK

1 oz. dry sherry
1 oz. Cynar
1 oz. Aquavit
2 dashes peach
   bitters

Pour ingredients into a shaker with ice. Stir into a martini glass. Garnish with a lemon twist.

TRIM THE TREE

CHAMPAGNE

MAKES 1 DRINK

2 tsp. apple brandy
½ oz. cranberry
   juice
4 oz. brut
   Champagne
1 sugar cube

Drop the sugar cube into a Champagne flute. Add the apple brandy and the cranberry juice. Slowly add the Champagne (it will foam up) and stir gently, trying not to disturb the sugar cube. Garnish with an apple slice on the inner rim of the flute, two thirds submerged, to soak up the flavor.

TRINIDAD SWIZZLE

MARTINI

MAKES 1 DRINK

1 oz. dark rum
1 oz. amber rum
1 oz. Grand Marnier
¼ oz. lime juice
2 dashes grenadine
½ oz. mango juice

Pour ingredients into a shaker with ice. Shake and strain into a martini glass. Garnish with a cherry, a mint leaf and a slice of orange.

TRINITY COCKTAIL

MARTINI

MAKES 1 DRINK

¾ oz. dry vermouth
¾ oz. sweet
   vermouth
¾ oz. gin

Pour ingredients into a shaker with ice. Stir and strain into a martini glass.

TRIPLE KISS

COLLINS

MAKES 1 DRINK

½ oz. triple sec
½ oz. peach
   schnapps
dash lemon juice
dash orange juice
dash lime juice
fill Sprite or 7-Up
dash grenadine

Pour first five ingredients into a Collins glass over ice. Stir. Add the Sprite or 7-Up to fill. Finish with a splash of grenadine. Garnish with a lemon wedge.

TROLLEY CAR

PARFAIT

MAKES 1 DRINK

1¼ oz. Amaretto
2 oz. strawberries
2 scoops of vanilla
   ice cream

Pour ingredients into a blender. Blend until smooth and pour into a parfait glass. Garnish with a fresh strawberry.

TROPICAL GOLD

HIGHBALL

MAKES 1 DRINK

1 oz. rum
½ oz. crème de
   banane
5 oz. orange juice

Pour ingredients into a shaker half filled with ice. Shake well and strain into a highball glass over ice. Garnish with an orange slice.

TROPICAL ICED TEA

COLLINS

MAKES 1 DRINK

½ oz. vodka
½ oz. rum
½ oz. gin
½ oz. triple sec
1 oz. sweet-and-sour
   mix
1 oz. pineapple juice
1 oz. cranberry juice
½ oz. grenadine

Pour all ingredients into a Collins glass over ice. Garnish with seasonal fruits.

TROPICAL RAIN FOREST

COLLINS

MAKES 1 DRINK

½ oz. lemon vodka
½ oz. cherry rum
½ oz. white tequila
½ oz. blue curaçao
½ oz. melon liqueur
cranberry juice
pineapple juice
orange juice

Pour the vodka, rum, white tequila, blue curaçao, and melon liqueur into a Collins glass over ice. Fill with equal parts cranberry, pineapple, and orange juice. Garnish with a paper parasol.

TROPICAL RAINSTORM

MARTINI

MAKES 1 DRINK

1½ oz. dark rum
1 tsp. triple sec
½ oz. cherry brandy
½ oz. lemon juice

Pour ingredients into a shaker half filled with ice. Shake well and strain into a martini glass.

TROPICAL SUNSET

HIGHBALL

MAKES 1 DRINK

4 oz. orange juice
2 oz. pineapple
  juice
½ oz. lime juice
½ oz. grenadine

Pour first three ingredients into a highball glass over ice. Stir. Drizzle grenadine on top.

TRUFFLE MARTINI

MARTINI

MAKES 1 DRINK

3 oz. strawberry-
  flavored vodka
½ oz. Grand
  Marnier
½ oz. chocolate
  liqueur

Pour ingredients into a shaker with ice. Shake and strain into a chilled martini glass. Garnish with an orange twist.

TUGBOAT COOLER

MARTINI

MAKES 1 DRINK

4 oz. red wine
1 oz. sweet-and-
  sour mix
1 oz. orange juice
1 oz. Sprite
splash crème de
  banane

Pour ingredients into a shaker with ice. Shake and strain into a martini glass. Garnish with orange and lime slices.

TURBO

COLLINS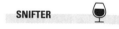

MAKES 1 DRINK

1 oz. tequila
1 oz. vodka
4 oz. tropical fruit punch

Pour ingredients into a shaker with ice. Shake well and strain into a Collins glass filled with ice.

TURF MARTINI

MARTINI

MAKES 1 DRINK

1½ oz. gin
1½ oz. dry vermouth
¼ oz. Pernod
1 tbs. lemon juice
2 dashes bitters

Pour ingredients into a shaker with ice. Shake well and strain into a martini glass. Garnish with an almond-stuffed olive.

TURKEY SHOOTER

SNIFTER

MAKES 1 DRINK

¾ oz. Wild Turkey bourbon
¼ oz. white crème de menthe

Pour ingredients into a shaker with ice. Stir and strain into a cordial glass or a brandy snifter.

TURTLEDOVE

MARTINI

MAKES 1 DRINK

1 oz. dark rum
¼ oz. Amaretto
4 oz. orange juice

Blend with 2 cups of ice until the mixture is slushy. Pour into a martini glass.

TUXEDO

MAKES 1 DRINK

2 oz. vodka
1½ oz. dry
  vermouth
½ tsp. maraschino
  liqueur
4 dashes orange
  bitters

Pour ingredients into a shaker with ice. Shake and strain into a chilled martini glass. Garnish with a lemon twist.

TWENTIETH CENTURY COCKTAIL   MARTINI

MAKES 1 DRINK

1½ oz. gin
¾ oz. Lillet
¾ oz. lemon juice
½ oz. crème de
  cacao (white)

Pour ingredients into a shaker with ice. Shake and strain into a martini glass.

TWILIGHT ZONE   COLLINS

MAKES 1 DRINK

¼ oz. light rum
¼ oz. dark rum
¼ oz. 151 proof
  rum
¼ oz. triple sec
splash orange juice
splash pineapple
  juice

Pour ingredients into a Collins glass over ice. Garnish with pineapple slices and cherries.

TWISTER   COLLINS

MAKES 1 DRINK

2 oz. vodka
lemon-lime soda
juice of ¹/₃ lime

Pour the vodka and lime juice into a Collins glass over ice. Fill with lemon-lime soda. Stir.

TWO TURTLES

MARTINI

MAKES 1 DRINK

1½ oz. Canadian
  whiskey
½ oz. B & B
½ oz. Cointreau

Pour ingredients into a shaker with ice. Stir and strain into a martini glass. Garnish with a cherry.

TWO-POINT CONVERSION

HURRICANE

MAKES 2 DRINKS

4 oz. white rum
4 oz. dark rum
3 oz. cranberry
  juice
6 oz. sweet-and-
  sour mix
6 oz. piña colada
  mix

In one blender combine rums, sweet-and-sour mix, cranberry juice, and ice. In another blender combine piña colada mix with ice. In two hurricane glasses alternate layers of each mixture. Garnish with an orange, lemon, or lime slice, and a cherry. Serve with a straw.

ULTIMO CHOCO MARTINI

MARTINI

MAKES 1 DRINK

1½ oz. vanilla vodka
½ oz. Frangelico
½ oz. white crème
  de cacao
½ oz. Godiva liqueur
½ oz. dark crème de
  cacao
½ oz. cream

Pour ingredients into a shaker with ice. Shake and strain into a martini glass. Garnish with chocolate square or chocolate twist.

UNCLE WIGGLEY

HIGHBALL

MAKES 1 DRINK

½ oz. Crown Royal
½ oz. Amaretto
cranberry juice
sweet-and-sour mix

Pour ingredients into a shaker with ice. Shake and strain into a highball glass. Fill glass with a 50/50 mixture of cranberry juice and sweet-and-sour mix.

U

UNFUZZY NAVEL (NONALCOHOLIC)   WINE

MAKES 1 DRINK

*3 oz. peach
    nectar
3 oz. orange
    juice
1 tsp. lemon
    juice
dash grenadine*

Pour ingredients into a shaker half filled with ice. Shake well. Strain into a red wine glass. Garnish with an orange, lemon, or lime slice, and a cherry.

U

UNO CINCO DE MAYO RITA   MARGARITA

MAKES 1 DRINK

*½ oz. tequila
½ oz. triple sec
½ oz. vodka
½ oz. gin
½ oz. rum
sweet-and-sour mix*

Pour the tequila, triple sec, vodka, gin, and rum into a salt-rimmed margarita glass over ice. Stir. Add sweet-and-sour mix to fill. Garnish with a slice of lime.

UNSUNG HERO   HIGHBALL

MAKES 1 DRINK

*1 oz. Kirsch
1 oz. apricot brandy
lemonade*

Pour ingredients into a shaker with ice. Stir and strain into a highball glass over ice. Garnish with an orange slice.

UPSIDE-DOWN PINEAPPLE MARTINI   MARTINI

MAKES 1 DRINK

*1 oz. vanilla vodka
1 oz. Irish cream
    liqueur
1 oz. butterscotch
    schnapps
2 oz. pineapple
    juice
maraschino cherry*

Pour the first four ingredients into a shaker with ice. Shake and strain into a martini glass. Drop in the cherry.

VALENCIA MARTINI

MARTINI

MAKES 1 DRINK

3 oz. gin
1 oz. Amontillado
  sherry

Pour ingredients into a shaker with ice. Stir and strain into a chilled martini glass. Garnish with an olive.

VALENTINE

WINE

MAKES 1 DRINK

4 oz. Beaujolais
1 tsp. cranberry
  liqueur
2 oz. cranberry
  juice

Pour ingredients into a shaker with ice. Shake well and strain into a wine glass.

VAMPIRE'S DELIGHT

CHAMPAGNE

MAKES 2 DRINKS

2 oz. rum
1 banana
2 scoops vanilla
  ice cream
grenadine

Pour the banana, rum, and ice cream into a blender. Blend until smooth. In two Champagne flutes, swirl the grenadine until the red syrup coats the insides of the glasses. Add the banana mixture in equal amounts to each glass. Serve with cherries.

VAMPIRE'S KISS

MARTINI

MAKES 1 DRINK

1 oz. vodka
½ oz. peach
  schnapps
½ oz. Razzmatazz
dash grenadine
cranberry juice

Pour ingredients into a shaker with ice. Shake and strain into a martini glass.

VANILLA BEAN

MAKES 1 DRINK

1 oz. vanilla vodka
1 oz. 7-Up
splash cola

Pour ingredients into a martini glass and stir. (Should taste like a cream soda.)

VANILLA FUDGE

OLD-FASHIONED

MAKES 1 DRINK

1½ oz. vodka
1½ oz. dark crème
  de cacao
1½ oz. Amaretto
¾ oz. half-and-half
1 tsp. vanilla

Pour ingredients into a shaker with ice. Shake and strain into an old-fashioned glass over ice.

VANILLA JESUS

COLLINS

MAKES 1 DRINK

2 oz. peach
  schnapps
1 oz. Absolut vodka
1 oz. Malibu rum
10 drops of vanilla
  extract

Pour all ingredients into a blender with 2 cups of ice. Blend on high until smooth. Pour into a Collins glass.

VEGAN EGGNOG

PUNCH

MAKES 12 DRINKS

21 oz. extra-firm
  silken tofu
2 cups soymilk
²/³ cup turbinado
  sugar, or light
  brown sugar
¼ tsp. salt
1 cup cold water
1 cup rum or brandy
4½ tsp. vanilla
  extract
20 ice cubes

Pour the tofu (crumbled) and soymilk into a blender with the sugar and salt. Blend until very smooth. Pour into a large bowl and whisk in the water, rum, or brandy, and vanilla. Cover, and refrigerate until serving time. To serve, blend half of the mixture with 10 ice cubes until frothy. Repeat with the other half. Serve with sprinkles of nutmeg.

VELOCIRAPTOR

HIGHBALL

MAKES 1 DRINK

1½ oz. vodka
4 tbs. chicken broth
3 dashes Tabasco sauce

Pour ingredients into a shaker with ice. Shake and strain into a highball glass over ice. Garnish with a slice of carrot.

VELVET CROCODILE

MARTINI

MAKES 1 DRINK

1 oz. gin
1 oz. grapefruit juice
1 oz. cranberry juice

Pour ingredients into a shaker with ice. Shake and strain into a martini glass over ice.

VELVET HAMMER

MARTINI

MAKES 1 DRINK

1½ oz. vodka
1 tbs. crème de cacao
1 tbs. cream

Pour ingredients into a shaker with ice. Shake and strain into a martini glass.

VELVET KISS

HIGHBALL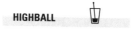

MAKES 1 DRINK

1 oz. gin
½ oz. crème de banane
½ oz. pineapple juice
1 oz. heavy cream
dash grenadine

Pour ingredients into a shaker with ice. Shake and strain into a highball glass.

VENTICELLO DI CARNEVALE

HIGHBALL

MAKES 1 DRINK

1 oz. gold rum
1 oz. Campari
2 oz. lemon juice
2 oz. lime juice
grenadine

Pour all ingredients into a cocktail shaker with ice. Shake and strain into a highball glass. Garnish with twists of lemon and lime.

VERMOUTH APÉRITIF

OLD-FASHIONED

MAKES 1 DRINK

2 oz. sweet
vermouth
lemon twist

Pour ingredients over ice into an old-fashioned glass. Add a lemon twist.

VERMOUTH CASSIS

HIGHBALL

MAKES 1 DRINK

2 oz. dry vermouth
1 oz. crème de
cassis
club soda

Pour vermouth and cassis into a highball glass nearly filled with ice. Add soda to fill. Stir gently. Garnish with a lemon twist.

VERTIGO

IRISH COFFEE

MAKES 1 DRINK

1 oz. Grand Marnier
½ oz. Kahlua
½ oz. crème de
cacao
4 oz. hot black
coffee

Pour into an Irish coffee glass or mug. Top with whipped cream.

VERY BLUE MARTINI

MARTINI

MAKES 1 DRINK

1½ oz. vodka
¼ oz. blue curaçao
4 oz. tart lemonade

Pour ingredients into a shaker with ice. Stir until chilled and strain into a martini glass. Garnish with a lemon slice.

VERY CHERRY

COLLINS

MAKES 1 DRINK

¾ oz. white crème de cacao
¾ oz. Amaretto
¾ oz. light cream
6 maraschino cherries
½ oz. maraschino cherry juice

Pour ingredients into a blender with ice. Blend thoroughly. Pour into a Collins or parfait glass. Garnish with a cherry. Serve with a straw.

VERY SCREWY DRIVER

HIGHBALL

MAKES 1 DRINK

1 oz. vodka
½ oz. gin
½ oz. tequila
4 oz. orange juice

Pour all ingredients into a highball glass nearly filled with ice. Stir well.

VESPER

MARTINI

MAKES 1 DRINK

3 oz. gin
1 oz. vodka
½ oz. Lillet blonde

Pour ingredients into a shaker with ice. Stir and strain into a martini glass. Garnish with an orange peel.

ICE PRESIDENTÉ (NONALCOHOLIC)

MARTINI

MAKES 1 DRINK

2 oz. pineapple
    juice
1 oz. lime juice
    or juice of
    ½ lime
½ oz. grenadine
1 tsp. fine
    sugar

Pour ingredients into a shaker nearly filled with ice. Strain into a martini glass.

VICTORY COLLINS

COLLINS

MAKES 1 DRINK

1½ oz. vodka
3 oz. lemon juice
3 oz. grape juice
    (unsweetened)
1 tsp. powdered
    sugar

Pour ingredients into a shaker with ice. Shake and strain into a Collins glass over ice. Garnish with a slice of orange.

VIENNA SOOTHER (NONALCOHOLIC)

OLD-FASHIONED

MAKES 1 DRINK

4 oz. cold black
    coffee
2 oz. cream
¼ oz. chocolate
    syrup
¼ tsp.
    cinnamon

Pour ingredients into a shaker with ice. Shake well and strain into an old-fashioned glass. Top with whipped cream and shaved chocolate.

VIENNESE DOCTOR

IRISH COFFEE

MAKES 1 DRINK

1 oz. Dr. McGillicuddy's
    Mentholmint
    schnapps
6 oz. hot chocolate
1 teaspoon General
    Foods International
    Coffee Viennese
    Chocolate Café

Pour into an Irish coffee glass or mug. Top with whipped cream.

VIEQUENSE

MAKES 1 DRINK

2 oz. rum
1 oz. Amaretto
2 oz. orange juice
2 oz. coconut
   cream

Pour ingredients into a shaker with ice. Shake well and strain into a hurricane glass over ice. Garnish with a cherry and an orange slice.

VIEUX CARRE

MAKES 1 DRINK

¾ oz. rye whiskey
¾ oz. brandy
¾ oz. sweet
   vermouth
splash Benedictine
dash Peychaud's
   bitters
dash bitters

Combine all ingredients in the order given in an old-fashioned glass over ice. Stir.

VINEYARD FIZZ (NONALCOHOLIC)

MAKES 1 DRINK

2 oz. grape
   juice
1 oz. lemon
   juice or juice
   of ½ lemon
½ tsp. fine
   sugar cream
   soda

Pour the grape juice, lemon juice, and sugar into a shaker half filled with ice. Shake well. Pour into a highball glass partly filled with ice. Add soda. Stir gently.

VIPER

MAKES 1 DRINK

1½ oz. Yukon Jack
½ oz. triple sec
1 oz. Rose's lime
   juice
½ lemon

Into a shaker filled with ice, squeeze juice from the lemon and add other ingredients. Shake well. Strain into a sugar-rimmed martini glass.

VIRGIN ISLAND (NONALCOHOLIC)   COLLINS

MAKES 1 DRINK

*3 oz. pineapple
   juice
1 oz. coconut
   cream
1 oz. lime juice or
   juice of ½ lime
½ tsp. orgeat syrup*

Pour ingredients into a blender with ice. Blend thoroughly. Pour into a Collins or parfait glass.

VIRGIN MARY (NONALCOHOLIC)   COLLINS

MAKES 1 DRINK

*10 oz. tomato
   juice
1 tbs. horseradish
5 dashes
   Worcester-
   shire sauce
1 dash celery salt
2 grinds pepper*

Pour all ingredients into a Collins glass with ice. Garnish with a celery stick.

VODKA ABYSS   MARTINI

MAKES 1 DRINK

*1 oz. vodka
½ oz. white rum
pineapple juice
½ oz. blue curaçao*

Pour all ingredients into a blender. Blend with ice until smooth. Pour into a martini glass. Top with an extra drizzle of blue curaçao.

VODKA AND TONIC   HIGHBALL

MAKES 1 DRINK

*2 oz. vodka
tonic water*

Fill a highball glass with ice. Add the vodka. Top with tonic. Stir. Garnish with a lemon wedge.

VODKA COLLINS

MAKES 1 DRINK

1½ oz. vodka
2 oz. sweet-and-sour mix
club soda or Sprite

Fill a Collins glass with ice. Add the vodka, sweet-and-sour mix, and the club soda or Sprite. Stir vigorously to work up a bit of a froth. Garnish with an orange slice and a cherry.

VODKA COOLER

MAKES 1 DRINK

2 oz. vodka
2 oz. club soda
1 tsp. fine sugar
ginger ale

Dissolve sugar in the club soda in a Collins glass. Nearly fill the glass with ice. Add the vodka. Fill with the ginger ale. Garnish with an orange, lemon, or lime slice, and a cherry.

VODKA DAISY

MAKES 1 DRINK

2 oz. vodka
1 oz. lemon juice or juice of ½ lemon
½ tsp. fine sugar
1 tsp. grenadine

Pour ingredients into a shaker with ice. Shake well and strain into an old-fashioned glass. Garnish with a cherry and an orange slice.

VODKA GIMLET

MAKES 1 DRINK

2 oz. vodka
½ oz. Rose's lime juice (or 1 oz. lime juice and 1 tsp. fine sugar)

Pour ingredients into a shaker with ice. Stir and strain into a martini glass. Garnish with a lime wedge.

VODKA MILLENNIUM

COLLINS

MAKES 1 DRINK

1 oz. peach brandy
1 oz. peach
  schnapps
1 oz. triple sec
1 oz. vodka
2 oz. cranberry
  juice
1 oz. grenadine
orange juice

Pour all ingredients except orange juice into a shaker with ice. Shake well and strain into a Collins glass over ice. Add orange juice to fill. Garnish with an orange slice.

VODKA ON THE ROCKS

OLD-FASHIONED

MAKES 1 DRINK

2 oz. vodka
lemon twist

Place a few ice cubes into an old-fashioned glass and add the vodka. Garnish with a lemon twist.

VODKA SLING

COLLINS

MAKES 1 DRINK

2 oz. vodka
1 oz. lemon juice or
  juice of ½ lemon
1 tsp. water
1 tsp. fine sugar
lemon twist

Pour ingredients into a Collins glass over ice. Stir. Add a lemon twist. Garnish with a slice of lemon and a cherry.

VODKA SOUR

SOUR GLASS

MAKES 1 DRINK

2 oz. vodka
1 oz. lemon juice or
  juice of ½ lemon
1 tsp. fine sugar
  (or 1½ oz.
  sweet-and-sour
  mix instead
  of lemon and
  sugar)

Pour ingredients into a shaker with ice. Shake and strain into a sour glass. Garnish with lemon and a cherry.

VODKA STINGER

MARTINI

MAKES 1 DRINK

2 oz. vodka
2 oz. white crème
  de menthe

Pour ingredients into a shaker with ice. Stir and then strain into a martini glass.

VOODOO SHOOTER

SHOT

MAKES 1 DRINK

½ oz. Tia Maria
rum cream
½ oz. 150 proof
  rum

Pour the Tia Maria into a shot glass. Layer the rum cream on top of the Tia Maria by pouring it over the back of a spoon. Float the rum on top.

WAIKIKI BEACHCOMBER

MARTINI

MAKES 1 DRINK

1½ oz. vodka
½ oz. raspberry
  liqueur
4 oz. guava juice
1 oz. lime juice or
  juice of ½ lime

Pour all ingredients except the raspberry liqueur into a shaker half filled with ice. Shake well and strain into a martini glass. Float the liqueur on top.

WARD 8

MARTINI

MAKES 1 DRINK

1½ oz. rye whiskey
½ oz. orange juice
½ oz. lemon juice
dash grenadine

Pour ingredients into a shaker half filled with ice. Shake well. Strain into a martini glass.

WARSAW MARTINI

MAKES 1 DRINK

2 oz. vodka
½ oz. dry vermouth
½ oz. blackberry
* brandy*

Pour ingredients into a shaker with ice. Shake and strain into a chilled martini glass.

WASHINGTON

MAKES 1 DRINK

2 oz. dry vermouth
1 oz. brandy
1 tsp. fine sugar
dash bitters

Pour ingredients into a shaker half filled with ice. Shake well and strain into a martini glass.

WASSAIL

MAKES ABOUT 12 DRINKS

¼ tsp. nutmeg
¼ tsp. cardamom
¼ tsp. powdered
* ginger*
2 cloves
2 cinnamon sticks
1 cup water
2 bottles medium
* dry sherry*
½ cup brandy
1 cup sugar
3 egg yolks
6 egg whites
4 baked apples

Simmer the spices in a large saucepan for 10 minutes. Add liquors and sugar; heat, but do not boil. Remove from heat. Lightly beat egg yolks and whites separately (they should be no more than frothy). Pour a cup of the warm sherry into a punch bowl and stir in the egg yolks. Add the rest of the liquor. Beat in the egg whites with a whisk until foamy. Float apples.

W

WATERMELON COOLER (NONALCOHOLIC) COLLINS

MAKES 8 DRINKS

18 oz. water, divided
4 oz. fresh lemon juice, divided
1 cup granulated sugar
3½ cups watermelon juice
16 oz. fresh orange juice
ice cubes
lemon slices

Pour 10 oz. water, 2 oz. lemon juice, and sugar into a saucepan. Boil, stirring, until sugar dissolves. Let syrup cool thoroughly. In a pitcher pour 8 oz. water, 2 oz. fresh lemon juice, watermelon juice, and orange juice. Add cooled syrup; mix well. Refrigerate several hours. To serve, pour mixture over ice in Collins glasses and garnish with lemon slices.

WATERMELON MARGARITA   MARGARITA

MAKES 1 DRINK

½ cup frozen watermelon
1¼ oz. tequila
½ oz. Rose's lime juice
½ oz. melon liqueur
½ oz. sweet-and-sour mix

Pour ingredients into a blender. Blend with ice until smooth. Pour into a salt-or-sugar-rimmed margarita glass. Garnish with a lime wedge.

WATERMELON MARTINI   MARTINI

MAKES 1 DRINK

1¹/₆ oz. Absolut vodka
½ oz. melon liqueur
2½ oz. watermelon juice
3 dashes gomme syrup
dash lemon juice

Pour ingredients into a shaker with ice. Shake and strain into a martini glass. Garnish with a sliver of fresh watermelon.

WATERMELON TIDAL WAVE   COLLINS

MAKES 1 DRINK

1 oz. watermelon schnapps
½ oz. Southern Comfort
½ oz. Amaretto
Mountain Dew

Fill a Collins glass with ice and add the watermelon schnapps, Southern Comfort, and Amaretto. Stir. Fill glass with Mountain Dew and stir again.

WAY TO JUAREZ (NONALCOHOLIC) HIGHBALL

MAKES 1 DRINK

*1 oz. orange
juice
2 oz. passion
fruit or
tropical juice
4 oz. lemon and
lime soda*

Pour juices into a highball glass over ice. Stir. Add the soda to fill. Garnish with an orange, lemon, or lime slice, and a cherry.

WEDDING BELLE

MARTINI

MAKES 1 DRINK

*1½ oz. gin
1 oz. Dubonnet
rouge
½ oz. kirschwasser
½ oz. orange juice*

Pour ingredients into a shaker half filled with ice. Shake well. Strain into a martini glass.

WEDDING BELLE 2

MARTINI

MAKES 1 DRINK

*¼ oz. orange juice
¼ oz. wild cherry
brandy
¾ oz. dry gin
¾ oz. Dubonnet*

In a mixing glass, stir well with cracked ice and then strain into 3 oz. martini glass.

WEDDING RECEPTION BUBBLES CHAMPAGNE

MAKES 1 DRINK

*½ oz. strawberry-
flavored vodka
1 oz. strawberry
liqueur
dry Champagne*

Pour the strawberry vodka and the strawberry liqueur into a Champagne flute. Add Champagne to fill. Garnish with a strawberry.

WEMBLEY MARTINI

MARTINI

MAKES 1 DRINK

3 oz. gin
½ oz. dry vermouth
1 tsp. apricot
brandy
1 tsp. calvados

Pour ingredients into a shaker with ice. Shake and strain into a chilled martini glass. Garnish with a lemon twist.

WEREWOLF

OLD-FASHIONED

MAKES 1 DRINK

1½ oz. Jack
Daniel's whiskey
1½ oz. Drambuie

Pour ingredients into a shaker with ice. Shake and strain into an old-fashioned glass.

WESTSIDE MANHATTAN

OLD-FASHIONED

MAKES 1 DRINK

2 oz. Irish whiskey
splash sweet
vermouth
2–4 drops bitters

Pour ingredients into an old-fashioned glass over ice.

WET DREAM

MARTINI

MAKES 1 DRINK

1 oz. gin
¼ oz. apricot
brandy
¼ oz. grenadine
dash lemon juice

Pour ingredients into a shaker with ice. Shake and strain into a martini glass.

WET KISS

MAKES 1 DRINK

½ oz. Amaretto
½ oz. watermelon
   schnapps
dash sweet-and-
   sour mix
dash 7-Up

Layer in the order given in a shot glass, or over ice into a highball glass. Garnish with a cherry.

WHISKEY COBBLER

WINE

MAKES 1 DRINK

2 oz. blended
   whiskey
2 oz. club soda
1 tsp. fine sugar

Pour club soda into a large wine glass or goblet. Add sugar and dissolve. Fill with crushed ice. Add whiskey and stir. Garnish with an orange, lemon, or lime slice, and a cherry. Serve with a straw.

WHISKEY DAISY

OLD-FASHIONED

MAKES 1 DRINK

2 oz. blended
   whiskey
1 oz. lemon juice or
   juice of ½ lemon
½ tsp. fine sugar
1 tsp. grenadine

Pour the liquor, lemon juice, sugar, and grenadine into a shaker half filled with ice. Shake well and strain into an old-fashioned glass. Garnish with a cherry and fruit.

WHISKEY DAISY 2

 OLD-FASHIONED

MAKES 4 DRINKS

10 oz. Wild Turkey
   bourbon
1¼ oz. grenadine
2.5 oz. lemon juice
10 oz. sparkling
   natural mineral
   water

Pour grenadine, lemon juice, and bourbon into a shaker with ice. Stir and strain into four old-fashioned glasses filled with ice. Top each glass with sparkling water.

WHISKEY FIX

HIGHBALL

MAKES 1 DRINK

2 oz. blended
   whiskey
1 oz. lemon juice or
   juice of ½ lemon
1 tsp. fine sugar

Add the lemon juice and sugar to a shaker half filled with ice. Shake and strain into a highball glass. Add ice and the whiskey. Stir. Serve with a straw.

WHISKEY MILK PUNCH

COLLINS

MAKES 1 DRINK

2 oz. blended
   scotch whiskey
1 tsp. powdered
   sugar
8 oz. milk

Pour ingredients into a shaker with ice. Shake and strain into a Collins glass. Sprinkle nutmeg on top and serve.

WHISKEY PUNCH

PUNCH

**MAKES ABOUT 20
DRINKS**

1 liter bourbon
½ cup curaçao
2 cups orange juice
½ cup lemon juice
2 quarts ginger ale

Pour all ingredients except ginger ale. Pour into a punch bowl over ice. Stir well. Add ginger ale just before serving.

WHISKEY SKIN

OLD-FASHIONED

MAKES 1 DRINK

1½ oz. rye or
   bourbon whiskey
1 lump sugar
boiling water
lemon peel

Put the lump of sugar into a hot old-fashioned glass and fill two-thirds with boiling water. Add the whiskey. Stir. Finish with a lemon twist.

WHISKEY SMASH

OLD-FASHIONED

MAKES 1 DRINK

2 oz. blended
whiskey
1 tsp. fine sugar
4 sprigs mint
1 oz. club soda

Muddle the sugar with the mint and club soda in an old-fashioned glass. Fill the glass with ice. Add the whiskey. Stir well. Finish with a lemon twist.

WHISKEY SOUR

SOUR GLASS

MAKES 1 DRINK

2 oz. blended
whiskey
1 oz. lemon juice or
juice of ½ lemon
1 tsp. fine sugar

Pour ingredients into a shaker with ice. Shake and strain into a sour glass, or over ice in an old-fashioned glass. Garnish with a lemon and a cherry.

WHISKEY STINGER

OLD-FASHIONED

MAKES 1 DRINK

2 oz. Crown Royal
Canadian whiskey
1 oz. white crème
de menthe

Pour the Crown Royal and the white crème de menthe into an old-fashioned glass over ice and stir.

WHISKEY SWIZZLE

COLLINS

MAKES 1 DRINK

2 oz. whiskey
1½ oz. lime juice or
juice of 1 lime
1 tsp. fine sugar
2 dashes bitters
3 oz. club soda

Pour the lime juice, sugar, liquor, and bitters into a shaker half filled with ice. Shake well. Strain into a Collins glass almost filled with crushed ice. Stir. Fill with soda. Serve with a swizzle stick.

WHISKEY TODDY

OLD-FASHIONED

MAKES 1 DRINK

1½ oz. rye or
bourbon whiskey
1 sugar cube
boiling water

Put sugar cube in a hot old-fashioned glass and fill two-thirds with boiling water. Add whiskey. Stir. Garnish with a slice of lemon. Grate nutmeg on top.

WHITE CACTUS

HIGHBALL

MAKES 1 DRINK

1 oz. tequila
ginger ale
splash lime juice

Pour tequila and ginger ale into a high-ball glass over ice. Nearly fill with the ginger ale. Finish with a splash of lime juice. Garnish with a slice of lime.

WHITE CHOCOLATE EASTER BUNNY

MARTINI

MAKES 1 DRINK

½ oz. vanilla vodka
1 oz. white
chocolate
liqueur
2 oz. eggnog
1 oz. half-and-half
jellybeans

Pour the vodka, white chocolate liqueur, eggnog, and half-and-half into a shaker with ice. Shake and strain into a martini glass. Drop jelly beans ("the Easter eggs") into the drink.

WHITE CHOCOLATINI

MARTINI

MAKES 1 DRINK

1½ oz. vanilla
vodka
1 oz. Godiva white
chocolate
liqueur
2 oz. half-and-half
white chocolate
shavings

Pour the first three ingredients into a shaker with ice. Shake and strain into a martini glass. Sprinkle the white chocolate shavings on top.

WHITE CHRISTMAS

MAKES 1 DRINK

*1 oz. vanilla-
   flavored vodka
½ oz. Godiva
   white chocolate
   liqueur
½ oz. peppermint
   schnapps*

Pour ingredients into a shaker with ice. Stir and strain into a chilled martini glass.

WHITE ELEPHANT

MAKES 1 DRINK

*2 oz. vodka
1½ oz. white crème
   de cacao
fill with milk*

Pour ingredients into a shaker with ice. Shake and strain into a highball glass.

WHITE LADY

MAKES 1 DRINK

*2 oz. gin
1 oz. Cointreau
½ oz. lemon juice*

Pour ingredients into a shaker with ice. Shake and strain into a frosted martini glass.

WHITE OR RED WINE COOLER

MAKES 1 DRINK

*4 oz. wine
2 oz. pineapple
   juice
club soda or
   sparkling water*

Pour the wine, juice, and soda into a large wine glass over ice. Stir gently. Garnish with a lemon or lime wedge.

WHITE ROSE

WINE

MAKES 1 DRINK

1¾ oz. gin
4 dashes
    maraschino
    liqueur
4 dashes orange
    juice
4 dashes lemon
    juice
1 egg white

Pour ingredients into a shaker with ice. Shake very well. Pour the egg white. Strain into a wine glass.

WHITE RUSSIAN

OLD-FASHIONED

MAKES 1 DRINK

1 oz. vodka
1 oz. coffee liqueur
half-and-half
    or milk

Pour the vodka, coffee liqueur, and half-and-half or milk into an old-fashioned glass over ice.

WHITE SANGRIA

WINE

MAKES 4 DRINKS

1 cup water
½ cup sugar
6 cinnamon sticks
1 bottle sweet white
    wine (not dry)
1 cup sparkling water
1 cup apple juice
½ cup orange juice
3 oranges cut in wheels
3 apples cut in chunks

Heat the water, sugar, and cinnamon sticks to a simmer. Continue to simmer for 5 minutes, and remove from heat. Let cool to room temperature. Remove the cinnamon sticks, and mix in all remaining liquid ingredients. Chill overnight in the refrigerator. Add the fruit when ready to serve for presentation.

WHITE SANGRIARITA

MARGARITA

MAKES 1 DRINK

1½ oz. tequila
1 oz. white wine
5 oz. sweet-and-
    sour mix

Pour the tequila, white wine, and sweet-and-sour mix into a blender with a cup of ice. Blend until smooth. Pour into a salt-rimmed margarita glass. Garnish with an orange, lemon, or lime slice, and a cherry.

WHITE SPIDER

MARTINI

MAKES 1 DRINK

1 oz. gin
1 oz. lemon juice
½ oz. Cointreau
1 tsp. dimple syrup

Pour ingredients into a shaker with ice. Shake and strain into a martini glass.

WHO'S YOUR DADDY?

COLLINS

MAKES 1 DRINK

1 oz. toffee liqueur
½ oz. Tuaca
½ oz. vanilla vodka
1 large scoop
*   vanilla ice cream*
half-and-half or milk
1 Sugar Daddy
*   caramel sucker*

Put the first four ingredients into a blender. Add about an oz. of milk or half-and-half to help the blending process. Keep adding milk or half-and-half and ice cubes little by little to achieve a thick but drinkable consistency. Pour into a Collins glass, and stick the Sugar Daddy on top.

WICKED WITCH'S SOCKS

SHOT

MAKES 1 DRINK

¹/₃ oz. coffee
*   liqueur*
¹/₃ oz. white crème
*   de cacao*
¹/₃ oz. Blavod black
*   vodka*

Pour the coffee liqueur into a shot glass. Gently pour the white crème de cacao over the back of a spoon to layer it on top of the coffee liqueur. Then add a layer of the black vodka the same way.

WIDOW'S KISS

MARTINI

MAKES 1 DRINK

2 oz. calvados
1 oz. yellow
*   Chartreuse*
1 oz. Benedictine
1 dash bitters

Pour ingredients into a shaker with ice. Stir and strain into a martini glass.

WIKI WAKI WOO

HURRICANE

MAKES 1 DRINK

½ oz. vodka
½ oz. rum
½ oz. 151 proof rum
½ oz. tequila
½ oz. triple sec
1 oz. Amaretto
1 oz. orange juice
1 oz. pineapple juice
1 oz. cranberry juice

Pour ingredients into a shaker with ice. Shake and strain into a hurricane or parfait glass. Garnish with an orange slice and a cherry.

WILD BLUEBERRY (NONALCOHOLIC)

COLLINS

MAKES 1 DRINK

5 mint leaves
handful of
  blueberries
2 spoons of sugar
  or Splenda
1 oz. water
7-Up
sprig of mint

Put the mint leaves, blueberries, sugar or Splenda, and water into a Collins glass. Mash all the ingredients together with a muddler or wooden spoon. Fill the glass with ice. Add the 7-Up to fill. Garnish with mint and blueberries.

WILD IRISH ROSE

HIGHBALL

MAKES 1 DRINK

1½ oz. Irish
  whiskey
1½ tsp. grenadine
½ oz. lime juice
club soda

Fill a highball glass with ice. Add the Irish whiskey, grenadine, and lime juice and stir. Fill with club soda.

WILD MARTINI

MARTINI

MAKES 1 DRINK

2 oz. Puerto Rican
  rum
½ oz. melon liqueur
splash dry
  vermouth
splash lime juice

Pour ingredients into a shaker with ice. Shake and strain into a chilled martini glass. Garnish with a lime twist and a cherry.

WILD THING

OLD-FASHIONED

MAKES 1 DRINK

1½ oz. tequila
1 oz. cranberry
*   juice*
1 oz. club soda
½ oz. lime juice

Pour into an old-fashioned glass over ice. Garnish with a lime wedge.

WILL ROGERS

MARTINI

MAKES 1 DRINK

1½ oz. gin
½ oz. dry vermouth
1 tbs. orange juice
1 dash triple sec

Pour ingredients into a shaker with ice. Shake well and strain into a martini glass.

WIND CHILL

MARTINI

MAKES 1 DRINK

1 oz. 151 rum
1 oz. dark rum
1 oz. blackberry
*   brandy*
1 oz. crème de
*   banane*
1 oz. Rose's lime
*   juice*
1 oz. grenadine

Pour the 151 rum, dark rum, blackberry brandy, crème de banane, Rose's, and grenadine into a blender with 2 cups of ice. Blend until smooth. Taste for sweetness. To make it sweeter, add a little more grenadine. Pour into a martini glass. Garnish with a paper parasol.

WINDEX SHOOTER

SHOT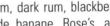

MAKES 1 DRINK

¾ oz. vodka
¾ oz. blue curaçao

Pour ingredients into a shaker with ice. Stir and strain into a shot glass.

WINE COOLER

MAKES 1 DRINK

any wine
citrus- or fruit-
flavored soda
(Sprite, 7-Up,
Fresca)

Put ice into a Collins glass and fill it half-way with the wine. Add the soda to fill. Stir. Garnish with an orange, lemon, or lime slice, and a cherry.

WINE SPRITZER

WINE

MAKES 1 DRINK

4 oz. wine, red or
white
2 oz. club soda or
sparkling water

Pour wine over ice into a large wine glass. Add the club soda. Stir gently. Garnish with a wedge of lemon or lime.

WINE TORCH

PUNCH

MAKES 25 DRINKS

3 cups apple juice
20 whole cloves
4 sticks cinnamon
1 lemon
750 ml red dinner
wine
750 ml port wine
4 oz. brandy

Squeeze juice from lemon. Remove pulp from peel and cut peel into slices. Simmer apple juice, cloves, cinnamon, and lemon peel 15 minutes. Strain; add lemon juice, red wine, and port. Simmer again, do not boil. Light the brandy and ladle it slowly into the hot wine. Serve in preheated mugs.

WINNER'S CIRCLE (NONALCOHOLIC)

PUNCH

MAKES 25 DRINKS

6 cups tea, chilled
2 cups sugar
2 cups orange
juice
3 cups pineapple
juice
½ cup lime juice
1 quart ginger ale

Pour all ingredients into a punch bowl over ice.

WINTER CARIBBEAN HEAT

IRISH COFFEE

MAKES 1 DRINK

*1 oz. Caribbean
    rum
1 oz. Frangelico
6 oz. hot chocolate*

Pour ingredients into an Irish coffee mug, and fill with hot chocolate. Top with whipped cream and chocolate shavings.

WINTER SPARKLER

PUNCH

MAKES 25 DRINKS

*1 lemon
1 lime
1 cup Southern
    Comfort
1 cup peach schnapps
2 750 ml brut
    Champagne
3 peaches
30 whole cloves
ice block*

Place ice in a punch bowl. Squeeze the juice of the lime and lemon. Add peach schnapps and Southern Comfort then stir. Pierce peach skin with cloves then add to bowl. Pour Champagne and stir gently. Serve in punch glasses.

WISH UPON A BURNING STAR

SHOT

MAKES 1 DRINK

*1½ oz.
    Goldschlager
¹/₈ oz. 151 rum
    (divided into
    2 equal parts)
sugar
cinnamon
bamboo skewer
star fruit slice*

Mix a tablespoon of sugar with a pinch of cinnamon. Skewer the star fruit and dip into the mixture. Pour Goldschlager into a shot glass. Float one half of the 151 rum on top and light. Pour the remaining rum over the skewered star fruit and hold over the flame to light. Make a wish, blow out the flames, drink the shot, and eat the star fruit.

WITCH'S BREW

COLLINS

MAKES 1 DRINK

*2 oz. Strega
½ oz. crème de
    menthe
1 oz. fresh squeezed
    lemon juice
1 oz. fresh squeezed
    orange juice
Pernod*

Fill an 8-oz. Collins glass with shaved ice. Shake above ingredients (except Pernod) well with ice and strain into the Collins glass; float three or four drops Pernod; decorate with seasonal fruit or fresh mint.

WOLFIE

IRISH COFFEE

MAKES 1 DRINK

½ oz. Kahlua
½ oz. Grand
  Marnier
3 oz. hot black
  coffee
3 oz. hot chocolate

Into an Irish coffee glass or mug, pour the hot chocolate and coffee. Add the liqueur. Top with whipped cream.

WOO WOO

OLD-FASHIONED

MAKES 1 DRINK

2 oz. vodka
1 tbs. peach
  schnapps
½ cup cranberry
  juice
lime wedge

Place the lime wedge into a shaker with ice. Add the other ingredients. Shake well. Strain into a chilled old-fashioned glass.

WOO WOO SHOOTER

SHOT

MAKES 1 DRINK

1 oz. cranberry
  juice
½ oz Amaretto
½ oz. peach-
  flavored brandy

Pour ingredients into a shaker with ice. Shake and strain into a shot glass.

WOODSTOCK

MARTINI

MAKES 1 DRINK

1½ oz. gin
1 oz. lemon juice or
  juice of ½ lemon
1 tbs. maple syrup
dash orange bitters

Pour ingredients into a shaker with ice. Shake well. Strain into a martini glass.

WOOLLY MAMMOTH

HIGHBALL

MAKES 1 DRINK

1 oz. tequila
1 oz. Archers
1 oz. Malibu rum
1 oz. Bacardi rum
1 oz. lime cordial
lemonade

Pour ingredients into a shaker with ice. Shake and strain into a highball glass. Drink slowly through a straw.

WORLD'S DRIEST MARTINI

MARTINI

MAKES 1 DRINK

2 oz. gin (chilled)
½ oz. vermouth

Pour vermouth into a chilled martini glass from the fridge. Swirl the vermouth in the glass and shake dry. Add the gin from the freezer.

X.Y.Z.

MARTINI

MAKES 1 DRINK

1 oz. rum
1 oz. Cointreau
½ oz. lemon juice

Pour ingredients into a shaker with ice. Shake and strain into a martini glass.

XENA MARTINI

MARTINI

MAKES 1 DRINK

2½ oz. honey vodka
½ oz. Zubrowka (or
*   any other bison*
*   grass vodka)*
1 tsp. Lillet (white)

Pour ingredients into a shaker with ice. Shake and strain into a chilled martini glass. Garnish with an asparagus spear.

X

XERES

MARTINI

MAKES 1 DRINK

2 oz. sherry
1 dash orange
*   bitters*
1 dash peach
*   bitters*

Pour ingredients into a shaker with ice. Stir and strain into a martini glass.

YACHT CLUB

MARTINI

MAKES 1 DRINK

¾ oz. gin
¾ oz. sweet
*   vermouth*
¾ oz. orange juice
2 dashes Campari
2 dashes simple
*   syrup*

Pour ingredients into a shaker with ice. Shake and strain into a martini glass.

YALE COCKTAIL

MARTINI

MAKES 1 DRINK

½ oz. dry vermouth
1½ oz. gin
1 tsp. blue curaçao
dash bitters

Pour ingredients into a shaker with ice. Stir and strain into a martini glass, and serve.

YARD SALE

IRISH COFFEE

MAKES 1 DRINK

½ oz. Irish cream
¼ oz. Frangelico
*   hazelnut liqueur*
½ oz. Grand
*   Marnier*
¼ oz. Tia Maria
5 oz. hot black
*   coffee*

Pour into an Irish coffee glass or large mug topped with whipped cream.

YELLOW BIRD

MARTINI

MAKES 1 DRINK

1½ oz. light rum
½ oz. Galliano
½ oz. triple sec
½ oz. lime juice

Pour all ingredients into a shaker half filled with ice. Shake well. Strain into a martini glass.

YELLOW FEVER

HIGHBALL

MAKES 1 DRINK

1½ oz. vodka
5 oz. lemonade

Pour into a highball glass. Garnish with a lemon wedge.

YELLOW JACKET (NONALCOHOLIC) OLD-FASHIONED

MAKES 1 DRINK

2 oz. pineapple
* juice*
2 oz. orange juice
½ oz. lemon juice

Pour all ingredients into a shaker nearly filled with ice. Shake well. Strain into an old-fashioned glass filled with ice. Garnish with a lemon slice.

YELLOW RATTLER

MARTINI

MAKES 1 DRINK

1 oz. gin
½ oz. sweet
* vermouth*
½ oz. dry vermouth
1 tbs. orange juice

Shake all ingredients with ice and strain into a martini glass. Garnish with a cocktail onion.

YODELER

MAKES 25 DRINKS

2 cups blueberries
2 cups strawberries
2 cups raspberries
2 750 ml bottles
*   brut Champagne*
8 oz. sherry
8 oz. honey liqueur

Into a large shaker filled with ice, pour the sherry and honey. Shake well and strain into a large punch bowl filled with fruit. Gently add Champagne. Serve with fruit in the glass.

YOGURT KISTRA (NONALCOHOLIC) COLLINS

MAKES 1 DRINK

6 oz. fruit puree
*   (strawberry,*
*   peach, or*
*   blueberry)*
3 oz. plain yogurt
3 oz. pineapple
*   juice*
¼ cup ice

Pour all ingredients into a blender. Blend until smooth. Serve in a Collins glass. Garnish with a cherry.

YOOHOO

HIGHBALL

MAKES 1 DRINK

¹/₃ oz. Kahlua
¹/₃ oz. Frangelico
¹/₃ oz. milk

Pour ingredients into a shaker with ice. Shake and strain into a highball glass. (If done right, it takes just like a Yoohoo.)

YULETIDE PUNCH (NONALCOHOLIC) PUNCH

MAKES 20 DRINKS

1 quart water
1 cup fine sugar
1 can frozen
*   lemonade*
1 quart cranberry
*   juice*
2 cups apple juice
1 cup orange juice
2 cups ginger ale

Heat water and sugar to boiling until sugar is dissolved. Cool. Pour all ingredients into a punch bowl over ice.

YUMMY CHOCOLATE STRAWBERRY MARTINI

MAKES 1 DRINK

3 oz. Stoli
  strawberry
  vodka
1½ oz. Godiva
  chocolate
  liqueur

Pour ingredients into a shaker with ice. Shake and strain into a martini glass. Garnish with a fresh strawberry.

ZAPPER COCKTAIL

OLD-FASHIONED

MAKES 1 DRINK

3 oz. Galliano
1 oz. white crème
  de menthe
1 lime (wedge)

Pour ingredients into a blender with 8 oz. of ice, and pulse twice. Pour into an old-fashioned glass, squeeze in a wedge of lime, then drop it in the glass.

ZAZA

MARTINI

MAKES 1 DRINK

¾ oz. gin
1½ oz. Dubonnet
1 dash orange
  bitters

Pour ingredients into a shaker with ice. Stir and strain into a martini glass.

ZIPPER

OLD-FASHIONED

MAKES 1 DRINK

1½ oz. triple sec
1½ oz. tequila
½ oz. cream

Layer in an old-fashioned glass.

ZIPPY MARTINI

MARTINI

MAKES 1 DRINK

3 oz. vodka
½ oz. dry vermouth
4 dashes Tabasco
* sauce*

Pour ingredients into a shaker with ice. Shake and strain into a chilled martini glass. Garnish with a jalapeño slice.

ZOMBIE

HIGHBALL

MAKES 1 DRINK

1¼ oz. lemon juice
1 oz. dark rum
¾ oz. orange juice
½ oz. cherry brandy
½ oz. light rum
½ oz. high-proof
* dark rum*
2 dashes grenadine

Pour ingredients into a shaker with ice. Shake well and strain into a highball glass over ice.

ZUMBO

MARTINI

MAKES 1 DRINK

1½ oz. gin
¼ oz. Cointreau
¼ oz. sweet
* vermouth*
¼ oz. dry vermouth
2 dashes Fernet
* Branca*

Pour ingredients into a shaker with ice. Stir and strain into a martini glass.

ZUMMY

MARTINI

MAKES 1 DRINK

¾ oz. Benedictine
½ oz. gin
¼ oz. dry vermouth
¼ oz. sweet
* vermouth*
1 dash Campari

Pour ingredients into a shaker with ice. Stir and strain into a martini glass.

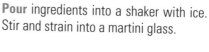

INDEX

242; Kentucky Black-Eyed Susan, 264; Lemon Love Shack Shake, 277; Menage à Trois, 306; Nicky Finn, 331; Panzerwagen, 344; X.Y.Z., 511

Crème de banana (banane): Banshee, 56; Beam Me Up Scotty, 63; Chocolate Monkey, 126; Climax, 131; Easter Egg, 174; Irish Green-Eyed Blonde, 252; Malibu Punch, 293; Monkey Shine Shooter, 319; Pousse-Café, 366; Shark Repellant, 418; Slow Kisser, 427; Surf's Up, 451; Texas Rose, 463; Top Banana, 474; Wind Chill, 507

Crème de cacao. *See also* **Dark crème de cacao**; **White crème de cacao**: Alexander Cocktail, 26; Alexander the Great, 26; Almond Joytini, 30; American Leroy, 34; Angel's Kiss, 36; Bushwacker, 102; Coffee Cacao Cream, 135; Coffee Nudge, 135; Grasshopper Shooter, 221; Jack Spratt, 255; Mom's Milk, 318; Neapolitan Shooter Sundae, 328; Peppermint Patty Shooter, 352; Russian Cocktail, 399; Velvet Hammer, 486

Crème de cassis: Heather Blush, 232

Crème de coconut: Almond Grove, 29; Coconut Concubine, 134

Crème de menthe. *See also* **Green crème de menthe**; **White crème de menthe**: Mocha Mint, 316; Pousse-Café, 366; Spanish Moss drinks, 439

Crème de noyaux: Pink Squirrel, 361; Pousse-Café, 366; Road Rage at the Traffic Light, 387; Ruptured Duck, 398

Crown Royal: Ace of Spades, 19; Bearded Clam, 63; Red Snapper 2, 382; Uncle Wiggley, 482; Whiskey Stinger, 501

Curaçao. *See also* **Blue curaçao**; **Orange curaçao**: Black Death, 72; Ethel Duffy Cocktail, 181; Marmalade, 300

Currant vodka. *See* **Black currant vodka**

Cynar: Trident, 476

Dark crème de cacao: Angel's Tit, 37; Chocolate Chip Cookie, 125; Creamy Mocha Alexander, 150; Foxy Lady, 193; Gaelic Coffee, 203; Girl Scout Cookie 2, 212; Gun Barrel, 227; Ice Breaker, 246; In the Mood, 248; Irish Dream, 251; Kissin' Candy, 268; Lover's Kiss, 287; Russian Bear, 399; Sacrifice to the Gods, 402; Ski Tip Coffee, 424; S'Mores, 402; Tootsie Roll, 473; Tootsie Rolltini, 474; Vanilla Fudge, 485

Dark porter: Black Velvet, 76

Dark rum: Abilene, 18; Adam, 20; Aloha, 30; Around the World, 48; Aunt Agatha, 49; Bat Bite, 60; BBC, 61; Big Chill, 68; Black Devil, 72; Black Monday, 75; Black Widow, 76; Blushing Reindeer, 84; Bossa Nova, 88; B. V. D. Cocktail, 50; Captain's Blood, 111; Caribbean Breeze, 112; Caribbean Coffee, 113; Coco Loco, 133; Coffee Nudge, 135; Dark & Stormy, 156; Detroit Daisy, 162; Four Wheeler, 192; Fox Trot, 192; Ginger Colada, 211; Golden Eggnog Grog, 216; Golden Oldie, 217; Hot Buttered Cider, 239; Hot Buttered Sugarplum, 240; Hot Cider-Cranberry Punch, 241; Hurricane drinks, 245; In the Mood, 248; Jamaican Cocktail, 256; Jamaican Firefly, 256; Keno, 263; Landed Gentry, 273; Lord and Lady, 285; Louisiana Lullaby, 286; Maiden's Blush, 292; Mai Tai Me Up, 292; Midnight Express,

310; Miss Belle, 315; Mumbo Jumbo, 325; Olympia, 338; Parisian Blonde Shooter, 345; Rendezvous Punch, 385; Rum Cobbler, 394; Rummy Moulin Rouge, 398; Scorpion 2, 409; Sex on the Slopes, 416; Shark Bite, 418; Shark Repellant, 418; Sloe Screw Against the Wall, 426; Slurricane, 427; Sunny Sour, 450; Swirl from Ipanema, 454; Tahiti Club, 455; Tiger's Milk, 468; Tiki Torch, 469; Tree Frog, 476; Trinidad Swizzle, 477; Tropical Rainstorm, 479; Turtledove, 480; Twilight Zone, 481; Two-Point Conversion, 482; Wind Chill, 507; Zombie, 516

Drambuie: Happy Hooker, 229; Mulligan's Downfall, 325; Papa Bear's Black Honey, 344; Tall Ship, 456; Werewolf, 498

Dr. McGillicuddy's Mentholmint schnapps: Viennese Doctor, 489

Dry gin: Bermuda Rose, 66; Burnt Martini, 102; B. V. D. Cocktail, 50; Casino, 114; Clover Club Cocktail, 131; El Cid, 177; Ginger Rogers Cocktail, 212; Leave It to Me, 276; Major Bailey Julep, 293; Marguerite Cocktail, 299; Montmartre Cocktail, 321; Ramos Gin Fizz, 377; Roma, 389; Russian Cocktail, 399; Star Daisy, 442; Wedding Belle 2, 497

Dry sherry. *See* **Sherry**

Dry vermouth: Admiral, 21; Allegheny, 29; Apocalypse Now (Shooter), 40; Bamboo Martini, 54; Baron Cocktail, 59; Bittersweet Martini, 71; Blackthorn, 75; Boston Tea Party, 89; Caruso, 113; Chrysanthemum Cocktail, 128; Coronation Cocktail, 143; Country Club Cooler, 146; Fifty-Fifty Martini, 187; Garbo Cocktail, 204; Go-for-Broke, 214; Imperial Cocktail, 248; Kissin' Cousin, 269; Latin Manhattan, 296; Mahogany, 291; Manhasset, 295; Metropole, 307; Midnight Martini, 311; Morning Cocktail, 321; Parisian, 345; Party Girl, 346; Plaza Martini, 363; Poet's Dream, 364; Queens, 375; San Francisco Cocktail, 404; Satan's Curled Whiskers, 406; Satan's Whiskers, 406; Scofflaw, 408; Tango, 456; Tip Top, 470; Trinity Cocktail, 477; Turf Martini, 480; Vermouth Cassis, 487; Washington, 495

Dubonnet: Alfonso, 27; Coronation Cocktail, 143; Dandy, 156; Dubonnet Cocktail, 172; Dubonnet Rouge, 172; Wedding Belle 2, 497; Zaza, 515

Everclear: Everglade, 181

Finlandia vodka: Asterix, 49

Forbidden Fruit Liqueur: Adam and Eve, 20

Frangelico: Anatole Coffee, 36; Bushwacker, 102; Butterfinger, 103; Celtic Twilight, 115; Coffee Nut, 135; Cottage Coffee, 145; Monk's Coffee, 319; Mount Creek Coffee, 322; Nutty Irishman, 335; Peanut Butter & Jelly Shooter, 350; Peanut Butter Cup, 351; Pocahontas Nuts & Berries, 363; Powder House Cocktail, 367; Ring of Fire, 387; Spread Eagle, 441; Toblerone, 472; Tomoko Koko, 473; Winter Caribbean Heat, 509; Yoohoo, 514

Galliano: Banana Italiano, 56; Captain's Stripes, 111; Copperhead, 141; Coral Snake Bite, 142; Galliano Stinger, 203; Golden Cadillac, 215; Golden Dream, 215; Illusions, 247; International Stinger, 250; Root Beer Float, 390; Sloe Screw Against the Wall, 426; Zapper Cocktail, 515